SPECIAL EDUCATIONAL NEEDS

Report of the Committee of Enquiry into the Education of Handicapped Children and Young People

Chairman: Mrs H M Warnock

Presented to Parliament by the Secretary of State for Education and Science, the Secretary of State for Scotland and the Secretary of State for Wales by Command of Her Majesty
May 1978

LONDON
HER MAJESTY'S STATIONERY OFFICE
Reprinted 1982
Cmnd. 7212   £12.95 net

MEMBERS OF THE COMMITTEE

Mrs H M Warnock (Chairman) – Senior Research Fellow, St Hugh's College, Oxford

Mr G V Cooke CBE (Vice-Chairman) – County Education Officer, Lincolnshire

Mrs J D Bisby – Senior Careers Officer, Sheffield

Sir Edward Britton CBE – Senior Research Fellow in Education, University of Sheffield. General Secretary of the National Union of Teachers until 1975

Miss M F Cairley – Assistant Head Teacher, Kirkriggs Special School for the Mentally Handicapped, Glasgow

Dr I Chesham – Specialist in Community Medicine (Child Health), Cheshire Area Health Authority

Mr D Coe – Assistant Director, Middlesex Polytechnic

Mr G H Dalziel – Headmaster, Thorn Park School for the Deaf, Bradford

Mr R A Davis – Headmaster, Pindar Comprehensive School, Scarborough, until December 1976

Dr R M Forrester – Consultant Paediatrician, Royal Albert Edward Infirmary, Wigan

Professor P J Graham – Consultant Psychiatrist, Hospital for Sick Children, Great Ormond Street, London

Mr D Guthrie OBE (resigned May 1975) – Director of the National Fund for Research into Crippling Diseases until November 1976

Mr J E Harding – Member of the Education and Training Committee, Scottish CBI and the Scottish TUC/CBI Joint Committee on the Employment of the Disabled

Mr L Macho – Headmaster, Pen-y-Bryn School for the ESN(M), Swansea

Dr J B Meredith Davies (appointed June 1975) – Director of Social Services, Liverpool

Mr J A D Michie – Director of Education, Grampian Region

Mr G P Newton OBE (resigned April 1975) – Director of Social Services, Wiltshire

Mr P H Priestley – Regional Psychologist and Head of Special Educational Services, Lothian Regional Council

Mr E J Richards – Senior Adviser, Special Education, Clwyd Local Education Authority

Lady Roth JP – Chairman of the Governors, Feversham Non-Maintained School for the Maladjusted, Newcastle-upon-Tyne, until July 1977

Mrs M E Thruston – Community Nurse Training Officer, Croydon Area Health Authority

Mrs W Tumim – Parent of two hearing impaired children and Chairman of the Education Committee of The National Deaf Children's Society

Dr M C Tyson – Professional Adviser/Senior Educational Psychologist for Special Education, London Borough of Hounslow

Professor P Williams – Professor of Educational Studies and Dean of the Faculty of Educational Studies, The Open University

Mr D Winnard – Secretary, Education Department, Trades Union Congress until September 1974

Mr D P T Woodgate – Headmaster, Priory Meadow School for Maladjusted Children, St Osyth

Mr P W Young – Tutor to the course in the education of children with learning difficulties, Cambridge Institute of Education, Chelmsford, until December 1977

ASSESSORS

Mr M A Walker (to September 1976) Mr V H Stevens (from October 1976) Mr J R Fish HMI	Department of Education and Science
Mrs N Munro (to May 1976) Mr R P C Macnab (from May 1976) Mr A Milne HMI	Scottish Education Department
Mr M W Stone HMI	Welsh Education Office
Mr P Tansley (to June 1977) Mr S Loveman (from June 1977)	Department of Employment
Dr E E Simpson Mr G M Bebb Mr R B Brown	Department of Health and Social Security
Dr J Ward (to May 1975) Dr J H Grant (June 1975 to August 1977) Dr M Hennigan (from September 1977)	Scottish Home and Health Department

SECRETARY

Mr J C Hedger (to May 1976) Miss I Luxton (from May 1976)	Department of Education and Science

The Rt Hon SHIRLEY WILLIAMS MP
Secretary of State for Education and Science

The Rt Hon BRUCE MILLAN MP
Secretary of State for Scotland

The Rt Hon JOHN MORRIS QC, MP
Secretary of State for Wales

March 1978

Dear Secretaries of State,

On behalf of the Committee of Enquiry into the Education of Handicapped Children and Young People, I have the honour to submit our report to you.

Our review has been a wide-ranging one, extending well beyond the education service. Our terms of reference required us to take account of the medical aspects of the needs of handicapped children and young people, together with arrangements to prepare them for entry into employment. We have also had regard to the social aspects of their needs, to relations between the different professionals engaged in meeting their needs, to the contribution of their parents and the parents' own needs for support and to the requirements for research and development.

We have been very much aware of the continuing financial constraints on central and local government, and have sought to be realistic in making recommendations which would entail additional expenditure. Some of the improvements which we have proposed could be achieved through a redeployment of existing resources; but in formulating proposals for the development of special education to the end of the century and possibly beyond, we have inevitably made some recommendations which would require substantial additional resources. Our priorities, however, are clearly stated.

We should like to emphasise that, though our Committee was large, and consisted of members from a variety of different professions, we are unanimous in submitting our report. On a very small number of issues, indicated in the text, there was difference of opinion among us. But these issues were minor. On all our main conclusions and recommendations we were in complete agreement.

Throughout our work we have been greatly helped by our assessors from Government Departments. In particular, we should like to express our gratitude to Mr Michael Walker and his successor Mr Vivian Stevens of the Department of Education and Science and to Dr Esther Simpson and Mr Bob Brown of the Department of Health and Social Security, who have helped us continuously for three and a half years. We are also deeply grateful to Mr John Fish, Mr Alastair Milne and Mr Malcolm Stone of Her Majesty's Inspectorate for their continuous help and advice.

Finally, it is a pleasure to record here the debt of gratitude we owe to the imaginative and thorough work of the Committee's two Secretaries, first Mr John Hedger and then Miss Imogen Luxton, who succeeded him half-way through our review. Their skill and patience are beyond praise.

To all these, as well as to our co-opted members, and others not mentioned by name we are deeply indebted.

Yours sincerely,

MARY WARNOCK

CONTENTS

INTRODUCTION

1. In November 1973 the Rt Hon Margaret Thatcher MP, then Secretary of State for Education and Science, announced that she proposed, in conjunction with the then Secretaries of State for Scotland and Wales and after consultation with the then Secretaries of State for Social Services and Employment, to appoint a Committee with the following terms of reference:

> "To review educational provision in England, Scotland and Wales for children and young people handicapped by disabilities of body or mind, taking account of the medical aspects of their needs, together with arrangements to prepare them for entry into employment; to consider the most effective use of resources for these purposes; and to make recommendations".

The Committee was established the following year and we held our first meeting in September 1974.

2. In view of both our size and the breadth of our terms of reference we decided early in 1975 to divide our work among four sub-committees. The division was as follows: the needs of handicapped children under five; the education of handicapped children in ordinary schools; day special schools and boarding provision; and the educational and other needs of handicapped school leavers. The sub-committees on special educational provision in ordinary and special schools were subsequently amalgamated and a further sub-committee was established in 1976 to consider arrangements for the training of teachers. In addition, small sub-groups met for varying lengths of time to discuss particular topics. These included the curriculum in special education; confidentiality and the flow of information; advice and support in special education; co-ordination of services; the SE Forms procedure; and research and development.

3. Although our membership covered a wide range of interest and expertise, we felt that we would benefit from the presence on our sub-committees of additional members with relevant knowledge and experience. We therefore co-opted a number of members, to whom we are indebted for their help. We list them below.

Mrs M Blythman – Head of the Special Education Department, Moray House College of Education, Edinburgh

Miss M Clarke OBE – Senior Adviser for Nursery, Infant and First School Education, Devon Local Education Authority

Miss K A Dougall – Headteacher, Inchview Primary School, West Pilton, Edinburgh

Mr M J K Flynn – Principal, Stretton House Hostel, Stretton, Derbyshire

Dr C Frain-Bell – Consultant Paediatrician (Educational Medicine), Community Child Health Services, Tayside Area Health Board

Mr D R Gray – Inspector (Special Education) City of Birmingham Education Department

Professor R Gulliford – Head of the Department of Special Education, University of Birmingham

Mr D Hutchinson – Head of the Work Orientation Unit, North Nottinghamshire College of Further Education

Rev R J Jones – Education Secretary, National Children's Home, until 1976

1

Mr P J Lowman – Production Director, Rosalind Foods Ltd, Great Yarmouth, until 1976

Miss M E Moyce – Principal Officer, Children's Services, London Borough of Lambeth

Mrs M de Paolo – Headteacher, New Fosseway School for the ESN(S), Bristol

Mr T E Thomas – Former pupil of a special school for the physically handicapped in Glamorgan

Mr G Vernon – Co-ordinator of In-Service Education, Leeds Polytechnic

Dr R I Woodger – Parent of a handicapped child

4. The sub-committees completed their work by May 1977 and their findings formed the basis of our report. We also took into account the many submissions of written evidence – nearly 400 – which we received from a variety of organisations and from individuals with a personal or professional interest in special education. We invited representatives of some of these organisations as well as a number of the individuals to discuss with us points of special interest in their submissions and we also asked other people with expertise in particular fields to meet us for discussion of specific topics. Those organisations and individuals who submitted written evidence or gave oral evidence to us in full Committee, in sub-committees or in sub-groups are listed in Appendix 1.

5. Our report also draws on the findings of a number of research projects undertaken on our behalf. A review of recent research in special education was produced for us by Mr C Cave and Mrs P Maddison. Two projects were concerned with provision for children under five and their parents: a survey of services for parents of handicapped children under five carried out under the co-direction of Professor M Chazan and Dr A F Laing of the University College of Swansea; and a study of pre-school education and handicapped and exceptional children in the Grampian Region of Scotland directed by Dr M M Clark of the University of Strathclyde. A project on the employment experiences of handicapped school leavers was commissioned from the National Children's Bureau and carried out by Mr A Walker. Two surveys were undertaken for us by the Department of Education and Science: one of the views of teachers in special and ordinary schools on various aspects of provision for children with special educational needs; and the other of the cost per place in special schools and special classes and units in nine local education authorities. Details of some of these projects are given in Appendices 5–8. We should like to express our thanks to those who undertook research projects for us, as well as to those parents, young people, professionals in different services and others who were the source of their information.

6. In the course of our work we made many visits, individually or in groups, to a wide range of institutions in England, Scotland and Wales. The places visited are too numerous to list but they included nursery schools and special nursery units, ordinary schools, maintained and non-maintained special schools, independent schools catering wholly or mainly for handicapped pupils, hospitals, assessment centres, colleges of further education, colleges of education and departments of education in polytechnics. We are extremely grateful to all those who received us in the course of our visits and, by answering our questions, helped us to formulate our views on the future development of special education.

7. Small parties of our members also visited a number of other countries. One party visited the United States of America and our Vice-Chairman visited Canada to study arrangements for special educational provision. Another group went to Denmark and Sweden to study the implementation of the policy of educating severely handicapped children in ordinary schools and the provision made for handicapped young people over 16. A third party visited Holland and West Germany to see a range of special schools in those countries. Although short, these visits were very valuable in enabling those who took part to re-examine particular issues from a different perspective.

8. One difficulty which confronted us in preparing this report was the existence of certain differences in terminology between England, Wales and Scotland. For example, the terms local education authority and social services department, which occur frequently throughout our report, are peculiar to England and Wales; their Scottish counterparts are education authority and social work department. The term "region" has a variety of meanings in England, depending on the context in which it is used: in the context of the education service it means a group of local education authorities. The term has no meaning in Wales, while in Scotland the region is the local authority. References to regional planning and co-ordination in Wales and Scotland, therefore, are meaningful only if "inter-authority" is substituted for "regional". Our report would, however, have been very cumbersome had we given both English and Scottish terms wherever neces-sary. For the sake of convenience, therefore, we decided to use the terminology current in England except when making proposals or recommendations specific to Scotland or Wales.

CHAPTER 1: GENERAL APPROACH

1.1 Ours was the first committee of enquiry specifically charged by any government of the United Kingdom to review educational provision for all handicapped children, whatever their handicap. The last such body to have terms of reference which approached our own in breadth was the Royal Commission on the Blind, the Deaf and Dumb and Others of the United Kingdom which reported in 1889. The Commission was originally appointed to consider the educational needs of the blind and although its remit was subsequently extended to the education of the deaf and dumb "as well as such other cases as from special circumstances would seem to require exceptional methods of education" the last phrase was interpreted as meaning only the mentally handicapped. Subsequent *ad hoc* committees of enquiry in this field have had fairly narrow terms of reference, restricted to a particular group or groups of the handicapped. The establishment of our Committee, therefore, provided a formidable challenge as well as a unique opportunity to take a comprehensive view of the way in which educational provision for handicapped children and young people, as well as arrangements for their transition from school to adult life, have developed and should develop in the future.

1.2 With regard to our terms of reference, we should like to make three preliminary points. First, we have not felt it part of our business to go deeply into the factors which may lead to educational handicap. We are fully aware that many children with educational difficulties may suffer from familial or wider social deficiencies. While for most children their family life enhances their development, others show educational difficulties because they do not obtain from their families or their social circumstances the quality of stimulation or the sense of stability which is necessary for proper educational progress. But regardless of the cause of such children's problems, familial or social, unless part of their educational provision is designed to compensate for the deprivation they have suffered, they will be unable to benefit from education in the ordinary sense. One cannot always keep these different strands apart. Secondly, we did not regard the problems of highly gifted children as falling within our remit, except insofar as these problems may result in emotional or behavioural disorders similar in effect to the problems of other children with whom we are concerned.* Thirdly, we have not attempted to offer comprehensive guidance on necessary improvements in special educational provision for each specific disability. Much of the content of our report and most of our recommendations are of a general nature, and references to particular types of disability and difficulty are mostly illustrative rather than comprehensive. It may well be that in the future, as in the past, working groups or committees will need to be set up to consider particular disabilities in more detail. Intensive study of each disability, however, was beyond our scope and indeed our competence.

---

* Procedures for identifying gifted children and various forms of provision for them are discussed in a recent publication *Gifted children in Middle and Comprehensive Secondary Schools*. Department of Education and Science HMI Series: Matters for Discussion 4 (HMSO, 1977).

1.3 The focus of our enquiry has been the EDUCATION of handicapped children and young people. It is natural that we should have worked with certain presumptions and presuppositions of a very general kind about what education is. We have not been concerned to draw absolute distinctions between education and neighbouring concepts such as training, therapy and care. Indeed we have endeavoured to take account of these other concepts wherever they bear upon our subject. We have, however, looked at the problems of handicapped children always with their education primarily in mind, and this has led us sometimes to distinguish between education and other related concepts.

1.4 We hold that education has certain long-term goals, that it has a general point or purpose, which can be definitely, though generally, stated. The goals are twofold, different from each other, but by no means incompatible. They are, first, to enlarge a child's knowledge, experience and imaginative understanding, and thus his awareness of moral values and capacity for enjoyment; and secondly, to enable him to enter the world after formal education is over as an active participant in society and a responsible contributor to it, capable of achieving as much independence as possible. The educational needs of every child are determined in relation to these goals. We are fully aware that for some children the first of these goals can be approached only by minute, though for them highly significant steps, while the second may never be achieved. But this does not entail that for these children the goals are different. The purpose of education for all children is the same; the goals are the same. But the help that individual children need in progressing towards them will be different. Whereas for some the road they have to travel towards the goals is smooth and easy, for others it is fraught with obstacles. For some the obstacles are so daunting that, even with the greatest possible help, they will not get very far. Nevertheless, for them too, progress will be possible, and their educational needs will be fulfilled, as they gradually overcome one obstacle after another on the way.

1.5 Broadly, our task has been to consider how teaching and learning can best be brought about wherever there are children who have particular obstacles to overcome, whether these are primarily physical, sensory, intellectual or emotional. For education, though concerned with the acquiring of knowledge, cannot be thought to be something which takes place only at school. Many children learn things without anyone specifically teaching them. They learn to walk, to speak, to get on with their companions by trial and error or by imitation. Learning these things may be regarded not as part of education, but merely as a normal part of the kind of learning which goes on for all of us all through life. But for some children, such knowledge will not be spontaneously acquired and has to be elaborately taught. For these children, education must start early and continue at home and at school and into adult life. Parents, as much as teachers, must see themselves as active educators, and both parents and teachers may need the help of other professionals in their endeavours. At every stage of our discussion, the contribution of parents and non-teacher professionals to the education of the child has been at the front of our minds.

1.6 The criterion by which to judge the quality of educational provision is the extent to which it leads a pupil towards the twin goals which we have described, towards understanding, awareness of moral values and enjoyment and towards the possibility of independence. It is progress towards these goals which alone can justify a particular course of education for anyone, whatever his abilities or disabilities. For some children, enjoyment and understanding may be confined to the hard-won, taught capacity to recognise things and people, and perhaps to name them. For some, independence may in the end amount to no more than the freedom of performing a task for oneself rather than having someone else do it, even if the task is only getting dressed or feeding oneself. For others the concepts of imaginative understanding, enjoyment and freedom have an infinitely richer content. But the direction of progress is the same.

1.7 Though the general concept of education may remain constant, its interpretation will thus be widely different in the case of different children. There is in our society a vast range of differently disabled children, many of whom would not have survived infancy in other periods of history. In the case of the most profoundly disabled one is bound to face the questions: Why educate such children at all? Are they not ineducable? How can one justify such effort and such expense for so small a result? Such questions have to be faced, and must be answered. Our answer is that education, as we conceive it, is a good, and a specifically human good, to which all human beings are entitled. There exists, therefore, a clear obligation to educate the most severely disabled for no other reason than that they are human. No civilised society can be content just to look after these children; it must all the time seek ways of helping them, however slowly, towards the educational goals we have identified. To understand the ways in which help can be given is to begin to meet their educational needs. If we fail to do this, we are actually increasing and compounding their disadvantages.

1.8 Moreover there are some children with disabilities who, through education along the common lines we advocate, may be able to lead a life very little poorer in quality than that of the non-handicapped child, whereas without this kind of education they might face a life of dependence or even institutionalisation. Education in such cases makes the difference between a proper and enjoyable life and something less than we believe life should be. From the point of view of the other members of the family, too, the process of drawing a severely handicapped child into the educational system may, through its very normality, help to maintain the effectiveness, stability and cohesion of the family unit.

1.9 We have been concerned, however, not only with the severely handicapped but with all those children who require special education in any form. The help needed may range from continuous support from specialist services, including an intensive educational programme in a special school for a child with severe and multiple disabilities, to part-time assistance from a specially trained teacher for a child with mild learning difficulties. It is perhaps useful to regard this range of special educational need as a continuum, although that is a crude notion which conceals the complexities of individual needs.

1.10 Our concept of special education is thus broader than the traditional one of education by special methods appropriate for particular categories of children. It extends beyond the idea of education provided in special schools, special classes or units for children with particular types of disability, and embraces the notion of any form of additional help, wherever it is provided and whenever it is provided, from birth to maturity, to overcome educational difficulty. It also embodies the idea that, although the difficulties which some children encounter may dictate WHAT they have to be taught and the disabilities of some HOW they have to be taught, the point of their education is the same.

1.11 Whatever else may come out of our report, we hope that one thing will be clear. Special education is a challenging and intellectually demanding field for those engaged in it. More research is needed, more experiments in teaching techniques, in curriculum development and in co-operation between different professions. Those who work with children with special educational needs should regard themselves as having a crucial and developing role in a society which is now committed, not merely to tending and caring for its handicapped members, as a matter of charity, but to educating them, as a matter of right and to developing their potential to the full.

CHAPTER 2: THE HISTORICAL BACKGROUND

INTRODUCTION

2.1 Special education for the handicapped in Great Britain is of relatively recent origin. The very first schools for the blind and deaf were founded in the life-time of Mozart; those for the physically handicapped awaited the Great Exhibition; day schools for the mentally handicapped and epileptic arrived with the motor-car; whilst special provision for delicate, maladjusted and speech impaired children is younger than living memory. Even so, the early institutions were nothing like the schools we know today and they were available only to the few. As with ordinary education, education for the handicapped began with individual and charitable enterprise. There followed in time the intervention of government, first to support voluntary effort and make good deficiencies through state provision, and finally to create a national framework in which public and voluntary agencies could act in partnership to see that all children, whatever their disability, received a suitable education. The framework reached its present form only in this decade.

I EARLY DEVELOPMENTS TO 1870

2.2 The first school for the BLIND in Great Britain was established by Henry Dannett in Liverpool in 1791. Named the School of Instruction for the Indigent Blind, it offered training in music and manual crafts for blind children and adults of both sexes. No education as such was given: child labour was the rule and pupils were taught to earn a living. The Liverpool foundation was quickly followed by other private ventures: the Asylum for the Industrious Blind at Edinburgh (1793), the Asylum for the Blind at Bristol (1793), the School for the Indigent Blind in London (1800) and the Asylum and School for the Indigent Blind at Norwich (1805). As at Liverpool, these institutions were solely concerned to provide vocational training for future employment, and relied upon the profits from their workshops.

2.3 The next schools, which came thirty years later, saw the beginnings of a genuinely educational element in the instruction. Thus the Yorkshire School for the Blind (1835) set out to teach arithmetic, reading and writing as part of vocational training; whilst the school established by the London Society for Teaching the Blind to Read (1838) regarded general education as the foundation for subsequent training in manual skills. The Society later opened branches in Exeter and Nottingham. The General Institution for the Blind at Birmingham (1847) combined industrial training with a broad curriculum in general subjects: and, following early concentration on training, Henshaw's Blind Asylum at Manchester (1838) eventually developed a thriving school with educational objectives. Nevertheless by 1870 there were only a dozen or so institutions for the blind, most of them in the nature of training centres; and only a small proportion of the blind benefited from their provision. However the first senior school for the blind had been founded in 1866 at Worcester and named "College for the Blind Sons of Gentlemen".

2.4 The first school for the DEAF in Great Britain was started by Thomas Braidwood in Edinburgh in the early 1760s. Mr Braidwood's Academy for the Deaf and Dumb, as it was called, took a handful of selected paying pupils to be taught to speak and read. In 1783 the Academy moved to London, where in 1792 the first English school for the deaf opened with six children under the direction of Braidwood's nephew. This Asylum for the Support and Education of the Deaf and Dumb Children of the Poor flourished: in 1809 it moved to larger buildings and later opened a branch at Margate. In 1812 another Braidwood School opened in Birmingham. Other schools for the deaf followed in the 1820s at Liverpool, Manchester, Exeter and Doncaster. By 1870 a further six schools had been founded, including the first in Wales at Aberystwyth (1847) and Donaldson's Hospital (now Donaldson's School) in Edinburgh. These early institutions for the deaf, no less than those for the blind, were protective places, with little or no contact with the outside world. The education that they provided was limited and subordinated to training. Many of their inmates failed to find employment on leaving and had recourse to begging.

2.5 The first separate educational provision for PHYSICALLY HANDI-CAPPED children was made in 1851, when the Cripples Home and Industrial School for Girls was founded at Marylebone. A training Home for Crippled Boys followed at Kensington in 1865. Both institutions set out to teach a trade, and education as such was rudimentary. The children came mainly from poor homes and contributed to their own support by making goods for sale. Little further was done for the physically handicapped until 1890.

2.6 Before the middle of the nineteenth century so-called MENTALLY DEFECTIVE children who required custodial care were placed in workhouses and infirmaries. The first specific provision made for them was the Asylum for Idiots established at Highgate in 1847. Like the institutions for the blind and deaf, the Asylum took people of all ages. By 1870 there were five asylums, only three of which purported to provide education. Admission was generally by election or payment. In the same year the newly created Metropolitan Asylum Board established all-age asylums at Caterham, Leavesden and Hampstead. The children were later separated from the adults, and those who were considered to be educable followed a programme of simple manual work and formal teaching. The staff were untrained and classes were very large. In Scotland, the first establishment for the education of "imbeciles" was set up at Baldovan in Dundee in 1852 and later became Strathmartine Hospital. An institution for "defectives" was founded later in Edinburgh: it transferred to a site in Larbert in 1863 and is today the Royal Scottish National Hospital. The Lunacy (Scotland) Act of 1862 recognised the needs of the mentally handicapped and authorised the granting of licences to charitable institutions established for the care and training of imbecile children.

II 1870–1902

2.7 The Forster Education Act of 1870 (and the corresponding Education (Scotland) Act of 1872) established school boards to provide elementary education in those areas where there were insufficient places in voluntary schools. The Acts did not specifically include disabled children among those for whom provision was to be made, but in 1874 the London School Board established a class

9

for the DEAF at a public elementary school and later began the training of teachers. By 1888 there were 14 centres attached to ordinary schools, with 373 children.[1] A number of other boards followed suit over the same period, but they were a small minority. Boards generally made no specific provision for the deaf; some had genuine doubts about their legal powers to do so, while others either did not have the money or believed that it was not in any case a proper charge upon the rates. Moreover school districts varied enormously in their size and resources and many of them had no school board.

2.8 It was equally so with the BLIND. Two years after the Scottish Act 50 blind children were being taught in ordinary classes in Scottish schools, and in 1875 the London Board first arranged for the teaching of blind children in its elementary schools. By 1888 there were 23 centres attached to ordinary schools, where 133 children were taught part-time by teachers who were themselves blind. The children received the rest of their education in ordinary classes, where they mixed freely with the other children. These developments were matched by a handful of other boards, including the Cardiff Board, which appointed a blind teacher to visit the ordinary schools attended by blind children.

2.9 Special educational provision for PHYSICALLY AND MENTALLY HANDICAPPED children was even slower off the mark. Those who attended elementary schools profited as best they could from the ordinary teaching. The more severely handicapped received care and sometimes education in institutions. However, in 1892 the Leicester School Board established a special class for selected "feeble-minded" pupils, and in the same year the London Board opened a school for the special instruction of physically and mentally defective children who could not be suitably educated by ordinary methods. The emphasis was upon occupational activity rather than formal education. By 1896 there were 24 special schools in London attended by 900 pupils and before the end of the century schools for defective children had been established by six other boards.

2.10 These first, hesitant efforts by a few school boards to cater for some handicapped children owed nothing to educational legislation. The middle of the nineteenth century had seen a stirring of social conscience over the plight of the disabled, especially of the blind, but it was primarily concerned to relieve their distress, not to educate them. Yet as the principle of universal elementary education took root, it could be only a matter of time before the educational needs of handicapped children began to be recognised. Six years after the Forster Act the Charity Organisation Society was pressing the right of blind children to receive education and the duty of school boards to provide it, and later applying the same arguments to the education of the deaf. The Society for the Training of the Deaf made approaches to government. Other bodies added their voices and through meetings, publications and propaganda created the climate of reform.

2.11 The time had come for an inquiry, and the Royal Commission on the Blind and Deaf was constituted in 1886. The Commission had started work the

---

[1] Royal Commission on the Blind, the Deaf and Others of the United Kingdom, Vol 2, Appendix 26. Cited in D G Pritchard, *Education and the Handicapped 1760–1960* (1963). The early part of this chapter draws extensively on Pritchard's history.

year before with a remit confined to the blind, but now extended to include the deaf. The amended terms of reference were to report on the provision for the education of the blind and deaf in the United Kingdom, the opportunities for their employment and the educational changes needed to increase their qualifications for employment. The Commission was also required to consider "such other cases as from special circumstances would seem to require exceptional methods of education". (We referred to the comprehensive nature of its remit at the beginning of this report.)

2.12 The Commission reported in 1889. It recommended the introduction of compulsory education for the blind from five to 16 and proposed that it should be provided by school boards either in their own schools or in institutions run by others if certified by the Education Department as being suitable. A two-stage arrangement was envisaged whereby pupils would receive elementary education to the age of 12 and thereafter follow a technical or an academic course. Boards should have the power to continue to pay grants beyond the age of 16 to assist pupils to establish themselves in a trade. At the elementary stage it was envisaged that the children would be taught in ordinary classes by ordinary teachers, although in town schools special instruction in reading might be given by visiting teachers or by attendance at a centre on certain days. There would be a need for special boarding schools for pupils who were delicate, neglected or lived too far from the nearest day school to be able to attend it without difficulty.

2.13 The Commission also recommended compulsory education for the deaf, to be provided by school boards, but with important differences. Since deaf children were generally less forward than hearing children they would not be ready to start school until the age of seven. Moreover, they would need to be taught not in ordinary classes but in separate schools or classes. There should be one teacher for every eight children where oral methods were used and one teacher for every 14 children for instruction by the manual system. The sexes should be educated separately. Teachers of the deaf should be paid higher salaries than ordinary teachers, their training should be under government supervision, and they should have qualified as ordinary teachers before beginning their special training.

2.14 The Commission's report was well received. Legislation quickly followed for Scotland in the Education of Blind and Deaf Mute Children (Scotland) Act of 1890, but three years elapsed before England and Wales were similarly covered by the Elementary Education (Blind and Deaf Children) Act of 1893. The Act required school authorities* to make provision, in their own or other schools, for the education of blind and deaf children resident in their area who were not otherwise receiving suitable elementary education. As the Commission had recommended, blind children were to receive education between the ages of five and 16 and deaf children between seven and 16. (The higher age of 16 was far ahead of contemporary provision for normal children, who, from the age of 11, might be given total or partial exemption from attending school.) Certified institutions were entitled to receive a *per capita* Parliamentary grant for each child received but had to be open to inspection.

---

* The term "school authority" includes school boards, and, for areas not under a school board, the district council where such existed, or otherwise the body responsible for appointing a school attendance committee for the area.

2.15 The new Act meant that all blind or deaf children would in future be sent to school as of right. The uncertainties of the 1870 Act which had affected the special provision made in board schools were thus finally removed, and monetary support assured. In most cases the extra places were provided by the extension of existing schools. The larger school boards generally made real efforts to maintain good standards in their own schools, but many boards, particularly those of small towns and country districts, were less efficient. Moreover there were some 20,000 voluntary schools, over which the school boards had no control, and these difficulties persisted until the creation of local education authorities in 1902.

2.16 Before the Forster Education Act the needs of MENTALLY HANDI-CAPPED children were little recognised. Mental disability was for many children no substantial handicap in coping with the simple demands of everyday life in a largely uneducated and relatively uncomplicated world, and institutional provision was available for those who needed looking after. Their needs first became apparent after 1870 when large numbers of children of below average or poor intellectual ability entered public elementary schools. Many of them made scarcely any progress and their presence hindered normal teaching. There were no systematic means of assessing their individual capabilities and requirements. The range of disability was very wide and there were unresolved questions of definition. Instruction was based upon the official Code for normal children; classes were large and there was no opportunity, even if teachers had the skills, to shape a special curriculum for them. Unlike the blind and deaf they had no organised opinion to plead their cause. Apart from isolated examples of private provision in London and elsewhere very little had been achieved when the Royal Commission on the Blind and Deaf reported in 1889.

2.17 The Commission had distinguished between the feeble-minded, imbeciles and idiots. The last group, having the greater degree of intellectual deficiency, were not generally considered to be educable. The Commission argued that imbeciles, having a lesser degree of deficiency, should not remain in asylums or workhouses, but school authorities should be responsible for ensuring their admission to institutions where they should wherever possible receive an education which concentrated upon sensory and physical development and the improvement of speech. This would be given by ordinary teachers. As to the feeble-minded, these should receive special education separately from ordinary children in "auxiliary" schools. The nature of the education to be given was not specified.

2.18 Following the Commission's report the Charity Organisation Society campaigned for the imposition of a duty on school boards to provide for the mentally handicapped and, to this end, sponsored in 1896 the National Association for Promoting the Welfare of the Feeble-Minded. The campaign drew support from the findings of Dr Francis Warner, who investigated 100,000 children in district poor law schools and the London Board Schools in the early 1890s and concluded that about 1% of the children required special care and training in separate schools on the grounds of their mental and physical condition. The Report of the Metropolitan Poor Law Schools Committee in 1896 also called for separate provision to be made for feeble-minded children. It recommended that they should be boarded out or placed in special training homes.

2.19 In 1896 the Education Department established a Committee on Defective and Epileptic Children, under its Chief Inspector of Schools. The Committee was asked to enquire first into the need for any changes in the system of education of feeble-minded and defective children not in charge of guardians and not idiots or imbeciles; secondly into the means of discriminating between educable and non-educable children and between those who could be taught in an ordinary school and those who should attend special classes; and thirdly into the provision of elementary education for children suffering from epilepsy.

2.20 Like the Royal Commission seven years earlier the Committee had to grapple with definitions. It decided that imbecile children were those who by reason of mental defect could not be educated to be self-supporting; and that feeble-minded children were those who, not being imbeciles, could not be taught in ordinary elementary schools by ordinary methods. Logically this distinction meant that all imbeciles would attend asylums and the feeble-minded would attend special schools or classes: but admission to asylums was only on the basis of certification, and many imbeciles were not certified. Thus some imbeciles would be presented for admission to special schools or classes. The Committee therefore concluded that the schools would need to exercise their own judgement on whether an individual child was capable of receiving proper benefit from special instruction. Dr Warner's study of London children had suggested that the children could be assessed by physical examination, and on this footing the Committee envisaged that a medical officer appointed by the school board would decide whether a particular child should be educated in an ordinary school, in a special school or not at all.

2.21 The Committee proposed that school authorities should have the duty to make special provision for all defective children in their area, and be given the power to compel attendance. Admission should be at age seven, and all children should remain until 14, unless the authority decided that they should stay until 16. Classes in special schools should be small, generally not greater than 20 or 30 in the case of senior classes. All headteachers should be qualified. The majority of assistant teachers should also be qualified and should moreover have additional training. None should be under 21. There would be not more than $4\frac{1}{2}$ hours of teaching each day, and lessons should be short. There should be a varied programme of activities with emphasis on manual and vocational training for senior pupils.

2.22 The Committee had classed the feeble-minded with PHYSICALLY HANDICAPPED children under the general description of "defective". It recommended that defective children of normal intelligence should attend ordinary schools, and be provided with transport, guides or boarding accommodation to enable them to do so. Even where a separate school was provided for them they should receive an ordinary education.

2.23 With regard to EPILEPTIC children the Committee proposed that where attacks occurred at intervals of a month or longer attendance at an ordinary class was possible: otherwise school authorities should be required to provide for them in residential special schools or to pay for their education and maintenance in a voluntary institution. Attendance should be compulsory.

2.24 The Committee reported in 1898. Its proposals were far ahead of contemporary ideas, made heavy organisational demands upon the boards and were, moreover, costly. Not surprisingly therefore the Elementary Education (Defective and Epileptic Children) Act of 1899 merely permitted school boards to provide for the education of mentally and physically defective and epileptic children. The Act applied to children who "not being imbecile, and not being merely dull or backward, are defective, that is to say . . . by reason of mental or physical defect are incapable of receiving benefit from the instruction in ordinary elementary schools but are not incapable by reason of such defect of receiving benefit from instruction in special classes or schools". Although an enhanced rate of grant was payable for this special provision, ten years later only 133 out of 327 local education authorities were using their powers under the Act.[2]

III 1902–1944

2.25 The Education Act 1902 abolished the school boards and established a two-tier system of local education authorities for elementary and secondary education respectively. The functions formerly exercised by school boards, including those relating to special education, were transferred to the new authorities for elementary education, whilst the higher education powers conferred upon county and county borough councils included the power to provide secondary education for blind, deaf, defective and epileptic children. With these changes the statutory foundation of special educational provision which had been laid in the last decade of the nineteenth century, though consolidated in the Education Act 1921, continued in broadly the same form until 1944. However, the Elementary Education (Defective and Epileptic) Act 1914 converted into a duty the earlier powers conferred on authorities by the 1899 Act to provide for the education of mentally defective children; and the Education Act 1918 did the same in respect of physically defective and epileptic children. Thus the intentions of the Committee on Defective and Epileptic Children were belatedly fulfilled and compulsory provision extended to all the categories of handicapped children which had so far been recognised.

2.26 New provision continued to be made, much of it by voluntary effort and of a pioneering nature. Open air schools, day and boarding schools for physically handicapped children, schools in hospitals and convalescent homes and trade schools all contributed to more varied facilities available to local education authorities and parents. Examples were the Heritage Craft Schools and Hospital at Chailey, Sussex (1903), the Swinton House School of Recovery at Manchester (1905), the London County Council's Open Air School at Plumstead (1907) and the Lord Mayor Treloar Cripples' Hospital and College at Alton (1908). The Manchester Local Education Authority had opened a residential school for epileptics in 1910: by 1918 there were six such schools throughout the country.

2.27 The education of MENTALLY HANDICAPPED children however faced a period of uncertainty following the report in 1908 of the Royal Commission on the Care and Control of the Feeble-Minded. After four years' investigation the Commission concluded that institutional provision for mentally defec-

---

[2] Annual Report for 1909 of the Chief Medical Officer of the Board of Education (HMSO 1910), p 152.

tive children on occupational lines was to be preferred to provision in special schools; it consequently recommended that the Elementary Education (Defective and Epileptic Children) Act of 1899 should be amended to exclude these children and that responsibility for their training should lie with local mental deficiency committees. In the event this proposal was not accepted and the 1899 Act remained intact. Instead the Mental Deficiency Act of 1913 required local education authorities to ascertain and certify which children aged seven to 16 in their area were defective. Only those who were judged by the authority to be incapable of being taught in special schools were to pass to the care of local mental deficiency committees. The duty to provide for the educable children which naturally followed was enacted a year later. In fact by 1913 175 out of 318 authorities had used their powers under the 1899 Act, about a third of them having established their own special schools: there were altogether 177 schools catering for some 12,500 mentally defective children.[3] By 1939 the number of children had risen to about 17,000.[4]

2.28 In Scotland, the Education of Defective Children (Scotland) Act of 1906 empowered school boards to make provision in special schools or classes for the education of defective children between the ages of five and 16, whilst the Mental Deficiency (Scotland) Act of 1913 required school boards to ascertain children in their area who were defective, and those who were considered incapable of benefiting from instruction in special schools became the responsibility of parish councils for placement in an institution. By 1939 the number of mentally defective children on the roll of special schools and classes had reached 4,871.

2.29 The education of mentally defective children again came under scrutiny with the appointment in 1924 of the Mental Deficiency Committee (the Wood Committee). This had been set up informally by Sir George Newman, Chief Medical Officer to the Board of Education, in association with the Board of Control. It set itself to inquire into the incidence of feeble-mindedness and to suggest what changes were necessary in the arrangements for the education of feeble-minded children. Reporting in 1929 the Committee concluded that some 105,000 schoolchildren were mentally defective in terms of the Elementary Education (Defective and Epileptic) Act 1914 and accepted evidence that only a third of them had been ascertained and that moreover only a half of these were actually attending special schools. The Committee also estimated that a further 10% of all children, though not mentally deficient, were retarded and failing to make progress in the ordinary school. (This broader concept of need found expression after 1944 in the category of educationally sub-normal pupils.)

2.30 The Committee's suggestions were very different from those of the Royal Commission twenty years before. Far from proposing the separation of mentally deficient children from the mainstream of education the Committee pressed for their much closer association with it. It proposed that the system of certification, which inhibited proper ascertainment of children's needs, should be abolished and that there should be a single system for dealing with the feeble-minded and the backward which allowed greater flexibility in the development of special

---

[3] Annual Report for 1912 of the Chief Medical Officer of the Board of Education (HMSO. 1913), p 239.

[4] D G Pritchard, *op cit.*, p 188.

schools and classes and the placement of pupils. It used these prophetic words: "We do not however contemplate that these [special] schools would exist with a different legal sanction, under a different system of nomenclature and under different administrative provisions. If the majority of children for whom these schools . . . are intended are, *ex hypothesi*, to lead the lives of ordinary citizens, with no shadow of a 'certificate' and all that that implies to handicap their careers, the schools must be brought into closer relation with the Public Elementary School System and presented to parents not as something both distinct and humiliating, but as a helpful variation of the ordinary school".

2.31 This view of special education as a variant of ordinary education had been expressed in relation to the feeble-minded only. But the Committee had, consciously or not, advanced a principle extending to all forms of disability; and also to all degrees of disability, because if no clear distinction could be drawn between feeble-mindedness and backwardness the same must also be true of feeble-mindedness and imbecility. However, forty years were to pass before the right of mentally handicapped children to education was recognised without qualification.

2.32 In contrast to the education of the physically and mentally handicapped that of BLIND and DEAF children had made substantial advances by the turn of the century. Provision for their education had been a statutory duty of the school authorities since 1893 and by 1902 most of the children were receiving education, either in maintained schools or in voluntary schools or institutions, and education was free to those children whose parents could not afford to contribute towards the cost. There were however three areas of deficiency. Their education was entirely neglected before they became of school age; moreover the statutory education of deaf children did not begin until the age of seven and even the blind were not in practice always able to gain admission to voluntary schools at five. Secondly, children with partial sight or partial hearing were at a disadvantage in ordinary schools, and even in special schools their usable sensory faculties were insufficiently exploited. Thirdly, whilst Worcester College provided an academic education for boys, there was no comparable provision for girls.

2.33 Nursery education for blind children originated in 1918 when the Royal National Institute for the Blind opened the first of its residential Sunshine Homes for deprived blind children. In 1921 the Institute also founded Chorleywood College as a secondary school for blind girls. The first provision for partially sighted children was made by the London County Council in 1907, when myopic children in the Authority's blind schools were taught reading and writing from large type instead of braille. The following year the Council established a special higher class for myopic children, which combined special instruction with attendance at ordinary classes for oral teaching. By 1913 eight English authorities were making provision for the partially sighted. Reporting in 1934 the Board of Education Committee of Inquiry into Problems relating to Partially Sighted Children recommended that so far as possible these children should be educated in classes within ordinary schools and should not be taught alongside the blind. The Committee had found that provision for 2,000 partially sighted children was being made in 37 schools and that a further 18 schools for the blind offered special education for the partially sighted. Nevertheless many partially sighted children were being educated as if they were blind.

2.34 So long as it was accepted that the formal education of DEAF children need not begin until two years later than that of the blind the question of nursery education for the deaf could hardly arise. They were not brought into line with the blind until 1938 (under the Education (Deaf Children) Act 1937). Although the need for a grammar school for the deaf was recognised before the Second World War no public provision was made until 1946, when the Mary Hare Grammar School for the Deaf was founded to take boys and girls sent there by local education authorities. The only earlier provision had been in private schools.

2.35 The first special school for partially deaf children was established by the Bristol Local Education Authority in 1906, and another by the London County Council soon afterwards. But most partially deaf children continued for many years to receive ordinary education or to be taught with deaf children in special schools. Their needs were examined by the Committee of Inquiry into the Problems relating to Children with Defective Hearing appointed by the Board of Education in 1934. Reporting four years later the Committee recognised that the needs of partially deaf children were different from those of deaf children, and were also varied. It suggested a three-fold classification: those capable of attending ordinary classes without special arrangements; those more severely affected who might either attend an ordinary school with the help of a hearing aid and support from visiting teachers of lip-reading or be taught in a special school (day or boarding) for the partially deaf; and those whose hearing was so impaired that they needed to be educated with the deaf. Teachers of partially deaf pupils should have the same qualifications as those of the deaf. The report led some authorities to provide residential schools for the partially deaf.

2.36 This period also saw the very beginnings of provision for the MAL-ADJUSTED. Before the turn of the century a psychological laboratory began to study difficult children at University College, London, and the British Child Study Association was founded in 1893. In 1913 the London County Council appointed a psychologist (Cyril Burt) to examine, among other things, individual cases referred by teachers, school doctors, care workers, magistrates and parents. Largely influenced by developments in America the concept of child guidance on multi-professional lines began to emerge, and in 1927 the Child Guidance Council, which later merged into the National Association for Mental Health, was formed. It aimed "to encourage the provision of skilled treatment of children showing behavioural disturbances". A number of clinics was subsequently started by voluntary bodies and hospitals. Provision by local education authorities came later, but by 1939 22 clinics, officially recognised as part of the school medical service, were wholly or partly maintained by authorities. However, since maladjustment was not officially recognised as a form of handicap calling for special education, practically no provision was made by authorities for these pupils before 1944, although some authorities paid for children to attend voluntary homes. In Scotland in the late 1920s an "educational" clinic was opened by Dr William Boyd of the Education Department of the

17

University of Glasgow and a "psychological" clinic was established by Professor James Drever in the Psychology Department at Edinburgh University. The term "child guidance clinic" was first used in 1931 when the Notre Dame clinic was opened in Glasgow. Glasgow was the first education authority to establish a child guidance clinic on a full-time basis, in 1937. Seven education authorities had child guidance clinics prior to the Education (Scotland) Act 1945.

IV 1944–1955

Approach to legislation

2.37 In June 1941 the Board of Education issued the Green Paper *Education After the War*. Although "strictly confidential" it received a wide circulation. The statutory framework of special education at that time was set out in the Education Act 1921. This had simply consolidated earlier enactments. Four categories of handicap were recognised – the blind, deaf, defective (comprising physical and mental disability) and epileptic. Local education authorities were required to ascertain and certify those children who were defective not being idiots or imbeciles. Blindness and deafness were not defined and there was no provision for the ascertainment and certification of these children. In effect the parents of children in any of the four categories were required to see that their child attended a suitable special school from the age of seven (or five in the case of blind or deaf children) until the age of 16. Local education authorities had the duty to secure the provision of such schools, and were empowered to provide continued education over the age of 16.

2.38 The Green Paper considered the care and education of handicapped children in the course of a separate chapter devoted to the "health and physical well-being of the child". It described school accommodation for blind and deaf children as being generally adequate, though much of it was old and ill-distributed. Less satisfactory was that for mentally defective and delicate children (now certifiable as physically defective). It suggested that provision for most of these children should be made in ordinary schools. Maladjustment should be recognised as an additional category of handicap and a small number of residential special schools should be established for these children on a regional basis. Indeed local education authorities should co-operate generally in the joint use of special schools in the interests of effective and efficient provision. The whole of Part V of the 1921 Act, which dealt with education of handicapped children, should be revised and updated. In particular the sytem of certification of defective children should be reconsidered. The idea was floated that when the ordinary school leaving age was raised to 15 that for defective children should be reduced to the same age.

2.39 Two years after the Green Paper the government issued its White Paper *Educational Reconstruction*.[5] As in the Green Paper handicapped children were included in a separate chapter devoted to health and welfare, but this time they were dealt with in two sentences: "Provision for the blind, deaf and

---

[5] *Educational Reconstruction*. Cmnd 6458 (HMSO, 1943).

other handicapped children is now made under Part V of the Education Act 1921. This part of the Act will require substantial modification".

2.40 The modest attention to special education in the consultations which preceded the introduction of the Education Bill in 1943 and also in the Parliamentary Debates which followed meant that the foundations of reform had already been laid. The view that provision for handicapped children should be regarded as an aspect, if a special aspect, of ordinary education had been steadily gaining ground before the war, and exactly accorded with the spirit of post-war reconstruction. There was now no disagreement on the need for a single framework of educational provision in which special education would have a distinctive but natural place.

The Education Act 1944

2.41 The provisions of Part V of the Education Act 1921 which (like earlier enactments) had treated the education of handicapped children as an entirely separate category of provision, were replaced by a requirement that local education authorities must meet the needs of these children, in the form of special educational treatment, within their general duty to provide a sufficiency of primary and secondary schools. Special educational provision was to be included in authorities' development plans for primary and secondary education. The 1921 Act had provided for handicapped children to be educated only in special schools or special classes. Now, the less seriously handicapped children might be catered for in ordinary schools (not necessarily in special classes), although those with serious disabilities would, wherever practicable, continue to be educated in special schools. The options were later extended by the Education (Miscellaneous Provisions) Act 1953 to include independent schools, subject to the Minister's power of veto in a particular case.

2.42 Other major changes were introduced. The duty of local education authorities to ascertain which children required special educational treatment, hitherto confined to defective and epileptic children, was extended to children with all types of disability. They were generally described in the Act as "pupils who suffer from any disability of mind or body" and definition of the types or categories was flexibly delegated to the Minister, acting under statutory regulations, instead of being written into the Act. Certification of defective children within the education system was abolished: any child considered to be educable would in future have access to schooling as of right. But children not considered to be capable of being educated in school were to be reported to the local authority for the purposes of the Mental Deficiency Act 1913. The lower age of compulsory school attendance at special schools was uniformly reduced to five years and the right to remain beyond the age of 16 was established.

2.43 For the purposes of ascertainment, authorities were empowered to require parents to submit their children for medical examination, subject to a lower age limit of two years: and they could not unreasonably refuse the parents' request that their child should be so examined. No specific provision was made for parental appeal against an authority's decision that their child required special educational treatment, but parents could appeal to the Minister against

19

an authority's refusal to consent to their child being withdrawn from a special school. Moreover, the normal procedures for the enforcement of school attendance applied, so that in the event of disagreement between the parents and the authority as to the school to be named in a School Attendance Order, the question could be referred to the Minister for his determination.

2.44 In Scotland, the Education (Scotland) Act 1945 repeated much of the content of the Education Act 1944, but with certain important differences. The duty of education authorities to ascertain which children required special educational treatment applied to children from the age of five. Education authorities were specifically empowered to provide a child guidance service in a child guidance clinic or elsewhere, its functions being to study handicapped, backward and difficult children, to advise teachers and parents as to the appropriate methods of education and training for these children and in suitable cases to provide special educational treatment in child guidance clinics. The creation of this service did a great deal to establish the importance in ascertainment procedures of the assessment of children by educational psychologists. In addition, the 1945 Act specifically recognised the educational importance of the early discovery and treatment of any disability of mind or body by placing upon education authorities the duty to make this known.

Planning the new structure

2.45 The intention of the 1944 Act, fulfilled by regulations made by the Minister in the following year, was to extend greatly the range of children's special needs for which authorities would be obliged to make specific provision, either in special schools or in ordinary schools. The Handicapped Pupils and School Health Service Regulations 1945 defined 11 categories of pupils: blind, partially sighted, deaf, partially deaf, delicate, diabetic, educationally subnormal, epileptic, maladjusted, physically handicapped and those with speech defects. Maladjustment and speech defects were entirely new categories. Partial blindness and partial deafness were extensions of existing categories, whilst delicate and diabetic children had previously been treated as physically handicapped. The categories (though not the detailed definitions) have remained unchanged since 1944 except that in 1953 diabetic children ceased to form a separate category and have since then been included with the delicate. The regulations prescribed that blind, deaf, epileptic, physically handicapped and aphasic children were seriously disabled and must be educated in special schools. Children with other disabilities might attend ordinary schools if adequate provision for them was available.

2.46 The new framework of categories entailed the development of existing and new forms of special educational provision. Detailed guidance on the provision to be made for each category by local education authorities in their development plans was issued by the Ministry of Education.[6] The small number of blind children (estimated to be about 1,200) would need to be educated in special boarding schools. Deaf children, though somewhat more numerous than the blind, might also require residential special schooling, except in the larger urban authorities, where special day school provision might be feasible. The

---

[6] *Special Educational Treatment.* Ministry of Education Pamphlet No 5 (HMSO, 1946).

more seriously affected partially sighted children should attend special schools (either day or boarding), but others could, with special help, be educated in regular classes in ordinary schools or in open-air schools. About half of partially deaf children might with suitable support be capable of attending an ordinary day school: others would require the more sophisticated services of a day or boarding special school. Provision for delicate children not in hospital schools should be in open-air day schools or in boarding schools for the delicate. The great majority of children would expect to return to ordinary schools within two years. Diabetic children should normally attend ordinary day schools, and be accommodated in special hostels if they could not receive adequate treatment and care whilst living at home. Epileptic children requiring regular medication should be sent to a boarding special school for epileptic children. The special educational needs of a maladjusted child should be assessed by an educational psychologist or a child guidance team and, depending on the assessment, might be met by his own teacher, with appropriate specialist advice; by periods of specialist teaching (often in a separate setting); by attendance at another day school (ordinary or special); or by transfer to a boarding special school. Local education authorities were reminded that effective assessment and placement called for proper arrangements for child guidance.

2.47 The guidance indicated that all children assessed as needing special educational treatment on account of physical handicap should be sent to an appropriate special school. Those with physical disabilities not requiring medical or surgical treatment or interfering with their progress in ordinary schools should not be regarded as physically handicapped. Aphasic children whose disability was not merely a defect of articulation should, given imperfect knowledge of the best methods of treatment, be admitted to a school for the deaf. Children with other speech defects should receive treatment at clinics whilst continuing to attend their own schools. A very large proportion of them could be expected to be cured by regular treatment.

2.48 The category of educationally sub-normal children was seen as consisting of children of limited ability and children retarded by "other conditions" such as irregular attendance, ill-health, lack of continuity in their education or unsatisfactory school conditions. These children would be those who for any reason were retarded by more than 20% for their age and who were not so low-graded as to be ineducable or to be detrimental to the education of other children. They would amount to approximately 10% of the school population. Detailed suggestions were made for provision. In large urban areas about 1–2% of the school population would need to be educated in special schools (including 0.2% in boarding schools); the remaining 8–9% of the school population would be provided for in ordinary schools. They should be taught in small groups, in attractive accommodation and by sympathetic teachers. They should not however be isolated, but should be regarded as full members of the ordinary school and should share in general activities. In the absence of well-tried methods there would be need for experimentation to discover the most effective ways of helping them. In small urban areas rather more provision (for 0.4% of the school population) might be required in boarding special schools: and where numbers were insufficient to support a day special school or a special class the remaining children would need to be educated in regular classes in ordinary schools.

The first ten years

2.49 The official guidance of 1946 had provided estimates for each category of handicap of the number of children who might be expected to require special educational treatment, not necessarily in special schools. In sum these amounted to a range between 14% and 17% of the school population. These were however planning objectives to be achieved in the fullness of time. The first task was to make good a shortage of places inherited from the war, through the interruption of school building and the effect of enemy bombing. In 1946 the number of children in special schools had for a variety of reasons fallen to 38,499 compared with 51,152 in 1939. Scarcity of building resources and the heavy demand for places to match the rapidly increasing post-war birth rate dictated the use of country mansions and other large buildings which were coming on to the market. Largely by these means the number of special schools increased between 1945 and 1955 from 528 to 743 (41%) and the numbers of pupils in them from 38,499 to 58,034 (51%). During the same period the number of full-time teachers in special schools rose from 2,434 to 4,381 (80%). Of 16,159 places provided between 1945 and the end of 1955, 68% were for ESN pupils, 14% for the physically handicapped and 7% for the maladjusted. Three out of five places were for boarders. In the same period 68 new boarding homes were provided, mainly for maladjusted pupils. The planning of these developments had been assisted by a series of regional conferences of local education authorities in 1946 and 1947 and again in 1954 and 1955.

2.50 By 1955 the guidance in Pamphlet No 5 had served its purpose. Provision for the BLIND AND PARTIALLY SIGHTED was judged to be adequate, and the partially sighted had been accommodated substantially in separate special schools. (The number of schools for both blind and partially sighted children had been reduced from 14 to three. This had been recommended by the Committee on the Partially Sighted in 1934, but was to be challenged later by the Vernon Committee in 1972.) Provision for the DEAF AND PARTIALLY HEARING had expanded rapidly to cope with the lower age of entry to school and was nearing sufficiency. The importance of early diagnosis, assessment and an early start to education was coming to be recognised. Advances in electronic engineering had made it easier to discover, measure and exploit the limited hearing that a deaf child might have; as with the partially sighted, provision for the partially hearing had been directed towards separate special schools.

2.51 Improvements in the methods of controlling EPILEPSY and increased willingness of teachers in ordinary schools to accept responsibility, with medical help, in less severe cases, suggested that existing places in special schools would fully meet foreseeable needs. The provision of 25 boarding schools in the decade 1945–55 had greatly eased the placement of children suffering from all kinds of PHYSICAL HANDICAP, including cerebral palsy. In January 1955 some 1,800 children with cerebral palsy were attending special schools other than hospital schools.

2.52 The first local education authority to employ speech therapists was the Manchester Local Education Authority in 1906. By 1945 70 authorities were employing them. But the development of provision for children with SPEECH

DEFECTS had been delayed by lack of qualified staff. Before 1945 there was no single recognised qualification, no agreed syllabus of study and some professional rivalry. In 1945 the College of Speech Therapists was formed and became the sole organising and examining body and mode of entry for speech therapists to the National Register of Medical Auxiliaries. The College's syllabus and final examinations were thereafter adopted by all training schools in England and Scotland. On this foundation, the number of speech therapists employed full or part-time by local education authorities increased from 205 to 341 in the five years 1949–1954 (an increase of nearly 90% on a full-time basis), whilst the number of children treated each year rose from 25,098 to 44,800. In 1969 the Quirk Committee,[7] reporting to the Secretaries of State for Education and Science, Social Services, Scotland and Wales, recommended unification of the speech therapy service, further expansion of professional staff, a broader based training at degree level and the establishment of a professional organisation. As a result the speech therapy services were reorganised in 1974 under area health authorities in England and Wales and under health boards in Scotland. But the government concluded that a fully graduate profession would need to be regarded as an aspiration for the future.

2.53 In 1955 12,000 DELICATE children were being educated in day and boarding open air schools in England and Wales. Considerable improvements in the standard of living and in the general health of schoolchildren resulting from the National Health Service and the provision of milk and meals in schools had both reduced and changed the nature of the need for special educational provision for this category of handicapped child, which from 1953 had included also diabetic children. Medical opinion also favoured a less spartan regime. A survey by medical officers, reporting in 1952, suggested that there was a continuing need for special schools for the delicate but little justification for expanded provision. It was thought that with reduced physical debility amongst schoolchildren these schools would increasingly cater for children who, for a variety of reasons (for example, asthma, the effects of illness or, in a few cases maladjustment*), found the life of an ordinary school too strenuous. The great majority of diabetic children, of whom there were estimated to be some 2,000 in 1955, were considered to be capable of attending ordinary day schools with care and treatment while living at home or at a hostel.

2.54 But if special provision for most categories of handicap appeared to be nearing sufficiency in amount (as distinct from quality) the needs of EDUCATIONALLY SUB-NORMAL pupils remained obstinately unsatisfied in spite of continuous expansion since 1945. By the end of 1955 nearly 11,000 new places had been provided and a further 8,000 places were in hand. The number of children in ESN special schools had nearly doubled between 1947 and 1955 (from 12,060 to 22,639) yet the number of children awaiting placement remained high at over 12,000. It was clear that the rate of ascertainment of these pupils was constrained by the number of special school places available. Indeed a special enquiry of authorities conducted in 1956 showed that although 12,437 had been

---

[7] *Speech Therapy Services*. Report of the Committee appointed by the Secretaries of State for Education and Science, for the Social Services, for Scotland and for Wales in July 1969 (HMSO 1972).

* In his first Annual Report (1908) the Chief Medical Officer had expressed the view that "nervous" children were likely to benefit from attendance at open air schools.

shown in the official returns as awaiting places in special schools, as many as 27,000 were considered to need such placement. These were children who were not being satisfactorily helped in ordinary schools.

2.55 Provision for MALADJUSTED pupils was also characterised by expansion in the decade 1945-55. Little had been done for them before the war. In 1945 the only facilities for examining maladjusted children were in 79 child guidance clinics (22 in 1939), some war-time hostels, a few independent boarding schools and two day special schools. Ten years later there were some 300 child guidance clinics, about two-thirds of them provided by local education authorities, 45 boarding homes or hostels, 32 boarding special schools, three day special schools and a number of special classes. Further, local education authorities had placed over 1,000 maladjusted children in 158 independent boarding schools and were providing education for seriously disturbed children in six children's departments of mental hospitals. This expanded provision had been accompanied by greater discrimination in the referral, assessment, placement and education of children. The importance of early referral and of prevention as well as cure was increasingly recognised, and maladjustment was seen as having manifestations in passive introverted behaviour as well as in disruptive or anti-social forms of conduct. Moreover the staff of clinics had expanded, though not in step with need. Whereas in 1945 clinics were generally run single-handed by a psychologist, in 1955 most of them were served by a team consisting of a child psychiatrist, an educational psychologist and a psychiatric social worker, and the teams worked more closely with the staff of special schools and hostels. A start had been made on providing courses of training for teachers and house-staff concerned with maladjusted children. Even so this branch of special education was recognised as being relatively undeveloped. With this in mind the Minister of Education had in 1950 appointed a Committee to enquire into and report upon the medical, educational and social problems relating to maladjusted children, with reference to their treatment within the education system. The Underwood Committee, as it was called, reported in November 1955. [8]

2.56 The special education of CHILDREN IN HOSPITALS had been safeguarded by the National Health Service Act of 1946. Section 62 empowered regional hospital boards and the teaching hospitals to arrange with a local education authority or voluntary body for the use as a special school of any premises forming part of the hospital. The number of hospital special schools grew from 95 in 1947 to 120 (15 run by voluntary bodies) in 1955. In addition to the 6,476 pupils who were being taught in the hospital schools, 1,425 children were receiving individual or group tuition. The education of these children was seen as posing special problems, deriving from the great variety of their medical condition and the nature of their treatment, the differing lengths of their stay, the necessary flexibility in organising classes, time-tables and school terms, the considerable interruption in the continuity of teaching and unequal standards of physical accommodation and equipment. It was recognised that successful education depended upon close and continuous co-operation between hospital and teaching staff.

2.57 In Scotland an attempt was made to bring together expert opinion on all forms of handicap. In 1947 the Secretary of State remitted to the Advisory

_____
[8] Report of the Committee on Maladjusted Children (HMSO, 1955).

24

Council in Scotland the task of reviewing the provision made for the primary and secondary education of pupils suffering from disability of mind or body or from maladjustment due to social handicaps. The Council produced between 1950 and 1952 seven reports which were valuable guides to education authorities on the provision for different handicaps, although their predictions of future need have not all stood the test of time. For example, it was thought that special provision should be made for 20,000 physically handicapped pupils, whereas the number of these children in special schools in 1976 was only 1,076: conversely the Council's estimate that four residential child guidance clinics would suffice to meet the needs of all children maladjusted because of social handicap has proved to be hopelessly inadequate. The Scottish Education Department Circular No 300[9] in presenting these reports placed special education within the mainstream of primary and secondary education. "Special educational treatment should not be thought of mainly in terms of the provision on a large scale of separate schools for handicapped children. . . . It is recognised that there must continue to be situations where it is essential in the children's interest that those who are handicapped must be separated from those who are not. Nevertheless as medical knowledge increases and as general school conditions improve it should be possible for an increasing proportion of pupils who require special educational treatment to be educated along with their contemporaries in ordinary schools. Special educational treatment should, indeed, be regarded simply as a well-defined arrangement within the ordinary educational system to provide for the handicapped child the individual attention that he particularly needs."

2.58 In the year prior to the issue of Circular No 300 Scottish regulations were made laying down definitions of the nine statutory categories of handicap. Delicate and diabetic children were not included as they were in England and Wales. These Regulations, together with the 1956 Schools Code, which prescribed maximum class sizes for the various categories of handicap, ensured for handicapped children in Scotland the benefit of favourable pupil-teacher ratios.

V 1955-1977

2.59 This section sketches the main events in special education from 1955 to the present day and looks at particular areas where significant developments have taken place with which we are especially concerned in this report.

Developments in child guidance

2.60 The important recommendations of the Underwood Committee on child guidance were brought to the attention of local education authorities in

---

[9] The Education of Handicapped Pupils: The Reports of the Advisory Council (21 March 1955). The titles of the Reports were as follows:

Pupils who are Defective in Hearing	(Cmd 7866)
Pupils who are Defective in Vision	(Cmd 7885)
Visual and Aural Aids	(Cmd 8102)
Pupils with Physical Disabilities	(Cmd 8211)
Pupils with Mental or Educational Disabilities	(Cmd 8401)
Pupils handicapped by Speech Disorders	(Cmd 8426)
Pupils who are Maladjusted because of Social Handicap	(Cmd 8428)

Circular 347.[10] The Circular accepted the Committee's report as the basis for the organisation and future development of child guidance. The Committee had urged that there should be a comprehensive child guidance service available for the area of every local education authority, involving a school psychological service, the school health service and child guidance clinics, all of which should work in close co-operation. Authorities and regional hospital boards should plan their provision in consultation. The Circular asked local education authorities, in consultation with hospital authorities, to give effect to these recommendations and to submit progress reports by June 1960. At the same time hospital and local authorities were asked by the Ministry of Health to co-operate with local education authorities. In their subsequent reports most local education authorities accepted the pattern of child guidance clinics suggested in Circular 347, whereby the authority would provide the premises and employ the psychologists and psychiatric social workers, whilst the hospital service would provide psychiatrists.

2.61 The major bar to progress was a continuing shortage of professional staff, demand for which was increased by the recommendation of the Underwood Committee (endorsed by the Ministry of Education in Circular 348[11]) that a maladjusted child should, wherever possible, continue to live at home during treatment and attend an ordinary school or special school or class. This had led the Department to ask authorities to consider the need for more day schools or special classes, and, through their regional machinery, to review the need for boarding provision in schools or homes. The number of child guidance clinics increased modestly each year from 162 in 1950 to 367 twenty years later, but that of professional staff continued to lag behind. The duties, training and supply of educational psychologists were considered by the Summerfield Working Party which reported in 1968.[12] The Working Party recommended new and expanded arrangements for training and a doubling of numbers. By 1977 the position had substantially improved. An investigation of the functions of clinical psychologists was similarly considered by a sub-committee of the former Standing Mental Health Advisory Committee (the Trethowan Committee) which reported in 1975. The contribution of social workers to child guidance was strengthened by the Health Visiting and Social Work (Training) Act 1962, which established national arrangements for the training of health visitors and social workers, as recommended in the Jameson[13] and Younghusband[14] reports.

2.62 In 1974, on transfer of responsibility for the school health service to area health authorities, the provision and organisation of child guidance was the subject of further advice,[15] jointly from the Departments of Education and

---

[10] Ministry of Education Circular 347, Child Guidance (10 March 1959).

[11] Ministry of Education Circular 348, Special Educational Treatment for Maladjusted Children (10 March 1959).

[12] *Psychologists in Education Services.* The Report of a Working Party appointed by the Secretary of State for Education and Science: the Summerfield Report (HMSO, 1968).

[13] *An Inquiry into Health Visiting.* Report of a working party on the field of work, training and recruitment of health visitors (HMSO, 1956).

[14] Report of the Working Party on Social Workers in the Local Authority Health and Welfare Services (HMSO, 1959).

[15] DES Circular 3/74, DHSS Circular HSC(IS)9, Welsh Office Circular WHSC(IS)5, Child Guidance (14 March 1974).

Science and Health and Social Security. This recommended that the child guidance service should be based on a multi-professional team, providing assessment, diagnosis, consultation, treatment and other help as needed by the child, his parents or other people in regular contact with him. Local and health authorities were asked to extend the available help to children with behavioural, emotional and learning difficulties, and to the families of these children through more flexible use of distinct but collaborating services, and to report their new arrangements. The Court Committee on Child Health Services [16] which reported to the Secretaries of State for Social Services, Education and Science and Wales in 1976 recommended "that the child guidance clinics and psychiatric hospital services should be recognised as part of an integrated child and adolescent psychiatry service". In its Circular advising health authorities of the government's conclusions on the Committee's recommendations, the Department of Health and Social Security accepted the need for further progress in the integration of services, in the sense of co-ordinated planning and working as distinct from fusion of the existing services into a new one.[17] The Circular also indicated that a document illustrating some aspects of good practice in the integrated services would be issued jointly with the Department of Education and Science during 1978.

2.63 In Scotland the child guidance service developed much more rapidly than in England and Wales. By 1966, 25 of the 35 education authorities had a child guidance service. The Education (Scotland) Act of 1969 made the provision of such a service a duty and the functions referred to in paragraph 2.62 were extended to include advice to social work departments, which had been established by the Social Work (Scotland) Act 1968. (The Scottish child guidance service has no direct medical component as in England and Wales and is organisationally similar to the school psychological service south of the border. The agreed ratio of educational psychologists to children in Scotland is 1:3,000, which it is hoped to attain by 1980.)

Child care

2.64 In England and Wales, effect was given to another recommendation of the Underwood Committee when in 1959 agreement was reached that the training courses provided under the aegis of the Central Training Council in Child Care should be extended to cover those intending to undertake the residential care of handicapped pupils in schools and boarding homes. Three types of courses were available: a basic one-year course for new entrants, a short refresher course for those in post, and a one-year advanced course for those aspiring to responsible posts. The Central Training Council in Child Care was succeeded in 1971 by the Central Council for Education and Training in Social Work (CCETSW), set up as a result of the recommendation of the Seebohm Report[18] that there should be one central body responsible for promoting the training of the staff of the personal social services. In 1977 CCETSW confirmed its intention of discontinuing its awards of the Certificate in Residential Social

---

[16] *Fit for the future*. The Report of the Committee on Child Health Services. Cmnd 6684 (HMSO, 1976).

[17] DHSS Health Circular HC(78)5 Local Authority Circular LAC(78)2, Welsh Office Circular WHC(78)4, Health Services Development (January 1978).

[18] Report of the Committee on Local Authority and Allied Personal Social Services. Cmnd 3703 (HMSO, 1968).

Work and the Certificate in the Residential Care of Children and Young People in view of its plans to provide alternative opportunities for training for work in residential establishments within courses leading to the award of the Certificate of Qualification in Social Work and schemes for the Certificate in Social Service.

Independent schools

2.65 The Underwood Committee had also recommended that local education authorities should be permitted to maintain maladjusted pupils only at those independent schools which were recognised by the Ministry of Education as efficient. This policy was accepted in principle in Circular 4/61[19] as being applicable to the placement of all handicapped pupils, and notice was given of the progressive elimination of placements in non-recognised schools, to be completed by June 1964. This intention was not in the event fulfilled. Although the Circular resulted in more rigorous control of the use of unrecognised schools, pupils continued to be admitted to them in substantial numbers. The decision of the Secretaries of State for Education and Science and for Wales, announced in 1977, to discontinue the recognition of independent schools from April 1978 meant that the policy in Circular 4/61 would need to be reviewed.

Mentally handicapped children

2.66 Increasing unease about the principle and practice of excluding large numbers of mentally handicapped children from school found expression in the Mental Health Act 1959. The Act replaced Section 57 of the Education Act 1944 (as amended) by less rigid provisions. Parents were allowed extra time in which to appeal to the Minister against a local education authority's decision that their child was incapable of being educated in school; and given the right to call for a review after one year, with like opportunity to appeal. Parents were to be given more detailed information about the functions of the local authority in relation to treatment, care and training, and, wherever possible, a statement of the arrangements proposed to be made for their child by the local authority in discharge of those functions. Thus co-operation between local education and health authorities was enforced by statute.

2.67 But whilst the 1959 Act was a response to unhappiness, particularly amongst parents, about the labelling of some children as not being entitled to education, it had merely tempered the procedures leading to segregation. Criticism of the system continued to grow, and moreover, the concept of special education was broadening to encompass needs hitherto regarded as beyond its reach. These tensions were finally resolved in April 1971 when local education authorities assumed responsibility for the education of mentally handicapped children, following the Education (Handicapped Children) Act 1970, which removed the power of health authorities to provide training for these children and required the staff and buildings of junior training centres to be transferred to the education service. In this way some 24,000 children in junior training centres and special care units, 8,000 in about 100 hospitals, and an uncertain number at home or in private institutions ceased to be treated as being mentally deficient and became entitled to special education. For this purpose they were to

---

[19] Ministry of Education Circular 4/61, The use of independent schools for handicapped pupils (27 March 1961).

be regarded as severely educationally sub-normal (ESN(S)), as distinct from the moderately educationally sub-normal (ESN(M)) who had previously made up the ESN category. Many of the children had other difficulties.

2.68 Detailed advice to local education authorities on the operation of the new arrangements was given in Circular 15/70.[20] Junior training centres would normally be approved by the Secretary of State as special schools. Provision in hospitals might take the form of hospital special schools or arrangements for teaching under the terms of Section 56 of the Education Act 1944. In the event about 400 new special schools were so formed. The training of teachers of mentally handicapped children would be integrated as soon as possible into the ordinary three-year initial teacher training: but to assist the transition special one-year courses would be provided at selected colleges for those teachers who held the Diploma of the Training Council for Teachers of the Mentally Handicapped and who could satisfy the minimum entrance qualifications. Apart from questions of staffing, many of the new special schools were accommodated in old outmoded buildings, and although their replacement became a major feature of special school building programmes since the 1970 Act was passed* a great deal remained to be done to achieve satisfactory standards in all schools.

2.69 In Scotland education authorities became responsible in 1947 for the education of children who were described as "ineducable but trainable". Those children were placed in junior occupational centres and trained by instructors, but following the Report of the Melville Committee[21] and subsequent provisions in the Education (Mentally Handicapped Children) (Scotland) Act 1974 the centres were re-named schools, and teachers were appointed in addition to the instructors. The 1974 Act also gave education authorities responsibility for the education of children who had previously been described as "ineducable and untrainable".

Community homes and List D schools

2.70 Under the Children and Young Persons Act 1969 a new system of community homes was established in England and Wales which called for new forms of collaboration between local education authorities and social services departments. The new system brought together establishments for the accommodation of children in the care of local authorities and the former remand homes and approved schools. Approved schools, which had been established in 1933, were residential institutions approved by the Home Secretary for the education and training of boys and girls who, with few exceptions, were ordered to be sent to them by the courts. They provided a general education, with considerable attention to craft training for the older children, but their primary objective was the social readjustment of the boys and girls in preparation for their return to the community. In Scotland all the functions of the former approved schools,

---

[20] DES Circular 15/70, Responsibility for the Education of Mentally Handicapped Children (22 September 1970).

* For example, of the 1974–75 special school building programme 42% was devoted to ESN(S) places: in 1975–76 the figure was 33%. Special school building was seriously interrupted during 1976–78.

[21] *The Training of Staff for Centres for the Mentally Handicapped.* Report of the Committee appointed by the Secretary of State for Scotland (HMSO, 1973).

including the provision of education, were transferred in 1971 to local authority social work departments under the terms of the Social Work (Scotland) Act 1968, and these institutions are now known as List D schools.

The school health service

2.71 The school health service originated in the Education (Administrative Provisions) Act 1907, which gave local education authorities the duty to provide for the medical inspection of children in public elementary schools and the power (which became a duty in 1918) to make arrangements, with the sanction of the Board of Education, for attending to their health and physical condition. The Education (Provision of Meals) Act 1906 similarly enabled authorities to provide or assist the provision of meals for children attending public elementary schools. In 1918 local education authorities were given the duty to provide for the medical inspection of children in secondary schools and the power to arrange for their medical treatment. The powers and duties of the Board of Education relating to the medical inspection and treatment of children and young persons were formally transferred under the Ministry of Health Act 1919 to the newly created Ministry of Health, but continued to be exercised, as permitted under the Act, by the Board on behalf of the Health Minister. The Chief Medical Officer of the Ministry of Health became also Chief Medical Officer of the Board, and subsequently of its successors, the Ministry of Education (1945) and the Department of Education and Science (1964). The Education Act 1944 and Education (Scotland) Act 1945 gave education authorities the duty to provide meals and milk for pupils at maintained schools; the duty to provide medical and dental inspection in all maintained schools; and the duty to provide or to secure for children attending maintained schools all forms of medical and dental treatment other than domiciliary treatment, without cost to parents. The National Health Service Act 1946 and the equivalent Act of 1947 in Scotland enabled education authorities by arrangement to use the services of regional hospital boards and teaching hospitals.

2.72 In April 1974 the school health service in England and Wales became absorbed into the National Health Service under the National Health Service Reorganisation Act 1973. A similar change took place at the same time in Scotland. The Act transferred responsibility for providing for the health of schoolchildren from education authorities to the Secretary of State for Social Services. From its inception, the school health service pioneered development in preventive medicine at a time when the importance of prevention was not generally recognised, and achieved much success in competition with therapeutic medicine, despite recurrent economic crises. Throughout its life the service has been particularly concerned with the needs of handicapped children; and the importance of continuing co-operation between the health, education and social services was stressed by the government in the White Paper that preceded the 1974 Act. Machinery was provided in Section 10 of the Act, which required health and local authorities to establish Joint Consultative Committees to promote the co-operative development of services.

Assessment

2.73 The construction of educational programmes for individual children with special needs depends for its success upon the accurate assessment of their needs. This was the theme of a joint departmental Circular issued in 1975.[22] It examined the composite process of discovery, diagnosis and assessment, emphasised its multi-professional character and stressed the value of informality and the importance of parental participation. It also introduced an improved set of forms for recording the educational, medical, psychological and other data required for deciding the nature of a child's special educational needs, and a summary sheet for use during the process of assessment, placement and review. Comments received in 1977 from local education authorities indicated their general satisfaction with the new procedures and their wish to develop them further.

2.74 In Scotland the 1960s had seen some confusion over the procedures for the assessment of handicapped children. Working parties examined the assessment of four groups of handicapped children: mentally handicapped, visually handicapped, maladjusted and hearing impaired. As a result major procedural changes were included in the Education (Scotland) Act 1969. The Act redefined special education in terms which excluded the concept of a fixed disability of mind or of body. It recognised the importance of early discovery by abolishing the minimum age at which a child could be ascertained by an education authority and established that the decision to ascertain a child was not exclusively a medical one. It required that in every case reports of psychological as well as medical examinations should be considered, with, wherever possible, the views of the child's parents and those of his teacher. It also recognised the widely held view that assessment is a continuing process.

Special qualifications of teachers

2.75 The enactment of compulsory education for blind and deaf children in 1893 was unaccompanied by any requirement relating to the training or qualifications of teachers. In 1886, when the Royal Commission on the Blind and Deaf was constituted, there existed three rival voluntary colleges which acted as examining bodies and issued certificates in the teaching of the deaf, but they were not recognised by the Education Department. The Commission recommended that training colleges for teachers of the deaf should operate under government supervision and that entrants to them should already be certificated teachers: but it made no proposals for compulsory further training or additional qualifications. In 1907, however, the three voluntary examining colleges were brought together to form a single joint examining body, and two years later the Board of Education approved its examination and recognised the diploma that it awarded. The Commission had offered no positive views about the training of teachers of the blind, but in 1907 the College of Teachers of the Blind was established as a voluntary examining and awarding body, and was also accepted by the Board. Thereafter the Board's regulations laid down that teachers in schools for the blind and deaf must obtain within two years of their appointment an approved qualification. The 1908 regulations have broadly continued to the present day.

---

[22] DES Circular 2/75, Welsh Office Circular 21/75, The Discovery of Children Requiring Special Education and the Assessment of their Needs (17 March 1975).

2.76 The McNair Committee (1944)[23] did not consider in detail the training of teachers of the handicapped, but the Fourth Report of the National Advisory Council on the Training and Supply of Teachers (NACTST) (1954) was devoted wholly to it. The Report recommended that with certain exceptions all intending teachers of handicapped children should, after experience in ordinary schools and some preliminary experience with handicapped children, take a full-time course of additional training. The Ministry of Education's Circular 324[24] accepted the recommendation in principle but declared it to be impracticable for the present. Teachers in special schools for blind, deaf and partially deaf pupils were already required to obtain a prescribed additional qualification within three years of taking up their appointment: whilst teachers in special schools taking classes of pupils who were both deaf (or partially deaf) and blind were required to hold a prescribed additional qualification for teachers of deaf and partially deaf children. The Circular urged that they should be encouraged to obtain also the qualification required of teachers of the blind. The requirement of an additional qualification was now extended to teachers of partially deaf pupils in special classes or units in ordinary schools.

2.77 The question of whether teachers of pupils with other kinds of disability should be required to have an additional qualification was considered again by the NACTST in 1962, but the Council concluded that the time was still inopportune. Ten years later the Vernon Committee[25] recommended that teachers of partially sighted children should (like those of the partially hearing) be required to have an additional qualification. This was also accepted in principle but not implemented. However a range of courses of in-service training continued to be available to teachers of handicapped pupils.

2.78 In Scotland following the first World War the National Committee for the Training of Teachers established a Central Executive Committee to make arrangements for the training of teachers of mentally defective children. In 1923 Kennedy Fraser was appointed to Jordanhill College of Education to be responsible for the endorsement course in special education. This was initially a one-year course but it had to be shortened to a term because of lack of numbers. For the next 30 years this course was the sole source of training of teachers in special education in Scotland. In 1956 a course was established at Moray House College of Education and by 1974 five such courses were available in Scotland. Until 1972 teachers of the deaf in Scotland were trained at Manchester. From that date, however, training was provided at Moray House College of Education and in 1972 the Scottish Centre for the Education of the Deaf was established in that College.

Integration

2.79 In 1928 the Wood Committee had stressed the unity of ordinary and special education. The philosophy of the Education Act 1944 had been explained

---

[23] *Teachers and Youth Leaders.* Report of the Committee appointed by the President of the Board of Education to consider the Supply, Recruitment and Training of Teachers and Youth Leaders (HMSO, 1944).
[24] Ministry of Education Circular 324, The Training and Supply of Teachers of Handicapped Pupils (29 May 1957).
[25] *The Education of the Visually Handicapped.* Report of the Committee of Enquiry appointed by the Secretary of State for Education and Science in October, 1968 (HMSO, 1972).

during the Debate on the Education Bill by the Parliamentary Secretary (Mr Chuter Ede) in these words: "May I say that I do not want to insert in the Bill any words which make it appear that the normal way to deal with a child who suffers from any of these disabilities is to be put into a special school where he will be segregated. Whilst we desire to see adequate provision of special schools we also desire to see as many children as possible retained in the normal stream of school life."[26] Accordingly, Section 33(2) of the Act provided for the less severely handicapped (the great majority of all handicapped) to be catered for in ordinary schools, and the ensuing departmental guidance to local education authorities contained detailed suggestions as to how this might be achieved. The post-war planning of special educational treatment thus proceeded on two main assumptions: first, that special educational treatment would be required for up to 17% of the school population; and secondly, that ordinary schools would have the major share in providing it.

2.80 These intentions were not in the event fulfilled: special educational treatment came to acquire a much narrower connotation than the official guidance had indicated; and its provision in ordinary schools failed to develop on the scale envisaged. With the benefit of hindsight it is possible to discern a number of interacting reasons why this happened. In the first place the statutory framework was not conducive to a broad conception of special educational treatment or to its positive development in ordinary schools. The children for whom special educational treatment was to be provided were defined in Section 8(2)(c) of the Education Act 1944 in a way which apparently excluded those whose needs did not spring from physical or mental disability. Further, Section 33(2) imposed a dichotomy between serious and less serious disabilities and, though stipulating that children with severe disabilities were to be educated in special schools wherever possible, merely permitted those with less serious disabilities to be educated in ordinary schools. The fact that ascertainment might entail resort to the compulsory procedure of medical examination and invariably meant formally assigning a child to one of the statutory categories of handicap, none of which might, in fact, fit his condition, was a disincentive to action. Inevitably ascertainment tended to be directed to children with more severe disabilities whom the law required to be educated in special schools. The widespread use of intelligence testing in determining the need for special education so far as mentally handicapped children were concerned also tended to perpetuate the notion of the separateness of such children.

2.81 Practical factors, too, impeded the development of special educational provision in ordinary schools. In the decade after the war local education authorities were hard pressed simply to maintain the fabric of the education service. Much school accommodation had been destroyed and many surviving buildings were in bad condition. Scarcity of building materials restricted work to essential needs including provision for raising the school leaving age, for the rapidly rising school population and for new housing estates, and the Building Regulations for schools allowed new building only on the basis of classes of 30 pupils in secondary schools and 40 in primary schools. Such classes were too large to enable effective special educational provision in ordinary schools to be developed. Nor was it a question of building alone. There were other shortages,

---

[26] Parliamentary Debates: Hansard Vol 398 Col 703 (21 March 1944).

for example of suitably trained teachers and other professionals required for effective assessment and treatment, and the quota of teachers then in operation did not allow for any appreciable reduction in the size of classes. For these reasons ordinary schools were badly placed to provide special education. The expansion of provision in special schools, in contrast, was greatly facilitated by the opportunities which existed for local authorities to purchase large town houses or country mansions relatively cheaply. In this way a large though not entirely adequate number of new special schools was provided, though at the price of their isolation. Since local authorities anxious to develop their special education could do so only in special schools, special educational treatment came to be associated with provision in special schools.

2.82 However, once the post-war difficulties had been overcome, developments followed which encouraged revival of the idea of special educational provision in ordinary schools. In particular, completion of the reorganisation of all-age schools in the 1960s and the progressive ending of selection for secondary education which followed the issue of Circular 10/65[27] enabled ordinary primary and secondary schools to broaden their educational programmes and to take greater account of children's individual needs. Special classes and units were established for children who had been ascertained as needing special educational treatment and a variety of forms of "remedial" education was developed for other children. Local education authorities were encouraged to minimise the formalities of ascertainment, to widen the basis of assessment and to diversify the provision. Integration became a topical subject of discussion.

2.83 Support for integration found Parliamentary expression in the Chronically Sick and Disabled Persons Act 1970, a private member's measure, which in Sections 25-27 required local education authorities, so far as was practicable, to provide for the education of deaf-blind, autistic and acutely dyslexic children in maintained or assisted schools. Although the legal description of the schools in which provision was to be made included special schools the intention was clearly that provision should, except for good reason, be made in ordinary schools. In Scotland, the same theme lay behind the report of the McCann Committee[28] on the secondary education of physically handicapped children. The Committee's report, whilst recognising that some physically handicapped children would require education in special schools, envisaged an ever increasing number of them being educated in ordinary schools.

2.84 This partial modification of the 1944 provisions was overtaken by the Education Act 1976, which in Section 10 required local education authorities to arrange for the special education of all handicapped pupils to be given in county and voluntary schools, except where this was impracticable, incompatible with the efficient instruction in the schools or involved unreasonable public expenditure, in which case it could be given in special schools or, with the Secretary of State's approval, in independent schools. The provision, which took the form of an amendment of Section 33(2) of the Education Act 1944, would come into force on a day to be appointed by the Secretary of State. In January 1977 the

[27] DES Circular 10/65, The Organisation of Secondary Education (12 July 1965).
[28] *The Secondary Education of Physically Handicapped Children in Scotland*. Report of the Committee appointed by the Secretary of State for Scotland (HMSO, 1975).

Secretary of State announced that before deciding to introduce the new provision she proposed to consult widely with the educational and other interests and also to await our findings. At the same time she made clear that the new legislation had not introduced a new principle, but had rather given a new impetus towards integrated provision, in which special schools would continue to have an important place.

CONCLUSION

2.85 Since the implementation of the Education (Handicapped Children) Act 1970 and the Education (Mentally Handicapped Children) (Scotland) Act 1974 all handicapped children, however serious their disability, have been included in the framework of special education.* Section 10 of the Education Act 1976, when implemented, will shift the emphasis of special educational provision within the framework in England and Wales significantly in the direction of greater integration and improved provision in ordinary schools. The quality of special education, however, cannot be guaranteed merely by legislation and structural change. The framework provides the setting within which people work together in the interests of children, and the quality of education depends essentially upon their skill and insight, backed by adequate resources – not solely educational resources – efficiently deployed. Our report is pre-eminently about the quality of special education, and in the following chapters we take up many of the themes that have emerged in this brief review of history.

---

* Also in 1970 The Transfer of Functions (Wales) Order provided for the Secretary of State for Wales to assume responsibility for a range of functions previously exercised by the Secretary of State for Education and Science, including special education.

CHAPTER 3: THE SCOPE OF SPECIAL EDUCATION

INTRODUCTION

3.1 We were appointed to review educational provision for children and young people handicapped by disabilities of body or mind. In this chapter we consider the meaning of handicap in an educational context and its usefulness as a concept. We urge the merits of a more positive approach, based on the concept of special educational need. We then turn to the need for a new system to replace the present statutory categorisation of handicapped pupils and conclude by advancing a broader view of special educational provision as a basis for a new framework of special education.

I HANDICAP IN AN EDUCATIONAL CONTEXT

3.2 In Chapter 1 we called attention to the wide range of things which a child needs to learn as part of his education. Besides his academic studies he must learn, for example, how to accommodate himself to other people. He must also learn what will be expected of him as an adult. Any child whose disabilities or difficulties prevent him from learning these things may be regarded as educationally handicapped, and it is with all educational handicaps that we are concerned in this report.

3.3 There is no agreed cut and dried distinction between the concept of handicap and other related concepts such as disability, incapacity and disadvantage. Neither is there a simple relationship between handicap in educational terms and the severity of a disability in medical or a disadvantage in social terms. Thus a boy with one leg suffers a gross and obvious physical disability which excludes him from many activities, but which may not prevent his making as good academic progress as his non-handicapped fellows. On the other hand, a child with impaired fine motor movements in his fingers has a physical disability which, though far from obvious and possibly not significant medically, may constitute a considerable handicap educationally since he will find great difficulty in writing. Again, a child suffering from extremely adverse social conditions may not have any difficulties in learning, whereas one whose home conditions seem only mildly unsatisfactory may nevertheless on starting school experience considerable educational difficulties.

3.4 Nor is there necessarily any direct relationship between handicap in educational terms and the degree of permanence of a disability or disturbance. For example there are some sensory disabilities which may be only temporary yet, while they last, have significant educational implications. An intermittent hearing loss or a partial hearing loss which becomes more severe at certain times may, for relatively short periods, be so handicapping to a child in school that intensive help in the form of specialist equipment and teaching techniques is necessary if he is to make educational progress. Moreover, the educational implications of a disability may vary at different stages of a child's development. A conductive hearing loss (one which is likely to be temporary and can respond to treatment) will affect an older child's understanding of language far less seriously than that of a younger child, whose vocabulary and skill in "guessing" at sentences are less well developed.

3.5 Whether a disability or significant difficulty constitutes an educational handicap for an individual child, and if so to what extent, will depend upon a variety of factors. Schools differ, often widely, in outlook, expertise, resources, accommodation, organisation and physical and social surroundings, all of which help to determine the degree to which the individual is educationally handicapped. Within a single school the impact of even a severe physical disability may vary from child to child according to its origin, the child's temperament and personality, his home circumstances, including the quality of the support and encouragement he receives within the family and neighbourhood, and the activities available to him out of school. In the case of maladjustment the relationship between a disability and the social setting in which it occurs may be even more complex.

3.6 It is thus impossible to establish precise criteria for defining what constitutes handicap. Yet the idea is deeply engrained in educational thinking that there are two types of children, the handicapped and the non-handicapped. Traditionally the former have generally been thought to require special education, and the latter ordinary education. But the complexities of individual needs are far greater than this dichotomy implies. Moreover, to describe someone as handicapped conveys nothing of the type of educational help, and hence of provision that is required. We wish to see a more positive approach, and we have adopted the concept of SPECIAL EDUCATIONAL NEED, seen not in terms of a particular disability which a child may be judged to have, but in relation to everything about him, his abilities as well as his disabilities – indeed all the factors which have a bearing on his educational progress. We discuss this concept further in the following section.

II THE EXTENT AND DIFFERENT FORMS OF SPECIAL EDUCATIONAL NEED

The extent of special educational need

3.7 The extent of special educational need is very difficult to assess. Some indication is given by the figures for the children ascertained as requiring special education IN THE TRADITIONAL SENSE OF SEPARATE SPECIAL PROVISION. Thus in January 1977 in England and Wales 176,688 handicapped children or 1.8% of the school population were attending special schools or special classes designated as such by local education authorities, were placed by authorities in independent schools catering wholly or mainly for handicapped pupils, were boarded in homes, were receiving education otherwise than at school or were awaiting admission to special schools. In Scotland 15,119 children or 1.4% of the school population were receiving separate special educational provision in the session 1976–77. However, the scale on which children are ascertained as being in need of special education varies widely from one authority to another. In England and Wales in January 1977 the prevalence of children ascertained as requiring special education ranged from below 120 per 10,000 of the school population in a handful of predominantly rural authorities to above 300 in a small number of counties with large conurbations. In only 44 out of 105 authorities was the figure within a range 10% above or below the average of 183. The prevalence of children ascertained as having particular handicaps varies even more widely between authorities; for example in one London borough in January 1977 ten times as many children were ascertained as maladjusted as in another. In Scotland a similar pattern is revealed. In the 1975–76 session the prevalence of children receiving special education ranged from 50 per 10,000 of the school population in a rural region to over 200 in a region with a large conurbation. Four out of nine regions were within a range 10% above or below the national average of 120.[1] Some of the variations between authorities may reflect variations in local policy and the strength of assessment services, but they also suggest a relationship between the rate of ascertainment and the availability of special provision.

3.8 Any estimate of the extent of the need for special education has also to take into account the children who spend at least part of their time in special classes set up on the initiative of individual schools. In 1976 classes of this kind were attached to 10,845 maintained schools in England and Wales – nearly 40% of all maintained primary, middle and secondary schools. They made provision, for varying periods of time each week, for 494,248 pupils, of whom 458,087 (4.7% of the school population) had difficulties in learning, or problems of an emotional or behavioural nature, or both. The great majority (82%) of the 458,087 spent less than half, and only 12% spent more than three-quarters, of their time in these special classes.[2]

3.9 Evidence from surveys of the proportion of children with special needs is variable since different surveys use different criteria of need. The most detailed study of the incidence of intellectual and educational retardation, psychiatric disorder and physical handicap was that carried out in 1964-65 on the Isle of Wight.[3] It covered the 2,199 children on the island aged between 9 and 11 years. For the purpose of the survey intellectual retardation meant an IQ of 70 or less; educational retardation meant a reading comprehension or accuracy 28 months or more below the child's chronological age or, in the case of specific reading retardation, 28 months or more below the level predicted from the child's age and IQ; psychiatric disorder was defined as an abnormality of behaviour, emotions or relationships sufficiently marked and prolonged to cause a handicap to the child himself or distress or disturbance in the family or community; and physical handicap was defined as a physical disorder which was chronic (lasting at least one year) and associated with persisting or recurrent handicap of some kind.

[1] Department of Education and Science and Scottish Education Department statistics. Note: The 1977 statistics for handicapped pupils in England and Wales quoted in this report are based on the returns to the Department of Education and Science, Schools Branch II, Special Education Division (SE1).

[2] Department of Education and Science statistics. (Comparable figures were not collected for 1977.)

[3] Ed M Rutter, J Tizard and K Whitmore, *Education, Health and Behaviour* (1970).

3.10 Of the 2,199 children, 354 were found to have one or more of these four types of handicap, that is 16% or roughly one child in every six of those in the middle years of their schooling. A quarter of the 354 had at least two handicaps: more precisely, 90% of the intellectually retarded, 43% of the educationally retarded, 36% of those with psychiatric disorder and 29% of those with a physical handicap had another handicap or handicaps.[4]

3.11 It is possible that the figures from the Isle of Wight survey may be an under-estimate rather than an over-estimate when applied to the country as a whole. The prevalence rates in other age groups generally are unlikely to be much lower and, as we explain below, may be considerably higher than for 9-11 year olds alone, while the social circumstances of the families studied on the Isle of Wight are likely to be typical only of populations living mainly in small towns where many of the adverse environmental circumstances associated with inner city areas are absent.

3.12 A study carried out in 1970 to compare the rates of "behavioural deviance" and psychiatric disorder in 10-year old children living in an inner London borough with those of children of the same age living on the Isle of Wight found that they were twice as high in the former as in the latter. The rate of "behavioural deviance", as assessed by the teachers' questionnaire, was 19.1% in the inner London borough compared with 10.6% on the Isle of Wight; while, on the basis of parental interviews, 25.4% of children in the inner London borough were estimated to show signs of psychiatric disorder compared with 12.0% on the Isle of Wight.[5] A study extending over the whole of inner London conducted by the Inner London Education Authority Research Unit using the same questionnaire found that the high rate of "behavioural deviance" was not specific to the one borough in the other survey. The average rate was found to be 19% with rates in different parts of inner London ranging from 14.2% to 25.3%.[6] The comparative study of children in the inner London borough and on the Isle of Wight also found that the rates of general reading backwardness (that is 28 months or more backward in either accuracy or comprehension) and specific reading retardation were over twice as high in the inner London borough as on the Isle of Wight: 19.0% compared with 8.3% and 9.9% compared with 3.9% respectively.

3.13 Other studies have used rather broader criteria in trying to establish the proportion of children with special needs. A study of an infants' school in a good residential area in England found that of the 500 children who left the school over a 6-year period 16% needed some additional help or consideration on account of learning, behaviour or emotional problems.[7] In 1971, after discussions with teachers, the Inner London Education Authority estimated, without

---

[4] *Ibid.*, pp 352–3. The figure for the total proportion of children with at least two handicaps (25%) is lower than that for the proportion of such children in each group because the multiply handicapped children were all included in more than one group *ie* they were all counted more than once.

[5] M Rutter, A Cox, C Tupling, M Berger and W Yule, "Attainment and adjustment in two geographical areas: I The prevalence of psychiatric disorder", *British Journal of Psychiatry*, 126 (1975), 493–509.

[6] Cited in ibid., 506.

[7] L Webb, *Children with Special Needs in the Infants' School* (1967).

attempting any breakdown, that between 12% and 20% of children of primary and secondary school age presented problems at some time or other in their school career and needed special attention for varying periods of time.[8]

3.14 The findings of the National Child Development Study with regard to the prevalence of special educational need nationally are broadly in line with those of local studies. The Study has followed up at the ages of 7, 11 and 16 years those children born in the week 3-9 March 1958. It found that at the age of 7 years 0.4% of the children were attending special schools; 5% of the children were receiving help within the ordinary school because of educational or mental backwardness; while there was a further 8% who, their teachers considered, would benefit from such help.[9]

3.15 At the age of 16 years 3% of the young people who were medically examined as part of the follow-up had been ascertained as currently in need of special education. 1.9% were attending maintained or non-maintained special schools. Of the young people in the sample who were in ordinary schools, 7% were receiving special help within the school because of educational or mental backwardness, 5% because of behavioural difficulties and 1% because of a physical or sensory disability. Special help in school was considered desirable by their teachers for a further 5.5%.[10] Thus some 20% appeared to need some form of special educational help. This may even be an under-estimate, for it proved impossible to obtain information about all the children for the follow-up, especially about those who had been receiving special education at the age of 11, were illegitimate, or had been in care by the age of 7.

3.16 The evidence of the Isle of Wight survey, the inner London survey, the study of the infants' school and the National Child Development Study broadly suggests, therefore, that at any one time about one child in six is likely to require some form of special educational provision. This is not of course an exact figure. It will vary from area to area according to local circumstances and will be influenced particularly by housing and other social factors and the character of individual schools, including their location, buildings, organisation and staffing, the effectiveness of their teachers and their approach to discipline. All these may affect the incidence of special educational need, especially in the realm of behaviour. Nevertheless the figure of one in six represents what we believe to be a reasonable judgement on the evidence and, indeed, is in line with the estimates of the number of children who might be expected to require special education which were given in 1946 and to which we referred in the last chapter.

3.17 While the special needs of some children will continue for relatively long periods and, in some cases, permanently, those of other children will, if promptly and effectively met, cease to exist. It follows that the proportion of children likely to require some form of special educational provision at any one time will be rather less than the proportion who may be expected to require such provision in the course of their school career. In the light of the information available to

---

[8] As reported in the minutes of the meeting of the Inner London Education Committee, 17 September 1974.

[9] M L K Pringle, N R Butler and R Davie, *11,000 Seven-Year-Olds* (1966), pp 37–39.

[10] ed K R Fogelman, *Britain's Sixteen-Year-Olds* (1976).

us, including the estimate made by the Inner London Education Authority in 1971 after discussions with teachers, we estimate that up to one child in five is likely to require special educational provision at some point during his school career. This means that a teacher of a mixed ability class of 30 children even in an ordinary school should be aware that possibly as many as six of them may require some form of special educational provision at some time during their school life and about four or five of them may require special educational provision at any given time. Again, we should stress that these figures will vary from class to class, school to school and area to area. The figures will however be an essential guide for planning purposes and *we recommend that the planning of services for children and young people should be based on the assumption that about one in six children at any time and up to one in five children at some time during their school career will require some form of special educational provision.*

Different forms of special educational need

3.18 Our conclusion that up to one child in five is likely to need special educational provision in the course of his school career does not mean that up to one in five is likely to be handicapped in the traditional sense of the term. The majority will be unlikely to have such a long-term disability or disorder. Their learning problems, which may last for varying periods of time, will stem from a variety of causes. But, unless suitable help is forthcoming, their problems will be reinforced by prolonged experience of failure. We refer to the group of children – up to one in five – who are likely to require some form of special educational provision at some time during their school career as "children with special educational needs".

3.19 In very broad terms special educational need is likely to take the form of the need for one or more of the following:

(i) the provision of special means of access to the curriculum through special equipment, facilities or resources, modification of the physical environment or specialist teaching techniques;

(ii) the provision of a special or modified curriculum;

(iii) particular attention to the social structure and emotional climate in which education takes place.

These are by no means exclusive and a child may very often have more than one of these forms of special educational need.

3.20 Special means of access to the curriculum may be required by children with impairments of sensory or motor functioning, including visual, hearing, speech and physical disabilities. For example, children with severe visual disabilities may need reading material translated into braille. A special or modified curriculum is likely to be required by children who are currently described as educationally sub-normal. Some children may have particular difficulty in meeting the social and emotional demands and adjusting to the constraints of an educational regime organised in the usual way. In their case special attention will need to be paid to the emotional climate and the social structure and organisation within the school, for example as regards the relationship between

41

the teachers and the ancillary and child care staff and that between the adults and children. Moreover, particular care will need to be given to the setting of limits to behaviour.

III A NEW SYSTEM TO REPLACE CATEGORISATION

The present system of categorisation*

3.21 It follows from what we have said about the different forms of special educational need that the particular form presented by an individual child is not necessarily determined by the nature of any disability or disorder suffered by him. Yet the principle of categorisation of handicapped pupils by type of disability or disorder has long been enshrined in education legislation in England and Wales and in Scotland. Moreover, it has exercised a powerful influence in practice on the ways in which assessment reports have been framed and educational provision has been organised.

3.22 It is generally accepted that in the early post-war years the list of statutory categories helped to focus attention on the existence and needs of different groups of handicapped children and offered a broad framework for planning special school provision which was generally found useful by local education authorities. There are some who believe that categorisation is still a valuable safeguard of the rights of a handicapped child to an education suited to his needs. They would probably accept that categories add nothing of substance to the existing general legal safeguards, such as those in Sections 8 and 34 of the Education Act 1944 (which require local education authorities in England and Wales "to secure that there shall be available for their area sufficient schools" and "to ascertain what children in their area require special educational treatment") and those in the equivalent Section of the Education (Scotland) Act 1945; but they argue that categories nevertheless underline the duties of local education authorities towards handicapped children. We return to this argument in paragraph 3.30.

3.23 These considerations have some force, but the use of statutory categories also has a number of disadvantages, as was pointed out by contributors to the written evidence, of whom a majority, although not an overwhelming one, favoured their abolition. First, their use pins a single label on each handicapped child and each special school. Many children suffer from more than one disability and this can present intractable problems of classification, especially as the major disability from a medical point of view may not, as we have pointed out already, be the most significant educationally; it also means that a wide variety of schools is required, with some catering for combinations of disabilities. Moreover, labels tend to stick, and children diagnosed as ESN(M) or maladjusted can be stigmatised unnecessarily for the whole of their school careers and beyond. More important, categorisation promotes confusion between a child's disability and the form of special education he needs. The idea is encouraged that, say, every child with epilepsy or every maladjusted child requires the same kind of educational regime. The confusion is heightened by the fact that only two categories – blind and deaf pupils – are defined in terms of

* The statutory categories of handicapped pupils are listed in Appendix 2.

educational methods positively required, whereas the other categories are defined in terms of disability which makes the pupils unsuited to the normal regime of ordinary schools. Moreover, although most local education authorities provide special help for children who in their opinion need it, even if these children do not readily fit into any of the statutory categories, a strict construction of Section 33(1) of the 1944 Act, or in Scotland Section 62 of the Education (Scotland) Act 1962 as amended, would prevent a child from being regarded as handicapped unless he came within one of the categories defined in regulations. However carefully a scheme of categorisation of handicaps is drawn up, there are always likely to be some children in need of special educational provision who will be excluded because they do not fit into any of the categories.

3.24 Whatever the weight attached to the preceding arguments, we believe that the most important argument against categorisation is the most general one. Categorisation perpetuates the sharp distinction between two groups of children – the handicapped and the non-handicapped – and it is this distinction which we are determined, as far as possible, to eliminate.

3.25 Furthermore, categorisation focuses attention on only a small proportion of all those children who are likely to require some form of special educational provision. We believe that the basis for decisions about the type of educational provision that is required should be not a single label "handicapped" but rather a detailed description of special educational need. *We therefore recommend that statutory categorisation of handicapped pupils should be abolished.*

Future forms of description of children with special educational needs and of special schools

3.26 We recognise, however, that for the sake of convenience descriptive terms will be needed for particular groups of children who require special educational provision. While the continued use of the existing forms of description for children with physical or sensory disabilities seems acceptable, we consider that it would be preferable to move away from the term "educationally sub-normal" or in Scotland "mentally handicapped", terms which can unnecessarily stigmatise a child not only in school, but when he comes to seek employment. "Educationally sub-normal" is, in any case, open to criticism on the grounds that it is imprecise and assumes agreement on what is educationally normal with regard to ability and attainment. It also suggests that a child so described suffers from an intrinsic deficiency whereas often the deficiency has been in his social and cultural environment. *We recommend that the term "children with learning difficulties" should be used in future to describe both those children who are currently categorised as educationally sub-normal and those with educational difficulties who are often at present the concern of remedial services.* Learning difficulties might be described as "mild", "moderate" or "severe". Children with particular difficulties, such as specific reading difficulties, might be described as having "specific learning difficulties". It will be argued that the practical effect of our proposal will be only to replace one label by another. We believe, however, that the term we have proposed, which will be used for descriptive purposes and not for any purpose of categorisation, is preferable to the existing label because it gives more indication of the nature of the child's difficulties, and is less likely to stigmatise the child.

3.27 The term "maladjusted" is also open to objection on the grounds that it can stigmatise a child unnecessarily; in addition, it can be criticised on the grounds that the concept of maladjustment itself is such a relative one that the description is meaningless without details of the child's circumstances.Worst of all, it tends to suggest a permanent condition and fails to give any indication of the type of special educational provision required. However, although there is a good case for referring to children as having emotional or behavioural disorders, we think that the term "maladjusted" also remains a serviceable form of description and should be retained. Indeed, we consider that the implication of this term (namely that behaviour can sometimes be meaningfully considered only in relation to the circumstances in which it occurs) is an advantage rather than a disadvantage. This consideration in our opinion outweighs the possible harm of stigmatisation.

3.28 Our suggestions as to the form of description of children apply also to the description of special schools. We hope, however, that our recommendation in Chapter 6 that each local education authority should produce a handbook giving details of special educational provision in its area will mean that knowledge of the facilities offered by particular special schools will be so widespread that in practice it will be unnecessary to describe them in terms of the pupils for whom they cater. It is already common practice in many areas to refer to special schools by a simple title, without mention of a particular disability, and we hope that this practice will become universal.

Statistical returns

3.29 Statutory categories of handicap have been used as a basis for statistical returns to the Education Departments from local education authorities and special schools. These returns show the special schools and special classes in existence and the number of handicapped children who are attending them or who have been placed by authorities in independent schools, hostels and so on. In England and Wales they also show the number of handicapped children awaiting places in special schools. The returns in England and Wales are misleading, in that all the children in a school for, say, delicate children tend to be shown simply as delicate, whereas the principal handicap of some may be, in current terminology, maladjustment and of others educational sub-normality; and there is no scope for showing additional handicaps. If, as we recommend, statutory categories of handicap are abolished, a new framework for statistical returns will be needed. We consider in the next chapter what form such a framework should take.

A system of recording children as requiring special educational provision

3.30 One argument in favour of categorisation of handicaps which does still weigh with us is that identified in paragraph 3.22, namely that it provides a valuable safeguard of the right of a child who fits into one of the categories to an education suited to his needs. We recognise that our recommendation that

44

statutory categories of handicap should be abolished may give rise to concern about how to safeguard the interests of children with severe, complex and long-term disabilities. We have found ourselves on the horns of a dilemma. On the one hand we are aware that any kind of special resource or service for such children runs the risk of emphasising the idea of their separateness, an idea which we are anxious to dispel, and of limiting the notion of special education to the provision made for such children. On the other hand, unless an obligation is clearly placed on local education authorities to provide for the special needs of such children, there is a danger that their requirement for specialist resources will be inadequately met.

3.31 In order to resolve this difficulty, we have tried to devise a system which, while avoiding the disadvantages inherent in categorisation, will preserve the advantages which it confers. *We recommend that there should be a system of recording as in need of special educational provision those children who, on the basis of a detailed profile of their needs prepared by a multi-professional team, are judged by their local education authority to require special educational provision not generally available in ordinary schools.* We shall elaborate this in the following chapter. There will be many children in ordinary schools whose need for special educational provision can be readily met with appropriate support in the school they are attending; these children will not need to be recorded as requiring special provision, since it will be unnecessary to formalise the obligation on authorities to provide education for them suited to their abilities and aptitudes. Only those children who have been assessed by a multi-professional team and, in the light of the team's assessment of their needs, judged by the local education authority to require special educational provision will be recorded by the authority in this way. The system of recording will thus safeguard the interests of the minority of children with special educational needs who have severe and complex disabilities or difficulties.

3.32 Our proposed system of recording children as in need of special educational provision will differ from the present system of categorisation in several important ways. First, it will lay an obligation on a local education authority to make special educational provision for any child judged to be in need of such provision on the basis of a profile of his needs prepared by a multi-professional team, whatever his particular disability. Secondly, it will not impose a single label of handicap on any child. Thirdly, it will embody a positive statement of the type of special provision required.

3.33 At the same time this system will be part of a much wider scheme designed to ensure that the individual needs of all those children – up to one in five – who require special educational provision at any time during their school career are appropriately assessed and met and that their parents* are involved as fully as possible. We hope that this scheme, which is developed in the course of this report, will help to eliminate the notion of two types of children – the handicapped and the non-handicapped – both in theory and in practice.

---

* References to parents throughout this report include both natural parents and those who care for children in place of their natural parents.

IV A BROADER CONCEPT OF SPECIAL EDUCATION

3.34 The view which we have stated of the nature and range of special educational needs and our estimate of the proportion of children who are likely to have such needs during their school career amount to a much wider concept of special education than any currently in use. We must therefore consider the precise way in which special education may be delineated.

3.35 We start from the concept of "special educational treatment" defined in Section 8(2)(c) of the Education Act 1944 as "education by special methods appropriate for pupils suffering from disability of mind and body". We note in passing that the definition is in the context of education in schools, and that there is no equivalent formulation applicable to further education. It has an institutional connotation, being linked to the provision of schools (principally special schools) and fixes the framework for later provisions in the Act for the ascertainment, categorisation and placement of the pupils covered by it.

3.36 Our concept is not tied to particular educational methods or particular categories of children. Nor is it associated with any particular institutional setting; the majority of children who are likely to require special educational provision in the wider sense that we are advocating will be in ordinary primary and secondary schools, which are not approved as providing a particular kind or kinds of education. The traditional view of special education as exclusively separate full-time provision in special schools or classes has in any case been substantially modified by recent practice, and has been explicitly called into question by Section 10 of the Education Act 1976 (which embodies the principle that handicapped pupils should be educated in ordinary schools wherever appropriate). This Section is to come into force in England and Wales on a day to be appointed by the Secretary of State for Education and Science. We consider its implications at length in Chapter 7.

3.37 We have already remarked on the negative quality of the definitions of most of the categories of handicapped pupils requiring special educational treatment, given as they are in terms of disability that makes the pupil unsuited to the normal regime of ordinary schools. The definition of special education in the Education (Scotland) Act 1969, although it has the merit of using terms which clearly apply to children with emotional or behavioural disorders as well as those with physical or intellectual disabilities, is similarly negative in tone: "education by special methods appropriate to the requirements of pupils whose physical, intellectual, emotional or social development cannot, in the opinion of the education authority, be adequately promoted by ordinary methods of education". Such a definition conveys nothing of the qualities or features which make special education "special".

3.38 Our view of special education is much broader and more positive than that contained in any of these definitions. It encompasses the whole range and variety of additional help, wherever it is provided and whether on a full or part-time basis, by which children may be helped to overcome educational difficulties, however they are caused. It thus embraces educational help for children with emotional or behavioural disorders who have previously been regarded as disruptive, as well as for children who have hitherto been seen as requiring remedial, rather than special, education. Both these groups in our view require special education.

3.39 At present "remedial" groups include children with a variety of difficulties which, though different in origin, are frequently treated alike. There are children who have been absent from school and need to make up work which they have missed; children with physical or sensory disabilities, sometimes temporary, sometimes permanent; children with varying degrees of learning difficulties and children who need to be temporarily withdrawn from the normal class for specific purposes. The term "remedial", like the term "treatment", suggests that these children have something wrong with them that can be put right. It is true that some of them are suffering only a temporary learning difficulty and, given appropriate help, are able to return rapidly to their previous classes having completely overcome their disability. Others, however, require special help and support throughout their school lives and to say that these children require "remedial" education is misleading. Children in these so-called "remedial" groups have a wide variety of individual needs, sometimes linked to psychological or physical factors, which call for skilled and discriminating attention by staff – in assessment, the devising of suitable programmes and the organisation of group or individual teaching, whether in ordinary or special classes. For these children the provision of special support is just as important as for those who have been ascertained as requiring special education. We conclude that a meaningful distinction between remedial and special education can no longer be maintained.

3.40 In attempting to delineate special education, we have sought to identify those features which make up its distinctive character wherever it is provided. Our approach is based upon the principle that if it is to be special, special education should afford access to teachers with additional training and, where appropriate, to other professionals; or access to an educational or physical environment appropriate to a particular child's special needs – for example, an environment where adequate physical support is available, or one in which a particular educational regime is followed. We propose that special educational provision for the children with whom we are concerned should, therefore, be understood in terms of one or more of three criteria :–

(i) effective access on a full or part-time basis to teachers with appropriate qualifications or substantial experience or both;

(ii) effective access on a full or part-time basis to other professionals with appropriate training; and

(iii) an educational and physical environment with the necessary aids, equipment and resources appropriate to the child's special needs.

In Chapter 12 we consider the nature of the qualifications that would be appropriate for teachers with responsibility for children with special educational needs.

3.41 We have described the distinctive characteristics of special educational provision as we conceive it and the children who will require it. The delineation will need to be given statutory expression. So far as England and Wales are concerned this entails three changes to Section 8(2)(c) of the Education Act 1944.

First, the term "special educational treatment" will need to be replaced by "special education"; secondly, there will be need to elaborate the references to children who suffer from disabilities in such a way as to establish that they include those with significant difficulties in learning, or with emotional or behavioural disorders, as well as those with disabilities of mind or body; and thirdly the reference to "special methods appropriate for persons suffering from that disability" will need to be replaced by a reference to "education by special means appropriate to their respective needs". The last amendment follows from our view that the form of special educational provision that a child requires is not necessarily conditioned by his disability alone, but should reflect a full assessment of his individual needs. This general reference to special means would be associated with a separate provision (replacing Section 33(1) of the Education Act 1944) requiring the Secretary of State to make regulations as to the means. These would be based on the criteria set out in paragraph 3.40.

3.42 The changes which we have outlined in the preceding paragraph apply *mutatis mutandis* to Scotland. *We therefore recommend that Section 8(2)(c) of the Education Act 1944 and Section 5(1) of the Education (Scotland) Act 1962 (as amended), which define the duties of local education authorities in relation to the provision of special educational treatment and special education respectively, should be amended to embody the broader concept of special education and the wider description of children which we have advocated in paragraphs 3.40–41.*

3.43 The new delineation of special educational provision that we propose would provide the point of reference for a general duty on the part of local education authorities to ascertain which children in their area require it, on the analogy of Section 34(1) of the Education Act 1944. By ascertainment we mean the whole process of discovery and assessment as we describe it in the following chapter. We indicate in that chapter the procedure whereby the duty of ascertainment should be fulfilled.

3.44 Only a minority of children who have been ascertained as needing special education will be recorded by the local education authority, as we have already explained. Their needs will require assessment and formulation by a multi-professional team. We consider these procedures and the composition of the record in the next chapter. It is however convenient to indicate here our intention that the local education authority should be given the specific duty to record those children whose needs cannot be satisfactorily met within the resources generally available to county and voluntary schools, and to provide special education as prescribed in the record. In support of these provisions the Secretaries of State should be required to make regulations as to the resources deemed to be not generally available in county and voluntary schools, as to the composition of the multi-professional teams and as to the form of the record. In addition there will be need for statutory provision for the enforcement of multi-professional assessment and for safeguarding the rights of parents. In the next chapter we set out our various recommendations for new statutory provisions that will be necessary to give effect to our proposed system of recording.

CONCLUSION

3.45 Thus we are proposing a general framework of special education which is much wider than the present statutory concept, and within that, though an integral part of it, the means of safeguarding the interests of the minority of pupils whose needs cannot be met within the resources generally available in ordinary schools. This framework is intended to establish once and for all the idea of special educational provision, wherever it is made, as additional or supplementary rather than, as in the past, separate or alternative provision.

CHAPTER 4: DISCOVERY, ASSESSMENT AND RECORDING

INTRODUCTION

4.1 We cannot emphasise too strongly in this chapter, as in the rest of our report, how essential it is for a child's education that any special needs he has should be discovered and assessed as early as possible. The broader, more flexible framework of special education which we believe is required in future will entail reform of the arrangements for the discovery and assessment of children's special needs. We contend that these arrangements have in any case now served their turn. Moreover, having been developed for some 2% of the school population, they would not necessarily be suitable for up to one in five children of school age, who present a very much wider range and variety of educational needs. In this chapter we consider procedures for the discovery and assessment of special needs that will be applicable to children of all ages, from birth to leaving school. We elaborate our proposal for a system of recording children as in need of special educational provision which will safeguard the interests of those with severe, complex and long-term disabilities, and we conclude by considering how statistical information about children requiring special educational provision should in future be collected.

I DISCOVERY

4.2 The discovery of handicapping conditions, which nearly always involves the identification of special educational needs, may take place at one of many different stages. Severe congenital abnormalities such as spina bifida, limb deformities or Down's Syndrome are usually recognised at birth, or in the first few days or weeks of a child's life. Other disabilities, physical, sensory or intellectual, or signs of handicapping conditions may be discovered in the early months or years of a child's life by parents and various professionals, including general practitioners, clinic doctors, health visitors, day nursery staff, social workers and teachers, all of whom need to be helped, through training, to appreciate the educational implications of these conditions. The difficulties of the large majority of children who are likely to require special educational provision, however, will become apparent for the first time in school and their needs will therefore have to be identified in that setting.

4.3 Very many contributors to the written evidence submitted to us were highly critical of present arrangements for discovering children with disabilities or serious difficulties. Many advocated the screening of the entire child population at various stages, ranging from birth and early infancy through to infant, junior and secondary school; while several among the associations of teachers and of local authorities recommended an extension of the use of registers of children at risk. In the following sections we consider how existing arrangements for discovery may be improved, and deal in turn with the contributions of parents and of different professionals and with systems of communication between hospitals and community health and other professional community services.

The role of parents

4.4 In many cases the first people to detect signs of those handicapping conditions or special needs which have not been discovered at, or soon after, birth are the child's parents. It is highly desirable that parents should be able to acquire knowledge about patterns of child development so that they can more easily detect any unusual features. Opportunities may be provided in a variety of ways: for example at ante-natal clinics or evening classes, through the medium of broadcasting or through magazines. Efforts are already being made by members of the health and education services and the broadcasting authorities to disseminate information about child development. We commend these efforts, but consider that they need to be taken further. *We recommend that information about child development and sources of expert advice on this subject should be still more widely disseminated to parents and prospective parents, fathers as well as mothers.* Moreover, parents should be reminded, through this information, of the need for their children's health to be regularly reviewed and of the availability for this purpose of the child health clinics provided under the preventive health services.

4.5 Even when parents express anxieties and suspicions about their child's development, these are too often disregarded by professionals. The fact that many parents have difficulty in convincing anyone that their children's problems are real came out very strongly from both the evidence submitted to us and the research project on services for parents of handicapped children under five which was carried out on our behalf under the co-direction of Professor Chazan and Dr Laing of the University College of Swansea.[1] Many parents need to be in contact with someone who can see that their anxieties are taken seriously and followed up. We propose that in most cases the health visitor, who will increasingly in future be working in collaboration with the general practitioner, should provide such a point of contact, and in the next chapter we develop this proposal in further detail.

Health surveillance and the role of the health visitor

4.6 As the Report of the Committee on Child Health Services (the "Court Report") recognised, periodical developmental assessment carried out by doctors and nurses trained for the job is an essential feature of the arrangements required for the early recognition of handicap.[2] Under the proposals contained in that Report, developmental assessment at specific stages of a child's life, supplemented by more intensive oversight of health and monitoring of developmental progress in the case of children with special needs, would be part of a standard programme of health surveillance. Suitable developmental screening tests might be applied to individual children in the course of such surveillance. Health surveillance programmes are already operated by nearly all area health authorities, but their effectiveness is limited by lack of resources and of suitable training for the staff. We are convinced that a basic programme of health surveillance involving a schedule of interviews between health care staff and a child and his parents, as proposed in the Court Report, would, if carried out by suitably trained staff and supported by the effective establishment and maintenance of

---

[1] See Appendix 5 for details of the research project.

[2] *Fit for the future.* The Report of the Committee on Child Health Services. Cmnd 6684 (HMSO, 1976), Vol 1, p 221.

51

contact with families, increase the likelihood of the early identification of disabilities or significant difficulties. *We therefore endorse the recommendation in the Court Report that a basic programme of health surveillance should be provided for all children.*

4.7 Registers of children considered to be "at risk" on account of medical and other factors in their history were widely used in the 1960s, but had been abandoned by many health authorities by the beginning of the present decade. The many problems encountered were set out in the Court Report, which, rightly in our view, recommended that their use should be discontinued.[3] In particular, the strict application of risk factors led to large and unwieldy numbers of children being included on the registers, whilst reduction of the number of risk factors led to a decrease not only in the size of the registers but also in the proportion of handicapped children on them. Moreover, reliance on such registers is open to the serious objection that it may lead to children who are not on them being overlooked, while causing possibly unjustified anxiety to the parents of those who are. The same problems would arise if registers were to be kept of children likely to suffer educational difficulties, on the basis of observed events in pregnancy and the perinatal period or the family history. We therefore reject any extension of the use of risk registers in relation to educational difficulties. We believe that there is no substitute for informed and systematic observation of all children.

4.8 Area health authorities are under a statutory duty to ensure that a mother is visited by a health visitor after the birth of her baby. Although health visitors have no right of entry to the home, their visits are generally welcomed and, in practice, they enjoy ready access to families with babies and young children. They also have close links with doctors and other nurses, particularly where they are attached to a general practice. They are thus well placed to detect disabilities which have not been discovered at birth; and in many areas, in conjunction with clinical medical officers and some general practitioners, they already use screening techniques designed to detect departures from normal development.

4.9 In practice the effectiveness of health visitors in detecting disabilities and significant delays in development has sometimes been limited by other demands on their time, arising from their responsibilities for patients of all ages, and by shortages of staff. These considerations led the Court Committee to propose the concept of a child health visitor and a considerable increase in the number of health visitors. We believe that it is important that the health visitor's tradition of special responsibility for children and parents should be preserved and that the health visiting service should be so organised that more time can be devoted to work with children under five. We welcome the proposal by the government that the service should be expanded in the period up to 1980–81 and we were pleased to note that in a recent statement on the Court Report the Secretary of State for Social Services indicated that work with children and families should be health visitors' top priority.[4]

---

[3] *Ibid.*, pp 139–40 and Appendix F, pp 413–5.

[4] *Priorities in the Health and Social Services. The Way Forward* (HMSO, 1977), p 10, and DHSS Health Circular HC(78)5 Local Authority Circular LAC(78)2, Welsh Office Circular WHC(78)4, Health Services Development (January 1978), Annex A.

4.10 In whatever way the health visiting service is organised, we strongly support the practice of giving health visitors additional training to enable them to add an understanding of young children with special needs to their existing knowledge of child development, and to make best possible use of the developmental information acquired in the course of their visits. *We recommend that this practice should be extended.* Health visitors also need to be helped, through training and contacts with the education service, to appreciate the importance of early educational opportunities for children showing signs of having special needs or problems. We see considerable scope for the organisation of some of their post-basic training on an inter-professional basis and in Chapter 16 we suggest possible ways of doing this. It is important too that their records should be designed to facilitate maximum use of their observations.

4.11 We have observed a number of different approaches to the work of the health visiting service in relation to young children with handicapping conditions. In some areas specialist health visitors are appointed; in others, senior specialist health visitors supervise and support the work of their non-specialist colleagues; in yet others, the pattern is still that of a generalist service. We see room for variations in the organisation of the service, but stress that in all arrangements those who are not specialists should have ready access to specialist advice and enjoy close working relations with other professionals concerned with the care and education of children with special needs.

Dissemination of information following birth

4.12 The discovery of a handicapping condition is of little value in itself unless it is followed by diagnosis and assessment of a child's needs. Where a child is born at home, it is essential that information about any special needs he may have is passed to the various community services as quickly as possible. In the case of children born in hospital, effective systems of communication between hospitals and community health and other professional community services are vital. We consider below what these systems should be.

4.13 In England and Wales, at present, documentation on an infant starts with the notification of his birth. The Area Medical Officer must by statute be notified within 36 hours of a birth; he is then able to pass the information to the appropriate health visitor and community doctor (usually the Specialist in Community Medicine (Child Health)). In 1963 a section was added to the form for notification of birth to allow the doctor or midwife to report the existence of any congenital abnormality observed at birth. Since, however, the completion of this particular section of the document is not required by law, and since doctors and midwives are understandably reluctant to complete it unless the parents have already been informed of the existence of such an abnormality, its value as a source of information about the existence of handicapped children is limited. The arrangements in Scotland, which are different from those in England and Wales, are currently being reviewed.

4.14 A second source of information which may reach the community doctor in the case of children born in hospital is the letter which is sent to the general practitioner when the mother is discharged from hospital, and which would be likely to refer to any serious abnormality. It is often the custom for a copy of this letter to be sent to the appropriate community doctor. The next source of information, and probably the most important, is the communication which is sent from the hospital to the general practitioner when the infant's neonatal period has been abnormal. This will provide medical details of what has occurred and a good indication of whether a child has or is showing signs of having a handicapping condition. It is the custom of many paediatricians, and some other hospital specialists, to send a copy of any such communication direct to the community doctor. Further letters from clinics where the child is subsequently seen may be sent to the general practitioner and, where it is the custom, copied to the community doctor over an indefinite period of time.

4.15 We have seen examples of the successful, systematic use of letters and documents in schemes designed to ensure that handicapped children are identified as early as possible and their individual needs recorded. The communication of information in this way should not give rise to problems of breach of confidentiality, since its disclosure is confined within the medical profession to those doctors directly concerned with the well-being of the particular child. *We therefore recommend that area health authorities should seek to ensure that all paediatricians and other hospital consultants send copy letters about handicapped children, exercising their discretion over content, to appropriate community physicians as a matter of course.*

4.16 The communication of information beyond the medical profession to, say, health visitors and other nurses, local education authorities or social services departments is essential if suitable provision is to be made without delay. The education service must be informed about children with special needs as soon as possible if early educational opportunities are to be provided for them, and the social services department must be informed if its support is to be provided for the family. The communication of such information does, however, raise problems of confidentiality. We consider that health visitors should be able to see copy letters containing information which they need in order to perform their services effectively. Other professionals will need to rely on the Specialist in Community Medicine (Child Health), who has the important task of abstracting from the documentation received from hospital specialists any information about children with special needs required by non-medical services in exercising their functions. It is desirable that, wherever possible, parental consent should be obtained to the passing of information about a child from community physicians to non-health services. The child's interests must, however, be regarded as overriding. Where the parent's consent cannot be obtained or is withheld and the child's welfare is considered to be at risk community physicians should ensure that professionals in other services are informed of any factors which suggest the need for special help, including early educational provision.

The role of the education and other services

4.17 Professionals in other services besides the health service may be instrumental in the discovery of handicapping conditions in children attending day nurseries, nursery schools, nursery classes and those playgroups with which they have effective contact. The staff of day nurseries and playgroups have excellent opportunities to discover such conditions among children in their care. Where

54

they make such a discovery, they should consult other professionals and, if necessary, point out to the parents that information about the child's condition will be needed by the headteacher when their child comes to attend school. The parent's consent to the communication of such information should be sought. The education service is clearly well placed to identify signs of special need among children in nursery schools and classes. Indeed, as one of the bodies submitting evidence put it, "one of the advantages of nursery education is that it eases the process of identification of pre-school children with less obvious potential educational difficulties, for example children who may become maladjusted if not helped in early life". As we stress in subsequent chapters, all professionals who come into contact with young children must be helped, through their training, to identify those showing signs of having special needs or problems, and to appreciate the educational implications of their special needs.

4.18 We have pointed out that the large majority of children with special educational needs will have to be identified within ordinary schools. It follows that the class teacher must be able to recognise early signs of possible special need and must take seriously parents' concern about their child's development. This requires that teachers should know how to identify the signs of special need and when and where to refer for further help; we return to this in Chapter 12. It is also important that each school should have a scheme for recording the progress of individual children so that, when a child begins to experience difficulties, head-teachers and staff are alerted, and thereafter have the means of judging the effectiveness of special help provided. We have noted the recent Circular which invited local education authorities in England and Wales to report on aspects of local curricular arrangements, including existing practices with regard to records of pupils' educational progress.[5]

Record keeping

4.19 Records of an individual child's progress should be clear, factual, up-to-date and reliable. We believe that two types of personal folder are needed for the maintenance of such records in school, of which one should be readily available for consultation and the other should be available only on a restricted basis. The first type of folder should be on the lines of that suggested a decade ago in the Plowden Report.[6] This envisaged that the compilation would include facts about illness, absence from school and composition of the family; examples of the child's work and the names of some of the books used and schemes of work followed by him; and results of attainment and, where applicable, diagnostic tests. The quality of the record and its effectiveness as an educational instrument will inevitably depend upon the skill and judgement of the teachers who prepare and use it. A full and carefully constructed folder will provide the information necessary for a composite picture of a child's strengths and weaknesses and of the background factors which influence his progress. Although the Plowden Report was concerned with children in primary schools, we consider that the principle of maintaining such a folder for each child should apply to all pupils in primary,

---

[5] DES Circular 14/77, Welsh Office Circular 185/77, Local education authority arrangements for the school curriculum (29 November 1977).

[6] *Children and their Primary Schools.* A Report of the Central Advisory Council for Education (England) (HMSO, 1967), pp 161–2.

middle and secondary schools. *We therefore recommend that a personal folder, containing records of his progress and other factual information about him, should be maintained in school for every pupil and should be readily available for consultation.*

4.20 Such a folder will go far to ensure the early detection and effective assessment of children with special educational needs, and its regular maintenance thereafter will be an indispensable condition of continuing effective educational provision. It will be essential for the purpose of marshalling all the information about the child's performance in school, and will be a useful, compact source of information about the child for any professionals involved in the assessment of his needs. It will, if properly maintained, contain a note of such professional consultations as have been arranged in school. (The detailed results of such consultations will be recorded in a separate, confidential folder, as we explain in paragraph 4.23.)

4.21 Parents should, as a matter of course, be able to see their child's folder. They should be consulted by the headteacher or the class or form teacher about information concerning, for example, the composition of the family and should be encouraged to help in the up-dating of the information in the folder. A pupil should also have access to his folder and help to select material for inclusion in it.

4.22 We agree with the Plowden Report that, to be of maximum value, the folders should be available to class teachers in primary schools and to those teachers and personal tutors in secondary schools concerned with the child. In addition, the folder of a child thought to require special educational help should be available to those professionals who contribute to the assessment of his needs. Most of the information in the folder, and certainly the details of a child's special needs and the action taken to meet them, should be passed on when he moves from one school to another. We endorse the point made in the Plowden Report that in such a case the value of written records will be greatly enhanced by direct contact between staff in the child's former school and those in his new one, and between the new staff and parents. Folders should also be available to careers officers in their consultations with pupils and parents and to establishments of further education and adult training centres in making suitable arrangements for young people with special needs.

4.23 *A second type of personal folder is needed for the results of professional consultations and sensitive information given in confidence about a child's social background or family relationships. This should be a confidential folder.* It would not be complete without significant medical information provided by the health authority. *The folder should be kept in the school and access to it controlled by the headteacher.* We would normally expect access to be readily granted to members of those professions concerned with meeting the child's needs. We discuss the handling of confidential material in Chapter 16.

The monitoring of whole age groups

4.24 Close and continuous observation of pupils' progress by their teachers needs to be supplemented by procedures of various kinds which assist the identification of children with special educational needs. The operation of such procedures with regard to reading and language development was considered in detail in the Bullock Report[7] and we support the notion of testing age groups at between seven and eight years and again at the secondary stage. We think that such procedures should be applied to whole age groups rather than groups of children considered to be at risk, in view of the difficulty of defining risk factors to which we have referred. Moreover, similar procedures, though not necessarily involving testing, should be used to discover other educational and behavioural difficulties. We are aware that some local education authorities have already instituted such procedures and we believe that this practice should be more widely followed. *We therefore recommend that local education authorities should operate procedures for monitoring whole age groups of children at least three or four times during their school life.*

II ASSESSMENT

The legal position

4.25 The process of determining which children require special education is described in Section 34 of the Education Act 1944 and Section 63 of the Education (Scotland) Act 1962 (as amended) as "ascertainment". This involves three stages: discovery, that is finding out which children have disabilities which may call for special help; diagnosis, that is the determination of the nature and causes of the disabilities; and assessment, that is the consideration of the implications of the disabilities, particularly in educational terms, and definition of individual needs. Under the above-cited Sections of the Education Act 1944 and the Education (Scotland) Act 1962 (as amended) local education authorities have a statutory duty to ascertain what children in their area need special educational treatment (described simply as special education in the Scottish Act) and, where they decide that a child needs such treatment, to make suitable provision unless the parents make suitable alternative arrangements. The Sections lay down certain formal procedures for ascertainment involving the medical and, in Scotland, the psychological examination of the child, which were designed for use when parents either objected to or might be expected to object to their child's attending a special school. As the Department of Education and Science Circular 2/75 (Welsh Office Circular 21/75)[8] explained, the number of cases in which the formal procedures have to be employed has greatly diminished.

4.26 When a child has been discovered to have a disability or is showing signs of having special needs or problems, the nature of the handicapping condition must be diagnosed and his needs assessed as soon as possible so that appropriate help can be provided. Since a handicapping condition can become manifest at any time from birth, and since early education is crucial to the development of young children with special needs, we see no justification for any limit to the age at which steps can be taken to provide for the special educational needs of children. In England and Wales, since the power of local education authorities to require parents to submit their child for medical examination for purposes of

---

[7] *A language for life.* Report of the Committee of Inquiry appointed by the Secretary of State for Education and Science under the Chairmanship of Sir Alan Bullock FBA (HMSO, 1975), Chapter 17.

[8] DES Circular 2/75, Welsh Office Circular 21/75, The Discovery of Children Requiring Special Education and the Assessment of their Needs (17 March 1975).

ascertainment, as well as their duty to comply with reasonable requests from parents to have their child medically examined, are restricted to children who have reached the age of two, in practice ascertainment and the provision of education do not at present usually take place before that age. The position is different in Scotland, where education authorities have a power to ascertain children from birth and a statutory duty in the case of children over five. They can invite parents to submit a child of any age for a medical and a psychological examination but can require them to do so only if the child is over five. They have a duty to comply with reasonable requests from parents to have their children medically and psychologically examined.

4.27 We also hold that full investigation of a child's disabilities calls for more than a medical examination. A psychological examination is necessary, as the Scottish legislation already recognises. In addition, as Circular 2/75 indicated, teachers and, in some cases, social workers have an important contribution to make to assessment. That Circular advised that, as a first step, a report should always be obtained from a teacher who knows the child well. It saw the next essential steps as being to obtain the opinion of a school doctor and an educational psychologist. It envisaged that for some children investigation by other medical specialists, therapists or specialist teachers or the involvement of a social worker would be necessary. Our later references to multi-professional assessment apply to investigations of children's needs in which a range of professionals as envisaged in Circular 2/75 is involved.

4.28 With continuing good relationships between parents, local education authorities and others concerned in the discovery and assessment of a child's special educational needs, we hope that the arrangements could normally be conducted by agreement and without formality. There will, however, be occasions when even the best practices break down for one reason or another, and there will be disagreement about the process or the outcome. We therefore consider that enforceable procedures will continue to be needed, in circumstances where parents believe that their child has special educational needs which are not recognised by the authority, or where the authority considers that a child has special educational needs which the parents do not accept. The statutory procedure should embody two features which we regard as indispensable: first, in line with our view that the need for special education may begin at birth, the procedure should be applicable to any child from birth; and secondly, the multi-professional nature of effective assessment to which we draw attention in later paragraphs requires that the procedure should not be restricted to a medical examination alone. *We therefore recommend that Section 34 of the Education Act 1944 and Section 63 of the Education (Scotland) Act 1962 (as amended) should be amended to give local education authorities the power to require the multi-professional assessment of children of any age (after due notice to parents) and to impose on them a duty to comply with a parental request for such assessment.* We hope that in practice local education authorities will rarely need to exercise their power to require the multi-professional assessment of children, particularly of very young children. For their part, parents of children with special needs should be made aware of their right to request such an assessment, and we suggest that this should be one of the functions of the Named Person who, as we explain in the next chapter, will provide a single point of contact for them.

Requirements of effective assessment

4.29 We believe that there are four main requirements of effective assessment. First, parents must be closely involved. No assessment of a child's needs can be complete without the information which his parents can supply and no educational programme prescribed to meet his needs can be complete without their co-operation. There may be a small number of cases where the early involvement of parents in their child's assessment will not necessarily be in the child's best interests. As a general rule, however, parents should be included in assessment procedures from the earliest stages, and informed of the results. In all cases where the child is already at school, parents should be consulted as soon as it is proposed that a specialist who is not a member of the school's staff be asked to carry out an assessment of the child's needs. We make proposals below for ways of enabling parents to contribute to their child's assessment.

4.30 A second basic requirement of effective assessment is that it should aim to discover how a child learns and responds over a period, and not merely how he performs on a single occasion. The educational psychologist, for example, needs time, not only to carry out tests, but also to observe the child in a variety of settings, taking into account factors such as curiosity, drive, attentiveness, distractability and the influence of different types of surroundings. He needs also to obtain the observations of teachers and others who know the child.

4.31 The third basic requirement is that assessment must include the investigation of any aspect of a child's performance that is causing concern. This will generally require only a limited range of specialist involvement. In some cases, however, depending on the nature and degree of the child's difficulty, a wide range of professional expertise will be needed if a full investigation is to be carried out. The assessment of a specific disability, such as impaired hearing or epilepsy, will usually call for the participation of different specialists to assess the effects of the disability on all aspects of the child's functioning. Although no hard and fast rules can be laid down, we do not regard as adequate an assessment which neglects any material point on which an appropriate specialist view is required.

4.32 Fourthly, the family circumstances as a whole must be taken into account in any assessment of a child's needs. A health visitor or home visiting teacher may have information about the family background in the case of young children, and the educational psychologist where older children are concerned. In most cases a social worker's contribution will be required to ensure that no material aspect of the child's background is overlooked.

4.33 Some handicapping conditions, particularly behavioural disorders, may be brought about or accentuated by factors at the school, such as its premises, organisation or staff. In such cases, assessment may need to focus on the institution, the classroom setting or the teacher as well as on the individual child and his family if it is to encompass a full consideration of the child's problems and their educational implications. This needs to be borne in mind by all who take part in assessment.

The assessment of children below statutory school age

4.34 Young children with handicapping conditions may be referred for a full investigation of their needs in a variety of ways. Those with severe congenital abnormalities apparent at birth, or severe or complex disabilities discovered in the early years of life will normally be referred directly for such an investigation by the paediatrician or hospital consultant. Others will be referred following initial assessment by one or more of a number of professionals such as a general practitioner or medical specialist, an educational psychologist, a social worker or, where a child is attending a nursery school or class, a teacher. We consider the assessment of children under five more fully in the next chapter.

Stages of assessment

4.35 It would clearly be both impracticable and unnecessary to offer the full process of multi-professional assessment to up to one in five of the school population. In order to make adequate arrangements for assessing the needs of such a large proportion of children, whose requirement for special help is likely to range from minor modifications in the regime of a regular class in an ordinary school to placement in a special school, well-defined procedures are needed which make the most effective use of specialist resources. These may vary between areas and between schools. As a general principle, however, we believe that the concept of different stages of educational assessment should be established. *We recommend that there should be five stages of assessment and that a child's special needs should be assessed at one or more of these stages as appropriate.*

School-based stages of assessment: Stages 1-3

4.36 We envisage that in the first instance the class teacher or form tutor will consult the headteacher about a pupil who is showing signs of having special educational needs. At STAGE 1 the headteacher will be responsible for marshalling all the information about the child's performance in school, together with other pertinent information that is available from medical, social and other sources including, wherever possible, the parents. For this purpose he will necessarily rely heavily on the information in the child's personal folder. In the light of all the available information about the child, the headteacher and class teacher or personal tutor will take a decision to make special arrangements for him within the competence of the school, or to continue his education without change but subject to further review, or to seek further advice. Whatever decision is taken at this or any subsequent stage, the child's progress must be carefully monitored and detailed records kept in his folder.

4.37 At STAGE 2 the child's difficulties will be discussed with a teacher with training and expertise in special education. Later in this report we stress that such a teacher should be readily available either as a member of staff or as a local advisory teacher. At this stage the headteacher will once again be responsible for marshalling all the available information about the child from the various sources, including the parents, and the teacher with special expertise or the advisory teacher may carry out a further assessment of the child's needs. The options for further action will be the same as those at Stage 1 with, in addition, the prescription of a special programme to be supervised by the specialist or advisory teacher.

4.38 If it is decided at Stage 2 to seek further advice or if a child who has been assessed at that stage subsequently fails to make as much progress as was hoped, assessment will take place at STAGE 3 by a professional or professionals brought in by the headteacher or school doctor, usually with the advice of the local advisory teacher. The professional consulted may be a peripatetic specialist teacher, such as a peripatetic teacher of the deaf, an educational psychologist or a member of the health or social services.

4.39 The options at Stage 3 will be to make special arrangements within the school or to refer the child for multi-professional assessment at Stage 4 or 5. We do not envisage that it will be necessary to refer a child for multi-professional assessment if his special educational needs, as assessed at Stage 3, can be met by the ordinary school's staff or resources, supplemented where necessary by, say, the part-time services of an additional teacher, but nevertheless readily available to or within the school. If, however, it is thought, in the light of the assessment at Stage 3, that he may require the provision of yet further help on a regular basis, which will be of a specialist nature and external to the school, then the child should be referred for multi-professional assessment, so that his needs can be more fully investigated. In this case, as we explain more fully below, the SE forms procedure should at this point be initiated by the headteacher.

4.40 The first three stages of school-based assessment allow for considerable flexibility in local or school arrangements, and would not be suitably defined in law. We suggest that they could be the subject of advice to local education authorities. It will be essential, however, that their development and conduct should be closely monitored by authorities. In practice this monitoring will be carried out by members of the local authority's special education advisory and support service outlined in Chapter 13, which will also be responsible for ensuring that the necessary information reaches the authority about any additional staff or resources required by ordinary schools to meet the needs of pupils assessed as requiring special educational provision.

Multi-professional assessment: Stages 4 and 5

4.41 Multi-professional assessment beyond Stage 3 should be carried out at one or both of two levels. The levels will be distinguished primarily by the degree and amount of specialist expertise involved. The professionals involved at Stage 4, who should be able to carry out assessment of a child's needs at short notice, will be able to judge whether or not more experts, particularly experts with more specialist expertise, should be brought in and a Stage 5 assessment conducted. As we explain below, we envisage that multi-professional assessment at both levels will take place in a variety of settings. In most cases these will be non-residential but there will be some children for whom a period in residence for the purpose of assessment will be positively desirable.

4.42 The professionals involved in assessment at STAGE 4 will usually be those with direct responsibility for local services for children with disabilities, for example a medical officer, health visitor, educational psychologist and social worker based in the locality, a teacher in a local school and a special education advisory teacher with local responsibilities. Some of these professionals may be referred to as having "district" or other responsibilities, depending on the service for which they work. They will be able to take decisions about the use of local facilities and resources or refer children, where necessary, for further investigation at Stage 5. In the case of a child already at school, the head of the school should be included in the process of assessment. We consider that, wherever possible, those taking part should meet at a school or, in the case of children not yet attending school, in another setting such as a day nursery or playgroup which affords opportunities for sustained observation of children's responses to learning. It is important, as we have already indicated, that they should be able to see children very quickly after referral.

4.43 At STAGE 5 the professionals involved may, in some cases, be the same as those at Stage 4 together with one or more other specialists, or they may be other experts with narrower specialisms, perhaps with geographically wider responsibilities. We recognise that there would appear to be considerable similarity between assessment at our Stage 5 and assessment by district handicap teams. Such teams have already been established in some areas and the principle of their establishment was recently accepted by the government in its response to the Court Report.[9] The range of professionals involved at our Stage 5 will in every case depend on the nature of the special needs of the individual child. It is essential, however, that professionals from the education service should always be included. The membership of some district handicap teams will therefore need to be extended if they are to carry out effective educational assessment at our Stage 5. *We recommend that, where a district handicap team exists, it should be augmented as necessary so that it can carry out among its functions the assessment of children with special educational needs.* New district handicap teams should be so constituted that they, too, can carry out effective educational assessment.

4.44 There already exist child guidance and child psychiatric teams concerned with the assessment and treatment of a wide range of learning difficulties and emotional and behavioural disorders. Their membership will often overlap that of district handicap teams. They will be well-placed to carry out multi-professional assessment at our Stage 5 of children with certain kinds of disability, provided that they have an educational component and include all those professionals whose skills are required. There is clearly a need for discussion at local level about the links between such teams and the education service and their relationship with district handicap teams.

4.45 Any team which is hospital-based is likely to develop a predominantly medically orientated approach. While this may be necessary for some children, particularly those with severe or complex disorders who require a period of specialist observation and testing, it is less likely to be suitable for those who, though they need special educational provision, do not require hospital treatment. *We therefore recommend that multi-professional assessment at Stage 5 should usually take place at a centre within the community other than a hospital.*

4.46 Where multi-professional assessment does take place in a specialised, hospital-based unit, it is essential that professionals from a wide range of services

[9] DHSS Health Circular HC(78)5 Local Authority Circular LAC(78)2, Welsh Office Circular WHC(78)4, Health Services Development (January 1978).

should nevertheless be involved. So far as the education service is concerned, a suitably trained and experienced teacher should be continuously present in the unit and, wherever possible, an educational psychologist or an appropriately trained clinical psychologist should contribute to the assessment. An officer of the local education authority, usually an adviser in special education, should also join the assessment team, since it is important that the team's recommendation for meeting a child's needs should be informed by his expertise and detailed knowledge of the local and other facilities available. For the same reason a member of the local authority social services department should be included in the team.

4.47 We recognise that in some rural, sparsely populated areas, particularly parts of Wales and the Highlands and Islands of Scotland, there may be difficulty in arranging multi-professional assessment at Stage 4. Where multi-professional assessment has to be conducted exclusively at Stage 5, facilities should be so organised that long delays between referral and assessment are avoided. It may be necessary for some children to have periods of residence at assessment centres, in which case they should normally be accompanied by a parent or someone else from their home or locality. Alternatively teams may visit outlying areas regularly.

Regional-based assessment

4.48 Regional-based assessment may be necessary for the small minority of children with extremely complex or unusual disorders. In view of the highly specialised personnel required, this will usually need to take place in a hospital setting and *we support the recommendation in the Court Report that regional multi-professional centres for children with relatively rare or particularly complex disabilities should be established in university hospitals. It is essential that the education service should be fully represented in these centres.*

4.49 Although our proposed stages of educational assessment have been described in terms of a progressive sequence, each stage involving more refined procedures and expertise than the last, the stages will not have to be gone through in order. Many children will not go beyond the first stage, while some may be referred immediately for multi-professional assessment at Stage 4 or 5. Moreover, if a Stage 1 assessment results in a call for further advice, this may in some cases be sought directly at Stage 3. Where the general monitoring of a whole age group reveals that a child has special needs it is important that the child's needs should be fully assessed at the appropriate stage of our assessment procedure. We believe that, because of its inherent flexibility, the procedure should be applicable to all children of school age showing signs of having special needs. There are groups of children, however, for whom the assessment of special needs will call for particular sensitivity, as we explain below.

The assessment of children whose first language is not English

4.50 We are aware that there are special problems in Wales and Scotland in assessing and meeting the special needs of children whose first language is Welsh or Gaelic. In order to cater effectively for children whose first language is Welsh, an increase in the numbers of Welsh-speaking teachers, psychologists and other professionals concerned with children with special educational needs is required. Education authorities in Scotland have a statutory duty to make adequate provision for the teaching of Gaelic in areas where it is spoken. The need for such provision naturally applies to, and may have considerable significance for, children in those areas with special educational needs.

4.51 Wherever a child's first language is not English, at least one of the professionals involved in assessing his needs must be able to understand and speak his language. The assessment of the needs and the placement of children from ethnic minorities may be a matter of special sensitivity. There has, for example, been concern in recent years that a disproportionate number of children from West Indian families has been placed in special schools or classes for children currently described as ESN(M). Any tendency for educational difficulties to be assessed without proper reference to a child's cultural and ethnic background and its effect on his education can result in a category of handicap becoming correlated with a particular group in society. We see this as a risk inherent in the present system of ascertainment and categorisation of handicap, and the uncertain relationship between remedial and special education. We hope that the broader concept of special education and the formulation of children's individual needs which we are advocating, together with the abolition of categories of handicap, will eliminate harmful associations of this kind. We obviously hold that all children, of whatever ethnic or cultural background, are entitled to the full benefits of our proposed procedures for the discovery, assessment and, where appropriate, the recording of special educational needs, and we would not wish to suggest any variation of these procedures for particular groups of children. Indeed we have emphasised that, for these procedures to be effective, there should be the fullest possible information available about a child's background, and this would clearly be incomplete without reference to his cultural upbringing. However we recognise that the incidence of learning difficulties which arise from living in a new cultural or ethnic setting is a matter of sensitive concern, and accordingly we consider it of the first importance that the assessment of children's special needs, at any of the five stages that we have proposed, and the subsequent educational prescription, should reflect a balanced consideration of all the relevant factors, be they cultural, social, medical, psychological, or educational. Further, as we have consistently stressed in this and other contexts, parents must be consulted and their views given full weight in the assessment of their children's needs; and this is especially true where decisions can touch deep-seated sensitivities. Finally, the practice of regular review and, where required, the re-assessment of children's needs and adjustment of the provision made for them, which we deal with in the following section, should encourage parents to view assessment not with suspicion but as offering the possibility of enhanced educational opportunity for their children.

Review of progress and re-assessment of needs

4.52 The needs of individual children change over time and no assessment can be regarded as final. It is important that, where a child has been discovered to have special educational needs and these have been assessed, his performance should be regularly monitored, so that any programme devised for him can be reviewed and if necessary modified, or further assessment carried out. Detailed records of his progress should be kept in his school folder. In most cases careful observation by class teachers will produce sufficient data for the record. In others, however, this may need to be supplemented by check lists and other procedures, including tests. These should be simple and easy to apply. Learning style, for example accuracy, pace and concentration, social relationships and attainments should all be covered.

4.53 *We recommend that the progress of a child with special educational needs should be reviewed at least annually, and that the headteacher of his school, whether an ordinary or a special school, should be responsible for initiating the review.* In some cases the headteacher may act in conjunction with a member of the proposed special education advisory and support service or other supporting service. In consultation with those teachers who have been observing the child's performance or monitoring his development and with the advice, where necessary, of a local advisory teacher or peripatetic specialist teacher, the headteacher should study the records of the child's progress maintained in his school folder and decide whether any special arrangements made for him need to be modified or his needs re-assessed. Parents should, of course, be able to seek a review of their child's progress at any time. *We recommend that responsibility for the oversight of reviews of progress should rest with the special education advisory and support service.*

4.54 The review of a child's progress may indicate that his needs should be re-assessed. The process of re-assessment may be carried out at any of the stages of our proposed assessment procedure. In most cases it will be suitably carried out at one of the school-based stages. Where, however, a child whose special educational needs have been assessed at Stage 4 or 5 moves from a nursery to a primary, or from a primary to a secondary school, it may, depending on his progress, be necessary to re-assess his needs at one or other of those stages. Re-assessment of special needs will be necessary at least two years before a young person with special needs is due to leave school. This process should always involve a careers officer and should usually include other professionals in the education, health and social services. We return to this in Chapter 10.

4.55 The Department of Education and Science Circular 2/75 (Welsh Office Circular 21/75) reminded local education authorities: "Though some children will prove to need to stay in a special school for the whole of their school life, no placement should initially be assumed to be final". The Scottish Education Department Circular 733 issued on 26 August 1969 also emphasised the importance of reviewing placements at regular intervals. The need to review a child's placement remains equally important in the context of our broader view of special education, irrespective of where it is provided. The variety of forms of special educational provision that we believe is required will give considerable scope for adjustment of the arrangements for individual children. Some pupils may simply require adjustment of their educational programmes without a change of placement. For others re-assessment may reveal the need for more intensive help, of a kind which calls for the pupil to be recorded as in need of special educational provision; or it may lead to a recommendation to the authority that the child's recording as in need of special educational provision should be cancelled, and that he should transfer from a special school, unit or class to an ordinary school or class, with or without additional help.

4.56 *We recommend that arrangements for any change of placement should always be carefully planned.* Where a change of school is indicated, the co-operation of the receiving school should be ensured. Wherever possible, the child should be prepared for the new setting by a period of attendance, either full or part-time, at the new school or class. This may be treated as a trial period although, in view of its limitations, the results of such a trial will need to be interpreted very carefully. Members of the proposed special education advisory and support service will usefully contribute to the arrangements for and appraisal of the results of any trial period. *A change of placement should always be subject to confirmation after a period during which the child's progress should be carefully watched by the headteacher, in consultation with the headteacher of the child's former school where the new placement entails a change of school.*

III THE SE FORMS PROCEDURE

4.57 We consider that the SE Forms procedure, modified in the way we suggest below, can provide an effective way of collecting information about and documenting the results of assessment of a child's special needs. *We recommend that it should be initiated when a child is referred for multi-professional assessment at Stage 4 or 5.*

4.58 The SE Forms for completion on individual children were introduced in Scotland by the Scottish Education Department's letter of 1 November 1971, in England by Circular 2/75 and in Wales by the Welsh Office Circular 21/75. There are three forms in use in Scotland: Forms SE1, SE2 and SE3, which are designed for completion by a child's teacher, an educational psychologist and a school doctor respectively. In England and Wales the sequence is different, in that Form SE2 is for the school doctor and Form SE3 for the educational psychologist, and there is an additional form, Form SE4, which is a summary and action sheet intended for completion and signature by an experienced educational psychologist or adviser in special education. The use of Forms SE1–SE4 is not mandatory. A recent survey carried out by the Department of Education and Science found that the forms were used by about two thirds of authorities in England and Wales; some of the others had devised their own equivalents of the SE Forms.

4.59 Although the SE Forms procedure was designed for children who are attending school, including those receiving nursery education, we see no reason why it should not apply also to children who have not yet started school. For pupils in school the procedure will continue, as at present, to be initiated by the headteacher using Form SE1. In the case of children under five who are not attending school, responsibility for referral will rest in other professional hands, and here a different initiating form may be used, suited to the professional context in which the referral is made.

4.60 We have stressed the need to involve parents in assessment procedures, not least because they can provide invaluable information about their child. None of the present SE Forms, however, is designed for completion by the parents and it is left to the headteacher on Form SE1 and the educational psychologist on Form SE3 (Form SE2 in Scotland) to record the parents' attitudes towards their child's needs. *We recommend that whoever refers the child for multi-professional assessment should inform the parents as soon as the SE procedure has been initiated and should give them a form on which to make their own statement about their child's needs.* This form should contain questions about significant events in their child's life as well as more general questions such as: What do you think is your child's main problem? What are his main strengths and special interests? What sort of special help do you think he needs? In addition, the form should ask for details of any professional consultations that have taken place about the child, and should give the parents opportunity to indicate whether or not they have any objections to the consultants' being approached for further information. The completed form should be returned by the parents either to the person who handed it to them, in which case he should forward it to the education officer of the local education authority with responsibility for special education, or, if they prefer, to that officer directly.

4.61 Some parents may need help to express their views and feelings adequately on the form. Advice should be readily available from their Named Person, who will provide a single point of professional contact for them, and whose functions we describe in the next chapter. The Named Person for parents will normally be the health visitor where the children are under school age or the headteacher where they are at school. In most cases, therefore, their Named Person will be the same person who gives them their form. Other sources of help in completing the form, particularly for parents of young children not attending school, may be their general practitioner, the social services department of the local authority, a local resource centre on handicap, a voluntary organisation concerned with the handicapped or a citizens' advice bureau. In every case the availability of help should be explained to parents when the form is handed to them.

4.62 *We recommend that the completed SE Form which initiates the SE procedure should be sent to the education officer of the local education authority with responsibility for special education.* We recognise that in practice he will wish to delegate responsibility for the SE procedure and *we recommend that a member of the special education advisory and support service should normally be given this responsibility.* That officer will then seek information about the child on the appropriate SE Forms from the different services.

4.63 At present the only professionals for whom the SE forms are designed are teachers, doctors and educational psychologists. We consider that the social services department should also be sent a document as part of the SE procedure in order both to inform its officers that a particular child is thought to require special educational provision and to obtain any information they consider should be supplied about the child's family background.

4.64 There has been much criticism from doctors in general and child psychiatrists in particular about the inadequacy of Form SE2 (Form SE3 in Scotland) and the lack of clarity about where, say, a psychiatric report is to be recorded. We consider that there should be better provision for contributions by medical professionals and by other health service professionals, such as speech therapists, physiotherapists or health visitors. *We recommend that contributions to Form SE2 by members of the health service should be co-ordinated by the Specialist in Community Medicine (Child Health) or a medical colleague designated by him, normally an officer with clinical responsibilities.*

4.65 Forms SE2 and SE3 have been widely criticised also for their lack of flexibility. In view of these criticisms *we recommend that Forms SE2 and SE3 should be revised, after due consultation with the appropriate professionals.* We hope that it will be possible to substitute structured documents which would give ample opportunity for full descriptions of various aspects of the child's functioning. It would be more useful and economical to have a briefer initial form, to which supporting information relating to particular areas of the child's functioning could be appended. *We further recommend that a document on lines similar to the revised Forms SE2 and SE3 should be drawn up for completion by professionals in social services departments.* The format of these documents should provide scope for the professionals concerned to give the fullest information in terms more in keeping with the best practices of their profession. For example, where a psychologist has had opportunities to observe a young child without formal testing but with various play and learning structures designed to bring out the child's progress in some area, it should be possible for him to record these observations in full, with their conclusions. Similarly, it should be possible for, say, a speech therapist to provide a full report of his findings. A short handbook will need to be compiled giving guidance as to the kind of information required.

4.66 We consider that the process of multi-professional assessment of a child's needs at Stage 4 or 5 should be concluded by the completion of Form SE4, re-numbered as necessary in the light of our proposals above. *We therefore recommend the introduction of Form SE4 in Scotland.* The detailed profile of the child's needs and the recommendation for the provision of special help entered on this form will, as we explain in the following section, provide the basis for a judgement by the local education authority as to whether the child should be recorded as requiring special educational provision. *We regard it as essential that the completion of this form should remain the responsibility of an officer of the local education authority, either an adviser in special education or an educational psychologist.* He should show the child's parents the completed form and give them an opportunity to indicate on it whether or not they concur with the statement of and prescription for their child's needs. *The form should then be forwarded to the officer of the local education authority responsible for the SE Forms procedure, who should ensure that copies are sent to the local authority social services department, the area health authority and, where the child is of school age or attending a nursery school or class, the headteacher of his school.*

4.67 Under our proposals the SE Forms will clearly be an integral part of procedures for multi-professional assessment at Stage 4 or 5. The profile of the child's needs contained in Form SE4 will need to be set out in a way that will be familiar to the local education authority in whose area the assessment is carried out and to any other education authority in whose area the child may subsequently live or attend school. In view of the strong desirability that the SE Forms should have national currency, *we recommend that their use by local education authorities in England, Wales and Scotland in a form to be determined jointly by the Secretaries of State should be mandatory*.

4.68 We are aware that there is often at present a considerable interval between the initiation and completion of the SE Forms procedure, with the unfortunate result that the provision of special education to meet a child's needs is delayed. We emphasise the necessity for speed in collecting information about the child from the various professionals concerned so that assessment can take place and special help be provided promptly. We suggest that it should be part of the function of the Named Person to seek to hasten the completion of the SE Forms by acting as a "progress chaser".

IV RECORDING OF CHILDREN AS IN NEED OF SPECIAL EDUCATIONAL PROVISION

4.69 As we indicated in the previous section, the completed Form SE4 will be the basis on which the local education authority will judge whether or not a child should be recorded as requiring special educational provision. We have considered most carefully whether such a system of recording could in practice tend to emphasise the separateness of the children concerned–an idea which throughout this report we are at pains to dispel. We think that such a possibility will be minimised by the confidential nature of the record and by the variety of settings, in many cases in ordinary schools, in which the children's special needs will in practice be met. Moreover, the broader concept of special education which we have proposed, linked to progressive stages of assessment and the regular noting of an individual pupil's needs and progress in a school folder, will, we hope, also work against the emergence of distinctive groups. However, to the extent that a system of recording may suggest a form of separateness we think that any possible disadvantages are outweighed by two considerations of practical importance. In the first place the needs of children who require the provision of regular special help outside the ordinary school greatly exceed those of children for whom special provision can be made wholly or mainly within the school: they call for greater resources and more complex organisation of services. Unless these needs and the corresponding means of meeting them are explicitly recorded there will be real danger of insufficiency or default in their provision. Secondly, even though regular specialist help may be available to the ordinary school which a child is currently attending there can be no guarantee, in the absence of a formulation of need and provision, that it will continue to be available if he moves to another school, whether in the same area or that of another local authority. *We therefore recommend that a duty should be imposed on authorities to maintain a record of children whom they judge to require special educational provision not normally available in the ordinary school, subject to the proviso that no child should be recorded without prior assessment by a multi-professional team.* We consider that authorities should have the power to record a child as requiring special educational provision from any age, although in practice, as we explain in the following chapter, we envisage that it would be unusual for them to use this power in the case of very young children. In support of this statutory provision, *we further recommend that the Secretaries of State should be required to make regulations as to the resources deemed to be not generally available in county and voluntary schools, as to the composition of the multi-professional teams and as to the form of the record.*

4.70 The process of recording a child as requiring special educational provision will entail entering in a file in the local education authority's offices the completed Form SE4 with a profile of the child's needs and a recommendation for the provision of special help, as well as a separate note on how that recommendation is being met in practice, together with the name of a person designated by the multi-professional team to provide a point of contact for the parents. These documents will form the record of the child. *The parents should have ready access to the documents comprising the record of their own child.* Beyond them, however, access to details of children recorded as requiring special educational provision should be restricted to those with a professional interest in a particular child and to those who can show on application to the local education authority that they have a *bona fide* reason for seeing the documents, for example for research purposes. It will be for the local education authority and, where necessary, the area health authority to decide, in the latter circumstances, whether access should be granted, and on what terms.

4.71 In order to protect their interests, *we recommend that, on the introduction of our proposed system, all children currently ascertained as requiring special educational treatment and also those who, though not so ascertained, are attending special schools or designated special classes or units should be recorded as requiring special educational provision.* Local education authorities may wish in due course to arrange for the needs of these children to be re-assessed by a multi-professional team so that up-to-date information is available against which to judge whether the educational provision being made for a particular child requires revision, or whether the child should continue to be recorded. *We also recommend that, in order to ensure continuity of specialist help for a pupil who, having been recorded as requiring special educational provision by one local education authority, moves to another area, a copy of the documents comprising his record should be passed to the authority into whose area he moves and that he should be automatically recorded by that authority.*

4.72 Arrangements should be made for children to cease to be recorded if they no longer need regular, specialist help external to the ordinary school. It will clearly be impracticable (and anyway in our view unnecessary) to insist that a recording can be cancelled only after full re-assessment by a multi-professional team. However, we consider that no decision should be taken until the child's needs have been re-assessed by more than one professional external to the school, if not by a full multi-professional team. If it is decided that the child should cease to be recorded, the documents held by the authority about his needs should be struck through.

4.73 The recording of children as in need of special educational provision will enable their parents to satisfy themselves that the children are receiving a suitable education. The profile of their child contained in Form SE4, as well as the document filed by the authority alongside Form SE4 recording how the child's needs are being met, will afford the parents a basis on which to make representations to the authority and subsequently, if necessary, to the appropriate Secretary of State if they consider that their child's needs have been incorrectly assessed, or that the recommendation for meeting them is inadequate, or that the authority is failing to make suitable provision.

4.74 Under Section 34 of the Education Act 1944 and Section 66A of the Education (Scotland) Act 1962 (as amended) parents have the right of appeal to the appropriate Secretary of State against a decision that their child requires special education. They have no corresponding right of appeal against a decision that he does NOT require special education although in England and Wales they could of course appeal under Section 68 of the Education Act 1944 on the general grounds that the authority was acting unreasonably. We believe that in future they should have explicit right of appeal against such a decision. *We therefore recommend that parents should have the right of appeal to the appropriate Secretary of State against a decision by a local education authority to record or not to record their child as in need of special educational provision.*

V STATISTICAL RETURNS

4.75 The statistical returns of handicapped pupils which are made by local education authorities to the Department of Education and Science, the Scottish Education Department and the Welsh Office are based on statutory categories of handicap. They show the numbers of handicapped pupils who are attending special schools, special classes or independent schools, who are receiving education in hospitals or at home and, in England and Wales, who are boarded in homes or who are awaiting places in special schools. The returns of pupils in England and Wales can be misleading in so far as the way in which an individual child is shown tends to depend on the type of disability for which his school caters rather than on his own primary disability. Moreover, they do not afford scope for showing any additional disabilities.

4.76 If, as we have recommended, statutory categories of handicap are abolished, a new framework for statistical returns will be required. We believe that this should be capable of yielding much more comprehensive statistical information than at present about children who require special educational provision (for example information about the number of children with different combinations of disability and the number with particular degrees of any given disability). This will be possible only if the information for each child is initially recorded on a grid, of which one axis lists a number of different areas of functioning under which the child's disability or disabilities can be shown, and the other takes the form of a scale on which the degree of disability can be indicated. *We therefore recommend that a feasibility study on the use of a grid for the purpose of statistical returns should be carried out in a sample of local education authorities and that, if it is found to be practicable, a grid should be introduced as a basis in future for such returns.* An example of a possible grid is given in Appendix 3: this would show on a five-point scale the degree of impairment of a child's functioning in each of a number of areas. There may be scope for improvement in its design. Detailed instructions for completion will of course need to be compiled.

4.77 It is clear that in practice it will be possible to complete such a grid only after multi-professional assessment of a child's needs. We therefore suggest that the grid should be filled in by the same person whom we have recommended to be responsible for completing and signing Form SE4, namely the adviser in special education or the educational psychologist. We envisage that it will be printed, along with a table showing the child's initial placement and any subsequent change, on the blank back page of Form SE4. While the information on the grid will be of use to the local education authority whether or not it decides that the child should be recorded as requiring special educational provision, *we recommend that the statistical returns to government departments based on the grid should be of those children actually recorded as in need of special educational provision.* The returns will thus have a uniform basis which will enable them to be used for comparative purposes and for planning the necessary provision. Information on the number of children with any particular combination of disabilities could be collected on the basis of the completed grids for individual children. The details entered on the grid for an individual child will need to be regularly up-dated to ensure that the returns are as accurate as possible. We suggest that they should be checked as part of any re-assessment of the child's special educational needs.

4.78 If local education authorities are to ensure that the necessary staff and resources are made available to meet the needs of all children who require special educational provision, not just those who are recorded, they will require information about children assessed as needing such provision at the school-based stages of our proposed assessment procedure. Such information will also be required so that authorities can put specialists such as specialist careers officers in touch, at the appropriate time, with pupils with special educational needs who are likely to require their help and advice. *We recommend that local education authorities should devise their own framework, which might be a simplified version of the grid, for collecting information from schools about pupils assessed at Stage 1, 2 or 3 as being in need of special educational provision.*

CONCLUSION
4.79 If appropriate special educational provision is to be made, and if it is to be made as early as possible, arrangements for the discovery and assessment of special educational needs must be effective, and must be carried out without delay. The procedures proposed in this chapter should, we believe, cater effectively for up to one in five of the school population, while providing a particular safeguard for the interests of the much smaller proportion of children with severe, complex and long-term needs. In subsequent chapters we consider particular aspects of these procedures in relation to the under-fives, children of school age and those leaving school.

CHAPTER 5: CHILDREN UNDER FIVE

INTRODUCTION

5.1 The earliest years of life have enormous significance for all aspects of a child's development. The survey of recent research in special education which was undertaken for us[1] drew attention to those studies which have stressed the very rapid physical, emotional and intellectual development that takes place during the first few years of life. The period between birth and four years of age is generally accepted to be that of the fastest intellectual development, while the years between one and three to four normally see a rapid development in language. Thereafter the rate of intellectual development progressively diminishes, and the learning of language becomes increasingly difficult. Education during the first five years of life is thus of crucial importance.

5.2 It is also widely held that there are periods, notably the very early stages in development, when a child is particularly sensitive to experience and quick to learn from it. The early experiences of children with physical, sensory or intellectual disabilities, and their opportunities for self-education, may however be very limited and their development correspondingly restricted. The development of young children, whether or not they have a disability, may also be hindered by difficulty in forming personal relations or by adverse social circumstances. As we pointed out in Chapter 1, children with disabilities or significant difficulties will need to be elaborately taught things which other children learn spontaneously. *Their education, therefore, must start as early as possible without any minimum age limit.* For some children educational help will need to be provided below the age of two. We understand that the law is ambiguous on the power of local education authorities to provide education for children under two. We consider that any doubts about their power to do so should be resolved and, if necessary, the law amended to give them this power.

5.3 *In the earliest years parents rather than teachers should be regarded, wherever possible, as the main educators of their children.* Parents of children with handicapping conditions will themselves have special needs, in particular the need for skilled support and help in developing in themselves behaviour and attitudes most conducive to their child's growth. The education service can help in these early years to widen the child's restricted range of experience and enable parents to give their child effective support.

5.4 If a suitable educational programme is to be devised at an early stage, it is vital that a child's special needs should be discovered and assessed without delay. In this chapter we draw attention to those aspects of the procedures described in the previous chapter for discovery and assessment which are particularly applicable to the under-fives; and we consider ways in which early

---

[1] Cyril Cave and Pamela Maddison, A survey of recent research in special education (to be published by the National Foundation for Educational Research).

educational opportunities may be provided. Throughout we consistently stress both the needs of parents and the contribution they can make to their child's development.

I DISCOVERY

5.5 Many severe congenital abnormalities are recognised at birth or in the first few days or weeks of a child's life. Other disabilities or signs of special needs may be discovered in the early years by many people, particularly parents, health visitors, general practitioners and clinic doctors as well as professionals in services other than the health service. These professionals need to be helped, through training, to recognise early signs of special needs and to appreciate that social disadvantage and the disruption of family relationships, as well as physical and other disabilities, may give rise to educational handicap. They also need to know when and where to refer for special help and to understand the importance of working closely with parents and colleagues in other professions concerned with children with special needs and problems. We recognise that, however effective the various services are in providing special help for children whose parents consult them, there will always be some parents who will not use them and with whom it will be extremely difficult to establish contact.

Disclosure to parents

5.6 The discovery of a handicapping condition at or soon after birth needs to be disclosed very carefully and sensitively to the parents, for whom it is a matter of the deepest emotional significance. Even allowing for the fact that this is an extremely delicate and difficult task and that the parents' recollections may be confused or incomplete, much of our evidence indicates that disclosure is often handled badly. The findings of the research project carried out for us on services for parents of handicapped children under five under the co-direction of Professor Chazan and Dr Laing reveal that many of the parents in each of the five areas surveyed were dissatisfied with the insensitive way in which their child's disability had been revealed to them; the inadequate and often confusing information which they had been given about the nature of the disability; and the lack of guidance which they had received on how to cope with the child at home.[2] Apart from the unnecessary suffering caused, a side effect of clumsy or insensitive disclosure may be embittered relationships between parents and the professional staff on whose assistance so much will depend over the years to come. There is also a danger that parents may look for less reliable help outside the health and other services.

5.7 We believe that the discovery of a handicapping condition in a child should usually be revealed to the parents without delay. We recognise that where such a condition is only suspected and not confirmed, the medical and nursing staff will need to exercise discretion in deciding whether or not to tell the parents of their suspicions and at what stage. Where, however, the existence of a handicapping condition has been established, parents should be informed with the least possible delay. They should be given the news in private and, wherever possible, together unless particular circumstances make this undesirable. In hospitals, a pre-arranged plan involving medical and nursing staff and social workers should

---

[2] For details of the research project see Appendix 5.

be implemented so that all those having contact with the mother and child act in concert. It is to be expected that, after the initial shock, parents will have further questions to ask about the handicapping condition, and they should have the opportunity to put these questions to the paediatrician or other hospital specialist in a further interview or interviews. Some of the mothers in the research project mentioned above felt that they had benefited from being accompanied at hospital consultations by a professional who could ask questions for them. We consider that, wherever parents feel in need of such support, they should be able to look to a particular professional, already known to them as a point of contact, to accompany them. We suggest below that this person should normally be the health visitor. Parents can also prepare themselves for interviews with medical and other consultants by formulating written questions in advance and they should be encouraged and helped to do so by the health visitor.

5.8 We regard it as important that, where the disability is discovered at birth, the mother should be allowed to keep her baby close to her unless there are medical reasons for removing the child, for example to an intensive-care unit. Even in this eventuality, as frequent contact as possible should be encouraged between mother, father and child. This may help to reduce the chance of rejection and prevent any disturbing fantasies relating to the disability if the child should not survive.

5.9 All parents of children with disabilities need practical advice and guidance about the implications of their child's problems. However uncertain the diagnosis and prognosis of the handicapping condition, *they should be given information at the time of disclosure about available facilities and supporting services* so that they do not have the immediate impression of having to cope with their child's problems alone. The information will usually have to be repeated, since few parents can absorb the shock of the disclosure of their child's disability and consider the practical implications at one session. They should be given the name of someone who will act as a point of contact for them and arrange for them to discuss particular aspects of their child's future, for example the educational facilities available, with the appropriate professional. Parents of children who are disturbed or whose development is mildly or moderately delayed, no less than those of children with disabilities about which they are informed in the way described above, will need appropriate practical help, guidance and support.

5.10 Both the needs of the child and the nature of the services available will change over time, and the information given to the parents must be consistently up-dated. Such information will include details of educational facilities and voluntary societies, advice on claiming allowances and on short-term residential relief and genetic counselling. Leaflets such as those currently issued by the Voluntary Council for Handicapped Children and the Scottish Education Department are useful sources of such information. In addition, we see a clear need in all areas for readily available information about the facilities provided by the local authority in its education and social services capacities as well as by the area health authority. In some areas guides for parents have already been produced; for example, the Sheffield handbook on children with special needs contains comprehensive information about area health services, education services, family and community services, benefits and allowances and voluntary societies and organisations. *We recommend that a handbook should be available for each area giving information about local facilities for children with special needs and their parents and that, where such a handbook is not already available, it should be produced under the aegis of the appropriate Joint Consultative Committee (or in Scotland the appropriate Joint Liaison Committee).*

5.11 Resource centres on handicap can offer parents and others concerned with meeting the needs of children with disabilities ready access to information. At our request, the Institute for Research into Mental and Multiple Handicap has prepared a booklet describing how to set up a resource centre on handicap, in the light of experience at its Community Resources Centre.[3] (This Centre, which was based at the Stockwell College of Education, Bromley, Kent from 1976 to 1977, was sponsored as a piece of research by the Institute.) We hope that the suggestions in the booklet, which include the collection and organisation of material for use in a resource centre, will be followed up, particularly by citizens' advice bureaux, voluntary organisations and groups of parents of handicapped children as well as local education authorities.

A Named Person for parents

5.12 Even if information about available facilities and supporting services is provided, few parents will be able to make the best use of them without help, and many will be confused. The research project on services for parents of handicapped children under five which was undertaken for us revealed that many of the parents in the survey were in great need of someone to whom they could turn for help and advice at any time. In one of the areas in the survey, for example, 11 of the 30 parents interviewed thought that it would be difficult or very difficult to obtain more specialist advice on any matter which concerned them. Families from ethnic minority groups are likely to face particular difficulty in obtaining help and support for children with disabilities or serious difficulties, through lack of knowledge of what is available and, in some cases, language difficulties. More seriously, many professionals lack knowledge of the special problems that result from differences in cultural patterns.

5.13 We believe that there is a clear need for one person to whom the parents of children with disabilities or incipient special needs can turn for advice on the different services available to meet their child's needs. This should be someone who is well known to and accepted by them. The principle holds whether the children are under five, of school age or making the transition from school to adult life. *We therefore recommend that one person should be designated as Named Person to provide a point of contact for the parents of every child who has been discovered to have a disability or who is showing signs of special needs or problems.* Where a handicapping condition has been discovered, this person should be available to advise the child's parents on which services to contact and introduce them to those services. She should also ensure that the local education authority is provided with information about the child and then give to the parents the telephone number of the person in the authority's offices to whom the information has been passed. Where children are showing signs of special needs,

[3] M Jobling and J Parfit, *How to set up a resource centre on handicap* (Institute for Research into Mental and Multiple Handicap, 1977).

her function will be to ensure that the parents' anxieties are treated seriously and that their concern about their child's development is followed up.

5.14 The interviews with parents conducted in the course of the research project mentioned above showed that, of those professional workers with whom parents came into contact, the health visitor was generally regarded as the most helpful. Indeed, in some areas in the survey the health visitor was the main source of information on aids, allowances and other forms of help available. In view of her ready access and general acceptability to families as well as her links with doctors and nurses *we recommend that the health visitor should act as Named Person in the early years for most parents of children with disabilities and for parents of children showing signs of special needs or problems*. In Chapters 9 and 10 we consider who should act as Named Person for parents of children with special needs at later stages in their child's life.

5.15 The health visitor should automatically assume the function of Named Person for the parents of every young child who has a disability or is showing signs of special needs, unless the child is referred for a full investigation by a multi-professional team. In that case it may be more appropriate for the Named Person to be someone who, besides being sensitive to the needs of parents, has particular expertise or interest in the area of the child's disability. *We therefore recommend that, where a child's special needs have been assesssed by a multi-professional team, the team should designate someone to serve as Named Person for the parents. In some cases they might nominate the health visitor to continue as Named Person, but in others they might decide that it would be preferable for the Named Person to be a social worker, educationist or other professional with particular expertise or interest in the area of the child's disability*. In order that the parents should feel assured that there is always someone to whom they can turn for help *they should be given the office telephone number of an officer of the local education authority who will have been provided with information about their child and, if the arrangement for their Named Person proves unsatisfactory, will put them in touch with another professional better placed to help them*.

5.16 Where a Named Person is designated for the parents of a child from an ethnic minority group, that person should be someone with appropriate experience which will enable him or her to understand the problems facing such a family on account of both their background and their child's special needs. He or she should ensure that, where the parents have language difficulties, they have access to a professional who speaks their own language or, failing that, to someone who can accompany them at interviews with medical or other consultants and act as interpreter.

5.17 We recognise that health visitors are already heavily burdened and that our proposal that they should act as Named Person in the early years for the majority of parents of children with disabilities or incipient special needs may seem, at first sight, to be likely to impose an additional load. We are not, however, proposing that the health visitor should in every case provide further support herself, but rather that she should be able to put parents in touch with those who can. We are confident, therefore, that our proposal represents a manageable undertaking, particularly if the health visiting service is expanded in the period up to 1980–81 as proposed by the government.[4]

5.18 It is crucial, however, that the health visitor should have close connections with the education, social and other services and should work within a multi-professional framework. She may need, for example, to put parents in touch with an officer of the social services department who can arrange short-term residential relief, home help or other day care services. Links with the education service are essential both to help her to appreciate the importance of early educational opportunities for young children with special needs or problems, and to enable her easily to pass on to the education service information about these children. She should be in close touch with members of the special education advisory and support service proposed in Chapter 13, particularly home-visiting teachers working with any of the children and their parents for whom she is Named Person. She should ensure that, when a child for whose parents she has been the Named Person goes to school, the headteacher is informed of his special needs; in many cases this information will be provided by the school medical officer, with whom she will need to work closely, but she should supply any additional information that she has. Throughout, the health visitor should work in close consultation with the general practitioner.

5.19 *Parents of children with disabilities or significant difficulties should also be informed at an early stage about voluntary organisations and associations of parents similarly placed.* These can offer support and encouragement to parents, give information about the different services available and, in many areas, provide pre-school opportunities for young children with disabilities.

5.20 Voluntary organisations may also be an important source of information about facilities for temporary residential relief about which, as we have recommended, parents should be advised when they first learn of their child's disability. Where children with severe disabilities are living at home, it is imperative for some such relief to be available to the parents. In addition to the overriding requirement for day-to-day support, parents and other members of the family need to be able to take occasional holidays on their own. Moreover, emergencies such as illness or the death of a relative may require the provision of relief for families from looking after a severely handicapped child. We consider in Chapter 9 the various ways in which relief may be provided.

II ASSESSMENT AND RECORDING

Assessment

5.21 In keeping with our view that the need for special education may begin at birth, it is important that there should be no lower limit to the age at which assessment can be carried out. In the last chapter we proposed that the statutory procedure for assessment, for which we saw a continuing need, should be applicable to any child from birth. Moreover, the concept of different stages of assessment, each requiring more refinement and a wider range of expertise than the one before and culminating in full multi-professional assessment, which we put forward in that chapter, can be readily applied to children below compulsory school age, as we explain more fully below.

---

[4] *Priorities in the Health and Social Services. The Way Forward* (HMSO, 1977), p 10.

5.22 Children with severe congenital abnormalities apparent at birth, or with severe or complex disabilities discovered in the early years of life, will normally be referred directly for multi-professional assessment at our Stage 4 or 5 by the paediatrician or hospital consultant. Others, however, may be referred for multi-professional assessment in a variety of ways, usually following initial assessment or assessments at what could be regarded as broadly equivalent to one or more of our Stages 1–3. In the case of children attending nursery schools or classes, the procedures would be the same as those outlined in the previous chapter for children of statutory school age.

5.23 Where parents are anxious about their child's development, they may seek advice from the health visitor, clinic doctor or their general practitioner. In some cases initial assessment of the child's needs by any one of these professionals may lead to the child's being referred directly for multi-professional assessment. In others, the health visitor or doctor may call on members of other services to carry out further assessments and to advise on whether a full investigation by a multi-professional team should be conducted. Where a child who is attending a playgroup or day nursery is presenting special problems, we would expect the staff, in close consultation with the parents, to seek advice through the health visiting service, the social services department or the proposed special education advisory and support service. The person consulted would then carry out an initial assessment and, in the light of the results, decide whether to refer the child directly for multi-professional assessment or to call on members of other services to conduct further assessments individually.

5.24 We have recommended that multi-professional assessment should be carried out at one or both of two stages, Stages 4 and 5, the second involving professionals with more specialist expertise. Stage 4, we considered, should take place wherever possible at a school or, in the case of children under five who are not attending school, in another setting which affords opportunities for sustained observation of children's responses to learning. This might be a nursery unit set up specifically to combine teaching with assessment, a day nursery or a play-group. Opportunity groups, which allow children with and without disabilities to play together and mothers of those with disabilities to meet each other (see paragraph 5.64), can provide a useful setting for assessment and one in which the mothers are very closely involved. Stage 5, as we recommended in the last chapter, should usually take place at a centre within the community other than a hospital. A hospital setting might, however, be suitable for some children, particularly those with severe and complex disorders, in which case it is essential that professionals from a wide range of services should be involved and the education service fully represented.

5.25 We are convinced that it is impossible to separate assessment from continuing treatment, care and education. Wherever assessment is carried out, it is a basic requirement that it should aim to discover how the child learns and responds over a period. The time required for effective assessment will depend on the particular difficulties and special needs of the individual child and in some cases may be considerable. Moreover, there may be a delay between assessment and the availability of a suitable placement, during which time the child may need to stay in the assessment unit. In these cases assessment, treatment, care and education will be inextricably linked. It is sometimes claimed that the provision of an element of care in all hospital-based assessment units would clog the units. We believe that such an element is indispensable, and that any congestion should be interpreted by the authorities as a sign of inadequate provision.

The SE Forms procedure

5.26 Although the SE Forms procedure was designed for children who are attending school, including those receiving nursery education, we see no reason why it should not apply also to children who have not yet started school. In their case the procedure will be initiated by the professional who refers the child for multi-professional assessment. The initiating form used will depend on the professional context in which the referral is made. The process of multi-professional assessment will be concluded, as in the case of children of school age, by the completion of Form SE4, re-numbered as necessary in the light of our proposals in the last chapter.

Recording as in need of special educational provision

5.27 We have recommended that local education authorities should have the duty to maintain a record of children whom, on the basis of a profile of their needs prepared by a multi-professional assessment team, they judge to require special educational provision. We think that authorities should be empowered to record a child as requiring special educational provision from any age. They may wish to use this power in the case of a very young child with a severe and complex disorder assessed by a multi-professional team as being likely to have a continuing need for specialist help on a regular basis. We envisage that it would be unusual, however, for this power to be used. It would be more usual for authorities to defer a decision as to whether or not a child should be recorded until it becomes clearer, in the light of regular re-assessment of his needs, whether his requirement for special help is likely to be a continuing one.

III EARLY EDUCATIONAL OPPORTUNITIES

5.28 It has long been recognised, both here and abroad, that children with impaired hearing need to start their education early. This is widely accepted as true also of those with other disabilities. Lack of opportunities to learn can restrict development in many ways and, in some cases, result in intellectual retardation or emotional disorder. Moreover, there is evidence that for children with severe learning difficulties the years before six may be critical for their grasp of language.[5] For all children with physical or sensory disabilities or showing signs of learning or behavioural difficulties, early education is the key to their individual development and the prevention or mitigation of later disturbances.

5.29 Wherever possible measures to stimulate or encourage the early development of children with disabilities or significant difficulties should be based on the home. The presence of wise and sympathetic parents and a favourable domestic setting will provide the best start in life. But if parental support is lacking or living conditions are unfavourable, compensatory measures may be needed if a child is to have the benefit of good care and education. Children in residential

[5] W Swann and P Mittler, "Language Abilities of ESN(S) pupils", *Special Education: Forward Trends*, 3 No 1 (March 1976), 24–27.

care, especially those in long-stay hospitals, will also have particular need of a warm relationship with one adult.

5.30 Among compensatory measures which may be taken we have been impressed by the "nurture groups" which have been started in a number of primary schools in London for children approaching or over the age of five who are socially and emotionally affected by severe deprivation in early childhood.[6] Many are from ethnic minority groups and are suffering from severe emotional disturbance produced by the disadvantages associated with living in an impoverished environment combined with cultural confusion and a poorly developed sense of identity. The "nurture groups" seek to provide, so far as possible, the normal relationships and experiences of early childhood which these children have missed. We believe that children under school age who are suffering from the effects of severe deprivation could also benefit from this specific, intensive kind of help.

5.31 Although we see parents as being the main educators of children wherever possible, we recognise that many parents will be unable to bear this responsibility without help and *we therefore recommend that reinforcement and skilled support should be provided for parents of children with disabilities or significant difficulties in the earliest years.* When a child has a handicapping condition, many of the parents' instinctive reactions are distorted. When a child with, say, a sensory disability fails to respond in the normal way with smiles or gurgles, the parents may find that, without skilled help, they are unable to give the child the stimulus he needs. So the natural difficulties of responding to the child may be compounded by a sense of helplessness on the parents' part, with serious consequences for the child's development.

5.32 *We recommend that a range of different forms of skilled support for parents of children with special needs should be available in every area.* The help given by a home-visiting teacher, for example, can be supplemented by the child's attendance at a normal playgroup or at an opportunity group where the parents are able to meet other parents of children with disabilities or disorders. The different ways of providing help and reinforcement for parents, which are by no means mutually exclusive, are considered below. A common feature is the central involvement of advisory teachers belonging to the proposed special education advisory and support service.

Home visiting teachers

5.33 A number of experimental projects in which parents of handicapped children have been trained to teach their children specific skills has shown that, with help and support, a large proportion of parents can contribute very substantially to their children's early development and education. In the Portage Project, based on a large rural area of Wisconsin, materials and procedures have been developed which enable visiting teachers to teach parents in their own home how to set and attain educational objectives for their children. Some of the teachers are professionals, others have no professional qualifications, but all

---

[6] M Boxall, *The Nurture Group in the Primary School* (Inner London Education Authority 1976).

receive special training of about one week and work under close supervision. They conduct a systematic programme of visits to plan with the parents a weekly scheme of directed activities based on continuing assessment and evaluation of the child's progress. Children with all types of disability and disorder aged between birth and six years who are shown through careful screening to have serious developmental delays are accepted. Recorded results show that some 60% of the parents have been able to follow the programme adequately, and that significant gains have been made by the children, compared with a control group, in the areas of language and academic and social skills.[7]

5.34 The materials developed by the Portage team have been used by the Health Care Evaluation Research Team headed by Dr Kushlick, under the auspices of the University of Southampton Faculty of Medicine, the Medical Research Council, the Department of Health and Social Security and the Wessex Regional Health Authority. A home teaching service has been organised to train parents with severely retarded children under school age to carry out systematic teaching activities with their child at home; the service covers, broadly speaking, the Winchester and Central Hampshire Health District and the areas of the corresponding social services. During its first six months the project revealed that parents were very keen to help their children by teaching them speci-fied activities. Even when away from home on holiday, most parents carried out some activities and recorded details of them. Moreover, where teaching activities ceased because of serious family difficulties, such as marital, health or financial problems, they were invariably resumed as soon as possible. Records of the children's development showed that several children made major gains in areas where they were particularly retarded and that all made progress.

5.35 We believe that a comprehensive peripatetic teaching service is needed which would show parents how to carry out systematic activities with the children and work directly with them. At present the only major peripatetic teaching service in England, Wales and Scotland providing home visiting teachers for young children with special needs is for those with impaired hearing. Members of the service visit children of all ages. The organisation of the service varies considerably between different authorities; some teachers work in isolation, some in groups and others in teams with a designated leader. Although peri-patetic teachers of the deaf work mostly with children under school age, some spend a good deal of their time visiting and supporting children in ordinary schools, of whom some have only a minimal hearing loss and might sometimes be more effectively helped in other ways, for example in suitably staffed resource centres in the schools. Moreover, very few peripatetic teachers of the deaf have had any special training in work with parents or in the development of young children.

5.36 Peripatetic services also exist for children with visual or mental disabili-ties, although they are less widely available than the service for the deaf. The Royal National Institute for the Blind provides an education advisory service for parents of visually handicapped children, which is regarded by the Institute as an advisory rather than a teaching service. The advisers are, however,

---

[7] M S Shearer and D E Shearer, "The Portage Project: A model for early childhood educa-tion", *Exceptional Children*, 39 (1972), 210–217.

teachers of the blind by training, and use their experience as teachers in advising both parents and professionals. An increasing number of local education authorities has appointed peripatetic teachers of the visually handicapped, but many of them have little experience of dealing with very young children or of working with parents. Several local education authorities have appointed peripatetic teachers to visit mentally handicapped children below school age. Another form of peripatetic service is provided by some teachers attached to various types of assessment unit who similarly visit all young children with special needs who are attending the unit.

5.37 *We recommend that there should be a comprehensive peripatetic teaching service which would cater, wherever possible, exclusively for children with disabilities or significant difficulties below school age. It should cover every type of disability or disorder* – hearing and visual impairment, physical disability, behavioural and emotional disorders and learning difficulties of any kind. As we have shown, peripatetic teaching is at an early stage of development in some of these fields and in others does not yet exist. A considerable expansion will therefore be needed if there is to be a comprehensive service covering the range of handicapping conditions. *We recommend that there should be scope for specialisation within the service; in particular, in view of the specific skills required for their teaching, children with sensory disabilities should be visited by teachers with related expertise.* Individual teachers, however, particularly in rural areas, might see children with disabilities outside their own specialism.

5.38 In some areas, particularly those with scattered populations, it might not be practicable to organise a peripatetic teaching service for children under five separately from that for children of school age. In such cases peripatetic teachers working with very young children with special needs will require special training on the lines proposed below.

5.39 We consider that peripatetic teachers should work with and provide support for parents. They must therefore have an understanding of parental needs and co-operate closely with other professionals. Unlike the home teachers in the Portage Project, however, some of whom were not professionally qualified as teachers, peripatetic teachers should spend part of their time working directly with children. We envisage that their job would be as follows:

(i) to assess children's educational needs on the basis of trained observation;

(ii) to work with parents towards an educational programme for their child in the light of his assessed needs;

(iii) to work directly with and teach children on a regular basis; and

(iv) to maintain contact with other professionals in the various services concerned with meeting the needs of young children with disabilities or significant difficulties and their parents.

In addition, they might have two further functions, where these are not already being performed by other professionals who are helping the parents:

(v) to encourage and participate in meetings of groups of parents of young children with special needs; and

(vi) to put parents in touch with toy libraries, local forms of pre-school provision – playgroups, opportunity groups, day nurseries or nursery schools or classes in ordinary or special schools – and voluntary organisations.

5.40 It is impossible to indicate precisely how many cases a peripatetic teacher could be expected to handle at any one time, since this will depend on the particular needs of the individual children and parents and on the amount of travelling involved. We would, however, stress that, where regular teaching sessions are considered desirable for a child, the teacher should have adequate time for preparation and discussion with the parents as well as teaching the child.

5.41 It has been suggested to us that peripatetic teaching should be based upon a school, particularly a special school, because this would enhance the teachers' standing with their colleagues in schools in the area. However, it would not always be possible for peripatetic teachers to work from a special school, especially in a rural area, and it is important that they should be seen to provide a service for all children with disabilities or significant difficulties under school age, whether or not they are likely to be placed in special schools. Furthermore, it would be difficult for peripatetic teachers who were individually attached to different schools to maintain close links with their colleagues who specialised in particular areas of disability and to discuss aspects of their counselling work with other members of the service. We consider it preferable for peripatetic teachers to be part of our proposed special education advisory and support service and for individual teachers to be usually attached to an assessment centre, so helping to ensure that their skills are deployed as widely as possible. This would not, however, preclude the possibility of those who specialised in particular areas of disability having a second base in a special school if one were conveniently placed; indeed, it would be desirable for peripatetic teachers with expertise in relatively rare or complex disabilities to have close links with special schools catering for those disabilities.

5.42 *We recommend that training for peripatetic teachers should be organised on an in-service basis. Training programmes should include inter-professional courses* so that peripatetic teachers are made aware of the work of professionals in other services concerned with young children with special needs and their parents and come to recognise their own limitations in providing help for families with such children. The training should aim to increase the teachers' knowledge and understanding of child development in the early years and to develop their skills in observation and counselling. By counselling, in this context, we mean helping parents by being ready to listen to their problems and assist them to explain their needs. If the problems are concerned with educational provision, peripatetic teachers may be able to give direct help; if not, they should put parents in touch or see that their Named Person puts them in touch with other professionals who can help them.

Toy libraries

5.43 Peripatetic teachers need access to a range of toys, books and play materials which they can lend or recommend to the families of young children with special needs whom they visit. Toy libraries have provided a very valuable service and we commend the effort which has been put into them by many voluntary and statutory organisations. Not only do they make materials available, but they enable mothers to meet other families with similar problems in an informal setting and stimulate interest in the purpose of play. We think that it is desirable that they should also be organised by the education service and that they should be available on a wider basis, for example in clinics, day nurseries and assessment centres.

Parents' workshops

5.44 Another form of support for parents of young children with special needs is the group session or "workshop". The workshops which have been run for groups of parents of mentally handicapped children at the Hester Adrian Research Centre, Manchester University have been designed to train the parents in child management, observation and teaching, on the basis that this will both help the child and serve to alleviate indirectly some of the root causes of parental problems, particularly feelings of inadequacy and perplexity. The success of the workshops in demonstrating the feasibility of involving parents in the early education of their children has led to suggestions that advanced courses should be established for parents who hope to be able to organise workshops for small groups of parents in their own neighbourhood. The leaders of the project at the Hester Adrian Research Centre recognise however that, even under expert guidance, parents' workshops are not always successful. They must meet the needs of parents who will differ in background, personality, intelligence and ability to express themselves; and a high degree of skill and sensitivity is required to run a small group of this kind.

5.45 Although some caution is therefore called for, we think that there is scope for extending the provision of workshops for parents of young children with special needs, so long as all the difficulties are understood. Where the children are attending schools there should be close contact between the workshops and the schools. Local education authorities may take the initiative in some cases; we have seen an effective approach in Devon, for example, where residential weekends are organised for parents of children with disabilities, involving lectures, discussions and opportunities for informal contact between parents and the professionals working with their children.

5.46 We hope that initiatives in organising group sessions will also be taken by other bodies. For example, voluntary organisations concerned with particular disabilities provide workshops, seminars and so on. It is unfortunate that these do not always attract the parents who most need help, many of whom are unknown to the organisations, or unwilling to join them. A voluntary organisation may, however, be able to reach the parents and bring some of them into a workshop if it has effective contacts with members of other agencies and professions such as health visitors, social workers and teachers, who will be in touch with a wider range of parents. Colleges and departments of education which have courses for teachers of children with special needs may also run workshops; and these are additionally helpful in giving teachers insight into parents' problems. Intensive group work in hospital settings, for example the Paul Sandifer Centre at Great Ormond Street in London, can also be most helpful where the hospital has special psychiatric and other resources. Within such major centres there are medical and other experts available to give talks, for example on genetic counselling, or psychiatric help when parents require it.

5.47 The initiative in organising group sessions and skilled support may also be taken by the parents themselves. In Southend, for example, where a group for parents of children with Down's Syndrome was set up by the local branch of the National Society for Mentally Handicapped Children at the suggestion of a local medical officer, group meetings have been successfully conducted by parents.[8] The leaders are in regular contact with the supporting services and different professionals attend group meetings whenever possible. We consider the conditions for the successful development of such groups in Chapter 9. Local radio can play an important part in furthering their establishment.

5.48 A group of parents of children with disabilities or significant difficulties may enlist the help of professionals to provide more specialist types of guidance. The Kith and Kids parents, for example, organised an intensive summer teaching programme for their children. In their "Two-to-One" project, two volunteers (who might be parents) were recruited, trained and assigned to carry out individual teaching programmes, worked out jointly by the professionals and the parents, for each of the children participating.[9] This sort of approach can have the salutary effect of requiring professionals to respond to needs identified by the parents themselves.

Schools, classes and units

5.49 Nursery education (which can be provided for children in nursery schools from the age of two and in nursery classes from the age of three, unless exceptional circumstances require earlier admission) is of immense value. It not only contributes to a child's early development but also provides opportunity for the early identification of signs of special needs or problems in young children. As we have indicated, it can provide a very useful setting, too, for the assessment of a child's needs. We believe that young children with special needs can benefit very considerably from nursery education, whether on a full or part-time basis, and that wherever possible they should be educated in ordinary nursery schools and classes.

5.50 Nursery education has expanded modestly in recent years, mainly on a part-time basis. The extent of the provision is still insufficient. The proportion of two, three and four-year olds attending maintained nursery schools and nursery classes in maintained primary schools in England and Wales in January 1977 on a full or part-time basis is shown below.

Age	2	3	4
Proportion	0.5%	15.3%	14.9%

---

[8] See G Pugh and P Russell, *Shared Care. Support services for families with handicapped children* (National Children's Bureau, 1977), pp 37–43.

[9] A Jones, *Two-to-One: A Kith and Kids Community Project* (Inter-Action Inprint, 1976).

In Scotland the position was marginally better, with nursery education being available in nursery schools and nursery departments in September 1976 for 16.6% of children aged three and four years.[10] Within these restricted numbers of children receiving nursery education the proportion of children with special needs appears to be very limited. In a survey of the provision for handicapped young children in the Grampian Region of Scotland, which was carried out for us by Dr Margaret Clark, 138 out of 2,441 children attending nursery schools and classes were considered to be handicapped (5.7%) compared with 63 out of 617 children (10.3%) in the sample of playgroups studied and 54 out of 321 children (16.8%) attending day nurseries.[11] (The children in the day nurseries were normally admitted on account of some form of social deprivation.) There is other evidence to indicate that in some authorities at least children with disabilities are not receiving any preferential selection for nursery education.[12]

5.51 While recognising the financial constraints, we should like to see a considerable expansion of opportunities for nursery education for young children with special needs on a part-time as well as a full-time basis. We do not, however, believe that it would at present be either practicable or desirable to seek to achieve this through a policy of positive discrimination in favour of those with disabilities or significant difficulties in the admission of children to nursery schools and classes. Rather, *we recommend that the provision of nursery education for all children should be substantially increased as soon as possible, since this would have the consequence that opportunities for nursery education for young children with special needs could be correspondingly extended.*

5.52 If ordinary nursery schools and classes are to make satisfactory provision for children with a variety of special needs, a number of conditions must be met. First, the attitudes of the staff and the parents of all the children must be favourable. Secondly, the accommodation and equipment must be suitable. Thirdly, staffing ratios for non-teaching as well as teaching staff must be generous. Fourthly, the implications for all the children of accepting children with different disabilities and difficulties must be carefully thought out by all those concerned. Fifthly, teachers must have regular advice and information from specialist and advisory staff, in particular from members of the proposed special education advisory and support service, educational psychologists, speech therapists, physiotherapists, doctors and nurses. These considerations are discussed in more detail in Chapter 7 in relation to provision in ordinary schools for children with special educational needs of statutory school age.

5.53 The importance of generous staffing (particularly so far as nursery nurses are concerned) and of adequate accommodation as conditions for the integration of children with disabilities or disorders in ordinary nursery schools and classes was stressed by teachers interviewed in the course of Dr Clark's research project in the Grampian Region. Most of the teachers expressed willingness to accept up to one in ten handicapped children in their class. A third of the teachers in

---

[10] Department of Education and Science and Scottish Education Department statistics.

[11] For details of this research project see Appendix 6.

[12] J Stevenson and C Ellis, "Which three-year-olds attend pre-school facilities?", *Child: care, health and development*, 1975, I, 397–411.

nursery classes, however, felt that their present staffing ratio was insufficient to cope with handicapped children, whilst a half considered their accommodation to be inadequate to take such children.

5.54 The admission of a child with a disability or serious difficulty to an ordinary nursery school or nursery class may be of inestimable value in helping to increase his self-confidence and pave the way for his successful integration into an ordinary primary school. If he is to be helped as effectively as possible, however, teachers must do more than merely accept him; they must devise for him such special programmes as they consider necessary, keep his progress under continuous review and encourage him to play with children without disabilities. The findings of Dr Clark's research project reveal that there is a need for much greater understanding by teachers in nursery schools and classes of the special needs of children with disabilities or significant difficulties and of the teacher's contribution to meeting them. In later chapters we consider how this understanding might be developed through training and closer relations with local authority advisers in special education.

5.55 Although we regard it as desirable that, wherever possible, young children with disabilities or significant difficulties should be educated in ordinary nursery schools and classes, some young children may require separate special facilities such as special nursery units attached to ordinary nursery or primary schools, special nursery classes attached to special schools or, for the very severely handicapped, special care units within special schools. *We therefore recommend that special nursery classes and units should be provided for young children with more severe or complex disabilities.*

5.56 We would expect a well-planned special nursery unit or class attached to an ordinary nursery or primary school to have the advantages over an ordinary class of being smaller and thus making it possible for the children to receive more attention, of providing more space and of facilitating the organisation of support services. Under our proposals in Chapter 12 a teacher in such a unit would be expected to have additional training in the teaching of children with special educational needs. A special nursery unit or class may be a more suitable form of provision than an ordinary class for a distractable, hyperactive child, for example, who needs to be in a small group.

5.57 Where facilities for nursing care, intensive treatment or teaching by special methods or with special programmes are needed, special nursery classes attached to special schools may be the most suitable form of provision. In some cases, early specialist assistance in such a class, for example in reading braille or in developing mobility and other specific skills, may enable a child to progress to an ordinary school. In others, where education in an ordinary school is likely to prove impracticable or ineffective, attendance at a special nursery class makes for educational continuity for young children. Attendance at the nearest suitable special school may however entail boarding away from home. In deciding whether or not very young children are to be sent away to boarding school a balance must be struck between the value of expert teaching and the inherent disadvantages of separation from family and home.

5.58 In all cases where a young child with special needs is attending a nursery school, class or unit, close links should be developed between the school and home, and *parents should be involved as closely as possible in the work of the schools and classes.* Those of us who visited Ysgol Delyn, Mold, were impressed by the way parents were encouraged to accompany very young severely handicapped children to the school and stay with them during the day.

Playgroups, opportunity groups and day nurseries

5.59 In order that the varying needs of children may be met as flexibly as possible, a range of provision for young children with special needs should be available, ideally in every area. We believe that this should include playgroups, opportunity groups and day nurseries as well as nursery schools and classes. It is important that there should be the closest possible co-operation between authorities and agencies, including voluntary bodies, providing services for the under fives, and some useful examples of different forms of local co-ordinating machinery were given in a circular letter issued jointly by the Departments of Education and Science and Health and Social Security in March 1976.[13] We return to the subject of co-ordination of services in Chapter 16.

5.60 If, as we propose below, playgroups and opportunity groups as well as day nurseries are to make an increasing contribution to the provision for young children with special educational needs, it is essential that their staff should have suitable training and that their links with the education and other services should be strengthened. We welcome the emphasis on the need to improve the educational content of the various forms of day care in a circular letter issued jointly by the Departments of Education and Science and Health and Social Security[14] to reinforce the one mentioned above and we consider below how such improvement might be achieved.

a. Playgroups and opportunity groups

5.61 Playgroups, which may be organised by a committee of parents or by private individuals, cater mainly for children over three years of age, although some accept children from two years. They have increasingly shown a willingness to accept young children with disabilities, who are thereby enabled to extend their range of experience by playing with other children, whilst their parents have an opportunity to meet those of children of the same age without disabilities and to see their child's abilities and disabilities from a different perspective. In addition, playgroups can offer parents support in working with their child. In the Grampian Region of Scotland, 10% of the children attending the sample of playgroups studied in Dr Margaret Clark's research project were perceived as handicapped, and all the staff in playgroups interviewed in the project were willing to accept some children with complex disabilities. The general attitude of the staff in the playgroups seemed to be one of acceptance of all children in the community whose parents wished them to attend.

[13] Local Authority Social Services Letter LASSL (76) 5 DHSS, Reference No S21/47/05 DES, Co-ordination of local authority services for children under five (9 March 1976).

[14] Local Authority Social Services Letter LASSL(78)1, Health Notice HN(78)5 DHSS, Reference No S47/24/013 DES, Co-ordination of services for children under five (25 January 1978).

5.62 We recognise that playgroups would find difficulty in coping with a substantial proportion of children with disabilities or serious difficulties and that they may be unable to give much help to severely handicapped children who need constant individual attention. We think that there is considerable scope, however, for an increase in the provision made by playgroups for young children with special needs and *we recommend that they should be prepared to accept young children with disabilities or significant difficulties wherever possible.* They should be encouraged to do so by local authorities who, together with area health authorities, can offer them significant help not only through financial grants but also by making available suitable premises and professional advice.

5.63 One of the main difficulties faced by playgroups, according to the Pre-School Playgroups Association in its evidence to us, is making contact with parents of children with special needs. There is clearly need for much closer liaison between local authorities, health services and voluntary bodies so that, where a playgroup is considered to be a suitable form of provision for a particular child, the parents can be introduced to a playgroup in their area. Local radio can help to disseminate information about those playgroups willing to accept children with disabilities.

5.64 A special form of playgroup is the opportunity group, which seeks to bring children with and without disabilities together and enable their mothers to meet each other. We were impressed by evidence from one such group that all their parents "were unanimous that the best support and understanding for parents of handicapped children comes from other parents of handicapped children". Opportunity groups range from informal clubs, where mothers chat and children play, to structured sessions devised and supervised by psychologists and therapists. They are a valuable source of provision for children with disabilities up to the age of five and are especially willing to take children under the age of three. As we have already pointed out, they can provide a useful setting for assessment, and one in which parents are closely involved. They may not be suitable, however, for certain children, particularly the profoundly deaf, who need highly specialised and intensive language teaching and experience and severely physically handicapped children who need medical supervision and frequent, perhaps daily, physiotherapy.

5.65 We regard successful opportunity groups as a most significant development, particularly on account of their spontaneity and *we recommend that much greater use should be made of opportunity groups as a form of provision for young children with disabilities or significant difficulties under school age.* The pattern of their development throughout the country has, however, been uneven and we very much hope that groups will be started in areas where they do not already exist and that local authorities will promote their establishment. Where they do exist, local authorities should be ready to offer them support without detracting from their voluntary and spontaneous character.

5.66 In view of the increasing willingness of playgroups to accept children with disabilities, and our proposal that the provision made for such children by both playgroups and opportunity groups should be increased, *we recommend that their staff should receive suitable training in helping to meet the special needs of young children with disabilities.* We welcome the development of short courses of training run by the Pre-School Playgroups Association and are glad to know that many playgroup leaders already have access to local authority training facilities. We would stress the importance of including particular reference in any training for playgroup and opportunity group staff to the problems of children with special needs. We also consider that such staff would have much to gain from courses of training organised on inter-professional lines, which we discuss further in Chapter 16. *We further recommend that professional help and advice from members of the various supporting services should be readily available to playgroups and opportunity groups, and that members of the proposed special education advisory and support service, including peripatetic advisory teachers, should be in close touch with the groups and help their staff to devise suitable programmes for those children with special educational needs.*

5.67 There is room, particularly in rural areas, for experimentation by local authorities with a multi-professional team approach to the support of different forms of provision for young children with special needs, such as playgroups and opportunity groups, day nurseries and nursery classes, which may be held in a variety of settings including play buses and caravans. We have learned with interest of the Canadian Mobile Team Project, which was designed to explore the feasibility of using hospital-based mobile treatment staff in a co-ordinated team approach to support the integration of multiply handicapped young children in local kindergartens and schools. The mobile therapists, together with a social worker, work closely with the children's teachers and parents on early developmental programmes, and in 1976 three mobile teams were supporting 107 children in the community. The assessment of the early results of the project is encouraging.[15] It is important that teachers should be closely involved in all such team approaches.

b. Day nurseries

5.68 Day nurseries are organised by the social services departments of local authorities or, in some cases, by voluntary or private bodies or by individuals, in which case they must be registered with the local social services department. They cater for children of all ages from six weeks to five years, usually from families in some category of social or economic need. Not only do they take younger children than do nursery schools but they are open for longer hours and remain open five days a week throughout the year. Some take a percentage of children with disabilities or significant difficulties or have a special unit for such children, and they are being increasingly used as assessment centres.

5.69 In some areas day nurseries are developing as a focus for all day care services in their locality and as a meeting place for groups of parents and child minders as well as mother and toddler groups and playgroups. A recent experimental project carried out as part of the Lambeth Inner Area Study in which a team of salaried child minders, specially recruited and trained for the purpose, was offered the support of a day nursery, found that the facilities of the nursery and the skills of its staff played a crucial part in improving the per-

---

[15] R Cripps (Project Director), Final Report on National Health Research and Development Project No 609-1006-20(A) (Mobile Team Project) January 1974 – November 1976 (unpublished).

formance of the team.[16] There is clearly considerable scope for the further development of day nurseries as day care centres in this way. *We recommend, however, that more educational opportunities should be provided for children attending day nurseries, particularly those with special needs.* Peripatetic teachers should visit day nurseries and their staff should have ready access to the proposed special education advisory and support service. Wherever possible, they should have a permanent teacher on their staff who would be appointed by the local education authority and seconded to the social services department for the purpose.

5.70 We welcome the development of combined day nurseries and nursery schools. They have the advantage of concentrating the intensive family support, care and education of children from an early age. They represent a particularly flexible form of provision, offering opportunities for children to spend varying amounts of time in the day nursery and educational settings, in accordance with their individual needs. They thus offer considerable scope for helping to meet the needs of children who require special help. *We recommend that the provision of combined day nurseries and nursery schools should be increased.* We recognise that one question which may arise is who should be in charge of combined centres. This raises a number of sensitive issues which will need to be tackled as soon as possible.

5.71 Although the basic course leading to the award of the Certificate of the National Nursery Examination Board or the Scottish NNEB gives nursery nurses a good basic knowledge of normal child development, it does not adequately equip them to recognise in children signs of special needs and help to meet those needs. We are therefore glad to note that pilot courses leading to an advanced certificate of the Boards have been established, which are designed to give nursery nurses a deeper knowledge of children with special needs. We hope that further courses of this kind will be established and that nursery nurses employed in day nurseries will be encouraged to take them. *Day nursery staff should also have opportunities to attend in-service courses organised on an interprofessional basis at which they would learn to recognise in children signs of special need and know when and where to refer for special help.* Such courses would also enable them to meet teachers and other professionals involved in working with children with special needs.

CONCLUSION

5.72 This chapter has had three main themes: the crucial importance of early educational opportunities for children with disabilities or who are showing signs of having special needs; the role of parents as educators of their children and the need to provide them with skilled help; and the need for close co-operation between the different professions concerned. The three themes come together in the idea of the Named Person, who will provide a single and constant point of contact for parents, will be able to see that their anxieties are followed up, will be able to put them in touch with members of the different supporting services and will herself appreciate, through her own close links with the

---

[16] *The Groveway Project: An Experiment in Salaried Childminding* (Department of the Environment, 1977).

different services, the importance of early education in the development of children with special needs. However this person is known, whether as a Named Person, an interpreter or by any other name, we believe that such a person should be designated as soon as possible for every parent of a child who has been discovered to have a disability or whose development is giving serious cause for concern. We regard this as one of the cornerstones of the service, which should be available for parents of children with special needs.

CHAPTER 6: SCHOOLCHILDREN WITH SPECIAL NEEDS: AN INTRODUCTION

INTRODUCTION

6.1 In recent years discussion of the education of handicapped children has tended to focus on where the education should be provided – in ordinary or special schools, day or boarding schools. Clearly the location of special education and the administrative arrangements for its provision merit deep consideration, and these are the subject of our next two chapters. As an introduction to those chapters, we consider the wide range of special educational needs and the corresponding variety of provision required to achieve an effective, sensitive and flexible matching of needs with services.

I RANGE OF SPECIAL EDUCATIONAL NEEDS

6.2 The idea of a continuum of special educational need is a concept which, though crude, is serviceable in conveying the idea of a spread of children's special needs, in contrast with the traditional system of discrete categories of disability. In practice, however, individual needs are extremely variable in their intensity and composition. A particular disability varies widely in its severity from child to child and is often complicated by interaction with other handicapping conditions. Thus a child with, say, impaired vision may additionally suffer to any degree from emotional disturbance or have additional learning difficulties. It is this kind of complexity which necessitates a variety of different kinds and degrees of specialist intervention. We see special education as a particular response to the complex needs of an individual child which have been assessed by the appropriate professionals.

6.3 As we explained in Chapter 3, in very broad terms special educational need is likely to be of three kinds, namely i. the need for the provision of special means of access to the curriculum, including specialist teaching techniques; ii. the need for the provision of a special or modified curriculum; and iii. the need for particular attention to the social structure and emotional climate in which education takes place. A child may very often have more than one of these forms of special educational need.

6.4 Need for the provision of special means of access to the curriculum may itself take a number of different forms. Modification of the physical environment may be required, perhaps the provision of ramps or handrails, or the acoustic treatment of classrooms. Special equipment may be needed: for example a comparatively simple hearing aid or, at the other extreme, a highly sophisticated and costly machine which affords a severely multiply handicapped child access to a learning programme. In some cases the need may be for specialist teaching techniques, for example techniques for assisting pupils who need part-time help in a special setting to overcome learning difficulties, or techniques for communicating with profoundly deaf children or for teaching through braille.

6.5 The basic elements of the curriculum may need to be interpreted differently for individual children. Thus, in the case of pupils with impaired hearing, particular emphasis will need to be placed on the development of language; or for some children mathematics may involve the binomial theorem, whereas for others it may not extend much beyond the recognition of shapes. Where learning difficulties are very severe, what amounts to a special curriculum may need to be developed. We consider the curriculum in more detail in Chapter 11.

6.6 Need for particular attention to the social structure and emotional climate in which education takes place may also take many different forms. Some children may depend upon the intimacy of small teaching groups to make educational progress. Some may need the reassurance which a small school can best provide; others a particular kind of organisation within a school, for example one which pays special attention to the setting of limits to behaviour.

6.7 Given that a child may have more than one of the three types of special educational need described in paragraph 6.3 and that each of these may itself take many different forms, it is clear that many combinations of individual need are possible. In the following section we consider the flexible range of special educational provision required if these different needs are to be adequately met.

II RANGE OF SPECIAL EDUCATIONAL PROVISION

6.8 It would be impossible for the many different combinations of individual need that occur to be matched exactly by a corresponding number of organisational arrangements. The organisation of the educational system as a whole, as well as the resources available, impose limitations on the number of formal arrangements that are possible. We believe, however, that there should be available as great a variety of organisational arrangements as is practicable if special educational needs are to be met effectively. There should therefore be a range of special educational provision.

6.9 Our conclusion that up to one in five children are likely to require special educational provision at some time during their school career means that the majority of children with special educational needs will have to be not only identified but also helped within the ordinary school. As part of the range of special educational provision which we are advocating, therefore, a number of different forms of such provision will be required in ordinary schools. Where a child's need for special means of access to the curriculum can be met through, say, special equipment such as a hearing aid, or the provision of ramps to classrooms, it may be possible for him, depending on the severity of his disorder, to continue his education full-time in an ordinary class with any necessary support. Where, however, a child requires a modified curriculum, specialist teaching techniques or the more intimate atmosphere of smaller teaching groups, some of his education will probably need to take place away from the ordinary class in a special class or other supporting base. If a child requires intensive specialist support for most of the time, he may need to receive most, if not all, of his lessons in a special class. Within each different form of special educational provision there should be scope for variety and flexibility in the way in which individual needs are met.

6.10 At the same time, we are entirely convinced that special schools will continue to be needed, particularly for the following three groups of children:

(i) those with severe or complex physical, sensory or intellectual disabilities who require special facilities, teaching methods or expertise that it would be impracticable to provide in ordinary schools;

(ii) those with severe emotional or behavioural disorders who have very great difficulty in forming relationships with others or whose behaviour is so extreme or unpredictable that it causes severe disruption in an ordinary school or inhibits the educational progress of other children; and

(iii) those with less severe disabilities, often in combination, who despite special help do not perform well in an ordinary school and are more likely to thrive in the more intimate communal and educational setting of a special school.

These groups broadly indicate the children who are likely to need to attend a special school at least for a period. Some of them may, after intensive help in a special school, be able to continue their education in an ordinary school. Others may need to attend a special school for the whole of their school career.

6.11 Although it is not exhaustive, the following list of different types of provision gives an indication of the range which we believe will be needed in future for children with special educational needs. Each of these types of provision is considered further in the course of the following two chapters.

(i) full-time education in an ordinary class with any necessary help and support;

(ii) education in an ordinary class with periods of withdrawal to a special class or unit or other supporting base;

(iii) education in a special class or unit with periods of attendance at an ordinary class and full involvement in the general community life and extra-curricular activities of the ordinary school;

(iv) full-time education in a special class or unit with social contact with the main school;

(v) education in a special school, day or residential, with some shared lessons with a neighbouring ordinary school;

(vi) full-time education in a day special school with social contact with an ordinary school;

(vii) full-time education in a residential special school with social contact with an ordinary school;

(viii) short-term education in hospitals or other establishments;

(ix) long-term education in hospitals or other establishments; and

(x) home tuition.

6.12 It is an essential feature of the range of provision described above that there should be the closest possible relation between ordinary and special classes or units and between ordinary and special schools. In both cases very careful planning is required. The organisation of ordinary schools to which special classes are attached must be such as to ensure that the children in the special classes have maximum opportunity to participate in the activities of the rest of the school. We consider this in more detail in the following chapter.

6.13 A number of experiments has already taken place in developing co-operation between ordinary and special schools, and we commend these. The evidence we received revealed a widespread conviction that ordinary and special schools should develop much closer links and should, wherever possible, share resources, for example the services of a specialist teacher or expensive plant such as craft workshops or a swimming pool. Arrangements for sharing resources or for pupils in one school to attend certain classes in another will, of course, be possible only when the schools are geographically close enough to permit an exchange of pupils without undue stress or waste of time. Moreover, such arrangements will require careful advance planning, including the co-ordination of time-tables, the dove-tailing of supporting services and, where necessary, the provision of special transport. Nevertheless, we entirely support the views of many of the contributors to our evidence that much closer links of these kinds should be developed and we return to this subject in Chapter 8.

6.14 Information about the range of special educational provision in any area needs to be widely available both to professionals and to parents. Lists of special schools are published by the Department of Education and Science (List 42) and the Scottish Education Department (List G) containing details of the category of handicap and age range of pupils catered for. We consider that these lists would be more useful if they were to include a description of the types of special educational need catered for. In particular this would facilitate the task of matching the needs of children recorded as requiring special educational provision with the provision available. We recognise that to produce such lists, and keep them up-to-date, would entail a considerable amount of work. *We recommend, however, that, at least in the case of residential special schools, the lists should in future include details of the types of special educational need catered for.* They will thus help those responsible for placing children in special schools outside their area, although they will not obviate the need for local education authorities to make their own enquiries about the suitability of placements for individual children.

6.15 Within each area information needs to be readily available to professionals involved in the assessment of special educational needs, and to parents, about different types of special educational provision. *We therefore recommend that each local education authority should produce and keep up-to-date a handbook containing details of special educational provision in its area for children recorded as requiring such provision. Like the lists referred to above, this handbook should include information about the types of special educational need catered for in individual schools. It should also contain the names, office addresses and telephone numbers of officers of the local education authority concerned with the provision of special education,* including the assistant education officer for special education and members of the proposed special education advisory and support service, so that parents know whom to contact, if necessary, about problems concerning provision for their child. This handbook might be issued

97

on its own or it might form a section of the handbook on local facilities of various kinds which we recommended in Chapter 5 should be produced under the aegis of Joint Consultative Committees (or in Scotland Joint Liaison Committees).

CONCLUSION

6.16 If the Named Person is one of the cornerstones of the service which should be available for parents of children with special needs, full information about the range of special educational provision in their area is another. The range of provision needs to be extensive and flexible, to match as nearly as possible the extremely varied and changing needs of individual children. It should embrace different forms of provision in ordinary schools, as well as separate provision in special schools and other institutions. In the following two chapters we consider these different forms in more detail.

CHAPTER 7: SPECIAL EDUCATION IN ORDINARY SCHOOLS

INTRODUCTION

7.1 In this chapter we move to the central contemporary issue in special education which has been earnestly debated far beyond the frontiers of the education service. The principle of educating handicapped and non-handicapped children together, which is described as "integration" in this country and "mainstreaming" in the United States of America, and is recognised as part of a much wider movement of "normalisation" in Scandinavia and Canada, is the particular expression of a widely held and still growing conviction that, so far as is humanly possible, handicapped people should share the opportunities for self-fulfilment enjoyed by other people. This recognition of the right of the handicapped to uninhibited participation in the activities of everyday life, in all their varied forms, has been aptly described by the Snowdon Working Party.[1] "Integration for the disabled means a thousand things. It means the absence of segregation. It means social acceptance. It means being able to be treated like everybody else. It means the right to work, to go to cinemas, to enjoy outdoor sport, to have a family life and a social life and a love life, to contribute materially to the community, to have the usual choices of association, movement and activity, to go on holiday to the usual places, to be educated up to university level with one's unhandicapped peers, to travel without fuss on public transport . . ." Although written with the physically disabled principally in mind, this passage catches the spirit of changing attitudes to handicap in all its manifestations.

7.2 The principle is not new to education. It has been long-standing government policy, confirmed in numerous official documents, that no child should be sent to a special school who can be satisfactorily educated in an ordinary one. There has in fact been a steady increase over time in the number of children ascertained as handicapped who have been placed in designated special classes and units in ordinary schools. It rose from 11,027 in 1973 to 21,245 in 1977, that is from 6.8% to 12.0% of all children ascertained as requiring separate special provision.[2] The children placed in these classes and units have been mainly those with moderate rather than severe disabilities, but all categories of handicap are represented. They still form quite a small proportion of all handicapped children for whom special education is provided, but the trend is likely to continue. Although the existence of such classes and units does not necessarily entail integration in any complete sense, nevertheless it is a proof that segregation is diminishing. Moreover, although figures are not available, placements of children with disabilities in ordinary classes, of which we give examples in paragraph 7.12 (i), are becoming more frequent.

---

[1] *Integrating the Disabled.* Report of the Snowdon Working Party (The National Fund for Research into Crippling Diseases, 1976), p 7.

[2] *Statistics of Education 1973 Vol 1* (HMSO, 1974) and DES statistics for 1977.

7.3 The wider concept of special education proposed in this report, embracing as it does all those children in ordinary schools who, though not at present accounted handicapped, need additional support in a variety of forms, is directly in line with the principle that handicapped and non-handicapped children should be educated in a common setting so far as possible. The great majority of these children will continue to attend ordinary schools in the future. Moreover, we have made very clear our determined opposition to the notion of treating handicapped and non-handicapped children as forming two distinctive groups, for whom separate educational provision has to be made. It follows that we wholeheartedly support the principle of the development of common provision for all children.

7.4 Section 10 of the Education Act 1976 is now on the statute book. This has the effect that, subject to certain qualifications and from a date to be appointed by the Secretary of State, handicapped pupils in England and Wales are to be educated in ordinary schools in preference to special schools. We regard this as a challenge to the educational system as a whole which it is our duty to take seriously, with all its implications. We have accordingly judged it more fruitful to concentrate on the practical requirements for the future than to continue to debate the advantages and disadvantages of integration. Moreover, the well-worn arguments for and against integration, being framed in terms of the 2% of children at present ascertained as requiring special education, do not fit our wider concept of special education.

7.5 Our consideration of arrangements for meeting special educational needs in ordinary schools is set in the much broader context of special educational provision for up to one in five children who may require it at some point during their school career. It also has particular regard to the needs of children with moderate learning difficulties or emotional or behavioural disorders who form the majority of children at present receiving separate special educational provision. We begin this chapter by discussing the different forms of integration. We then proceed to consider in detail those types of special educational provision identified in the last chapter which may be made in ordinary schools, and the conditions for their success. Finally, we examine the implications of Section 10 of the Education Act 1976.

I THE DIFFERENT FORMS OF INTEGRATION

7.6 We have distinguished three main forms of integration. They are not discrete, but overlapping, and although each has a validity of its own they represent progressive stages of association. They provide a serviceable framework for discussion both of the nature of integration and of the means of planning its effective provision.

7.7 The first form of integration relates to the physical LOCATION of special educational provision. Locational integration exists where special units or classes are set up in ordinary schools. It also exists where a special school and an ordinary school share the same site. It may be the most tenuous form of association, especially if contact with other children is not carefully organised. Even so it can bring worth-while gains. In the case of children attending special units or classes, their parents may be encouraged by the mere fact that their children attend an ordinary school; it is good that a child with a disability or significant difficulty should be able to attend the same school as his brothers or sisters of like age; moreover there is opportunity for children in the ordinary classes to be aware of children with special needs, and for children with disabilities to observe the behaviour of their contemporaries. These outcomes can be promoted by careful planning of the disposition of ordinary and special accommodation. In Sweden, where it is often claimed that the integration of even severely handicapped children has been widely achieved, the form which it takes is, in many cases, mainly locational, as those of us who visited that country observed. Some of the special classes are effectively separated from the rest of the school in all respects; those which are imaginatively planned and organised, however, offer handicapped and non-handicapped children the opportunity of familiarising themselves with the other, and they represent a first stage towards full integration. These benefits can also accrue when a special school is on the same site as an ordinary school.

7.8 The second form of integration which we have identified relates to its SOCIAL aspect, where children attending a special class or unit eat, play and consort with other children, and possibly share organised out-of-classroom activities with them. Social interchange of this kind between children with special needs and others in the same school, or on the same campus, will have a different significance at different ages. Young children are generally able to accept individual differences more readily and more naturally than older children, whose growing self-consciousness and conformity to group behaviour can often inhibit the development of easy relationships with others outside their chosen circle. It is therefore important that social interchange should begin at as early an age as possible, and so be received as the natural order of communal life and lay the foundation of more significant relationships later on. Even for children with profound learning difficulties, the friendship and society of other children can effectively stimulate personal development.

7.9 The third and fullest form of integration is FUNCTIONAL integration. This is achieved where the locational and social association of children with special needs with their fellows leads to joint participation in educational programmes. It is the closest form of association, where children with special needs join, part-time or full-time, the regular classes of the school, and make a full contribution to the activity of the school. Functional integration makes the greatest demands upon an ordinary school, since it requires the most careful planning of class and individual teaching programmes to ensure that all the children benefit, whether or not they have special educational needs. We deal extensively with these issues later in this chapter and in our discussion of the curriculum in Chapter 11.

7.10 The concept of these three characteristic forms of integration – locational, social and functional – sharpens discussion of its meaning. Each element of the triad has a separate validity, although the functional element is perhaps uppermost in most people's minds when they speak of integration. Together these elements provide a framework for the planning and organisation of new arrangements for the education of children with special educational needs jointly with other children, and for later judgement of how effectively it has been achieved. They also bring home very forcibly the truth that if integration is to bring all the desired benefits there must be a sufficient proportion of the activities of a school, physical, social and educational, in which a child with a disability or significant difficulty can participate on equal terms with other children, and by means of which he can come to enjoy the realisation of personal achievement and gain acceptance as a full member of the school community by pupils and staff.

7.11 Such an outcome will not occur spontaneously. Nor will it be achieved by legislation alone. It has to be contrived and patiently nurtured. It means greater discrimination in favour of those children with special needs, in proportion to the severity of their disabilities. The planning, initiation and sustaining of integrated education calls for considerable knowledge, skill and sympathetic dedication by everyone concerned – parents, teachers, administrators and other professionals of different kinds. This chapter is about the QUALITY of special education in ordinary schools, for that will substantially determine attitudes to integration in future years.

II TYPES OF SPECIAL EDUCATIONAL PROVISION IN ORDINARY SCHOOLS

7.12 The three forms of integration identified in the last section can be illustrated by examples of different types of special educational provision. In the last chapter we identified the main types of such provision which, in our view, will be needed in the future. Here we consider in somewhat greater detail those which are located in the ordinary school, with particular attention to the scope they offer for interaction between those children with special educational needs and other children, and with examples of existing practice.

(i) *Full-time education in an ordinary class with any necessary help and support*

Full-time education in an ordinary class should be the aim for many children with special educational needs. It should be possible to achieve this aim in the case of the majority of children with mild learning difficulties, many of whom are at present the concern of remedial services, provided that adequate support is available from teachers with additional training or expertise in special education and from members of the special education advisory and support service proposed in Chapter 13. Some children with mild learning difficulties, however, will need more specialised provision of the type described in (ii) and (iii) below, as will most of those with moderate learning difficulties.

For many children with other handicapping conditions full participation in the curriculum of an ordinary class can be made possible by various measures like the provision of ramps and other aids to movement, space for a wheel-chair, special equipment such as a hearing aid, the presence of non-teaching aides, and individual teaching within the ordinary class, supported where necessary by special materials, such as books with large print. Already many children with handicapping conditions, particularly those with physical disabilities, have been successfully placed in ordinary classes in this way.

102

A small number of children with more severe disabilities, in very favourable conditions, have also been successfully placed in ordinary classes. There are two schemes in England designed to integrate blind children in ordinary classes, both based on residential special schools – Tapton Mount in Sheffield and St Vincent's in Liverpool.[3] The Tapton Mount scheme, which was launched in 1969, included fifteen pupils up to 1977-78: the children attend a comprehensive school in the city and return in the evening to a hostel attached to Tapton Mount School for the blind. Two teachers from Tapton Mount, designated "resource teachers", run a small resource centre on the comprehensive school campus where they produce maps, diagrams and braille texts and arrange for volunteer readers. In the St Vincent's scheme, which began in 1961 and in which 13 pupils have so far taken part, the pupils attend two Roman Catholic grammar schools in Liverpool and return to St Vincent's for a specified period of homework every evening. A counsellor, based at St Vincent's, supervises and assists the pupils with their homework but has little contact with the local grammar schools. The propinquity of the participating schools and the rigorous procedures for selecting pupils favour the success of both schemes. To be selected a pupil must display high academic potential, emotional and social maturity, adequate mobility and expertise in braille and typing.

There is also a small number of schemes for the integration of deaf children in ordinary classes. In the London borough of Haringey some deaf children are being integrated into ordinary classes in their local primary and secondary schools. Each child in the scheme receives a daily visit of up to 45 minutes from a teacher of the deaf, and visits of up to five half days a week from a supporting teacher who has undertaken a brief induction course in helping deaf children. The amount of additional help that each child needs varies according to his age, hearing loss, personality, the size of the school class and the way the class is organised. Schemes for the integration of individual deaf children are also operating in Norfolk and Worcestershire, where over 80% of the children who wear hearing aids attend local ordinary schools. The success of such schemes depends on the availability of special equipment and the way in which local services are organised, in particular the extent to which the teacher of the deaf is a member of a co-ordinated team on which he can draw for professional support.

We regard it as an important condition of the success of all schemes for integrating children with disabilities or significant difficulties into ordinary schools that there should not be so many of these children in any one school as will change the nature of the school, or even encourage the formation of a separate sub-group. We make a recommendation to this effect in relation to special classes and units in paragraph 7.38. Any special arrangements for the integration of a child with a disability into an ordinary class must be compatible with the interests of other children in the class, and specialist teachers must be available to review the arrangements, to support the ordinary

---

[3] See M Jamieson, M Parlett and K Pocklington, *Towards Integration. A study of blind and partially sighted children in ordinary schools* (National Foundation for Educational Research, 1977), pp 63–69.

teacher in his work and to tutor the child, where necessary.

(ii) *Education in an ordinary class with periods of withdrawal to a special class or unit or other supporting base*

Some children, though enabled by measures of the kind described in (i) to profit from substantial attendance at an ordinary class, need at least some additional provision which the ordinary class cannot offer. They are likely to include those who require a form of modified or supplemented curriculum, specialist teaching techniques in particular areas of learning, access to some types of special apparatus, materials or accommodation, or perhaps simply the occasional enjoyment of the intimate influence of a smaller teaching group. A variety of arrangements has been developed along these lines, including some for children with moderate learning difficulties. In one primary school to which a partially hearing unit is attached, for example, close co-operation over the years between the staffs of the school and the unit has resulted in a number of partially hearing children receiving substantial periods of education in ordinary classes. Careful preparation and continued support on the part of the unit staff, some additional training for teachers in the ordinary classes and the provision of a special resource in the form of a radio-microphone system have all helped to make this possible. In Chapter 3 we noted that special classes, other than designated special classes, have been set up in some 40% of maintained schools in England and Wales. In 1976 they catered for 458,087 children (4.7% of the school population) with learning difficulties, emotional or behavioural problems or a combination of these, of whom 82% spent less than half of their time in the special classes.[4] In some schools resource rooms, suitably equipped and staffed, have been established as a supporting base for children with special educational needs, and we make a recommendation about these in paragraph 7.32. Whatever the form of separate provision, it should be interwoven with the programmes of the ordinary class that the child attends, and it should be directed, wherever possible, to enabling the child eventually to attend the ordinary class full-time.

(iii) *Education in a special class or unit with periods of attendance at an ordinary class and full involvement in the general community life and extra-curricular activities of the ordinary school*

This arrangement implies that a pupil's special needs are such that the major part of his education must take place outside the ordinary classes of the school. In most cases he will therefore be on the roll of the special class or unit, in contrast to the arrangement in (ii) where the ordinary class will be the home base. Nevertheless we take the view that the slightest participation in ordinary class activities can be strikingly beneficial to children with special needs, and that their total exclusion should therefore not be accepted before every possibility has been thoroughly considered. Of necessity the range of educational

---

[4] *Statistics of Education 1976 Vol 1* (HMSO, 1977) and unpublished DES statistics. (Comparable figures were not collected for 1977.)

opportunities available in a special class or unit may be limited. It is therefore important that children who are able to do so should take part in a wider range of activities, particularly at the secondary school stage. We recognise that the provision of these wider opportunities may present practical difficulties, which will vary according to the nature and extent of the children's disabilities and their age; the problems will be different in secondary schools, where frequent class changes are necessary, from those in primary schools. We believe that these difficulties can, and should, be overcome and we see scope for making arrangements of this kind for children with a wide range of difficulties and disorders, including emotional and behavioural disorders. Indeed, such an arrangement has been successfully operated for pupils with emotional and behavioural difficulties as well as those with moderate learning difficulties at the Bicester and Cooper Schools at Bicester, and we give further details in paragraph 7.30. Full involvement in the communal life and extra-curricular activities of a school is clearly an important feature of the education of all the pupils, particularly those with special needs: but it acquires additional significance where such involvement is the major or only means whereby a severely handicapped pupil is able to establish his place as an active member of the school. Those responsible for the planning of out-of-class activities should therefore constantly have in mind the interests of pupils in special classes or units and contrive the means for their full involvement, wherever possible.

(iv) *Full-time education in a special class or unit with social contact with the main school*

Where a child's special needs are such that he is quite unable to join an ordinary class for any part of his education he may, for the same reasons, be prevented from full involvement in out-of-class activities. If such children are to live in the community, and if their fellows are to understand their problems, some special interaction is essential. Particularly if the attendance of children with very severe disabilities at the ordinary school is to have any justification they must be allowed opportunity for regular contact with other children and teachers in the school. This contact might be achieved through other children and teachers coming into the special class or unit or through the teachers and children in the special class or unit visiting the main school, if only for social interchange. Careful arrangements to this end will need to be made which take into account individual conditions and capabilities. The arrangements will require to be consciously planned no less than the pupil's formal education, and for this reason should be the responsibility of a particular member of the school staff. Every effort must be made to ensure that the special class or unit is an integral part of the school.

7.13 Within each of the forms of provision described above there will in many cases be wide scope for teachers, through skilful use of their resources, to achieve an even finer tuning of the provision to be made for a particular child.

(The scope may be more limited in small schools and schools in rural areas.) Certainly the quality of special education depends as much on the skill and insight of teachers, supported by adequate resources, as on the institutional or organisational form that it takes.

III THE CONDITIONS FOR THE EFFECTIVE PROVISION OF SPECIAL EDUCATION IN ORDINARY SCHOOLS

7.14 On the basis of the evidence received and our own observations of good practice in schools, of which some examples were given in the last section, we have identified a number of conditions for the effective provision of special education in ordinary schools. The character of a school, its size, premises, staffing and organisation all affect its capacity to make effective special educational provision. These conditions are discussed in detail in the following paragraphs.

7.15 If provision is to be effective, a framework is needed within which children may use AS OF RIGHT the general facilities available at school and also receive the special help that they require. There must be maximum opportunity for children in the ordinary school to share experience through both curricular and extra-curricular activities. It will not be enough for such activities to be encouraged: they have to be planned. Although such opportunity will inevitably be restricted in particular cases by a child's need for special teaching in a separate setting, or by other constraints imposed by his particular condition, this should be the guiding principle applicable to all the different forms of special educational provision in ordinary schools. It entails the creation of individual learning, including therapeutic, programmes, based upon a full and accurate assessment of individual need, and the relating of these programmes to each other and to ordinary teaching programmes. It makes new and formidable demands upon the capabilities of teachers and calls for extra provision in the shape of accommodation, equipment, and on-the-spot supporting services. We cannot envisage any substantial move towards the integration of children with disabilities or significant difficulties unless these conditions, which we discuss in greater detail below, are satisfied.

The children

7.16 Special educational provision, in whatever shape, will be effective only if informed by an accurate assessment of all the factors – physical, mental and emotional – which condition a child's performance. Teachers must have full information about any special educational needs of the children for whose education they become responsible. The assessment procedures which we proposed in Chapter 4 should enable this condition to be met. For most of those children, up to one in five of the school population, who are likely at one time or another to experience special educational difficulties, assessment at one of our school-based stages should be sufficient; a child with more severe difficulties who requires regular specialist support over and above what the school itself can offer will have been assessed by a multi-professional team. The team will have completed a profile of his needs which, if he is subsequently recorded by the local education authority as requiring special education, will form the basis of the authority's duty to provide it.

106

7.17 The attitudes of other children in the school also affect the success of arrangements for those with disabilities or significant difficulties. It is important that, where children with severe or complex disabilities are accepted, the other pupils should be helped to understand that, while they have certain special needs, these children are in other respects no different from them.

The parents

7.18 Throughout this report we have consistently stressed the need for the closest possible involvement of parents in the assessment of the child's educational needs and in the provision made. It follows that we regard such involvement as an important feature of any form of special educational provision in ordinary schools, no less than in special schools. Moreover, the parents of children who are on the roll of a special class or unit should be treated in exactly the same way as parents of other children in the school with regard, for example, to invitations to school functions and membership of governing bodies. We recognise that attending school functions regularly may involve parents in rural areas in considerable expense and we hope that, wherever possible, local education authorities will offer assistance by arranging transport or contributing to the costs.

7.19 Since problems in integrating individual children with disabilities or significant difficulties in ordinary schools may sometimes stem from their incomplete acceptance by the family, parents must be assisted to understand their child's difficulties. They must also be helped to adopt attitudes to him most conducive to his feeling that he is accepted and has the same status in the family as any brothers or sisters. This sense of acceptance by the family is likely to be a prerequisite of the successful integration of an individual child in an ordinary school. We discuss the various forms of advice and support required by parents of children with special needs in Chapter 9.

7.20 The integration of children in ordinary schools, particularly those with severe or complex disabilities or disorders, may be prejudiced if the parents of other pupils are not conversant with the arrangements. It is important that they should be clearly informed of the nature of the special provision being made and should have the opportunity to discuss this with the staff.

The staff

7.21 Without whole-hearted commitment by teachers to the reception of children with disabilities, particularly severe or complex ones, the most careful planning is unlikely to be successful. An understanding by teachers of what will be involved is essential, and in Chapter 12 we suggest how this might be developed in the course of training. Understanding does not however go the whole way: it must be combined with helpful and constructive attitudes which encourage but do not patronise. A recent survey of special classes and units for physically handicapped children found that although many of the handicapped children were benefiting academically and socially from attendance at ordinary classes, much greater interaction with non-handicapped children would have resulted had integration been a major objective of all the staff, and had more thought been given, from the planning stage onwards, to the means of its achievement.[5] Since the aim of integration is to enrich the education of both handicapped and non-handicapped children this loss of opportunity represents a double deprivation. *We recommend that before a child with a disability or severe difficulty enters an ordinary school the teaching staff should discuss among themselves and agree a plan for securing the maximum educational and social interaction between him and others in the school, and should strive collectively thereafter to implement the plan.*

7.22 The importance of favourable staff-pupil ratios if individual pupils with disabilities are to be successfully assimilated into ordinary classes was confirmed by the responses from headteachers and teachers in ordinary schools to a survey which was conducted on our behalf by the Department of Education and Science of the views of teachers in England, Scotland and Wales about provision for children with special educational needs.[6] Staffing ratios which facilitate smaller classes in general, and smaller teaching groups in particular, were considered to be the most important factor contributing to successful integration.

7.23 We strongly endorse the need for adequate staff and resources to be made available to ordinary schools to meet the needs of children assessed as requiring special educational help. These staff must have additional training or substantial experience in special education, and the nature of the training required is considered in Chapter 12. Moreover, as the Circular on staffing in special schools and special classes issued jointly by the Department of Education and Science and the Welsh Office in 1973 and the Consultative Document issued by the Scottish Education Department in the same year rightly emphasised,[7] adequate numbers of competent ancillary workers are also needed in special classes. This, we would add, is particularly necessary where a special class or unit or ordinary class contains children with severe disabilities.

7.24 If there is to be a FUNCTIONAL UNITY within an ordinary school, there must be close relations between teachers responsible for children with special educational needs and other members of staff. Where a special class or unit is attached to a school, teachers in the class or unit should have the opportunity to do some teaching in other parts of the school; conversely teachers in the ordinary classes should have the opportunity to share in some of the teaching in the special class or unit. Such interchange will promote the unity of the school, help teachers to understand each other's interests and concerns, and encourage children in the special class or unit to regard themselves as equal members of the school. We recognise however that this may present difficulties in secondary schools in Scotland under present regulations if the teacher concerned does not hold a qualification for secondary teaching.

The governing body

7.25 The endeavours of local education authorities and teachers to promote

---

[5] C Cope and E Anderson, *Special Units in Ordinary Schools* (University of London Institute of Education, 1977).

[6] For details see Appendix 8.

[7] DES Circular 4/73, Welsh Office Circular 47/73, Staffing of Special Schools and Classes (6 March 1973). Scottish Education Department Memorandum, Revision of Schools (Scotland) Code 1956 (October 1973).

and sustain the spirit and practice of a unified system of ordinary and special education will be strongly assisted by an informed and sympathetic managing or governing body of the ordinary school. It is therefore important that the managing or governing body should appreciate the fact that a significant proportion of the pupils in a school is likely to require special educational help at any time, and the implications of the acceptance of children with severe difficulties. The members should be consulted before arrangements are made to establish a special class or unit in the school. Thereafter they should be ready to give attention to this aspect of the school's activity and should be helped to do so. To this end *we recommend that where a special class or unit established by a local education authority is attached to an ordinary school, a member of the managing or governing body should be specifically concerned with that class or unit.* We do not suggest that this need entail a new appointment. We have in mind, rather, that an individual member, who may or may not already have related experience, should be especially charged with informing himself of this aspect of school activities and with generally equipping himself to promote discussion of matters relating to special education. He should be able to consult informally both the headteacher of the school and the local education authority's advisory and support service on any matters on which he requires information or which are causing him concern.

Premises

7.26 The nature of the school premises is a major determinant of the effectiveness of special educational provision in ordinary schools. Any impediments to easy movement around the school will need to be overcome through adaptations to premises if children with severe physical disabilities are to be enabled to join ordinary classes and share in school activities. Other more general considerations, such as the degree of open planning, may affect the suitability of a school for children with emotional disorders or with impaired hearing. We return to this in the following section.

Organisation, methods and curriculum

7.27 The extent to which an ordinary school is able to meet the special needs of pupils will be influenced by its organisation and by its ability to adapt to new demands. The demands may be relatively simple or more complex and varied according to circumstance. The principal factors in each case will be on the one hand the nature of the special needs, and, on the other, the flexibility of organisation and planning by means of which they are to be met. In Chapter 11 we consider the general principles of the planning of the curriculum for children with special educational needs.

7.28 In general terms, the headteacher will exercise oversight of special educational arrangements in his school in the manner laid down by the articles of government and will be responsible to the governors for the implementation of agreed policy. He should work closely with our proposed special education advisory and support service, and should collaborate with the headteacher of any special school in the vicinity to foster interchange between the schools, including the planning of joint activities for all pupils and the sharing of resources wherever possible. *We recommend that the headteacher should normally delegate day-to-day responsibility for making arrangements for children with special needs to a designated specialist teacher or head of department.* Such a teacher should be free to plan provision, including the curriculum, in consultation with the headteacher and members of the proposed advisory and support service.

7.29 Where special classes or units are set up, interaction between the pupils in them and other pupils can be further promoted through the skilled planning of extra-curricular activities. If the integration of children with severe disabilities who are unable to attend lessons in ordinary classes is to be at all real, there must be some activities in which they can mix and participate on equal terms with other children in the school. Extra-curricular activities such as visits, social functions and clubs provide such opportunity. At the same time some activities, particularly sporting activities, may be more satisfying for children with special needs if carried out separately rather than organised jointly with their non-handicapped fellows. Opportunities should be provided for children with physical disabilities and those who, for example, cannot easily co-ordinate their movements, to share physical activities with others who have similar difficulties. Arrangements of this kind should be an integral feature of local plans for special educational provision.

School-based resource centres and non-designated special classes

7.30 If ordinary schools are to be enabled to take an increasing share in the education of children with special needs in the ways described in the last section, including effective interchange with special schools, they will require support. In particular there will be need for the increasing development in ordinary schools of special facilities, and of teaching in a variety of ways, to enable as many children as possible who require special educational provision to receive it in ordinary classes. We have already referred in paragraph 7.12 (ii) to the special classes which have been established informally for this purpose in some 40% of maintained schools in England and Wales. Other arrangements include the establishment of resource rooms, specially equipped according to the children's needs and staffed by a teacher or teachers with special qualifications, and progress units. Those of us who visited the Bicester and Cooper Schools at Bicester were impressed by the progress units in those schools, which provide specialist help and support for pupils with learning difficulties as well as a more informal and intimate atmosphere beneficial to pupils with emotional or behavioural difficulties. In each school the pupils with learning difficulties belong both to an ordinary form group and to the unit. The resources of the latter are readily accessible to other pupils in the school, some of whom have themselves asked to attend the unit.[8]

7.31 The development of resource centres in ordinary schools has been taken further in a number of other countries, including Denmark and the USA. In Denmark they are used as a way of providing additional help both for children with learning difficulties and for those with emotional or behavioural problems. The centres may take one of three forms: the reading "clinic", found in most schools, consisting of a small room equipped with the technical resources needed

---

[8] E J Garnett, " 'Special' Children in a Comprehensive", *Special Education*, 3, 1 (1976), 8–11 and G Webster, M Forder and J Upton, "Action for the Vulnerable Child", *Special Education*, 4, 4 (1977), 26–28.

for the teaching of reading and writing; the observation "clinic" for children with emotional or behavioural problems; and the resource room equipped for children with special learning difficulties. Each of these forms of resource centre offers special facilities and specialist teaching for children for varying periods of time according to their needs. The children continue, however, to be regarded as belonging to the ordinary class. In some schools in the USA the staff in resource centres provide special programmes for children for part of each day and support individual children in ordinary classes for the remainder.

7.32 We see a resource centre as a room, or suite of rooms in a large school, where special materials and equipment are kept and to which groups of children may be withdrawn for special help. In some instances it may also be the class base for children from which they join ordinary classes for a considerable part of the normal school day. We also see it as a base in which visiting specialist teachers may work with children with special needs and where the school's special education teachers can prepare their work when they teach children elsewhere. Such a base would be the principal resource for helping children whose needs have been assessed at one of our school-based stages. Whilst the establishment of such a base in every school, regardless of its size or the incidence of pupils needing special education, would not be justified, there is likely to be a clear need in most large secondary schools. Accordingly *we recommend that where one does not already exist, some form of resource centre or other supporting base should be established in large schools to promote the effectiveness of special educational provision.*

7.33 We deal below with special classes and units which are formally designated by the local education authority. It will be important that every resource centre, special class or base which is organised internally by the headteacher should have as much material support related to its needs as would be given to one formally designated by the local education authority. At present many remedial departments fare badly in terms of premises, equipment and staffing. Their resources and staffing will in many cases need to be improved if they are to function effectively as resource centres in future. In order to avoid the possibility of disparity of provision we think that the proposed special education advisory and support service should be responsible for ensuring that information reaches the authority about the staffing and the pupils who have been assessed as needing this form of special support. *The authority should then arrange for the necessary staff and other resources to be made available to the school and should ensure that they are used for that purpose.*

Designated special classes and units

7.34 Special classes and units designated as such by a local education authority and providing wholly or mainly for the ascertained handicapped are of two main types. They may be attached to an ordinary school and regarded by the children as their home base within the school, or they may be unconnected with a school. Some of those unconnected with a school are attached to a child guidance clinic or other centre. Others are unattached to any establishment. These function under a teacher who is on the staff of a local special school or under a teacher who is responsible to the local education authority adviser or assistant education officer for special education. Even when attached to an ordinary school, a class

111

or unit may in practice be physically or organisationally separate from it. The terms "special class" and "special unit" are often used interchangeably, but "special unit" sometimes has the connotation of a special class (or group of special classes) which caters for children with one particular disability and which, whether or not formally attached to an ordinary school, functions as a distinct entity. It is, to all intents and purposes, a separate special school.

7.35 We have indicated our view (in paragraph 7.7) that the location of special educational provision can materially assist the achievement of worthwhile interchange between children with and without disabilities. For example, it at least affords opportunity for them to become acquainted and at best opens up the possibility of friendship and understanding, as well as effective functional integration. In the interests of promoting such interchange *we recommend that special classes and units should wherever possible be attached to and function as part of ordinary schools rather than be organised separately or attached to another kind of establishment such as a child guidance centre.*

7.36 Unless protected by careful arrangements children in special classes and units may experience a number of disadvantages, particularly where only one class or unit is attached to an ordinary school. In particular, the age range and variety of disabilities of pupils may be undesirably wide, with consequent restriction of their opportunities for progression in their education; and, secondly, the pupils may be exposed to too frequent changes or absences of staff. We recognise the need for discretion in the organisation of special classes and units, particularly in small towns and rural areas where numbers are small. We consider this further in paragraph 7.39. In relation to changes and absences of staff *we recommend that local education authorities should ensure that a school with a special class or unit is allotted an extra specialist teacher to its staffing complement.* Where possible the number of teachers in the special classes (including the class or classes within a unit) attached to a school should always exceed the number of such classes. Where this is not possible, for example in small schools and rural areas, other arrangements for re-inforcing the staffing of the special classes should be made. An arrangement on the lines recommended would not only safeguard the continuity of special education but also facilitate the release of teachers in special classes or units to attend courses of in-service training or to participate in other activities designed to extend their knowledge and improve their qualifications.

7.37 The efficient deployment of specialist teaching and of other professional expertise available to a local education authority and the need to maximise the use of that sophisticated equipment which the education of many children with severe disabilities requires is likely to suggest the concentration of certain special classes or units in selected schools. For example, blind or deaf children may need extensive teaching and material support over and above the facilities of an ordinary school which it might be unrealistic to expect more than a few schools to provide. The availability of specialist medical, therapeutic and other supporting services may for the same reason point to a similar pattern of selective location of provision. Moreover, logistics apart, it may be desirable to ensure that a severely handicapped child has the companionship of a sufficient number of those with similar difficulties if he is not to feel an overwhelming sense of isolation in an ordinary school. The principle of selected concentration of special educational provision is followed in Denmark, where special classes are grouped at a number of ordinary schools to form a special education centre.

7.38 We see both the utility and the desirability of a measure of concentration of special educational provision in particular schools. However, effective integration implies as we have said a functional unity within the ordinary school, and the difficulty of achieving this will increase in proportion to the number of pupils with special needs and the range and severity of the needs those pupils have. *We therefore recommend that children in special classes or units, whether attending full or part-time, should not form such a high proportion of the school roll or present such a range of needs as would substantially change the nature of the school.* It should be noted that in some deprived inner-city and remote rural areas many schools already contain a very high proportion of children with mild or moderate learning difficulties or emotional or behavioural disorders. Such schools need considerably better than average facilities for special educational provision for these children and the assimilation of more children with disabilities and significant difficulties would need to be undertaken with great caution.

7.39 In small towns and rural areas there are unlikely to be sufficient children with the same basic disability to justify the provision of a separate class for that disability, particularly if it is a disability of generally low incidence. The difficulty is accentuated in Wales and certain areas of Scotland by the co-existence of two languages and the need for even finer grouping according to the child's first language. As a result "multi-handicap" classes or units have been established in some areas which cater for a mixture of disabilities. This arrangement is acceptable if adequate resources are applied and the character of the school is not distorted. It will entail the regular attendance of visiting teachers and other specialists commensurate with the number of pupils and the range and severity of their educational needs, and careful and systematic monitoring of each child's progress. Where a wider range of milder disability is catered for a child's progress may be such that he is able to join an ordinary class, at first part-time but progressively moving towards full-time attendance. We hope that this kind of progression will become general practice in the future.

Supporting services

7.40. We hope that our recommendation in paragraph 7.32 that some form of resource centre or other supporting base should be available in ordinary schools to provide special facilities and teaching for children with special educational needs, as well as our proposals for teacher training, will mean that in future there will be at least one member of staff in most large schools with additional training and expertise in special education. All schools, however, whether or not they have such a teacher on their staff, will need access to sources of specialist educational advice and support if they are effectively to assess and provide for the needs of up to one in five children who may require special educational help. This is the basis of our recommendation in Chapter 13 that there should be a special education advisory and support service, and of our recommendations in Chapter 8 touching the future functions of special schools.

7.41 Ready access to other supporting services, particularly the school psychological, health and social services, is also needed if ordinary schools are to provide effectively for children who require special help. Moreover, careers officers and their specialist colleagues should be closely involved in the assessment of the special needs which many young people in schools may have and in offering advice and guidance to them on opportunities in further or higher education and employment. A recent survey of special units for physically handicapped children in ordinary schools found that it appeared to be easier for teachers in special schools than for teachers in special units, particularly those for junior pupils, to obtain advice from psychologists and other members of the education service.[9] The survey mentioned in paragraph 7.22 also revealed that teachers in special classes and units had less regular contact than those in special schools with speech therapists and physiotherapists.[10] It is axiomatic that the quality and regularity of specialist support for both children and teachers in special classes and units must be the same as that provided in good special schools.

7.42 At present a child in a special school who requires regular medical, nursing and other professional support may have the advantage over a child with similar needs placed in an ordinary school that he is able to receive treatment at the school, thus reducing the disruption to his education, and enabling the teachers to be associated with the treatment. Ideally we should like to see physiotherapy, speech therapy and treatment for children in ordinary schools who require such support provided in the school rather than at a clinic or other centre; as a corollary, local education authorities would need to provide the necessary facilities and area health authorities the necessary professional support. In practice, however, we recognise that this must be a long-term aim, to be achieved when resources permit. In the meantime a child's need **for** regular treatment and the degree of interruption that this would cause to his education if he were placed in an ordinary school and had to travel to a clinic or other centre must be taken into account, along with other relevant factors, in decisions about his placement.

7.43 We recognise that even in the long term, with improved services, it will not be possible to provide therapy or treatment in every school. For this reason alone it will in some cases be necessary to concentrate certain special classes and the related provision of therapy and treatment at particular schools. The local education authority will need to discuss these questions with the health authority before drawing up its arrangements for special educational provision.

IV INTEGRATION AND THE LAW

7.44 In November 1976 Parliament enacted an amendment to Section 33(2) of the Education Act 1944, operative from a day to be appointed by the Secretary of State for Education and Science, which requires that the arrangements made by local education authorities for special educational treatment in England and Wales shall provide for the education of handicapped pupils in county and voluntary (ie "ordinary") schools, in preference to special schools, unless this

---

[9] C Cope and E Anderson, *op cit.*

[10] For details see Appendix 8.

would be impracticable, incompatible with the efficiency of the school or would involve unreasonable public expenditure. In this section we consider these qualifying conditions in the light of our more general discussion in the last section of the conditions for the effective provision of special education in ordinary schools.

7.45 The amendment embodied in Section 10 of the Education Act 1976 should be read against Section 8(2)(c) of the Education Act 1944 which requires that, in fulfilling their duty to secure that there are sufficient schools available, local education authorities should have regard to the need for securing that provision is made for pupils who suffer from any disability of mind or body by providing, either in special schools or otherwise, special educational treatment. Being set within the present statutory framework of ascertainment, categorisation and treatment, Section 10 will need to be amended in line with the new concept of special educational provision which we proposed in Chapter 3. We deal with it here in the context of our broader view of special educational provision.

7.46 The principle embodied in Section 10 is not new or revolutionary, but rather it accords with a consensus of public feeling that handicapped people should, so far as possible, be enabled to take their place in the general community. Our present purpose is to consider what the new legislation means for special education in practice and how it is likely to affect the future development of special educational provision in ordinary schools.

7.47 Although Section 10 is ostensibly about the location of special educational provision, it goes very much wider than that. The attachment of important qualifications to the main requirement evidences Parliament's concern with the QUALITY of special education as well as its LOCATION. We would emphasise that, if children with special needs are to benefit from the normal facilities of the ordinary school, and if they are to participate, as of right, in its educational and social activities, there has to be a functional unity within the school. The qualifications also reflect Parliament's recognition that there are inevitable constraints on integration, in some cases so severe as to make the aim altogether inappropriate. For some children very careful and sometimes difficult decisions will have to be taken as to where the balance of advantage lies between education in an ordinary school and in a special school.

7.48 The implementation of Section 10 will therefore call for the very careful and comprehensive planning by local education authorities of their general arrangements for the area. It will be necessary to decide what special help ordinary schools can provide with reasonable support, in which schools special arrangements will be made, and the variety and severity of needs that they will meet. Moreover, the co-ordination of and continuity between provision at the primary, middle and secondary stages will be essential. Local education authorities will have to consult area health authorities, social services departments and other providing services, as well as other local education authorities, where it would be sensible to make shared provision. Teachers and others working in particular schools will have to plan to ensure that the general principles are put into effect. The need for all teachers to have an insight into special educational

115

needs, and for some to have an additional qualification in special education, the distribution of resources, including specialist equipment, the arrangements for transport and residential accommodation, the future structure of administrative and professional support, the deployment of scarce specialist staff and resources in the health and social services, the developing relations between ordinary and special schools – these and other aspects of provision will need a co-ordinated approach if the danger of piecemeal development is to be avoided. *We therefore recommend that each local education authority should have a comprehensive and long-term plan for special educational provision within which the arrangements for individual schools will take their place.* Those authorities which have already prepared plans for the future provision of special education will need to revise them in the light of Section 10 and the more extensive ambit of special education that we have identified; the others should draw up comprehensive plans as soon as possible. The need for regional planning is considered further in the following chapter and in Chapter 16.

7.49 The three qualifying conditions set out in Section 10 (practicability, efficiency and cost) are open to many interpretations. We assume, however, that their paramount aim is to ensure a high quality of special educational provision. The following comments illustrate our general approach. The circumstances in which integrated provision in an ordinary school might be impracticable will vary depending on the abilities and disabilities of different children. Integrated provision in an ordinary school might be impracticable for a variety of reasons. It would be impracticable if the physical conditions were not suitable and could not be made so, for example because the site was small or the buildings so planned or designed as to be incapable of alteration or extension. Equally the test of practicability would rule out the use of unsuitable buildings before necessary adaptations or improvements had been undertaken. Integration would be impracticable if requisite nursing and therapeutic services could not be conveniently provided or if traffic conditions adversely affected travel to and from the school. The list can be extended, and the considerations will vary in relation not only to different kinds of disability but also to individual children. For example, adaptations to the premises of a school might make integration in that school practicable for children in wheelchairs but not for those with calipers. Moreover, integration in an ordinary school might be impracticable for children with impaired hearing if the school was adjacent to a main road. Each case will have to be considered individually in the light of the child's needs and the physical conditions of the school. The importance of this qualification, as we see it, is that integration is unlikely to be successful and could be retrogressive, if put into operation without full regard to the kinds of considerations we have indicated.

7.50 The second qualification requires that the provision of special education in an ordinary school should be compatible with the provision of efficient instruction in the school. "Efficient instruction" must be taken to mean the same as "good education". This requirement is therefore absolutely indispensable. We would emphasise that it applies to THE SCHOOL AS A WHOLE and therefore to all the pupils in the school, whether they have special educational needs or not. It follows that the arrangements must not work to the disadvantage of any group of pupils in the school, for example in the allocation of resources or amenities, or in the range of academic or social opportunity. Further, we read "efficient instruction" as encompassing the "wholeness" of need which individual pupils may have, their need, for example, for the companionship of children of like age, condition and background, or in some cases for the intimate community that a small school is especially able to provide.

7.51 Educational efficiency can be considered in four different aspects. First, it depends in part upon the physical organisation of facilities. A school on more than one site could not be efficient if, as a result of the number of sites, some pupils were barred from full participation in school activities. The possibility of moving around the school without stress, not only between classes but for corporate social and recreational activities, is an essential element in the concept of efficiency. Thus special facilities, in the form of handrails, ramps or lifts, will be needed to enable severely handicapped children to make their way from one part of the school to another, and suitable washing and toilet arrangements will need to be adapted for their use in various places. Blind children must be able to circulate within and outside the school buildings without danger to themselves or to others, whilst deaf children must not be at risk through inability to hear instructions or warning sounds. Those children who require constant personal care or attention should be able to receive it wherever they may be at any time or place within the school; and should not be restricted to a particular location on that account. In the same category we would place the dovetailing of educational and supportive programmes: thus a physically handicapped child who needs physiotherapy should be able to obtain it without detriment to his education, and it should be co-ordinated with the teaching programme, for example in physical education. Where the efficiency of a child's education depends upon the provision of special accommodation, equipment or materials, such as audiological aids or books in braille, these must clearly be available wherever the curriculum requires it. Before any scheme of integration is introduced its implications in physical terms must be thoroughly studied and appropriate provision made.

7.52 Secondly, efficient education requires scrupulous planning of the curriculum so that the special needs of children are met so far as possible within or in association with ordinary teaching programmes. This is particularly important so far as children with moderate learning difficulties are concerned. Much planning may need to be done on an individual basis. We deal with this in Chapter 11.

7.53 Thirdly, to be compatible with efficient instruction, integration must be planned from the standpoint of children's emotional needs. Some children, for instance, find it difficult to flourish in a large school and need the reassurance of a more intimate community. Similarly, in the case of some forms of disability, particularly profound hearing impairment, there must be a sufficient number of children in a special class with the same condition if individuals are not to feel isolated. Children are not different from adults in needing opportunities to form special relationships with those who share their particular condition, interests and perspectives. Conversely the emotional needs of some children may be incompatible with those of others. Thus very careful arrangements will be needed, if children whose maladjustment takes the form of seriously disruptive behaviour are to be educated in ordinary schools. For many of these children

117

separate provision in special schools may be essential, particularly where boarding education is required.

7.54 Fourthly, educational efficiency depends on the expertise of the teaching staff. Integration requires that all teachers have some knowledge of special educational needs and that those with a defined responsibility for teaching such children have additional training or substantial experience in special education. We return to this in Chapter 12.

7.55 The final qualification in Section 10 – the avoidance of unreasonable public expenditure – will obviously have different applications at different times according to the state of national prosperity and the ordering of priorities. If resources were unlimited it would theoretically be possible for all schools to be enabled to cater for all children in the catchment area, whatever their special needs might be. In practice resources have to be deployed with economy insofar as this is consistent with good standards. Moreover, public spending on education cannot be determined independently of other public sector needs. The provision of special facilities of a comparable standard to those in the best existing special schools will involve a very considerable amount of public expenditure and whether or not such expenditure is justifiable will be a matter of judgement by those responsible for the allocation and management of public resources. Moreover, the costs involved will have different implications depending on, for example, whether a particular area is sparsely or densely populated, rural or urban. At some stage it may be desirable to develop guidelines of reasonable cost in relation to different forms of special provision. However, it would be short-sighted to judge a particular proposal solely on an immediate cost-efficiency basis. Section 10 refers to local education authorities' arrangements as a whole, and this implies a general plan or scheme of future provision into which the separate proposals fit. We have urged that local education authorities should prepare such a plan. The cost of each proposal should therefore also be looked at in terms of its contribution to the general plan, since it might well facilitate the later introduction of other components of the plan, with compensating savings at the later stage.

7.56 One thing is clear. As a number of contributors to our evidence, including the associations of local authorities, pointed out, the integration in ordinary schools of children currently ascertained as handicapped, if achieved without loss of educational quality, is not a cheap alternative to provision in separate special schools, and there is no short cut. Indeed, leaving aside the capital costs of making buildings suitable for handicapped children, the dispersal over many schools of the specialist teaching and supportive services at present concentrated in few schools will be considerably more expensive.

7.57 Arrangements for special educational provision in ordinary schools, particularly for children with severe disabilities, will need careful monitoring. We welcome the initiative of the Department of Education and Science in commissioning a research project, now being conducted by the National Foundation for Educational Research, to monitor some recently developed schemes for the education of handicapped children in, or in association with, ordinary schools, and in Chapter 18 we suggest that the monitoring and evaluation of changes following the implementation of Section 10 should receive attention as an area of research which deserves priority. We hope that local education authorities, through the proposed special education advisory and support service, will monitor arrangements in their own areas.

7.58 In addition to establishing the circumstances in which special educational provision may be made in schools which are not maintained by local education authorities, Section 10 also provides that such schools shall be those which are currently accepted by the Secretary of State as being suitable for the purpose. Clearly a non-maintained school which had been approved by the Secretary of State as a special school under Section 9(5) of the Education Act 1944 would automatically be deemed to be suitable for the purposes of Section 33(2) of the 1944 Act as amended by Section 10 of the Education Act 1976. We deal with registered independent schools in Section IV of Chapter 8 and there make separate recommendations in relation to their acceptance for the purposes of Section 33(2) of the Education Act 1944, as amended.

7.59 Finally, Section 10 is to come into force on a day to be appointed by the Secretary of State. We have observed that Section 10 is the legislative expression of a principle which is widely supported, and that provision for handicapped children has been increasingly made in ordinary schools. We would expect this trend to continue irrespective of Section 10. The new provision therefore supports the natural growth of integration by a positive requirement that local education authorities are in future to plan their arrangements in line with the principle. The extent to which authorities have built up experience of integrated arrangements varies considerably. The 21,245 handicapped children who in 1977 were educated in special units or classes attached to ordinary schools represented 12% of all children who had been ascertained as requiring separate special educational treatment (176,688) and, of the 21,245, 64% were in present terminology ESN(M), 17% were partially hearing and 11% were maladjusted. Thus integration has so far taken place on a limited, though increasing, scale and substantially in relation to particular disabilities. We have pointed to the need for a co-ordinated approach and have urged that each local education authority should draw up a comprehensive plan setting out its arrangements for special educational provision. *We recommend that before Section 10 comes into force the Secretary of State for Education and Science should issue comprehensive guidance to local education authorities on the framing of their future arrangements for special educational provision.* We would expect the Secretary of State for Social Services to contribute to the guidance in respect of those aspects which concern the health and social services.

7.60 The guidance issued to local education authorities would need to be drawn up in accordance with the new concept of special education and the procedures for assessment and recording that we propose. We have pointed to the need for Section 10 to be amended in these terms; indeed, we envisage that it will be embodied in the legislative provisions which our proposals require and which we outlined in Chapters 3 and 4. Section 10 is to come into force on a day to be appointed by the Secretary of State, but by no means all authorities will be ready on that day to extend their special educational provision in ordinary schools. Its implementation must necessarily be a long-term development, and it should take place within the new framework of special education proposed in this report.

CONCLUSION

7.61 Our report envisages a considerable improvement in special educational provision in ordinary schools to meet the needs of a significant proportion of their pupils who are likely to require such provision, including those often regarded at present as requiring "remedial" education. We also expect an increasing proportion of the children who at present receive separate special education to be educated in ordinary schools. If all this is to be successfully achieved, a great deal of planning and determination will be required. We believe that the conditions identified in this chapter, particularly (i) special training for teachers with responsibilities for children with special needs, (ii) sustained support at a high level from the various services and (iii) suitable facilities, must all be fulfilled if special educational provision on the scale envisaged is effectively to meet the wide range of needs presented.

CHAPTER 8: SPECIAL EDUCATION IN SPECIAL SCHOOLS

INTRODUCTION

8.1 We are in no doubt whatever that special schools will continue to feature prominently in the range of provision for children with special educational needs. This view was supported by the weight of the evidence submitted to us, which was in favour of a continuing place for special schools, alongside a move in the direction of educating a greater proportion of handicapped children, including more severely handicapped children, in ordinary schools. The Inner London Education Authority in its evidence to us affirmed that "in many respects, the special school represents a highly developed technique of positive discrimination". We believe that such discrimination will always be required to give some children with special educational needs the benefit of special facilities, teaching methods or expertise (or a combination of these) which cannot reasonably be provided in ordinary schools. In this chapter we consider the organisation of special schools and of other forms of special educational provision located outside the ordinary school. We do not follow precisely the classification of such provision given in Chapter 6 but we do cover the various forms listed there.

I SCALE OF PROVISION

8.2 The last twenty-five years have seen a very considerable expansion of the provision made for handicapped children outside ordinary schools. The number of special schools (including hospital schools) in England and Wales increased from 601 in 1950 to 1,653 in 1977 and the number of handicapped children attending them full-time from 47,119 to 135,261. In Scotland the number of special schools increased from 84 in 1950 to 229 in 1976, the number of pupils attending them from about 10,000 to 12,322.[1]

8.3 The scale of special educational provision outside ordinary schools that will be required in future, however, is likely to be considerably reduced, for a number of reasons. First, the size of the school population itself will be declining and may be accompanied by a reduction in the number of pupils with severe disabilities. The latest school population projections for England and Wales show a decline in pupil numbers beginning in the late 1970s and continuing into the 1980s, with the prospect that by 1988 or 1989 the school population may have fallen from its present level of 9 million by about $1\frac{1}{2}$ or 2 million. Thereafter the projections envisage the beginnings of an eventual upswing in total pupil numbers, the upturn in primary schools having begun in 1986. In Scotland the school population is also expected to continue to decline until about 1988-89, when it will be about 225,000 below the present level of just over one million.

---

[1] Department of Education and Science and Scottish Education Department statistics.

and then begin to grow.[2] The projections are, of course, based on a number of different and, in many respects, uncertain assumptions. Nevertheless, the decline in the school population is already occurring in many areas and, while its duration and magnitude over the country as a whole cannot yet be closely forecast, it will certainly continue for ten years or more.

8.4 The decline in the school population could produce conditions which might themselves tend to reduce the demand for places in separate special schools. In particular, improvement in staff-pupil ratios and reduction in over-crowding in schools should make it easier to prevent the educational difficulties of individual children from becoming more severe. Moreover, as spare accommodation becomes available, there should be opportunities to set up more supporting bases for children with special needs in ordinary schools.

8.5 Secondly, improvements in preventive health services will result in a reduction in the number of children who are likely to require special educational provision outside ordinary schools. These improvements include the greater use and effectiveness of genetic counselling; advances in diagnostic methods in the early stages of pregnancy with opportunities, where the foetus is found to be defective, for the termination of pregnancy; immunisation against rubella; and continuing advances in obstetrics and peri and post-natal care.

8.6 Thirdly, the implementation in England and Wales of Section 10 of the Education Act 1976, which embodies the principle that, wherever possible, handicapped children should be educated in ordinary schools, will clearly work towards a reduced need for places in special schools. But whilst it may lead to a reduction in their use, Section 10 by no means signifies the end of special schools. The point has been very clearly stated by the Secretary of State for Education and Science in these words: "The new law . . . does not herald the precipitate dismantling of the very valuable work of special schools, particularly those for children with severe disabilities . . . a minority of handicapped children will always need the help that only a special school can give, and it will be important to ensure that integration does not force them into isolation".[3]

II THE ROLE OF SPECIAL SCHOOLS

8.7 There are three types of school in England and Wales for handicapped children: maintained special schools run by local education authorities; non-maintained special schools provided by voluntary bodies; and independent schools catering wholly or mainly for handicapped pupils. The first two types are subject to the Handicapped Pupils and Special Schools Regulations 1959 made under Section 33 of the 1944 Education Act. In Scotland the corresponding types of school are those run by education authorities; grant-aided residential special schools provided by voluntary bodies; and independent schools catering wholly or mainly for handicapped pupils. Wherever we refer to special schools, we include both maintained and non-maintained, or in Scotland education

---

[2] *The Future School Population.* DES Report on Education No 85 (Department of Education and Science, June 1976), and Scottish Education Department statistics.

[3] Speech by the Secretary of State for Education and Science, Mrs Shirley Williams, at the opening of Inkersall Green Special School at Staveley, Derbyshire on 21 January 1977.

authority and grant-aided, schools; independent schools catering wholly or mainly for handicapped pupils are the subject of a separate section later in this chapter.

8.8 We identified in Chapter 6 three groups of children for whom provision in special schools is particularly likely to be needed in future. These are:

(i) children with severe or complex physical, sensory or intellectual disabilities who require special facilities, teaching methods or expertise that it would be impracticable to provide in ordinary schools;

(ii) children with severe emotional or behavioural disorders who have very great difficulty in forming relationships with others or whose behaviour is so extreme or unpredictable that it causes severe disruption in an ordinary school or inhibits the educational progress of other children; and

(iii) children with less severe disabilities, often in combination, who despite special help do not perform well in an ordinary school and are more likely to thrive in the more intimate communal and educational setting of a special school.

The groups of children identified above provide a broad indication of those children who are likely to attend a special school, some of them on a residential basis, at least for a period of their school life. Some may need to attend a special school all their school life; others may, after a period in a special school, be able to pursue their education in an ordinary school.

8.9 Special schools will thus have a continuing and important function in offering separate special educational provision for certain groups of children with special needs. Further, *we recommend that their facilities and expertise should be more widely available to provide intensive specialised help on a short-term basis and sometimes at short notice*.

8.10 The future development of special schools as institutions catering mainly for children with more severe or complex disabilities will have important implications for the teachers in them. In particular, it will mean that their work will become more specialised and that the nature of both the demands on them and the personal rewards will change. It will be more than ever necessary to guard against the schools' becoming isolated from the mainstream of educational developments. We referred in Chapter 6 to the widespread conviction among those who submitted evidence to us that there should be much closer co-operation between ordinary and special schools including, wherever possible, the sharing of resources by pupils in both types of school, and *we recommend that firm links should be established between special and ordinary schools in the same vicinity*. Wherever possible we believe that there should be some sharing of educational programmes between special and ordinary schools. Where this is not possible, there should at least be opportunities for the pupils to share social experience on as regular a basis as possible.

123

8.11 Arrangements for links between special and ordinary schools require very careful planning. If children attending special schools are to be enabled to receive part of their education in an ordinary school and if children with special needs in ordinary schools are to attend special schools part-time there must clearly be joint planning of the curriculum and time-tables, as well as careful attention to the administrative and organisational aspects, including the dovetailing of supporting services and the provision of transport. More than this, there must be a common basis of commitment and interest on the part of all the staff concerned if the arrangements, however faultless in form, are in practice to succeed. Staff in either school will need to collaborate at all stages of the preparation of schemes, to consult regularly on their execution and to join in periodical appraisal of the outcome for individual pupils, so that any necessary adjustments can be made. Where these conditions are met we are convinced that very considerable benefits to both pupils with special needs and other pupils, as well as to teachers, can result from shared arrangements of this kind. For example, we know of one school for the partially sighted which is situated on the campus of a comprehensive school where pupils from the special school attend lessons in science, French, German, home economics and technical subjects in the ordinary school and some pupils from the comprehensive school with learning difficulties join pupils in the special school who have similar difficulties for tuition from a teacher with a qualification in special education. The sharing of social experience must also be positively constructed if the interest of all the pupils is to be sustained and there is to be genuine interaction between them. The mere bringing together of children may not of itself produce real benefit, nor will invitations to school occasions. More natural interaction in social activities should be sought. The occasions may need to be selected and organised and members of the staff of the participating schools should be unobtrusively available to exert their influence, as may be needed, to ensure that individual children benefit. Links of both an educational and social kind are obviously easier to establish when special and ordinary schools are close together. We therefore suggest that when any new special schools are built in future, consideration should be given to constructing them in close proximity to ordinary schools so as to facilitate the development of positive collaboration between the two types of school.

8.12 We also think that the staff in ordinary and special schools have much to gain from closer relationships. The expertise in special schools is likely to be of considerable benefit to teachers in ordinary schools in a range of areas, particularly the following: the teaching of children with sensory disabilities; the care of physically handicapped children and appreciation of the level of achievement which can be expected of them; and curriculum planning for children with special educational needs. In addition, teachers in schools for the maladjusted should be able to offer expertise on the management of children with emotional and behavioural problems and the development of personal relations with them. Teachers in ordinary schools will need this kind of experienced help if they are to cater effectively for increased numbers of children with disabilities or significant difficulties. Moreover, by collaborating with staff in ordinary schools teachers in special schools will avoid the professional isolation which many of them feel at present and which would otherwise tend to increase if, as we envisage, special schools become more specialised institutions than they now are. We would expect the headteachers of ordinary and special schools in the same area, as well as members of the special education advisory and support service proposed in Chapter 13, to take the lead in establishing and encouraging contact between staff in the two types of school.

8.13 While all special schools should provide support for teachers in ordinary schools, we envisage that some of them will be formally established as resource centres, that is centres of specialist expertise and of research in special education, in which teachers in the area would be closely involved. Such centres would be used for curriculum development and in-service education for teachers, and also as places to which parents and other professionals could refer for advice on special education and where parents could meet each other. The preparation, storage and loan of specialised equipment and materials for use elsewhere, and the development of audio-visual materials for training would support the main functions outlined. In some instances the centres might also provide bases for advisory teachers working with pupils in ordinary schools. The number of such centres which it would be practicable to have in any one area would depend on the nature and size of the area and the type of special schools in that area. In a large conurbation it might be feasible to think in terms of a number of such centres: for example, one for the deaf and partially hearing; another for the physically handicapped; another for children with severe learning difficulties; and another for children with emotional or behavioural difficulties. *We therefore recommend that within each local authority area some special schools should be designated and developed as resource centres.*

8.14 We see a need for another kind of resource centre, also based in a special school, which would be developed in collaboration between local education authorities and would specialise in relatively rare or particularly complex disabilities, such as severe visual, hearing or physical disabilities, severe speech or language disorders, severe epilepsy and severe conduct disorders. Centres of this kind would provide facilities for specialist assessment, short and long-term day and residential education, and specialist advice and support to teachers and pupils in other schools as well as to other professionals. They would also be places where parents of children with the same type of disability could meet together. (Some special schools already carry out these functions.) *We therefore recommend that a number of special schools should be designated as specialist centres for relatively rare or particularly complex disabilities, and should be developed as such by groups of local education authorities.* The number of such centres would depend on the incidence of the disabilities concerned in the various parts of the country. We consider the planning of such centres further in paragraph 8.31.

Residential special schools

8.15 Our proposals for the extension of the functions of special schools, including the provision of intensive, specialised short-term help, and the development of some schools as resource centres apply to residential as well as non-residential schools. Further, the proposed specialist centres for relatively rare or particularly complex disabilities would be based in residential special schools, or schools with some residential facilities.

8.16 Education in residential special schools is likely to continue to be needed in the following circumstances which call for a co-ordinated approach to a child's learning and living:

(i) where a child with severe or complex disabilities requires a combination of medical treatment, therapy, education and care which it would be beyond the combined resources of a day special school and his family to provide, but which does not call for his admission to hospital;

(ii) where learning difficulties or other barriers to educational progress are so severe that the whole life of the child needs to be under consistent and continuous educational influence, for example where a child is suffering from severe sensory loss, extensive neurological damage or malfunction, severe emotional or behavioural disorder or severe difficulties of communication;

(iii) where a child has a severe disability and his parents cannot provide at home the sustained attention that he needs, or could not do so without unacceptable consequences for family life and the well-being of other children in the family;

(iv) where poor social conditions or disturbed family relationships either contribute to or exacerbate the child's educational difficulty.

We consider the organisation of residential special schools later in this chapter.

8.17 In addition to residential special schools of the traditional type, we see a need for other, more flexible types of boarding school which would cater for children with varying needs for residential accommodation and education on or off the premises. *We therefore recommend that a range of different types of boarding special school should be available.* The schools in this range would make provision for the following groups of children:

(a) those who need residential accommodation and full-time education under the same roof;

(b) those who may be able to attend a local day school (either ordinary or special) but require the support and special expertise of a boarding school of the hostel type for some very important aspects of their education; and

(c) those who can live at home but who need special education which can most suitably be provided by attendance as day pupils at a boarding school. Examples are blind children with a boarding school for the blind near their homes; and children who have been boarders at a local boarding school and who no longer need to live away from home, but for whom attendance at the school as day pupils provides a transitional stage before they go to a local day school.

Since individual needs will be varied and changing, there would be advantages if some of the boarding schools in the range were to make provision for all three groups of children.

8.18 We consider that boarding special schools should extend their functions in the future in a number of ways. First, they should offer facilities for residential

126

assessment. Secondly, they should provide short-stay facilities for children with severe disabilities whose parents and families need a respite from looking after them. (We return to the subject of relief for parents in the following chapter.) Thirdly, they should afford opportunities for young people with disabilities to widen their horizons and increase their independence by a period of residential experience. Fourthly, they should offer intensive short courses of specialist teaching for pupils in ordinary day schools who need additional help to maintain their progress. Fifthly, they should provide recreational and leisure activities for children and young people with disabilities or significant difficulties, particularly those in ordinary schools, for whom opportunities to follow such pursuits are often limited. *We therefore recommend that boarding special schools should be prepared to accept children and young people with disabilities or significant difficulties for short periods wherever this meets a need.* We recognise that this may be more practicable during school holidays than during term time; it may, however, become feasible throughout the year as spare accommodation becomes available in special schools.

8.19 There is a small number of children who need 52-week care because, for example, they have no families to return to, or because their families are unable to cope for any part of the year. Where what is required is a substitute home with 52-week care, but without any special educational provision, responsibility for providing this should rest with the local authority in its social services, not its educational, capacity. Where special educational provision as well as a substitute home is required, a decision on the child's placement should be made jointly by the social services and education departments, in the light of the assessment of the child's needs.

8.20 We are aware of the importance to all children attending residential special schools of knowing that there is a home to which they belong and to which they can return during school holidays. This is particularly so in the case of children who need 52-week care. We would therefore urge local authority social services departments to make every effort to ensure that a stable home is provided for such children which, so far as is possible, is the same for every holiday. This is most likely to be possible when the child is placed with foster parents. We recognise that there may be some children for whom this will be impossible, particularly those with very severe disabilities, and that, until facilities in the community are developed further, a minority will have to return to hospital during the holidays. Where this is necessary, care should be taken to ensure that adequate staff are available and that stimulating activities are arranged for them. Children for whom, for whatever reason, a stable home cannot be arranged during the holidays might well benefit from continued attendance at school and we see a need, therefore, for the premises of some special schools to remain open during the school holidays. We consider the practical implications further in the next chapter.

Non-maintained special schools

8.21 Non-maintained special schools are non profit-making concerns and they have to meet a number of other conditions for approval as special schools, laid down in the Handicapped Pupils and Special Schools Regulations 1959, as

127

amended; in return they may receive grants from central funds towards capital projects. In Scotland the grant-aided residential special schools also receive grants towards expenditure on maintenance. The schools are thus part of the national system of special educational provision in a way that independent schools, which we consider in a later section of this chapter, are not.

8.22 There were 112 non-maintained special schools in England and Wales in 1977, of which 102 were residential, and 13 grant-aided residential special schools in Scotland in 1976. Although the number of handicapped pupils attending non-maintained special schools full-time in England and Wales in 1977 represented only 6% of all full-time pupils in special schools, it included 82% of all blind children and 45% of all deaf children in special schools for the blind and deaf respectively. The comparable figures for Scotland in 1976 were 4%, 76% and 28% respectively. Further, non-maintained special schools in England and Wales catered for 32% of all handicapped pupils attending residential special schools in 1977 and grant-aided residential special schools in Scotland catered for the same proportion (32%) in 1976. More specifically, they made provision for 82% of the blind (94% in Scotland), 72% of the deaf (49% in Scotland), 49% of the physically handicapped (80% in Scotland) and 23% of the maladjusted (38% in Scotland) who were in residential special schools.[4]

8.23 In the past the voluntary bodies providing non-maintained special schools and, in Scotland, grant-aided residential special schools have done extremely valuable pioneering work for a wide variety of disabilities. Some of them continue to innovate and experiment, for instance in providing for combinations of disabilities or in trying out new methods of treatment for individual disabilities. Without wishing in any way to underrate the pioneering work which has been carried out in the maintained sector, we recognise that it may have been easier in the past for non-maintained special schools to try out new ideas than it has been for special schools maintained by local education authorities.

8.24 Although some non-maintained special schools receive financial support from charities or trusts, the running costs of the majority are met almost entirely out of fees paid by local education authorities for pupils placed at the schools. Yet, with a few exceptions in some parts of the country, which we commend, there is little contact between non-maintained special schools and either the authorities which send pupils to them or the authorities in whose areas they are situated. Local education authority officers, including advisers in special education, have no right of access to the schools and can visit only by invitation. Further, authorities are not always represented on the governing bodies of schools in their area. As a result, it is often difficult for authorities to monitor the standards of provision in the schools, while for their part some of the schools have difficulty in keeping in touch with the mainstream of educational developments. Although it is true that Her Majesty's Inspectors visit the schools, their visits are less frequent than we would wish, because of other demands on their time.

8.25 We believe that in future non-maintained special schools should be subject to much closer oversight by local education authorities and, so far as

---

[4] Department of Education and Science and Scottish Education Department statistics.

possible, by Her Majesty's Inspectorate. *We therefore recommend that the standards of educational provision in non-maintained special schools should be closely monitored both by Her Majesty's Inspectorate and increasingly by the proposed special education advisory and support service*, particularly in the light of the effects of the declining school population and of Section 10 of the Education Act 1976, which may affect the viability of many of the schools. In order to facilitate this, *we further recommend that there should be much closer links, to the benefit of both sides, between non-maintained special schools and local education authorities.* Visits to the schools by members of our proposed special education advisory and support service and opportunities for their teachers to attend in-service training courses run by the authorities will help to bring the schools into the mainstream of educational developments. On their side, the authorities have much to gain from a closer knowledge of, and interest in, non-maintained schools, both those at which they already take up places and those at which they might wish to do so.

8.26 If members of the special education advisory and support service are to visit non-maintained schools, they will need to be assured of access to them. We suggest that local education authorities might consider making the placement of a child in a non-maintained special school conditional upon the school's granting access to their officers, and to those of the authority in whose area the school is situated. Alternatively this requirement might be included in the statutory regulations governing the approval of special schools. We hope, however, that our recommendation in Chapter 4 that a child's progress should be regularly reviewed and, where necessary, his special needs re-assessed by professionals with appropriate expertise will, if implemented, itself lead to the development of closer links between the schools and local education authorities. As a further way of developing such links, *we recommend that every non-maintained special school should have its own governing body and that this should include at least one representative of the local education authority in whose area it is situated, or of one of the authorities making particular use of it.*

8.27 In certain parts of the country there is a concentration of non-maintained special schools catering for children with the same kinds of disability; for example schools for children with epilepsy are concentrated in the north west and the south east. Some schools for children with particular disabilities may wish to explore with local education authorities, either directly or through the regional machinery considered in Chapter 16, the possibility of making provision for children with kinds of disability different from those of the children for whom they currently cater. Indeed, we understand that a few are already doing so. We recognise that the extent to which a change of this kind will be possible may depend on the nature of the schools' trust deeds. It is important that the non-maintained special schools and the voluntary organisations which provide them should be closely involved in the planning by local education authorities of future arrangements for special educational provision, which we consider further in the following section.

III ORGANISATION OF SPECIAL SCHOOLS

Planning by local education authorities

8.28 We urged in the last chapter that, in the light of Section 10 of the Education Act 1976, each local education authority should draw up a long-term plan for special educational provision in its area. This would provide a framework within which arrangements for individual schools, special as well as ordinary, would take their place. The preparation of such a plan would give local education authorities the opportunity of re-appraising the aims of the special schools which they maintain or use, many of which are at present uncertain about the direction of their future development.

8.29 In their forward planning of special educational provision, local education authorities will need to take into account the fact that handicapping conditions often overlap, with the result that special schools, though mostly designed for children with the same main disability, may find themselves catering in practice for a very wide range of disabilities. A few of those who presented evidence to us argued in favour of a broadening of the range of disabilities for which individual schools are designed. In particular, the Association of Municipal Authorities commended the development of larger special schools catering for a greater number of handicapping conditions. They argued that such large "multi-handicap" schools would helpfully encourage the concentration of scarce specialist staff and resources and offer improved career prospects for staff and a wider range of opportunities for pupils. We recognise that there are administrative arguments in favour of the development of such schools but we hold strongly that educational considerations must be overriding. In our view the most important of these is that each school should operate as a functional unity. It follows that the special educational needs of its pupils must be broadly similar. Moreover, in line with the views advanced earlier in this chapter, such schools should have close links with ordinary schools in their area and any new ones should be built in geographically close proximity to ordinary schools, in order to facilitate close collaboration between them.

8.30 The planning of special educational provision requires close consultation between local education authorities (and between them and health authorities and social services departments), particularly where it is sensible to make shared provision. We strongly support the principle of regional self-sufficiency which the Department of Education and Science invited local education authorities to consider at their regional conferences held in 1975. It was recognised that even wider arrangements might be needed to provide adequately for children with certain disabilities of infrequent incidence, and we would also point to the desirability of effective co-operation across the regional boundaries. Since 1975 the regional conferences have made useful progress in reviewing special educational provision within their regions. We believe that the conferences need to be strengthened and their membership widened so that they co-ordinate provision yet more effectively, and we suggest in Chapter 16 how this might be achieved.

8.31 We have recommended that groups of local education authorities should develop a number of specialist centres for relatively rare or particularly complex disabilities based in special schools. If no suitable special school for the purpose exists in a particular part of the country, steps should be taken by the local education authorities in the region to establish one jointly and develop it, in collaboration where appropriate with voluntary organisations, as a specialist centre. If a suitable school exists but is not suitably located to serve the region, consideration should be given to the possibility of moving it to a more convenient location. In the event of a new capital programme being required, joint funding arrangements will need to be worked out between authorities. Where several schools are candidates for selection, local education authorities in the region will have to make a choice. In doing so they should consider how the selection of a particular school or schools would affect the regional pattern of special school provision and, in consultation with the voluntary bodies concerned, how any resulting imbalance could be corrected, for example by certain schools agreeing to cater for a different type of special educational need.

Size

8.32 One of the most important benefits that many special schools can offer their pupils is their smaller size, which makes it possible for them to provide more individual attention and better opportunities for children to relate to each other and to members of staff. With the future contraction which seems probable in special educational provision in separate schools, however, some special schools may decrease in size to a point where authorities will have to consider closing them or amalgamating them with other special schools. In all such cases, however, authorities will need to weigh the advantages and disadvantages of either of these courses of action against those of keeping them open as separate units. A variety of factors will apply, for example the cost of transport to and from the children's homes under the different options. But above all the needs of the children must be considered. Thus, if amalgamation of a particular special school with another school is likely to result in its pupils receiving less individual attention and being subjected to a variety of new pressures, the authority should be prepared to provide the necessary staff and resources to enable that school to continue as a separate unit. Similar considerations will apply to the future use of non-maintained special schools. If such a school is significantly declining in size, the voluntary organisation concerned will need to examine all the factors in discussion with the constituent local education authorities of the regional conference for special education and with any authorities outside the region who take up places. Every case must be looked at separately and for this reason we do not propose to offer advice on the minimum size of a special school or class, which we believe could be misleading.

Age range

8.33 The size of schools is affected by their age range. All-age special schools, though doubtless first established in order to concentrate resources, are able to offer their pupils certain advantages. They may provide a more flexible use of facilities and resources, including staff, than is possible in separate primary and secondary schools. More importantly, they are able to provide continuity of education for their pupils. On the other hand, there is a tendency to look on all-age schools as extended primary schools, with the result that the opportunities available to older pupils may be unduly limited. This effect is compounded by the relatively small numbers of senior pupils in all-age schools and the attendant difficulties of arranging subject options. On balance, we consider that the disadvantages of all-age schools outweigh their advantages and *we recommend that, wherever possible, separate special schools should be provided for senior and junior pupils.* Since the peak age for the admission of children to special schools

131

(including those currently ascertained as ESN(M)) is 8–9, it may be sensible for the break to come later than 10–11 (the usual point of transition to secondary school in England and Wales) – perhaps at 12 or 13. For children with emotional or behavioural disorders there are other advantages in a break at a later age: the problems of adolescents are often different in kind from those of younger children. Some flexibility however should be allowed in the age of transfer to suit the varying needs of individual children. We would draw particular attention to the needs of autistic children, whose language development, cognitive ability and emotional maturity may vary widely. Since the effects of change on these children can be particularly adverse, the age of transfer must be as flexible as possible and the transfer itself very carefully organised.

8.34 We recognise that geographical or other considerations may sometimes preclude the establishment of efficient separate primary and secondary schools. *Where the only practicable form of provision is an all-age school* – for example, to cater for one of the less common disabilities in an urban area or for several disabilities in a rural area – *we recommend that the school should be organised in separate departments, with a clear difference in the approach to children of secondary school age.* In such a case each department should have at least some teachers wholly committed to it.

School hours and school terms

8.35 We regard it as most unsatisfactory that the school day in many special schools, particularly those for children currently ascertained as physically handicapped, maladjusted or ESN(S), is so short. It often lasts only from 9.30am to 3.00pm, and preparations for going home may start before 3 o'clock. This can seriously restrict opportunities, particularly for physically handicapped children whose education has, in any case, to be interrupted for treatment. There is a number of factors which need to be taken into account in considering what should be the length of the school day. For example, an extended day could mean a very long period away from home for some children at special schools in rural areas. In order to avoid this, it is important that, as a general rule, children should not have to spend more than three-quarters of an hour travelling to or from school. Moreover, the special needs of children who, for example, tire easily, must be borne in mind. *We recommend that, so far as is possible, the length of the school day in special schools should be the same as that in ordinary schools, with scope for variation according to the age and needs of the pupils.*

8.36 In practice the possibility of extending the length of the school day often depends upon the arrangements for transport. The difficulty which authorities have in attracting tenders for transport contracts from private hire firms and the practical necessity for vehicles to make a number of stops for individual children mean that arrangements for transport tend to be very inflexible. We consider that there is more scope in urban areas for the use of public transport, particularly by older pupils; some schools are over-protective about this. In rural areas, however, special arrangements will invariably need to be made. We therefore suggest that local authorities should explore different ways of making arrangements for transport which would enable the school day in special schools to be lengthened. One local education authority in its evidence to us suggested that "ultimately the answer may be for local authorities to run their own transport fleets for the handicapped or resort increasingly to escorts taking two or three children to school, or providing individual schools with mini-buses and ambulances with appropriate driver support to enable the schools to transport their most severely handicapped pupils". Some authorities already have their own fleet of buses and certainly this allows special schools more scope to extend the school day. Moreover, it can enable children to remain after school for youth club and other activities and still be taken home – something which is often very difficult at present. We are aware that the widespread maintenance by local authorities of their own fleet of buses would be expensive, particularly in the early stages, but in the long term it could prove cheaper than the various alternatives.

8.37 School holidays, particularly the long summer holiday, are often difficult times for parents of children with disabilities. A number of those who submitted evidence to us argued in favour of a four-term year on the grounds that it would both maintain the continuity of the children's education and reduce the strain on families. We concur with the general feeling, however, that special schools should keep in step with ordinary schools in the organisation of the school year. We consider that instead arrangements should be made for the premises of some special schools to stay open for at least part of the school holidays and we discuss this further in the next chapter.

Weekend arrangements in residential special schools

8.38 Residential schools may be divided into three groups so far as their policy on weekend arrangements is concerned:

(i) those where boarding education implies residence for the full term apart from half-term breaks, but where weekends at home may be allowed at the parents' request;

(ii) those where regular visits home are encouraged, either weekly or every fortnight or so, but where the school aims to provide a more personal and intimate weekend regime for those pupils who cannot return home or in some instances choose to remain in school for the weekend; and

(iii) those where boarding is organised on a weekly basis and the school closes at weekends.

There has been a trend in favour of a policy of weekly boarding; in some cases this is being forced on schools because of the difficulty of obtaining staff at weekends; in others it is a matter of deliberate choice. While boarding schools stand to make some savings if they close completely at weekends, there is less scope for savings if they remain open for some pupils. Consequently, schools are tending to offer boarding on either a termly or a five-day a week basis.

8.39 It is thus becoming increasingly difficult to offer a child a choice of boarding arrangements within a particular residential school. Yet children for whom five-day boarding is desirable at the time of initial placement may, by reason of a change in family circumstances, subsequently require residential facilities at weekends. Conversely, children who need termly boarding at first may come to want the opportunity to return home at weekends. In both cases a change of placement will be required, even though the school continues to meet the child's educational needs, unless the boarding arrangements are flexible. *We therefore recommend that residential special schools should be organised on as flexible a basis as possible, and should retain the capacity to remain open at weekends so that there is a genuine choice as to whether or not the children return home at weekends.* We recognise that residential schools may face staffing difficulties at weekends and that the scope for savings will be reduced if they do not close completely. However, we strongly hold that placements should be made on the basis of what is educationally most suitable for a particular child and should not be conditioned by rigidity in the arrangements for weekend provision. Flexibility in the organisation of schools is therefore essential.

8.40 We believe that parents should have opportunity to visit their children at school or to have them at home at weekends if they so wish, and that they should not be prevented from doing so by restrictions on the part of the school. Boarding special schools are, however, often situated at a considerable distance from the homes of many of the children who attend them and, although most local education authorities have schemes for meeting the costs in certain circumstances, particularly where a school is organised for weekly boarding only, the cost of regularly visiting or bringing home their child can be very burdensome to some parents. In recommending to a local education authority the residential placement of a child with special educational needs, the assessment team should always express a view about the arrangements for his being visited by his parents or for his returning home at intervals. In so doing the team should take into account not only their own assessment on educational grounds but also the wishes of the parents, which in our view are of the greatest importance. *We recommend that where the multi-professional team which assesses a child's needs at Stage 4 or 5 of our proposed assessment procedure concludes that he should return home or that his parents should visit him at weekends or other regular intervals, the local education authority should meet all or a substantial part of the cost. Even where no such recommendation has been made by the multi-professional team, the local education authority should be prepared to meet all or part of the cost if subsequent review of a child's progress suggests that he would benefit from weekend visits home or visits by his parents.* In all other cases where parents wish to visit their children or have them at home at weekends, we would urge authorities to contribute at least the difference between the transport costs and the financial savings made by the parents by not having to care for their children during the week.

Teachers and other staff

8.41 We welcome the flexible approach to staffing standards shown in the Circular on the staffing of special schools and classes, which the Department of Education and Science and the Welsh Office issued in 1973; and in the Consultative Document issued by the Scottish Education Department in the same year.[5] The staff-pupil ratios suggested in these documents are not based upon a rigid concept of the size of classes, but rather allow for the work of each school to be

---

[5] DES Circular 4/73, Welsh Office Circular 47/73, Staffing of Special Schools and Classes (6 March 1973). Scottish Education Department Memorandum, Revision of Schools (Scotland) Code 1956 (October 1973).

134

organised in teaching groups ranging for different purposes from individual tuition to 20 or more. *We recommend that the staff-pupil ratios suggested in the Circular and the Consultative Document should be regarded as a minimum requirement.*

8.42 The staffing ratios suggested in these documents are based on the assumption that adequate numbers of suitable ancillary staff are available, and attention was drawn to the particular value of ancillary staff in schools catering for younger children or those suffering from very severe physical or learning difficulties. *We recommend that guidance should be issued in a further Circular on the numbers of ancillary staff that should be regarded as adequate.* We make suggestions for a scale of staffing provision for classes catering for children in different age groups and with different types of disability in Chapter 14.

8.43 Ancillary staff can greatly help children with disabilities or serious difficulties, particularly those with physical disabilities, to become as self-sufficient as possible. Their support is of particular value to teachers at certain times of the day, especially in dealing with severely disruptive children, including those with difficulties of an autistic or hyper-active kind. Whilst we would not wish to see hard and fast lines laid down, it is clearly important that there should be broad agreement between local education authorities and teacher and other unions concerned about the respective functions of teachers and ancillary staff. This is necessary in the interests of effective co-operation and also as a basis for training. Ancillary staff should have opportunity to undertake training for their work in the classroom and should be encouraged to do so; likewise teachers should have access to courses which include training in how to use the services of ancillary helpers to best advantage. We consider the supply and training of ancillary staff further in Chapter 14.

8.44 Child care staff in residential special schools spend at least as much time with the children as do the teachers. Demarcation lines between child care and teaching are rightly blurred. The two overlap; a teacher may put the child to bed and a child care worker may help with a group of children with learning difficulties. For child care staff as well as for teachers satisfactory staff ratios, career opportunities and training are imperative, and we make suggestions as to what these should be in Chapter 14.

Specialist support

8.45 We are firmly of the view that more specialist support is needed for both teachers and pupils in special schools. The survey of teachers' views conducted by the Department of Education and Science found that of those teachers in maintained special schools who replied to questions about contact with particular categories of specialist half had only irregular contact with advisers in special education, educational psychologists and social workers, and well over half never had contact with peripatetic or advisory teachers. Between one-third and one-half of those responding to these questions indicated that they would like more contact with advisers in special education, educational psychologists, social workers and speech therapists.[6] We consider the need for support for teachers

---

[6] For details of the survey see Appendix 8.

from advisers in special education at length in Chapter 13 and discuss the supply of other professionals employed by the education service, including educational psychologists, in Chapter 14. Aspects of the work of the social services are considered in Chapter 15. In the following paragraphs we turn to the provision of support from professionals in the health service. Some aspects of their work and of the work of teachers overlap, and should be recognised as doing so. It follows that there must be the closest possible co-operation between them in meeting the needs of children in the school.

8.46 Many children in special schools need regular supervision and treatment by medical specialists, such as orthopaedic surgeons, paediatricians, urologists, otologists, ophthalmologists and psychiatrists. We received evidence, confirmed by our own observations, that the arrangement of children's visits to hospitals and clinics for supervision and treatment sometimes requires much effort on the part of the teachers and also wastes valuable educational time. These difficulties can be overcome if, as already happens in some special schools, clinics are held by visiting specialists in the school. *We therefore recommend that local education and area health authorities should provide the necessary space, equipment, nursing and secretarial help to enable medical specialists to hold their clinics in the school.* Further, we commend the practice in some residential special schools of inviting a visiting specialist to spread his work over two days and spend the intervening night at the school. This can provide a unique opportunity for the school staff to join in discussions about individual children, and should be more widespread. Parents should be strongly encouraged to attend medical consultations at the school and, where decisions about changes of treatment or operations are to be taken, the local education authority responsible for placing the child should be prepared to meet the cost of their transport.

8.47 In many schools where their services are needed by the pupils, physiotherapists and occupational or speech therapists are members of the school team, either full or part-time. Their effectiveness within the school depends on a variety of factors, including the facilities and conditions offered to them, the extent of their contact with medical and orthopaedic specialists, and their relations with teaching and care staff and with parents. It is important that they should work closely with other members of the school staff and with parents and enlist their help in the re-inforcement of treatment. Moreover, *we recommend that area health authorities should ensure that continuity of treatment is provided for children during the school holidays.* We consider the provision of services by professionals in the health service in more detail in Chapter 15.

8.48 Nursing support for special schools may vary from intermittent visits by a single school nurse to one school to the presence of a nursing team with three or more full-time members in another, depending on factors such as the size of the school and the needs of the children attending it. The wide variations in the school nursing service provided from one area health authority to another, so far as staffing, conditions of service and administration are concerned, emerged very clearly from a report of a recent study on the provision of nursing care in special schools.[7] We consider in Chapter 15 the nursing requirements of

---

[7] Department of Health and Social Security Circular CNO(78)1, Provision of Nursing Care in Special Schools (9 January 1978).

special schools. We would emphasise here the importance of nurses being encouraged and helped to work closely with, and so far as possible to share some of their duties with, other members of the school staff. Moreover, *we recommend that continuity of nursing support, as of treatment, should be provided during the school holidays.*

Governing bodies in England and Wales

8.49 Although special schools were excluded from the terms of reference of the Taylor Committee on the management and government of schools in England and Wales which reported in September 1977,[8] we consider that many of that Committee's recommendations are equally applicable to them. Moreover, in principle we regard it as desirable that so far as possible the constitution, duties and powers of the governing bodies of special schools should be the same as those of the governing bodies of ordinary schools, since this will help to reduce the separateness of special schools from the rest of education. We recognise that the governing bodies of non-maintained special schools may differ in certain respects from those of maintained special schools, depending on the nature of their trust deeds, but we consider that their constitution should be based on the same principles and our following remarks therefore apply to both types of school. We urge that, subject to what is said below, any decisions that may be taken in England and Wales on the governing bodies of ordinary schools in the light of the report of the Taylor Committee should apply also to all special schools.

8.50 There is a number of changes which we regard as particularly desirable so far as the governing bodies of special schools are concerned. First, like the Taylor Committee, we are convinced that there are serious disadvantages in the grouping of several schools under one governing body. In particular, group governing bodies tend to be very large and cumbersome, their members often lack a personal identification with the schools in the group and there is little sense of partnership between the schools and the governing body. Indeed, we heard of a headteacher of one special school grouped with six others under one governing body who was not even aware that the school had a governing body. We recognise that there may be exceptional circumstances, for example in rural areas, which make the grouping of special schools expedient on practical grounds, but the principle remains the same. *We therefore recommend that, as a general rule, every special school should have its own governing body.*

8.51 Secondly, we consider that membership of the governing bodies of all special schools needs to be broadened in the way proposed by the Taylor Committee for ordinary schools to include representatives of the local education authority, parents, school staff and the local community, though not necessarily in the proportions which the Committee recommended. *We recommend that special arrangements should however be made to ensure that the governing bodies of those special schools which have catchment areas extending beyond the locality reflect the wider communities that they serve.* Thus parent members and representatives of the community should not be confined to those who live close to the

---

[8] *A New Partnership for our Schools.* Report of the Committee of Enquiry appointed jointly by the Secretary of State for Education and Science and the Secretary of State for Wales under the Chairmanship of Mr Tom Taylor, CBE (HMSO, 1977).

school. Moreover, where a special school takes children from more than one local education authority area, the local education authority representation on the governing body should not be confined to the authority in whose area the school is situated.

8.52 Thirdly, *we recommend that, wherever appropriate, the governing body of a special school should include a handicapped person*. This would be in keeping with the spirit of the Chronically Sick and Disabled Persons Act 1970, Section 15 of which requires a local authority to have regard to the desirability of appointing chronically sick or disabled persons to committees of the authority. It would be desirable that the person concerned should be particularly knowledgeable about the needs of the children for whom the school catered.

8.53 We share the Taylor Committee's view that it is undesirable for an individual to serve simultaneously on a very large number of governing bodies of schools catering for children in the same age range and believe that the principle holds for special as well as ordinary schools. Nevertheless, we endorse the view expressed by the Taylor Committee that a primary or secondary school governor should be able to serve also as governor of a special school, whatever the age group of the children attending that school.

School councils in Scotland

8.54 Until the Local Government (Scotland) Act 1973 there was no provision for the appointment of governing bodies for schools in Scotland. That Act provided for the appointment of school councils with the duty of discharging any functions of management and supervision of schools that the education authority might decide to give them. The Act did not, however, specify the functions that should be given to school councils or their membership, whether each school should have its own council or whether a number of schools might be grouped under one council. As a result, since 1974, when the new provisions came into operation, many different arrangements have been made in various parts of Scotland; all of these involve the grouping of schools. Research funded by the government is currently being carried out by the University of Glasgow into the relative value and effectiveness of different arrangements and the results are expected before the end of 1978. We understand that the government intends to consider what changes, if any, would be desirable in the light of this research.

8.55 So far as the management of special schools is concerned, we consider it preferable, wherever possible, for each school to have its own school council rather than to be grouped under a school council responsible for the management and supervision of a number of schools. We recognise that arrangements for grouping can have the advantage of reducing the isolation of special schools from ordinary schools, but we would regard it as essential that such arrangements should not preclude the appointment of a separate governing body – be it a school council or other body – with effective powers in relation to each special school. We think that it should be possible for this object to be achieved without any major change in the present provisions. If, for example, grouping of ordinary schools continues, provision might be made for the appointment of an individual school council for each special school with the proviso that a representative of that school council should be appointed *ex officio* to the school council for other schools in the area. We hope that this will be borne in mind in any review of the Scottish arrangements.

IV INDEPENDENT SCHOOLS CATERING WHOLLY OR MAINLY FOR HANDICAPPED PUPILS

8.56 At the end of June 1977 there were 160 independent schools in England and Wales which catered wholly or mainly for handicapped pupils. In January 1977 7,237 handicapped pupils were placed in independent schools by local education authorities, of whom 89% were boarders. Within this total of 7,237 there were, in current terminology, some 4,211 maladjusted children (58%), 853 physically handicapped, 625 ESN(S), 573 ESN(M) and 335 deaf children. In Scotland in September 1976 there were 13 independent schools which catered wholly or mainly for handicapped pupils. These provided some 500 places. About 200 of the children placed in them were, in current terminology, mentally handicapped (40%), 160 maladjusted (32%) and 60 physically handicapped (12%). [9]

8.57 Independent schools which cater wholly or mainly for handicapped children have in the past carried out useful pioneering work; and some of them continue to innovate and experiment in the same way as some non-maintained special schools do. Some are also readier to admit children aged over 13 than maintained and non-maintained special schools are. There is, however, a much greater variation in the quality of individual independent schools and in their approach to the task of educating children with disabilities or significant difficulties. At one extreme, some of the very best schools in the country for children with certain disabilities, particularly for spastic and for autistic children, are run by voluntary bodies who prefer for their schools the greater freedom which independent status confers. At the other extreme, some individual proprietors appear to view the provision of boarding special education as a commercial venture which should yield a profit. Moreover, the schools are often isolated from the mainstream of education and, having few contacts with ordinary schools, they tend to accentuate the present division between handicapped and other children.

8.58 At present, because of the inadequacy of their own provision, local education authorities have no choice but to make use of independent schools for placing children with certain types of disability or disorder, particularly those with emotional or behavioural disorders and those with severe learning difficulties who require residential education. Thus in England and Wales in 1977 independent schools catered for 30% of all children ascertained as maladjusted who were in special schools or placed by authorities in independent schools. Until the economic recession of the early 1970s some progress was being made by a number of authorities in increasing their residential provision for these children; but the subsequent reduction in capital programmes has led authorities to rely more than ever on independent schools, often a long way away, to fill gaps in the local provision. *We recommend that where special school provision in the maintained sector is inadequate, as it is particularly for children with emotional or behavioural disorders and those with severe learning difficulties, it should be*

---

[9] Department of Education and Science and Scottish Education Department statistics.

increased to the point of sufficiency. This will mean that the necessary use by authorities of independent schools catering wholly or mainly for handicapped pupils will progressively decrease. For the present, however, we expect that authorities will continue to have to use independent schools where suitable arrangements cannot be made in other ways, and we believe that much closer supervision of these schools is required.

Supervision of independent schools in England and Wales

8.59 The Department of Education and Science and the Welsh Office exercise less stringent control over independent schools than over non-maintained special schools. Independent schools do not have to meet conditions laid down in statutory regulations. Moreover, there is no limitation on the length of time for which an independent school, having been provisionally registered, can continue without final registration, which calls for a further inspection by Her Majesty's Inspectorate. Finally, as from 30 April 1978 the present arrangements for the recognition by the Secretaries of State for Education and Science and for Wales of certain independent schools as efficient, which though not in the nature of a measure of control did confer a special mark of approval on the schools concerned, are to be discontinued.

8.60 The Secretaries of State for Education and Science and for Wales do, however, have powers to control the use by local education authorities of independent schools under Section 33(2) of the Education Act 1944 as amended by the Education (Miscellaneous Provisions) Act 1953. This provides that in certain circumstances local education authorities may make arrangements for the special educational treatment of handicapped pupils in schools not maintained by a local education authority other than those notified by the Secretary of State to the authority as being, in his or her opinion, unsuitable for the purpose. Section 33(2) is amended by Section 10 of the Education Act 1976 (operative from a date to be appointed by the Secretaries of State for Education and Science and for Wales). In its amended form, Section 33(2) will continue to allow the use of schools that are not maintained by local education authorities but with the Secretary of State's agreement expressed positively (ie that the school in question is suitable). The Secretary of State's statutory approval is presently exercised under arrangements set out in Circular 4/61.[10] Schools recognised as efficient are automatically regarded as being suitable: those not so recognised are regarded as being unsuitable, unless in a particular case the Secretary of State, on application by a local education authority, decides to make an exception (either generally or for a particular pupil or category of pupil).

8.61 Supervision of independent schools which cater for handicapped pupils is needed for two purposes: to ensure that any such school is of an adequate standard at the time of a child's placement; and that it continues to achieve this standard. Recognition as efficient provided a serviceable means of helping to determine a school's suitability. Its discontinuance will call for new machinery. We do not think that registration can be a satisfactory substitute. The standards required for recognition as efficient were more stringent than those required for

---

[10] Ministry of Education Circular 4/61, The use of independent schools for handicapped pupils (27 March 1961).

registration. Moreover registration is itself a separate statutory process. An independent school may appeal to the Independent Schools Tribunal against a decision of the Secretary of State that it should not be registered or should cease to be registered and we do not think that a school's suitability for the education of handicapped children should, in effect, be determined by a body instituted for another purpose. We think, rather, that the Department of Education and Science and Welsh Office should establish separate criteria for the statutory acceptance of an independent school as being suitable for providing special education and that no school should be accepted without very full and thorough inspection by Her Majesty's Inspectorate. Its continued acceptance should likewise be subject to periodical inspection. *We recommend that the Department of Education and Science and the Welsh Office should maintain and publish a list of independent schools which are accepted by the Secretaries of State for the purposes of Section 33(2) of the Education Act 1944 as it will be amended by Section 10 of the Education Act 1976.*

8.62 The statutory acceptance of an independent school under Section 33(2) of the Education Act 1944 will not by itself guarantee that the needs of particular pupils are being met. These may be pupils of any age, ranging from the under-fives to the post-sixteens. It is therefore important that local education authorities should regularly review their placement of a child with special needs in such a school. *We recommend that responsibility for following up the placement of a child in an independent school catering for handicapped pupils and, where necessary, for initiating a new placement should rest with the person designated by the multi-professional team which assessed the child's needs to act as Named Person for the child's parents.* As we explained in Chapter 5 in relation to young children and as we point out in Chapter 9 in relation to children of school age, we would expect this person to be someone with particular expertise or interest in the area of the child's disability. It is a corollary of our recommendation that children should be placed in schools as near as possible to their home, so that the Named Person can follow their progress without difficulty.

8.63 In general, if local education authorities are to develop closer links with independent schools which cater for handicapped pupils, as we believe they should, and monitor the standards of the schools which they use, they will need to have full access to those schools. At present they have no right of access to independent schools and, indeed, because of this, are often reluctant to share with other authorities any information which they obtain about the standards of provision in such schools. *We therefore recommend that, as a way of ensuring that local education authorities have access to independent schools used for handicapped pupils, part of the conditions for acceptance of the use of such a school under Section 33(2) of the 1944 Act as it will be amended should be that the Secretary of State is satisfied that the school will offer access to officers of both the sending authority and the authority in whose area the school is situated.*

8.64 Contact between local authorities and independent schools in their area would also be facilitated if representatives of the authority were to be members of the governing bodies of the schools. *We therefore recommend that all independent schools which cater for handicapped pupils and are accepted by the Secretaries of State for the purpose of Section 33(2) of the Education Act 1944* (*as it will be amended*) *should have governing bodies and that the membership of those bodies should include a representative of the authority in whose area they are situated.* We recognise that in some parts of the country where there is a concentration of such schools, particularly the south east and the south west, this will call for large numbers of local authority representatives to serve as governors but we believe that the benefits will be considerable.

Supervision of independent schools in Scotland

8.65 The system of registration of independent schools in Scotland is in some respects different from that in England and Wales and there is no category of schools which are recognised as efficient. Provisional registration is granted by the Scottish Education Department on receipt of a valid application and final registration is given only when the school meets the inspection standards of Her Majesty's Inspectorate and the fire precautions have been approved by the local firemaster. If the school does not meet the standards for final registration, the Department may consider serving a notice of complaint on the school proprietors under Section 112 of the Education (Scotland) Act 1962. All independent schools providing special education for the handicapped are included in List G (Provision for Handicapped Children in Scotland) and if they fail to continue to provide special education they may be removed from the List. In view of his responsibility for health, education and social work, the Secretary of State for Scotland is well placed to ensure that appropriate advisers are available when premises are being inspected to determine the suitability of the school for its intended purpose. Schools included in List G are regularly inspected at not more than two yearly intervals. *We recommend that the Secretary of State for Scotland should make the inclusion in List G of independent schools catering for handicapped pupils conditional on their proprietors agreeing to allow officers of both the sending authority and the authority in whose area the school is situated access to the school.* Every encouragement should be given to the school to invite a member of the authority in whose area it is situated to serve on the board of management.

The placement of children in care in independent schools

8.66 A local authority in its social services capacity is *in loco parentis* in relation to any child who is placed in care, and so assumes the duty imposed on parents by Section 36 of the Education Act 1944 to secure that the child receives efficient full-time education. The same authority, in its education capacity, has a duty under Section 37 to take action if it is not satisfied that the requirements of Section 36 are being met. We do not propose here to comment on local procedures in a general sense, but within our terms of reference we hold that these two duties, which usually lie upon the same local authority acting in different capacities, call for full consultation between the social services and education departments whenever the educational placement arises of a child in care who has been assessed as needing special education. *In particular we recommend that no child with special educational needs who is in care should be placed in an independent school without agreement between the local education authority and the social services department.* Although the provisions of Section 33(2) of the Education Act 1944 (to which we referred in paragraph 8.60) do not apply to placements in independent schools by social services departments we consider that no such placement should be made in any independent school not accepted by the Secretaries of State for the purposes of Section 33(2) of the Education Act 1944 as amended.

V RESIDENTIAL PROVISION IN OTHER ESTABLISHMENTS AND HOME TUITION

8.67 There is a number of residential establishments other than boarding special schools and independent schools in which educational provision may be made for children with special needs. In the following sections we consider two types of such establishment, namely community homes and hospitals, and then conclude by examining arrangements for home tuition.

Community homes

8.68 Since the Children and Young Persons Act 1969 and the Personal Social Services Act 1970 all institutions for the accommodation and maintenance of children in the care of local authorities have been designated community homes. There are three types of such home: community homes with observation and assessment facilities; community homes from which the majority of children attend local schools; and community homes with education on the premises. In 1976 these three types of community home catered for 4,976, 23,412 and 6,784 children respectively in England and Wales. Responsibility for the homes rests with the local authority in its social services capacity or the voluntary organisation if the home is "assisted".

8.69 In our view there is a considerable similarity between the educational needs of children in community homes with education on the premises (CHEs) and those of children with emotional or behavioural disorders in special schools. At the same time we recognise that children who are placed in CHEs require a period of treatment which aims at social readjustment. As a basic principle, we believe that education in community homes should be seen as an essential element of an integrated programme of treatment and that the quality of the educational provision made for children in CHEs should be the same as that for children with similar educational needs in special schools.

8.70 We are concerned, however, that in practice, mainly because of the professional isolation of the teaching staff in CHEs, the quality of the educational provision in CHEs may not match that in special schools. A survey of educational provision in community homes carried out by the National Association of Schoolmasters/Union of Women Teachers and submitted to us as evidence confirmed our impression that staff in CHEs and community homes with observation and assessment facilities lack information about courses of in-service training organised by the local education authority. Opportunities for them to take part in courses are limited and they receive inadequate support from local authority advisory and support services. It would seem to follow that the quality of the education provided in CHEs and observation and assessment centres must suffer.

8.71 In some areas teachers are seconded to the social services department by the local education authority to work in a CHE. This practice is far more widespread in the case of teachers in observation and assessment centres. We recognise that there are considerable differences between the terms and conditions of service and employment of teachers in community homes and those in other sectors of education; these stem from the need to provide residence, care and education for children in community homes on a year-round basis. This consideration does not, however, outweigh the advantages which we believe would ensue if all teachers in community homes were employed by local education authorities. *We therefore recommend that, as a first and major step in improving the quality of educational provision in CHEs and observation and assessment centres, teachers in those establishments should be in the service of local education authorities.* They should be appointed by a panel consisting of the head of the establishment and the chairman of the managing body, where such a body exists, together with officers of the local authority education and social services departments. Moreover, teaching in community homes should be regarded as part of the career structure for all teachers rather than a separate profession. We consider that the minimum teacher-pupil ratios in CHEs should be those suggested for maladjusted children in the Circular on staffing standards in special schools and classes issued by the Department of Education and Science and Welsh Office in 1973 and in the Consultative Document issued by the Scottish Education Department in the same year.[11]

8.72 In addition we see a need for other close links between CHEs and the education service, as suggested in the Joint Circular issued by the Department of Education and Science, Department of Health and Social Security and Welsh Office in 1973.[12] In particular, teachers in CHEs need the support of the local education authority advisory service and, as the National Union of Teachers emphasised in evidence to us, opportunities to develop their professional skills through in-service training courses. We consider that our proposals in Chapter 12 regarding the training of teachers with responsibility for children with special educational needs should apply to teachers in CHEs and that, as soon as it becomes practicable, they should be required to have a recognised qualification in special education. *We therefore recommend that opportunities for teachers in community homes to undertake courses of in-service training should be improved and that regular support should be provided for them by members of our proposed special education advisory and support service.*

8.73 We also see a need for much closer contact between staff in observation and assessment centres and other local authority staff concerned with the assessment of children with special educational needs. The present separation between the two is often wasteful of the time of scarce specialist staff, since in some cases a child's special needs may be assessed by two separate groups of professionals. We are supported in this view by the recommendations in the Joint Departmental Circular on child guidance issued in 1974[13] for the development of a network of separate but collaborating services for dealing with those children and their families whose problems call for a combined approach. As a further step in

---

[11] DES Circular 4/73, Welsh Office Circular 47/73, Staffing of Special Schools and Classes (6 March 1973). Scottish Education Department Memorandum, Revision of Schools (Scotland) Code 1956 (October 1973).

[12] DES Circular Letter Schools Branch II (SE) 1/73, DHSS Circular 42/73 and Welsh Office Circular 194/73, Children and Young Persons Act 1969 – Arrangements for education in community homes (31 August 1973).

[13] DES Circular 3/74, DHSS Circular HSC(IS)9, Welsh Office Circular WHSC(IS)5, Child Guidance (14 March 1974).

strengthening the educational component of CHEs and observation and assessment centres *we recommend that the educational representation should be strengthened on the managing bodies of homes and centres where such bodies exist.*

8.74 We have doubts whether the various changes which we have proposed will suffice to bring about the much closer contact between CHEs and the education service which we regard as imperative. We have therefore considered a proposal for a more fundamental change in the community home system involving the transfer of the management of CHEs to the education service. We have found merit in this proposal; in particular it would have the advantage of making for a wider and more flexible range of special educational provision for children with emotional and behavioural disorders. On balance, however, most of us consider that such a radical change would be undesirable at the present time, given that the Children and Young Persons Act 1969 has not yet been fully implemented. Our recommended changes should nonetheless be regarded as the minimum necessary if the educational needs of children in CHEs are to be adequately met.

List D schools in Scotland

8.75 List D schools are residential establishments to which children under the age of 16, and those over 16 but under 18 who are already subject to a supervision requirement of a children's hearing, may be sent by children's hearings or on the direction of the Secretary of State for Scotland following committal by courts under Sections 206 and 413 of the Criminal Procedure (Scotland) Act 1975. Although the appropriate local authority is responsible for the children sent to residential establishments by hearings, the responsibility for children committed under Sections 206 and 413 rests with the Secretary of State.

8.76 There are 26 List D schools, with some 1,700 places, which provide the main resource for the accommodation of boys and girls considered by the children's hearings to be in need of compulsory measures of residential care or placed there by the Secretary of State as a result of court orders. Two of the schools are managed by Strathclyde Regional Council, and the rest by independent bodies of voluntary managers.

8.77 We consider that our recommendations on the educational aspect of CHEs are generally in accord with the terms of the Secretary of State for Scotland's Consultative Document issued in December 1976 on the future of List D schools[14] and we propose that these recommendations be taken into account during the discussions on the future of List D schools.

Education in hospital

8.78 Education whilst in hospital is the right of every child over the age of five. In England and Wales it may be provided either in hospital special schools approved under Section 9(5) of the Education Act 1944 or in other ways under Section 56 of the Education Act 1944, which enables a local education authority to provide education otherwise than at school. In January 1977 there were 152

---

[14] Future Administrative and Financial Arrangements for List D Schools (Scottish Education Department, 9 December 1976).

hospital special schools (68 exclusively for children currently ascertained as ESN(S)). Official statistics indicate that 8,979 children were attending these schools, of whom 5,029 were in schools for the ESN(S) and 3,950 in other hospital special schools.[15] In addition, other handicapped children were receiving education in hospital under Section 56 arrangements. In Scotland in September 1976 there were 867 children in 15 mental deficiency hospital schools, of whom 845 were, in present terminology, mentally handicapped or severely mentally handicapped. In addition, 508 children were receiving education in 45 hospitals under arrangements made under Section 14 of the Education (Scotland) Act 1962.[16] The statistics for children taught in hospital on a particular date may not however accurately reflect the normal situation; there are seasonal flows of children into hospital and in January, when the statistics are collected, admissions and re-admissions may not have built up again after the Christmas holiday. We are aware, however, that very many children are taught in hospital and *we recommend that for administrative purposes all education in hospital should be regarded as special educational provision.* Thus, within a local education authority it would be the responsibility of the assistant education officer for special education or designated senior officer for special education and, as we propose in paragraph 8.87, support for the teaching staff would be provided by our proposed special education advisory and support service.

8.79 Responsibility for the education of children in mental handicap hospitals, along with that of other mentally handicapped children who would previously have been regarded as unsuitable for education at school, was transferred to the education service in 1971 in England and Wales and in 1975 in Scotland. Since then there have been considerable improvements in mental handicap hospital schools in the staffing ratios and the proportion of teachers who are qualified; and there has been some improvement in the grouping of children for teaching purposes, the planning of programmes for both groups and individuals and the stimulation of children's responses to teaching. Serious problems continue to exist, however, as regards accommodation and staffing and as regards relations between teaching, medical, nursing and other staff, to which we return in paragraph 8.86.

8.80 The nature of the educational provision in hospital is the product of the individual hospital, its patients, methods, history and geographical position. We have identified two groups of children in hospital who require particular consideration. First, there is a group of children who are not receiving education, either because they are dispersed in adult or other wards and their presence is unknown to the responsible local education authority, or because they are subject in the hospital to a waiting period before they can start hospital schooling. We recognise that there may be excellent medical reasons for postponing the start of education in hospital for a child who, for example, is in an acute, serious or exhausting phase of his illness. Sometimes, however, a variable waiting period is imposed by local education authorities for financial reasons. *We recommend that arrangements should be made for all children to receive education as soon as possible after their admission to hospital.*

---

[15] Department of Education and Science statistics.
[16] Scottish Education Department statistics.

146

8.81 The second group about whom we are particularly concerned is that of children who live in hospital because they have no other home. We cannot over-state our view that, where children who have been abandoned by their families do not require hospital care, new homes must be found for them by local authority social services departments. We recognise that on occasions short periods in hospital may provide the only possible solution to joint educational and medical problems but as a general principle we hold that no child should ever enter hospital solely to receive education.

8.82 Educational activities need to be separated, so far as possible, from the other activities of the hospital so that a child can feel that he is "going to school". We share the view expressed in the Department of Education and Science Circular 5/74 (Department of Health and Social Security Circular HSC(IS)37)[17] on the education of mentally handicapped and other long-stay children in hospital that, wherever it is practicable, such children should attend school in the community. This will be increasingly important with the trend towards smaller mental handicap units, which may make it impracticable to have a school on the hospital site. There will, however, be children with profound disabilities in both mental handicap and other hospitals who need continuous nursing care and for whom education will need to be provided in hospital. *We recommend that, wherever possible, educational premises should be specially provided in the hospital for children who are unable to leave the hospital to attend school.* Where such premises do not exist or are inadequate, the children should nevertheless be taught in different surroundings and should be taught in the wards only if no other arrangement can be made.

8.83 It is important that children who are in hospital for long periods should, wherever possible, have contact with the outside world. The most effective way of achieving this will be through their attending schools in the community. If this is not possible, then links with children in local schools should be developed through, for example, reciprocal visits to each other's schools, the exchange of diaries and participation in joint projects. We have heard of one mental handicap hospital where children with severe and multiple learning difficulties lead a very full life, enjoying shopping, riding, swimming and camping as well as joining in the activities of a local youth club and playgroup – all of which bring them into regular contact with life outside the hospital. We have noted the view expressed in the Court Report[18] that where a child is in hospital for more than three months, there should be a comprehensive review of his need for services including education. We see no need to wait until three months have elapsed. *We recommend that a comprehensive review of a child's need for services should take place as soon as it becomes clear that he needs long-term hospital treatment, without waiting for any fixed period of time.*

8.84 The vast majority of children who receive schooling in hospital, however, are there for a very short time. We consider that education has an indispensable contribution to make in helping them, through its very normality, to come to

---

[17] DES Circular 5/74, DHSS Circular HSC(IS)37, The Education of Mentally Handicapped Children and Young People in Hospital (21 May 1974).

[18] *Fit for the future.* The Report of the Committee on Child Health Services. Cmnd 6684 (HMSO, 1976), Vol 1, p 278.

terms with a brief, but perhaps traumatic, period of hospital care. Many of these children will be very young and, in keeping with our view that the need for special education may begin at birth, we believe that there should be no lower limit to the age at which education can be provided in hospital. We recognise that children already have considerable opportunity for structured play in hospital. Educational programmes for young children in hospital will clearly need to be organised in co-operation with the existing play services and with the full involvement of parents. Children whose stay may be short or intermittent, no less than those who are in hospital for long periods, need to retain a sense of continuity in their education and in their contacts with their family, friends and neighbourhood. Their present or future schools could contribute significantly to smoothing their transition from home to hospital and vice versa, and this process should be facilitated by local education authorities in collaboration with local health and social services.

8.85 We believe that there is a need for some educational provision to be made in hospitals during the school holidays, particularly for children who are there for a long time and whose educational programmes may be seriously interrupted by the holiday break and for children who are able to attend residential special schools but for whom hospital is for the time being their home during the holidays. Moreover, given the rapid turnover of junior doctors and junior nurses, teachers on the wards and in hospital schools can provide a much needed element of continuity and stability for the children. We commend the practice which already operates in some hospitals of staggering teachers' holidays and hope that it will become more widespread.

8.86 We have already referred to the problems which exist in mental handicap hospitals as regards relations between teaching, medical, nursing and other staff. The problems are not confined to mental handicap hospitals but exist in other types as well. In particular, there may be a reluctance on the part of medical, nursing and other staff to give full recognition to the contribution which education can make to the development of all children, however serious their disabilities. Much closer communication needs to be established between teaching and other staff in hospitals in the interests of breaking down the barriers that too often exist between them. It is desirable that nursing staff should be closely associated with the educational programmes devised for individual children.

8.87 Teaching in hospitals is a demanding occupation which calls for the capacity to deal with disability, deformity and death, as well as the ability to teach children who are gravely ill or disturbed. It is essential that teachers in hospitals should receive support from our proposed special education advisory and support service and *we recommend that within the service there should be advisers who specialise in education in hospital.* Their task would be to ensure that the educational needs of children in hospital are adequately met, to provide support and advice to the teachers and to ensure that there is close co-ordination between teachers in hospital schools and local ordinary and special schools.

8.88 In the past there have been difficulties over the financing of educational provision in hospitals within the framework of another service. We believe that

148

there is a need for collaboration between health and local education authorities both in the planning of such provision and in the joint financing of suitable projects. *We recommend that the arrangements which currently exist for joint financing of health and personal social services should apply also to health and education services.*

Home tuition

8.89 There may be a variety of circumstances in which home tuition is needed, for example when a child has been discharged from hospital but has to receive continued treatment at home before he can return to school. As soon as it is known that such a child will be leaving hospital, the hospital and local education authority should invariably collaborate in good time to ensure that he continues to receive a suitable education, without a break. At present home tuition is also provided for children who suffer from school phobia. We do not think that home tuition is the right form of provision for these children and consider that their needs will be more suitably met in centres such as the tuition centres which have been set up by a number of local education authorities.

8.90 We are aware that many home teachers suffer from a feeling of professional isolation. In order to reduce their isolation, *we recommend that home teachers should have close links with individual schools, particularly special schools designated as resource centres, and with centres such as tuition and diagnostic centres.* They also need access to advisers who can offer them professional support and guidance on their future careers. *We therefore recommend that within our proposed special education advisory and support service there should be advisers who specialise in home tuition.*

CONCLUSION

8.91 For special schools the future holds both challenge and opportunity. The challenge consists in the call to adapt to a changing pattern of special education, in which ordinary schools will increasingly feature. We have pointed to the opportunity: whilst there will probably be some decrease in the number of special schools, we see a secure future for them as the main providers of special education for severely and multiply handicapped children in increasingly close collaboration with ordinary schools; as pioneers of new and more effective ways of satisfying children's special needs; and as sustainers of the quality of special education in ordinary schools through the mediation of their indispensable knowledge and expertise. These are vital tasks which carry the prospect of purpose and fulfilment.

CHAPTER 9: PARENTS AS PARTNERS

INTRODUCTION

9.1 We have insisted throughout this report that the successful education of children with special educational needs is dependent upon the full involvement of their parents: indeed, unless the parents are seen as equal partners in the educational process the purpose of our report will be frustrated. But the parents with whom we are at present concerned (mainly, though not exclusively, those of more severely handicapped children) have burdens to bear of which other people may have no conception. It is therefore an essential part of our thesis that parents must be advised, encouraged and supported so that they can in turn effectively help their children. The evidence we have received strongly confirms this view. For instance a local association of parents of ESN children wrote as follows (and they may be allowed to speak for others as well):—

> "Parents almost always care for a child for a larger part of each day than any professional. They endure the disturbed nights and the disruption of social life which a handicapped child brings. Their view of the child is vital to any treatment plan and their co-operation vital to its success. No attempts by teachers or other professionals to communicate with parents about their children are a waste of time. It may take parents years to understand or to spare the energy to respond. Parents of an ESN child may be assailed by guilt, shame, frustration and disappointment but almost always they will want to listen to someone who is on their side in efforts to love and understand the child. It is for the professionals to persist and persist in explaining, giving practical advice and listening to the parents' story."

9.2 In other parts of our report we make recommendations relating to the support of parents (see Chapters 4, 5, 7 and 8). The appearance of such recommendations in so many chapters is evidence of the central place of parents in our view of special education. Moreover, in making proposals for the support of parents in this chapter we are aware that those who take the place of parents, no less than natural parents, require support in attending to the special needs of children in their care, particularly where the children have missed the normal relationships and experiences of early life.

9.3 Just as the special needs of children take a great variety of forms, so do those of their parents. Any discussion of these needs in general terms must not be allowed to obscure the truth that they are individually "special". Wherever we refer to parental needs in this report we are mindful that no two cases are the same; that each represents a unique combination of distinctive strands. The needs of an individual parent will clearly reflect the nature of his child's disability, particularly its degree of severity and the weight of dependence upon parental and family support that it entails. They will also reflect the family circumstances. Cramped or inconvenient accommodation (such as a top flat in a tower block) will obviously severely hamper parents in looking after a disabled child: likewise a large family, particularly where there are young children, imposes its own constraints. Parents are obviously more able to cope if they are themselves in good health, are free from financial or other anxieties, and have helpful neighbours, relatives or friends. The point needs no further elaboration.

9.4 Nor is it simply a question of practicalities. Some children with disabilities are more resilient than others in striving to overcome them. Equally parents differ widely in their attitudes, temperament, insight, knowledge, ability and other personal qualities – all of which powerfully influence the extent and nature of the help that they require. Indeed, the problems of some children may stem from disturbed relationships within the family and will need to be tackled from that standpoint.

9.5 All these factors go to make up the particular needs that parents have. Some parents may merely wish from time to time to discuss their difficulties with someone who can shed light on particular aspects of dealing with them. Others will require elaborate advice and practical help, sometimes intermittently but more often on a regular and continuing basis. Between these two extremes there lies a gradation of intensity and complexity of individual needs, which are, moreover, dynamic and which change with time. We are therefore looking for a pattern of flexible services for parents which matches the different forms of help that they require, not only when the needs arise, but also as they develop thereafter. Special arrangements may need to be made to help parents of children from ethnic minorities who have difficulty in speaking and understanding English.

9.6 We make a further, general point of great importance. We have chosen the title of this chapter deliberately, as expressing our view of the relationship between parents and members of the different professions who may be helping them at any time. It is a partnership, and ideally an equal one. For although we tend to dwell upon the dependence of many parents on professional support, we are well aware that professional help cannot be wholly effective – if at all so – unless it builds upon the parents' own understanding of their children's needs and upon the parents' capacity to be involved. Thus we see the relationship as a dialogue between parents and helpers working in partnership. We prefer this description to others such as "counselling", which may wrongly suggest a one-way flow between those who dispense and those who receive enlightenment. Professionals have their own distinctive knowledge and skills to contribute to parents' understanding of how best to help their handicapped child, but these form a part, not the whole, of what is needed. Parents can be effective partners only if professionals take notice of what they say and of how they express their needs, and treat their contribution as intrinsically important. Even where parents are unable to contribute a great deal themselves, at any rate to start with, their child's welfare will depend upon the extent to which they understand and can apply the measures recommended by professionals and can help to monitor their effects. Parents will often be able to point to an aspect that the professional has overlooked or has insufficiently considered.

151

9.7 In this chapter we bring together and summarise the forms of support that we believe parents are entitled to expect from the different services which contribute to the education of children with special needs. We begin with those aspects which will be handled within the dialogue to which we have referred. We then turn to the point of contact with the various services that every parent needs and deal finally with the forms of relief that should be available to parents to assist them in coping with their handicapped children.

I DIALOGUE WITH PARENTS

9.8 Parents of children with special needs require three principal forms of co-operative support – information, advice and practical help. If support is to be effective, it must be given promptly and consistently. For many parents the need begins as soon as their child is born.

Information

9.9 Whenever a child is discovered to have a handicapping condition his parents need to know what is wrong with him. It is sometimes a delicate and difficult task to impart this information and we have discussed in Chapter 5 how it might best be handled when a disability is revealed at or soon after birth. Whatever the timing or manner of the discovery, however, parents should be taken into professional confidence. They should be informed of the nature and degree of severity of the disability and its possible consequences for the child. Even where the parents had previous suspicions the confirmation that their child has a handicapping condition is bound to come as a shock, and may well lead to a sense of helplessness and isolation. It is therefore essential that when told of the existence of a disability parents should also be informed of the range of facilities and supporting services available to help them and their child. The services will include genetic counselling where a disability may have arisen through hereditary factors.

9.10 As we pointed out in Chapter 5, a number of useful leaflets has been produced on services available, both nationally and locally, for children with disabilities or significant difficulties. It is very desirable that a collection of such leaflets should be available locally in an information centre: this might be in, say, a citizens' advice bureau, the premises of a voluntary organisation, a toy library, a school, a college, a general practitioner's surgery, a child health clinic or a hospital. Some resource centres on handicap already exist to provide this information. Where the centre is set up in an institution with other functions, a special room should wherever possible be set aside so that parents of children with special needs can enjoy a measure of privacy in studying the literature and meeting other parents with similar concerns for discussion and exchange of information.

9.11 We also drew attention in Chapter 5 to the need for a comprehensive handbook for each area giving information about local facilities for children with special needs and their parents. We recommended that, where such a handbook or pamphlet is not already available, it should be produced under the aegis of the appropriate Joint Consultative Committee (or in Scotland the appropriate Joint Liaison Committee). It will need to be kept up-to-date if the information is to continue to be useful. We recognise that parents of young children with special needs are likely to be particularly concerned about the educational facilities available, especially where the child's needs are such that they may need to be recorded by the local education authority under our proposed system of recording. We therefore recommended in Chapter 6 that each local education authority should produce and keep up-to-date a handbook containing details of special educational provision in its area for children recorded as requiring such provision, in particular information about the types of special educational need catered for in individual schools and details of the officers of the local education authority concerned with the provision of special education. This information might be provided as a section of the comprehensive handbook about local facilities or as a separate publication.

9.12 We believe that parents of children with special educational needs cannot receive too much information about the special provision made in individual schools. We welcome the Circulars issued by the Department of Education and Science and the Welsh Office in November 1977 providing guidance on the kind of information which should normally be made available to parents about the schools their children are attending or may attend.[1] The guidance should include the name, address and telephone number of the school, the hours during which it is open and the dates when terms begin and end, the names of the headteacher and senior staff, the number of pupils, the characteristic features of the school and how the teaching is organised, details of extra-curricular activities and information on how parents may arrange to visit the school. Although the Circulars refer only to ordinary schools, we consider that equivalent information about facilities in special schools must also be made available to parents. Moreover, the information about ordinary schools suggested in the Circulars will not be complete unless it provides details of any special educational facilities that the schools provide.

Advice and support

9.13 The dissemination of information in these and other ways about the services available to children with special needs will go a long way to show their parents where to look for help. Such help will include advice and practical support, and much of it will be organised within the special education advisory and support service proposed in Chapter 13. We make no apology for repeating that the relationship between parents and those professionals who help them is a reciprocal one. It is of course very necessary that each professional – teacher, doctor, nurse, health visitor, social worker – should be knowledgeable about the application of his particular skills to children with special needs: it is no less important that he should exercise his skills in alliance with the parents and shape his contribution around the parents' own understanding of what is required. This makes heavy demands upon the time of professionals. But unless they can devote as much time as is necessary to parents and are actively concerned to work with them in partnership their contribution cannot be fully effective. The research into services for parents of handicapped children under five which was undertaken for us under the co-direction of Professor Chazan and Dr Laing revealed that from the mother's point of view medical teams often

---

[1] DES Circular 15/77, Welsh Office Circular 201/77, Information for Parents (25 November 1977).

seemed to be operating without including the parents of the child. The report on parents' opinions in one of the areas in the survey stated: "From comments it was obvious that for many parents their perception was of a 'them' and 'us' situation with the specialist treating their children, often very skilfully, without a great deal of reference to them."[2] There is a lesson to be learned here by all the services concerned in meeting children's special needs.

9.14 We drew attention in Chapter 5 to the importance of peripatetic teachers in providing support for parents of young children with special needs, and the necessity for expanded peripatetic teaching services to cover all types of disability and disorder. These teachers will be responsible for devising appropriate educational programmes which are suitable for the parents to carry out. They will help parents to work with their children and by working directly with the children will themselves provide a model of how such programmes can be effectively carried out. They will direct parents to such other advice as may be needed. These tasks will require the ability to work sympathetically with parents and to share the concerns and problems of parents. The teachers will need insight and skill in judging how far they are able to help directly and when to call on others. They will need to be prepared for these tasks by suitable training and to have close contacts with colleagues in the proposed special education advisory and support service and with members of other services.

9.15 The nature of the parents' attitudes to a child with a disability or significant difficulty and the support which they are able to give him may determine not only the rate of his early development but also the ease with which he can be integrated into an ordinary school. As we indicated in Chapter 7, problems in integrating children in ordinary schools may sometimes stem from their incomplete acceptance by their family. Where this circumstance exists parents will need help in dealing with it. The need for help may persist well beyond the child's early years and we would expect the professional who serves as Named Person for the parents (see Section II) to be able and ready where necessary to introduce them to someone qualified and ready to give such help.

9.16 In some families of children or young people with special educational needs, wider problems may arise which call for additional support. Sometimes, for example, problems associated with a child's disability or disorder may give rise to marital tensions or even breakdown or may adversely affect other children in the family. Such difficulties are better prevented than tackled after they have appeared. They can be overlooked altogether by hard-pressed services working to the limits of their resources. We see scope for voluntary organisations as well as the local health, social and other services in helping to forestall or mitigate the strains and stresses that handicap can bring to any family.

9.17 The need for personal counselling of adolescents and young adults is discussed in Chapter 10. It should not, however, be forgotten that the parents may also need advice on how they can contribute to their children's future life through a more complete understanding of the personal problems that their children may face. Here also, the Named Person, who will usually at this stage be the careers officer or his specialist colleague, should point the parents to sources of skilled help that may be needed.

---

[2] For details of the research project see Appendix 5.

9.18 Advice is by no means exclusively the province of professionals. Non-professionals have much to offer too, particularly in the field of human relationships, and may have one advantage over professionals that they are less constrained by time. Where they have intimate knowledge of a particular disability, because for example either they, or perhaps one of their children, suffer from it, they may be able to offer advice of a very special value. It is important that all who undertake advisory work, professionals as well as non-professionals, should have adequate and appropriate training. However, we would emphasise our view that the effective giving of advice is much more than a question of technique. Above all, it calls for knowledge shaped by experience, discrimination and human sympathy. Not all of these qualities can be taught.

9.19 The relationship between parents and the school which their child is attending has a crucial bearing upon the child's educational progress. On the one hand if parents are to support the efforts of teachers they need information and advice from the school about its objectives and the provision being made for their child: on the other, a child's special needs cannot be adequately assessed and met in school without the insights that his parents, from their more intimate experience of him, are able to provide. Close links between schools and parents must therefore be established and maintained, as we have stressed throughout this report.

9.20 Formal means of collective co-operation between parents and the school may be established by the appointment of parent representatives to governing bodies, as the law already requires in respect of school councils in Scotland, or through parent-teacher associations. The case for parental representation on the governing bodies of ordinary schools in England and Wales has been urged by the Taylor Committee.[3] Parent-teacher associations have proved to be a useful way of bringing parents together and establishing closer relationships between them and teachers. For individual parents however there can be no substitute for personal access to the school whenever they require information about their child's education or wish to discuss his progress. It is essential that parents of children with special educational needs should have the opportunity to visit their child's school regularly and without ceremony and be able to talk to his teachers or to the headteacher who, as indicated in Section II, is likely to be their Named Person. Where a child is attending a day special school in the same area but some distance from his home the local education authority should be ready to consider using school transport to help his parents to make such visits, or should be prepared to assist them with their expenses. We urged in the last chapter that parents of children attending residential special schools should have opportunity to visit their children at school or to have them at home at weekends if they so wish. In these circumstances the staff must regularly advise the parents about the best ways of re-inforcing the work that their children are doing at school and of maintaining any programmes of treatment during weekends and holidays.

9.21 We have stressed the importance of the contribution which parents can

---

[3] *A New Partnership for our Schools.* Report of the Committee of Enquiry appointed jointly by the Secretary of State for Education and Science and the Secretary of State for Wales under the Chairmanship of Mr Tom Taylor, CBE (HMSO, 1977).

make to their child's educational progress. Its importance should not be under-rated either by the parents themselves or by the school, whether it be an ordinary school or a special school. However, some parents will not, for a variety of reasons, realise the value of their re-inforcing what is done in school, while other parents may feel diffident about offering their contribution to what they see as a matter for experts. It is for these reasons necessary to create a climate in which parents are encouraged to have an active share in meeting their child's special educational needs. This is particularly necessary where a child's difficulties come to light for the first time in the school setting. We envisage that some parents might be invited to spend some time in their child's school on a regular basis and be assisted with their travelling expenses to do so.

9.22 Some appointments have been made in schools of teacher-counsellors, guidance teachers or home-school liaison teachers with responsibilities for working with the parents of pupils who have special needs and for maintaining the school's links with other services and agencies. For example, one primary school in the East End of London for children categorised as ESN(M) has appointed a "teacher for home and school contacts", with a part-time teaching commitment, who visits children's homes and tries to promote greater understanding between parents and teachers by organising weekly afternoon visits to the school by small groups of parents, Saturday outings for parents, and children's and parents' evenings. Such teachers can effectively promote good relations between home and school and we see scope for their further appointment in both ordinary and special schools. In addition, as we explain more fully in Chapter 14, many special schools will also need the services of social workers.

9.23 We particularly commend, as an example of the other ways in which schools may work with individual parents, the use of home-school notebooks, in which teachers and parents record progress made at school and at home respectively. We have seen a number of successful examples of the use of such notebooks in special schools, which we believe could be extended to children with special educational needs in ordinary schools. They can help to encourage parents to take a close interest in their child's education, and the progress recorded can be a source of information and encouragement to parents, children and teachers.

9.24 We identified in Chapter 5 a range of different forms of skilled support that should be available, separately or in combination, in every area for parents of children under five with special needs. They included home visiting teaching services, parents' workshops, playgroups and opportunity groups, nursery schools and classes and day nurseries. Some parents of children with special needs may themselves take the initiative in organising group activities. We referred in Chapter 5 to the group meetings organised at Southend for parents of Down's Syndrome children and their successful leadership by parents. There, training in group leadership comes about through participation in the group, and several highly competent leaders have emerged. The main conditions for the successful development of such groups appear to be: professional recognition of the parents as the key to child development; the initial help of a committed professional or parent with successful experience in this field; a capable group leader; well co-ordinated services for children with special needs so that parents are referred to a group as soon as possible; and the availability of the right kind of professional support whenever a group runs into difficulties. Besides the indirect benefits which they bring to the children concerned, the advantages of groups of this kind are that they reduce the isolation felt by many parents, by enabling them to share their feelings and ideas with other parents; and they give parents the satisfaction of learning how to encourage the development of their children's skills from birth, or at least a very early age. Local education authorities, social services departments and health authorities should make facilities available and actively encourage and support such groups.

Practical help

9.25 Depending on the nature of their child's disability or difficulty the parents of children with special needs require above all practical help. We have in different chapters called attention to forms of practical help that are already available and suggested improvements where we see deficiencies. Mobility and attendance allowances are critical for those parents qualified to receive them in respect of their children. Both they and many other parents have great need of help with the provision of transport – to visit school, hospital or clinic, to enable their children to take part in social activities of various kinds, or perhaps to take their disabled child on an outing or a similar excursion. Voluntary organisations are particularly helpful in these matters, both in the direct support that they can give and in their ability to involve parents in the actual arrangements. Some parents need practical help in providing, maintaining or modifying aids or appliances of different kinds or in re-arranging accommodation at home in ways which facilitate the movement of their disabled child. The need is for prompt, effective and efficient help. Delay, for whatever reason, is damaging both to the child and to good relations with the parents.

II A SINGLE POINT OF CONTACT

9.26 As we indicated in Chapter 5, even if information about supporting services is readily available, many parents will be unable to make the best use of such services without help. We therefore recommended that one person should be designated as Named Person to provide a point of contact for the parents of every child who has been discovered to have a disability or is showing signs of special needs or problems. The main function of the Named Person will be to introduce parents to the right services or, in the case of parents of children showing signs of special needs, to ensure that any concern which there may be about their child's development is followed up. We envisage that in most cases the health visitor will be the Named Person in the early years, and as the child approaches the time for going to school she will be able to facilitate the change from home-based to school-based education by making suitable arrangements with her successor as Named Person within the education service.

9.27 We consider that all parents of children with special needs should be able to look to a Named Person to provide them with a single point of contact with the local education service and expert counsel in following their child's progress through school. We have considered the suitability of various professionals for this assignment, including the educational psychologist, the adviser in special education, the education welfare officer, the teacher with training in social

157

work and the school-based social worker. The consideration that has weighed most heavily with us is that most parents who are seeking advice about their child's progress in school turn naturally in the first place to the headteacher. He, for his part, is favourably placed to stimulate the interest of diffident, discouraged or apathetic parents and is, moreover, an easily identifiable person whom parents should have no difficulty in finding and contacting, especially if information about the school is issued to parents as proposed in paragraph 9.12. *We therefore recommend that the headteacher of the child's current school should be the Named Person for most parents of schoolchildren with special educational needs.* The parents should be told that the headteacher will be their point of contact for information and guidance about their child's progress at the same time as they are informed of the results of the assessment of their child's special needs at one of the school-based stages of our proposed assessment procedure.

9.28 In primary schools and small secondary schools, the headteacher should usually be able to act personally as Named Person for the parents of those pupils who require special educational help. Even in large schools the headteacher should continue to retain responsibility for acting as Named Person, although he may have to delegate much of the day-to-day work which the function of being Named Person entails. Where this is the case, the person to whom the work is delegated should, wherever possible, be a member of staff with training and expertise in special education.

9.29 Some parents of children with special educational needs may wish to discuss the suitability of the provision being made by the school for their child with a professional in the education service who is outside the school. *We therefore recommend that, in addition to having a point of contact in the headteacher, parents should have direct access to the proposed special education advisory and support service.* They should be able to obtain from the local education authority's handbook information about how to make contact with members of the service. Arrangements for them to contact members of the service may also be necessary during the school holidays.

9.30 We pointed out in Chapter 5 that, where a young child has severe or complex developmental problems requiring multi-professional assessment at Stage 4 or 5 of our proposed procedure, it may be more suitable for the Named Person to be someone with particular expertise or interest in the area of the child's disability. We consider that this will also apply where a child of school age is referred for multi-professional assessment at Stage 4 or 5 and, in the light of a profile of his needs drawn up by the multi-professional team, is recorded by the authority as requiring special educational provision. In this case the Named Person will need to be someone familiar with the child's particular form of disability; in contact with members of a range of specialist services; prepared to provide considerable support for the parents not only during term time but also during school holidays if required; and able to follow up the child's placement and at the right time arrange for its continuing suitability to be reviewed.

9.31 We regard it as axiomatic that the parents should be able to continue to consult the headteacher of the school in which their child is placed—whether the same school as before or a new one – after a decision has been taken by the local education authority to record him as in need of special educational provision. But they may also need someone to whom they can turn outside the school. *We therefore recommend that the Named Person for the parents of a child recorded as requiring special educational provision should be someone designated by the multi-professional team which assessed the child's needs.* The identity of the Named Person, who will normally be in the education service, should be conveyed with the completed Form SE4 to the officer of the local education authority responsible for the SE Forms procedure. Where a decision is taken to record the child as requiring special educational provision, the parents should be informed of the identity of their Named Person at the same time as they are told of their child's being recorded. As we proposed in Chapter 4, the identity of the person designated as Named Person for the parents of a child recorded as requiring special educational provision should comprise part of his record, and the documents forming the record should be readily accessible to the parents.

9.32 When a child who requires special educational help but who is not recorded moves from one school to another, whether or not in the same area, the headteacher of the new school should succeed that of the child's former school as Named Person and should contact the parents at the time of transfer. Where the move entails a change of local education authority and the child has been recorded as requiring special educational provision, the documents comprising his record, including the identity of his Named Person, should, under our proposals in Chapter 4, be passed to the new authority. The assistant education officer for special education in the new area should ensure that a new Named Person is designated, normally with qualifications and experience similar to those of the previous one, and the parents informed of his identity. The Named Person in the area from which the child has moved should satisfy himself wherever possible that the parents know the name of his successor and where to contact him.

9.33 We recognise that the arrangements made by the multi-professional team for a Named Person for the parents of a child recorded as requiring special educational provision may sometimes prove unsatisfactory. It is important, therefore, that parents should have access to an officer of the local education authority who can introduce them to another professional better placed to be their Named Person. *We recommend that they should be given the office telephone number and address of the officer who completed their child's Form SE4, that is either the adviser in special education or the educational psychologist.*

9.34 The need of parents for the services of a Named Person in the circumstances that we have described will continue up to and beyond the time that their child leaves school. Morever, during the transition from school to adult life the need for a Named Person will be shared by the young person himself. In the next chapter we propose that the careers officer or, in the case of young people with more severe or complex disabilities, the specialist careers officer is likely to be the person best placed to provide such a continuing link.

III RELIEF

9.35 Where children with severe disabilities are living at home, their parents need periodical relief from their day to day pre-occupation with looking after them. A day out or a short holiday with other children in the family or an opportunity to do some of the things that have had to be set aside, such as decorating a room, visiting friends or relations or reading an interesting book – in fact all the normal activities that most families are able to take for granted – can be a luxury for some parents of severely handicapped children, particularly where there are no friends or relatives conveniently placed to lend a hand. The sudden occurrence of an emergency such as illness or death among the family or near relations can present insuperable problems if no relief is available. *We therefore recommend that a variety of forms of short-term relief should be available to parents of children with severe disabilities who are living at home.*

9.36 There should be opportunity for parents to seek, if necessary at short notice, the presence of someone who can look after their child at home for part of a day or even a day or two whilst they are attending to family business or need to be away from home for any reason. We have heard with interest of a community befriending system in one town in which a volunteer family is matched with and provides social support for a family with a handicapped member. We envisage that a stand-in or befriending service would be provided by the local social services department, in co-operation with voluntary organisations in the area. We return to the contribution of voluntary organisations in providing social support for families in Chapter 17.

9.37 Longer-term relief can be provided in a number of ways. Some purpose-built day schools for physically handicapped children have small residential hostels attached to them where children (not necessarily pupils in the school) can be looked after for short periods when parents either need a rest or have unforeseen or inescapable commitments. In other cases, children are admitted to hospitals. In some areas this may be the only place able to receive them. We regard such placement as a last resort and urge that wherever possible other facilities of a non-institutional kind should be provided, such as care in homes or with foster parents which some social services departments are able to arrange. An arrangement like Honeylands in the West Country[4] can be very beneficial in combining proximity to the paediatric service of a district general hospital with effective day-to-day relief for parents in which they may participate if they wish. As we indicated in the last chapter we see much greater scope in future for the provision by boarding special schools of short-stay facilities for severely handicapped children whose parents and families need a break from looking after them.

9.38 One complaint often heard from parents, where their children are already attending school, is the lack of support during school holidays, particularly the long summer holiday. As we indicated in the last chapter, there was some support in the evidence for a four-term year in special schools. Our own view is that special schools should be in step with ordinary schools over the organisation of the school year, but that arrangements should be made for the premises of some special schools to be available for at least part of the school holiday. This would require local education authorities (or the governors in the

---

[4] F S W Brimblecombe, "Exeter Project for Handicapped Children", *British Medical Journal* 1974, 4, 706-709.

case of non-maintained schools) to provide for people to be in charge of the premises and their use during these periods. *We recommend that ways of enabling the premises of some special schools to remain open during the school holidays should be further considered by the local authorities' and teachers' associations and, where appropriate, school governors.* We envisage that the use of school premises during holidays will in future become a much more widespread practice than at present.

9.39 It is sometimes forgotten that even with considerable support parents of children with severe disabilities may be facing such chronic stress that residential placement is in the long term interests of both child and family. However, recent official emphasis on the advantages of community care as against residential placement has led to many parents being pulled in two directions. On the one hand they may be intolerably overtaxed in trying to look after a child with severe difficulties, yet in agreeing to his going away they may be beset by feelings of guilt induced by suggestions that they have somehow failed. It is important that parents whose children leave home for residential education and care are encouraged to overcome this feeling, so that what should be a relief does not become an additional anxiety. When it is available the kind of intensive support provided by voluntary organisations such as the Invalid Children's Aid Association will be particularly beneficial.

CONCLUSION

9.40 The form and extent of parents' need for support will depend on a multiplicity of different factors, including the nature and degree of their child's disability or disorder, his age, the family circumstances and, not least, the parents' own resources and independence. The support, however and wherever given, must be seen as taking place within a partnership between parents and the members of the different services. To the extent that it enables parents more effectively to help their children at home and at school the support should be an integral part of the provision made for children with special educational needs, which parents have the right to expect.

CHAPTER 10: THE TRANSITION FROM SCHOOL
TO ADULT LIFE

INTRODUCTION

10.1 The transition from school to adult life can be difficult for many young people. For those with special educational needs it is likely to be a period of particular stress. Unless skilled support is available to them and their parents at this stage all the efforts made to meet their special needs during their school career may come to nothing. Indeed, the more successful their school has been in meeting their needs, the worse the experience of leaving school may be for them. The support they must have will obviously vary according to the nature and extent of their individual requirements. It may be temporary and specific, for example to bridge the immediate transition from school to a place of further or higher education or to employment; or it may take the form of continuing and comprehensive help with all aspects of life. In this chapter we start by emphasising the importance, well before a young person is due to leave school, of re-assessing his special needs, of guiding him in the choice of a career, and of preparing him at school for the demands of adult life. We go on to describe the pattern of educational provision and the opportunities for vocational training and employment required by young people over statutory school leaving age who have special needs. We then examine the contributions of the various services towards meeting their needs for counselling, health care, financial assistance, accommodation and other aids to living and working. Finally, we consider ways in which the most severely handicapped, who are unable to enter any form of employment, may be helped to achieve significant living without work.

10.2 Provision for young people over 16 with special educational needs has received little attention in the past, as our historical review in Chapter 2 clearly indicated. The field is relatively uncharted and is extremely complex, not least because of the very disparate needs of the young people themselves. The young people with whom we are concerned in this chapter include those with special educational needs of long standing which continue to the time of school leaving and beyond, and also those whose special educational needs become apparent only as they prepare to leave school or after they have left school. They are thus a wider group than those described as "handicapped" in the traditional sense (requiring separate special educational provision while at school), or "disabled" in the employment sense (being registrable as such for employment purposes, under the Disabled Persons (Employment) Acts). However, in the context of employment and of supporting services, we have been particularly concerned with young people with more severe or complex disabilities. In this chapter we seek to put forward a framework within which the very disparate needs of the individual young people may be met as flexibly as possible by a range of different services.

162

10.3 We believe that the young people with whom we are concerned have much to contribute to society, although society has so far all too often failed to recognise this. Our approach to preparing such young people for adult life, whatever the nature or degree of severity of their disability, disorder or other difficulty, is based on the view that they should be given the chance to reach the highest level of achievement possible for them. All young people, whether or not they have special needs, must learn to accept and work within their limitations, but an unduly pessimistic expectation will discourage them, their parents and their teachers from making efforts to succeed. This approach does not ignore the fact that many people will need extra help, a number of them throughout their lives, and some in an intensive form. Rather, it implies that not only should their disabilities be recognised and accommodated, but they should also be helped to use their abilities to the utmost. Though such an attitude is often adopted towards a child at school, in the world beyond school it is regrettably far less common.

10.4 It is in society's own interest to invest more in opportunities for education, training, and other forms of support for these young people in order to minimise their disadvantages. Our own experience and impressions from visits to schools, colleges, training establishments and other institutions suggest that people with special needs are often unemployed or under-employed, simply because they are not provided with the right help at the right time. We are convinced that resources spent on further education and training facilities and on support for these young people before and after they leave school will in the long term reduce their dependence on the social and health services, and thus the cost to the community of supporting them. For example, a small amount of extra help for school leavers with moderate learning difficulties or emotional or behavioural disorders may enable them to hold down a job and reduce the chances of their entering a cycle of frequent changes of job, leading to long-term unemployment and dependence on social and psychiatric services. Responsibility for providing whatever extra help a re-assessment of needs dictates should be clearly assigned to one or more services before the young person leaves school.

10.5 At the same time, we are aware that greater independence, particularly for those with more severe disabilities, will not be achieved simply by administrative measures or the injection of more resources. In the end, changes in the nature of education, training and supporting services and in opportunities for work and other forms of personal fulfilment will depend on changes of attitude. Teachers and parents can be over-protective and expect too little; many employers who have never had any seriously handicapped employees imagine that a single disability will mean all-round incapacity and incompetence; and the community at large regrettably tends to think of people with obtrusive disabilities as less than human in their emotional and social needs. We cannot over-emphasise the urgency of finding ways of changing attitudes so that such people are accepted as ordinary people who merely have certain special needs.

I ASSESSMENT AND CAREERS GUIDANCE

Assessment and re-assessment

10.6 The procedure for assessment outlined in Chapter 4, involving five possible stages each requiring a wider range of expertise than the last, applies to pupils who are nearing the end of their school career no less than to others. Thus, special educational needs which become apparent only in the last years at school should be assessed at the appropriate stage of the proposed procedure. In some cases they may arise from conditions which first become apparent during adolescence; in others they may result from illness or from injuries sustained in accidents. It should be a feature of the assessment of special needs in the last years at school that, whether the assessment is school-based or external to the school, a member of the careers service should be involved.

10.7 Where a young person has been found to have special educational needs earlier in his school career, it is essential, as we stressed in Chapter 4, that careers guidance should start early and that his special needs should be re-assessed well before he leaves school. *We recommend that a pupil's special needs should be re-assessed with future prospects in mind at least two years before he is due to leave school.* A range of different professions may be concerned if all the implications of the young person's particular difficulties for his future are to be considered and the suitability of the opportunities available to him for continued education in school, further or higher education, vocational training or employment fully explored. *We therefore recommend that the process of re-assessment of special needs at this stage should always involve a careers officer and should usually include other professionals in the education, health and social services.* All the available information about the young person's progress and needs should be taken into account as well as his own and his parents' aspirations for and apprehensions about the future. A compact source of information about his progress will be the personal folder which should be maintained in school, as we recommended in Chapter 4. Wherever possible, the process of re-assessment should be carried out in the school. In the light of the outcome, the need for any special programmes of study or therapy should be discussed with specialist teachers or other professionals and the different services concerned should be informed of the young person's future needs so that continuity of support can be ensured.

10.8 Where a young person with special needs, who is about to leave or has left school, experiences particular difficulty in obtaining employment, more specialist assessment specifically directed to employment may be necessary. Indeed, unusual difficulty in obtaining employment may be a sign of the existence of special needs which have not previously been identified. We have observed or learned of a number of examples of specialist assessment. At the Work Orientation Unit of the North Nottinghamshire College of Further Education at Worksop, for example, which caters for young people with a variety of disabilities and learning difficulties, a full programme of assessment of the student's needs and of his prospects for employment is undertaken. It deals with all the qualities required to do a job and hold it down. At Banstead Place the Queen Elizabeth's Foundation for the Disabled now provides residential assessment as well as training for severely physically handicapped and immature young people previously regarded as unemployable or untrainable.

10.9 We consider that, wherever possible, assessment of a specifically vocational kind should be carried out locally so that the young people and their parents have easy access to advice. The school, college or establishment which the young person is attending is likely to be the most suitable setting, but if he is not attending any such institution or if the advice of scarce specialists is required the assessment may have to be conducted elsewhere. In particular, regional assessment centres are likely to continue to be necessary to provide specialist facilities for the intensive vocational assessment of young people with severe impairment of sight or hearing or severe, multiple physical disabilities.

10.10 The normal procedures for professional assessment and consultation may need to be supplemented by case conferences to deal adequately with the needs of young people in special or ordinary schools who have severe disabilities. The conferences need not necessarily be very large. Their professional composition will vary, but they will normally include members of the education, health and social services; and both the parents and young people should usually be invited to attend. Members of the Employment Medical Advisory Service may also be included in some conferences. The headteacher of the school should be responsible for calling the conference.

Careers guidance*

10.11 Our strong impression is that existing arrangements for the provision of careers guidance for young people with special needs generally fall far short of what is required. Evidence we received from young people with a variety of disabilities and disorders suggested that even in schools where careers guidance is readily available, fixed ideas are usually entertained about occupations suitable or unsuitable for young people with particular disabilities, irrespective of the degree of disability or other factors. Other contributors to the evidence complained that specialist advice on the problems associated with different disabilities or disorders is often not readily available, particularly to handicapped pupils in ordinary schools. As a result, at one extreme, potential difficulties may be ignored: at the other, badly informed teachers and members of other professions, or parents with inadequate knowledge, may discourage a pupil from attempting a job which is within his or her capacity. It is not always recognised that even if a pupil with a disability or significant difficulty is successfully integrated in an ordinary school, he may still need specialist help with decisions about further or higher education, training and a career.

10.12 The findings of the research project conducted for us by the National Children's Bureau on the employment experiences of a number of handicapped school leavers[1] confirm our own impression. According to the recollections of the young people themselves, the proportion of young people in the sample

---
* We use the term "careers guidance" to cover careers education as well as guidance, though we recognise that these can be distinct activities, carried out by different people.

[1] For details see Appendix 7.

165

ascertained as handicapped who had attended schools without a careers teacher was three times that of the non-handicapped. Moreover, a greater proportion of the handicapped than of the non-handicapped young people in the sample said that they had not heard of the careers service or, if they had heard of the service, had not talked to a careers officer in it.

10.13 Careers guidance of a high standard needs to be available in schools, whether ordinary or special schools, for young people with special educational needs. We welcome the request to local education authorities in England and Wales, as part of their review of curricular arrangements, to report on the policy in their areas for careers education, the appointment of careers teachers, and relations with the careers service.[2] In Scotland, formal systems of guidance – personal, vocational and curricular – have been introduced in secondary schools, and the recommendation in Circular 826 for the establishment of approximately one promoted post in guidance for every 150–200 pupils has been generally accepted.[3] It was pointed out in evidence to us, however, that the guidance staff in the schools need more specialist training if they are to be able to provide suitable advice and guidance for pupils with special educational needs.

10.14 We believe that in all secondary schools and all-age special schools there should be at least one careers teacher with special understanding of the particular problems facing young people with special educational needs. He should be enabled to acquire and, at intervals, up-date this understanding in a variety of ways; for example, through short full-time courses, part-time courses or courses organised on the basis of distance teaching. *We therefore recommend that a teacher with special responsibility for careers guidance should be appointed in every special school which caters for older pupils and that in every ordinary secondary school there should be at least one careers teacher with additional training or expertise in understanding the careers implications of different types of disability or disorder.* Moreover, these teachers should have very close links with members of the careers service in their area: they should ensure that information about pupils with special educational needs is directed to the careers officer in good time and that the careers officer is aware of the need to collaborate closely with them.

10.15 We have recommended that the careers officer should always be concerned in re-assessment of the special needs of young people which should take place at least two years before they leave school. It is important that the officer, or a specialist colleague, should then work closely with each young person before and after he leaves school. If this is to be practicable, information about young people's special needs must be given to establishments of further education or training centres to which they move. We consider the dissemination of such information more fully in Chapter 16. It will also be necessary for the careers service to be considerably strengthened and the number of careers officers increased. *We recommend that, as a general guide and on the understand-*

[2] DES Circular 14/77, Welsh Office Circular 185/77, Local education authority arrangements for the school curriculum (19 November 1977).

[3] SED Circular 826, The Structure of Promoted Posts in Secondary Schools in Scotland (HMSO, 1971). *Guidance in Scottish Secondary Schools.* A Progress Report by HM Inspectors of Schools 1976 (HMSO, 1976).

ing that adequate support will be provided, at least one full-time specialist careers officer should be appointed for every 50,000 of the school population (or for a substantial proportion of 50,000). This ratio of staff to school population, however, will leave specialist careers officers with a manageable case load only if there are sufficient careers teachers with suitable training in ordinary and special schools, as we recommended in the last paragraph, and if all careers officers are trained to be aware of special needs and their implications, to start working with pupils with such needs well before they leave school, and to know when to call in their specialist colleagues. We return to the training of careers officers in Chapter 14.

10.16 Where children are attending boarding special schools outside their own local education authority area and some distance from their home, it is often difficult for the home careers officer to visit them and regularly consult other professionals in the education, health and social services about their special needs. If the case-loads of specialist careers officers make it impossible for them to maintain contact with children from their area who are away in residential schools, other solutions must be sought. Current procedure is for the specialist careers officer in the area where the school is situated to have responsibility for the children in the school and to ensure that careers service colleagues in the home area of the children are well informed of their special needs. Another solution, where a school has appointed a home-school liaison teacher, might be for that person to have responsibility for ensuring that information is passed to the responsible careers officer in the home area.

10.17 It is important that careers teachers and careers officers should find time to see, and if necessary visit, parents of children with special educational needs and discuss with them the opportunities for their child to undertake further or higher education or training or to enter employment. In doing so they will be able to influence parental expectations, which in our judgement are more often too low than too high and which may dissuade young people from taking advantage of the best opportunities open to them. Moreover, as we explain in paragraphs 10.92-94, we envisage that the careers officer or his specialist colleague will be the person who either provides a single point of contact for young people with special educational needs and their parents, or ensures that someone else does, during the transition from school to adult life. Close links between the careers service and the parents of young people with special educational needs should therefore be established at as early a stage as possible.

Preparation at school for the transition to adult life

10.18 It is obviously important that pupils with special educational needs, whether they are in ordinary or special schools, should acquire the basic educational skills. It is equally important that they should develop social competence as well as vocational interests, which will give them a realistic awareness of employment opportunities and help them to achieve personal satisfaction in their future life. In the case of pupils with disabilities so severe that they may never be able to work, basic education and instruction in the skills of daily living such as shopping or using public transport should go hand in hand. Moreover, a special effort should be made to enable pupils who have spent their entire school career in special schools to overcome any feelings of isolation and to cope with adult life, in particular to share as closely as possible in the everyday activities of other people without disabilities.

10.19 There is a variety of ways in which pupils with special educational needs can be helped to gain some experience of and prepare themselves for further education or employment and we consider below linked courses and different forms of preparation for work. Particular care needs to be taken, however, in planning the curriculum for such pupils to ensure that their career opportunities are not unnecessarily narrowed by any restriction of educational opportunities. The range of school courses available should be carefully reviewed in the case of individual pupils and we suggest that this should be carried out at the time of re-assessment of special needs which, as we have already recommended, should be at least two years before the end of schooling. *We recommend that both ordinary and special schools should give pupils with special educational needs more help to acquire the basic skills and to develop social competence and vocational interests.*

Linked courses

10.20 Linked courses, which are courses planned and conducted jointly by schools and colleges of further education and in which pupils spend between half a day and two days a week at the college, can be a useful way of introducing pupils to the possibilities of further education and of widening their horizons. It is important, however, that the courses should have clear objectives and should not be focussed too closely or narrowly on vocational subjects. They should be planned by the school and college in concert as part of the school leaver's programme and be closely linked with the rest of the curriculum. Both the children and the school and college staff need to be adequately prepared; and arrangements must be made for school and college to exchange information about individual children's special needs or aptitudes. We recognise that the organisation of linked courses may present difficulties, particularly in the case of pupils at special schools who have examination commitments and also need special transport arrangements. We therefore suggest that some linked courses should be organised in the early evening or during school holidays. The importance of providing opportunities for linked courses for pupils with a wide range of ability and the need for careful planning were emphasised in a Circular issued by the Scottish Education Department in 1976.[4]

Preparation for work

10.21 In the case of those young people with special educational needs who are likely to seek to enter employment immediately after leaving school significant elements of work preparation, designed to enable them to gain some insight into the demands of employment and conditions of work, should feature in the concluding stages of the curriculum. Work preparation can include arrangements in which young people are placed in simulated working conditions; works visits or "work tasting" to provide pupils with opportunities to see at close hand

---

[4] Scottish Education Department Circular 948, Courses for School Pupils in Further Education Colleges (8 March 1976).

a number of different jobs and different working conditions; and work experience in the form of a planned period of supervised employment in industry, commerce or the public service. It is important that, whatever form it takes, work preparation should be positively and carefully planned as an integral part of the school curriculum and in relation to the particular needs of individual pupils. In a number of special schools work preparation is part of a wider programme which includes training in a variety of aspects of everyday life, including use of the telephone and public transport, and talks from members of the careers service and speakers from a range of different occupations. In the best of these schemes the pupils are expected to keep careful records of their activities and experiences; and, through discussions within the school, they are encouraged to recognise both their strengths and limitations. Pupils with special needs in ordinary schools could well benefit from participating in such a scheme, where one has been developed in a nearby special school. At the same time, however, we should like to encourage ordinary schools to develop their own schemes for school leavers with special needs.

10.22 Facilities for work preparation for people over statutory school age are made available by the Employment Service Agency at 14 Employment Rehabilitation Centres (ERCs) and we consider these in Section III. We are aware that there can be overlap between the work preparation courses offered at an ERC to young people over the age of 16 and the work preparation programmes provided for pupils in their final year at school by the local education authority. In Sheffield, for example, the work preparation programmes provided for pupils in their final year by the local education authority are very similar to parts of the work preparation course at the ERC, to which the authority seconds a full-time teacher. Under present legislation on school leaving dates in England and Wales, however, pupils of compulsory school age cannot enter regular full-time employment or transfer to further education, and thus work preparation courses in ERCs cannot be made available to them. We have considered whether to recommend that the legislation in England and Wales should be amended to enable young people below school leaving age with special educational needs to attend such courses in their last year at school. We recognise, however, that there is already a heavy demand for ERC places by older people and that any appreciable intake of schoolchildren could be achieved only at the expense of reducing the intake of young people over statutory school age for the special courses and of adults for normal courses. Moreover, some of those under 16 may not be sufficiently mature for the organised setting and pace of work in an ERC. We do not therefore propose any change in the present arrangements for the provision of work preparation for young people of compulsory school age. In Scotland education authorities have discretion to allow exemption from school attendance in exceptional cases in order to allow a pupil to begin a full-time course of formal further education. We have noted the guidance in the Scottish Education Department Circular 956, however, that where there is any restriction on the number of places available, pupils should not generally be admitted to further education courses at the expense of those who have already reached the leaving age.[5]

---

[5] Scottish Education Department Circular 956, The Education (Scotland) Act 1976, School Leaving Arrangements (11 June 1976).

10.23 Work experience provided under the Education (Work Experience) Act 1973 is not intended to be a substitute for the provision of induction training by employers. It seeks merely to increase a young person's understanding of industrial or commercial life. It must be integrated with the school's educational programme, and schemes with appropriate safeguards must be approved by the local education authority. While some of us question the value of work experience for young people under 16, most of us think that it has positive benefits and should be increasingly developed. We recognise that work experience can never be entirely realistic for schoolchildren since they cannot be paid wages or be subject to industrial discipline and can be placed only in jobs for which no previous training is required. Nevertheless, we accept that work experience can, in appropriate cases and when properly linked with the rest of the curriculum and well organised and prepared, help to bridge the gap between the sheltered world of school and the harsher world of work; and we also believe that it may lead to a more realistic choice of occupation. We hope that more and more employers will be able and willing to offer satisfactory facilities for work experience for schoolchildren with special educational needs.

10.24 It is a prerequisite of the effective organisation of linked courses and the different forms of work preparation that schools should have the closest possible links with local establishments of further education and with local industry and commerce. The local education authority careers service has a very important part to play in promoting them.

II EDUCATIONAL PROVISION FOR YOUNG PEOPLE OVER STATUTORY SCHOOL LEAVING AGE

10.25 For the great majority of young people with disabilities or significant difficulties the year in which they are 16 marks the end of formal education. In January 1977 only 5,945 16-year-olds and 1,069 17-year-olds were attending special schools in England and Wales compared with 15,019 15-year-olds. In Scotland in September 1976 758 16-year-olds and 168 17-year-olds were attending special schools compared with 1,447 15-year-olds. Moreover, of the 18-year-olds in the sample studied in the research project carried out for us by the National Children's Bureau, five times as many of the non-handicapped as of those ascertained as handicapped were still at school or in further education. (Further details are given in paragraph 10.56.)

10.26 A considerable number of contributors to the evidence submitted to us stressed the need for education to be available to young people with disabilities or significant difficulties beyond the age of 16. It was argued that far more encouragement needs to be given to pupils to remain at school beyond 16, and a handful of contributors suggested a return to a higher statutory school leaving age for handicapped young people. There was very wide support for an expansion of opportunities for such young people in further education.

10.27 We recognise that relatively few young people with disabilities or significant difficulties have achieved by the age of 16 either their full educational potential or an adequate degree of maturity to make a smooth transition to adult life. Some young people with handicapping conditions will have experienced interruptions to their schooling for health or other reasons; some will be slow in developing personally as well as educationally. Educational provision must therefore be far more widely available to such young people beyond the age of 16. This is a principle of which we are firmly convinced. It applies to all young people with special educational needs, and particularly to those with language problems, including young people whose first language is not English, those with impaired hearing, those with specific speech problems and some of those with learning difficulties. Their needs obviously vary, but the importance of intelligible speech and adequate language skills as components of social competence cannot be over-emphasised. Parents must be strongly encouraged to seek continued education for their children and the children themselves strongly encouraged to undertake it, either in schools or in establishments of further education.

10.28 Local education authorities have a duty, which is not widely recognised, to provide for all young people who want continued full-time education between the ages of 16 and 19, either in school or in an establishment of further education, though not necessarily whichever of the two the individual prefers. It is essential that they should fulfil this duty and ensure that adequate numbers of places in schools and establishments of further education are available to and taken up by young people with special educational needs. In practice a flexible range of arrangements is required, as we explain below, if an educational setting appropriate to the young person's special needs is to be provided.

10.29 The need for continued education does not stop when young people with special needs enter work. In their case, however, opportunities need to be provided on a part-time basis. Evening study may be impracticable for many of these young employees, but day release from work could provide an ideal basis for continued education. The TUC has for many years urged the case for universal day release for further education for all young workers up to the age of 18 years and in their evidence to us both the TUC and Scottish TUC supported the case for compulsory day release, whether for continued general education or for vocationally orientated courses. We considered recommending compulsory day release for further education for young workers with special needs but concluded that compulsion would be likely to deter employers from engaging them. At present employers are willing to contemplate day release when the qualifications or training will benefit the firm, for example where the employees have entered apprenticeships or where improved qualifications will lead to their promotion. Many employers will, however, need a great deal of persuasion to release employees for continued general education. Any substantial improvement in the opportunities for young people with special needs to continue their education will depend on general developments in the provision of opportunities for further education, and an extension of the present arrangements for day release. In the meantime, we urge that a sustained effort should be made to convince employers in both the public and private sectors that courses of continued general education will significantly enhance the general competence of those young employees with special needs. To this end there should be much closer links between local industry and commerce and establishments of further education, and joint discussion of the courses provided for young workers with special needs.

Provision in school

10.30 Until the statutory school leaving age for children in ordinary schools was raised to 16 from the beginning of the school year 1972-73, the school leaving age for children in special schools was higher by a year than that for children in ordinary schools. We would not wish to see any such special provision re-introduced since it would have the unfortunate effects of reinforcing the division between the handicapped and the non-handicapped which we are determined to see eliminated and of making for rigidity in the arrangements for continued education beyond 16. At the same time we should like to see a much higher proportion of young people over 16 with special needs continuing in full-time education. We recognise that for some children with special needs a change of educational setting may be preferable at the age of 16, but there are others who will benefit from staying on at school, particularly where the school offers specially designed programmes for those over 16. *We therefore recommend that, where it is in their interests, children with special educational needs should be enabled to stay at school beyond the statutory school leaving age.* Since some parents may be deterred by financial considerations from encouraging their children to stay at school, it is important that local education authorities should look sympathetically on the families of pupils with special needs who remain at school beyond 16 in deciding whether to make an educational maintenance allowance. We return to this in paragraph 10.104.

10.31 Our comments in the previous section on the need for the inclusion in the final stages of the curriculum for pupils with special needs of elements of preparation for the next phase in life apply equally to the curriculum for young people over statutory school leaving age, whether in schools or in establishments of further education. There is considerable scope at this stage for the organisation of all forms of work preparation and, indeed, work experience in particular might be offered more appropriately at this stage than previously. We recognise that our recommendation that pupils with special needs should be enabled to stay at school where it is in their interests will have considerable implications for many special schools and special classes which at present cater only for pupils up to 16. They will need to extend the scope of their provision and ensure that suitable courses for young people over 16 are developed.

10.32 At present some pupils in special schools who would benefit from taking a sixth form course are precluded from doing so because their school does not have a sixth form. We believe that wherever possible arrangements should be made for them to pursue their studies with any necessary support in the sixth form of an ordinary school or a sixth form college in the vicinity. *We therefore recommend that, where it is in their interests and possible to arrange, pupils with special educational needs should have access to sixth forms or sixth form colleges.* We discuss the need for adaptation of examination syllabuses to suit pupils with particular disabilities, particularly impaired vision, in the next chapter.

Further education

10.33 A variety of arrangements is needed for young people with special educational needs in establishments of further education. In all cases it is essential that careers guidance should be readily available and that careers officers should participate in the construction of educational programmes. For many young people an establishment of further education will be a more appropriate setting than a school in which to continue their general education. The need for the provision of courses in further education directed towards helping school leavers of low educational achievement and social competence, many of them deficient in the basic skills of literacy and numeracy, was identified in the Holland Report[7] and was emphasised in a Joint Circular by the Department of Education and Science and Welsh Office in September 1977 and a Circular by the Scottish Education Department in October 1977.[8] Courses of this kind will clearly be of great value to many young people with special needs and we hope that they will be made widely available. As the Holland Report pointed out, young people tend to respond better when courses are related to the world of work, and we therefore hope that they will be planned with close reference to local industry and commerce.

10.34 We believe that a positive effort should be made by colleges of further education to develop day or block release courses suited to the requirements of young workers with special needs. We are pleased to know that young people with disabilities are able to take part in the pilot schemes of unified vocational preparation introduced by the government in 1976.[9] These are designed to help those young people who leave school with few or no qualifications to assess their potential and think realistically about jobs and careers, to develop basic skills which will be needed in adult life, to understand their society and how it works, and to strengthen the foundation of skill and knowledge on which further education and training can be built.

10.35 For those young people who, for whatever reason, are unable to take advantage of such courses in further education, we note here the opportunity which exists for them to develop basic skills through adult literacy classes. We were interested to learn that, of the young people ascertained as handicapped in the sample studied in the National Children's Bureau's research project who had undertaken some form of further education since leaving school, over half were receiving tuition in adult literacy classes. The actual number of people concerned was small (13) but it included all ten of the young people classified as ESN(M) who had taken some form of further education. While we hope that curricular developments in schools will result in far fewer young people leaving school deficient in literacy and numeracy, we believe that more encouragement should be given to those who do so to attend adult literacy classes.

10.36 In addition to courses designed to help school leavers to acquire basic skills, a range of courses of a more vocational nature is required for young people with special educational needs in further education. In practice far more young people with special needs are likely to take such courses than to take

[7] *Young People and Work*. Report on the feasibility of a New Programme of Opportunities for Unemployed Young People (Manpower Services Commission, 1977).

[8] DES Circular 10/77, Welsh Office Circular 165/77, Unemployed Young People: Th~ Contribution of the Education Service (30 September 1977) and Scottish Education D~ ment Circular 996 (7 October 1977).

[9] DES Circular 6/76, Welsh Office Circular 104/76, Government Statemen~ Vocational Preparation (21 July 1976) and Scottish Education Department Ci~ July 1976).

courses of higher education. Existing provision in further education, however, has developed in a piecemeal and unco-ordinated fashion. We consider that opportunities in further education should be increased and a coherent pattern of provision developed. We describe below what this should be and examine the conditions for its effective development.

10.37 In line with the principle we have supported in schools of the development of common provision for all children, *we recommend that wherever possible young people with special needs should be given the necessary support to enable them to attend ordinary courses of further education.* The support required may take the form, for example, of adaptations to premises, special equipment or help from advisory teachers with specialist training. We recognise that not every establishment of further education will be able to provide the different forms of support necessary. Consultations will be needed between local education authorities within a region on the support which can be provided in individual establishments and on the sharing of special equipment and specialist staff between different establishments. Moreover, area health authorities and social services departments will need to be consulted on the supporting services required. In many cases, however, the most important factor will be the attitude of the staff. We are convinced that a deeper and more sympathetic understanding on the part of staff in colleges of further education could enable many more young people with special needs to take part in and benefit from ordinary courses without the requirement of substantial additional resources.

10.38 Some young people with special needs will be able to master the content and attain the standards of ordinary courses of further education if some modification is made in, say, their duration or presentation. It may be desirable, for example, to extend a course or alter the entrance requirements, say, for the benefit of students with learning difficulties. *We therefore recommend that some establishments of further education should experiment with modified versions of ordinary further education courses for young people with special needs.*

10.39 Some special courses for young people with special needs will also be required, particularly special vocational courses at operative level. It is important that such courses should not be based on traditional school methods but should take advantage of the adult environment and the range of facilities available in a college of further education. We also referred in paragraph 10.33 to the need for special courses designed to help school leavers of low educational achievement to attain basic skills of literacy and numeracy. In the case of young people with disabilities or disorders, training may also be needed in social competence and independence. *We therefore recommend that some establishments of further education should provide special vocational courses at operative level for students with special needs and special courses of training in social competence and independence.*

10.40 There is also a need for special courses designed more specifically for young people with moderate or severe learning difficulties or physical or sensory disabilities. These must be backed up by special facilities and support, if necessary of an intensive kind, from different services. If specialist resources for this purpose are to be deployed as effectively as possible, they will need to be concentrated in a number of special units. *We therefore recommend that within each region there should be at least one special unit providing special courses for young people with more severe disabilities or difficulties which would be based in an establishment of further education.* The special unit would also act as a supporting base for handicapped students following ordinary courses of further education in the college. Some special units already exist, but others will need to be established. The criteria for selecting the colleges in which the units would be based should include the facilities available, the interests and experience of the staff, and the ease of access within a region. In many parts of the country residential accommodation will be a crucial element of the special facilities which need to be provided. This should be organised flexibly, with opportunities for students to return home at weekends if they wish.

10.41 A number of conditions will need to be fulfilled if the development of further education provision for young people with special needs is to be as effective as possible. First, such provision requires a higher status. At present the high level of understanding and skills required to teach students with special needs is not sufficiently recognised and work with such students has a low professional status in further education. We believe that provision for young people with special needs should be clearly recognised as an integral and very important part of further education. Secondly, all teaching staff in further education must be aware of and understand the special needs which many young people have; and those teachers specialising in work with them must have specialist training for this purpose. We make proposals for the training of teachers in further education in Chapter 12. Thirdly, more attention needs to be given to curriculum development in further education, and we return to this in the following chapter. Fourthly, any necessary adaptations to premises must be made and special equipment together with help from supporting services, including financial support, provided as required.

10.42 It will be important, if the necessary support is to be provided, that there should be a member of staff in every place of further education to whom students with special needs, whether they are taking ordinary, modified or special courses of further education, can turn for help and advice on any problem which they face. Moreover, this person should be able to advise other members of the teaching staff about the students' special needs. *We therefore recommend that every establishment of further education should designate a member of staff as responsible for the welfare of students with special needs in the college and for briefing other members of staff on their special needs.*

10.43 A fifth condition of the coherent development of provision for young people with special needs is a co-ordinated approach by local education authorities. We have already pointed to the need for local education authorities within a region to consult each other on the provision of the necessary facilities and to consult the area health authorities and social services departments on the supporting services required. *We recommend that a co-ordinated approach to further education provision for young people with special needs should be adopted and publicised by the local education authorities within each region against a long-term plan within which arrangements for individual institutions will take their place.*

Further, the institutions themselves should publicise their policy on the admission of students with special needs as well as the courses and special facilities which they provide for them.

10.44 There are some national colleges which at present provide further education and vocational training for young people with particular disabilities. With the exception of Hereward College at Coventry, they are run by voluntary bodies. They were intended to provide vocational training, and became engaged in further education only because prospective students could not acquire their minimum entrance qualifications. We consider that most of these colleges will eventually perform a more useful function as part of the pattern of further education provision in their region rather than as national centres catering for particular areas of disability. Experience at Hereward College, for example, has shown that, after completing their foundation year, some 50% of its students continue at local colleges. Moreover, as we have already emphasised in Chapter 3, special educational needs are not necessarily determined by the particular disabilities of the young people. It follows that more emphasis should be placed on making provision for common educational needs than for particular disabilities. *We therefore recommend that the national colleges which currently provide further education or training for young people with disabilities should in time all become part of their regional patterns of further education for students with special needs.* Indeed, we understand that one or two of the colleges are already moving in this direction. We recognise that, in the case of the colleges run by voluntary bodies, the extent to which changes can be made may depend on the terms of their trust deeds, as in the case of non-maintained special schools.

10.45 It is impossible at present to predict accurately the likely level of demand for further education on the part of young people with special needs, since there is little experience to go on and it may be expected that demand will grow with provision. The best guide will be the experience of local education authorities and other bodies who provide places for such young people in further education, and we therefore suggest that they should monitor carefully the extent to which places are taken up and whether a waiting list is formed.

10.46 There is also scope for young people with special needs, particularly those with disabilities which restrict their mobility, to pursue courses of further as well as higher education through distance teaching, using the medium of broadcasting or correspondence. We have noted that the Scottish Business Education Council runs correspondence courses in business studies, with some tutorial sessions, which were originally intended for the Highlands and Islands, where the distance between establishments of further education makes day release schemes impracticable, but which now cater also for physically handicapped students. Distance teaching offers a useful way of extending further education opportunities to young people with disabilities who might be unable to continue their education by other means, provided that it is accompanied by a significant amount of group work and tutorial sessions, which can help to avoid the sense of isolation that the young people might otherwise feel.

Higher education

10.47 Some universities and polytechnics have taken steps to enable students with disabilities to pursue courses of higher education. The University of Sussex, for example, provides facilities for deaf students, as well as a small purpose-built residential unit for physically handicapped students with medical facilities and support staff. We welcome these initiatives and hope that other establishments will emulate them.

10.48 The Open University has always made special arrangements for disabled students. They have been exempted from the usual "first come, first served" basis of admission and from the normal minimum age limit of 21. Some are excused summer school and receive extra tuition locally instead; some have taken examinations at home or in hospital. A Liaison Committee with the Disabled was set up in 1970 which includes representatives of national organisations and assessors from the Departments of Education and Science and Health and Social Security. In 1972, the University appointed a senior counsellor with specific responsibility for disabled students and we understand that it is planning to introduce improvements in assessment, counselling, special facilities and teaching methods when additional resources are available. The report of the Open University Committee on Continuing Education[10] recommended that the University's concern for the special needs of disabled students should extend to those who enrol for new courses as part of a continuing education programme outside the University's undergraduate programme, and we hope that this recommendation will be implemented.

10.49 *We recommend that all universities and polytechnics as well as other establishments of higher education should formulate and publicise a policy on the admission of students with disabilities or significant difficulties and should make systematic arrangements to meet the welfare and special needs, including careers counselling, of those who are admitted.* Because of the relatively small numbers of students, it will be desirable to concentrate special facilities and skills. Where institutions have already developed a bias towards certain disabilities (such as the facilities for deaf and physically handicapped students at the University of Sussex) these should be strengthened; and similar centres should be established for other disabilities. On the other hand, we do not wish to see prospective students deprived of any choice between institutions because of their disability. While this may be difficult to avoid for students who suffer from a relatively rare or particularly complex disability, we wish to see as many institutions as possible equipped to deal with students who are less severely handicapped.

10.50 The National Bureau for Handicapped Students has taken a valuable initiative in encouraging all establishments of further and higher education to become more aware of the needs of handicapped students and in providing information on facilities available for such students throughout the United Kingdom. We hope that it will receive adequate financial support to continue its valuable work.

---

[10] *Open University. Report of the Committee on Continuing Education* (December 1976).

Adult training centres, day centres and hospitals

10.51 Young people at the age of 16 who are currently described as severely educationally sub-normal may be at a critical stage in their development, both educational and social, and unless suitable educational provision is made for them they may not only fail to make any further progress but actually fall back. Continued education in a special school will be right for some, but it may be difficult for others to mature in such a setting, particularly if the school caters for children of all ages. At present the only other option may well be an adult training centre, run by the social services department of the local authority. In parts of the country where there is a shortage of places in adult training centres, however, some young people may have to wait at home for a period of up to two years after leaving a special school before they can enter an adult training centre. We regard it as essential that a range of provision should be available to them on leaving school. It should include not only adult training centres and day centres but also intermediate centres with a strong educational bias, such as that provided by the local education authority in Clwyd for the 16-21 age group: and full-time courses of general education in places of further education such as those lasting two to three years provided in Leeds. The latter type of course would probably best be offered in special units on a regional basis, as we envisaged in paragraph 10.40. Enough places should be available in these different establishments to enable all severely handicapped young people to be accommodated after leaving school without a waiting period. Time wasted at this stage may make all the difference between a life of total dependence and one of reasonable freedom and purpose.

10.52 As a survey carried out for the National Society for Mentally Handicapped Children showed, in practice there is very little agreement as to what the purpose of adult training centres should be.[11] Although there were some examples of successful educational projects being carried out in adult training centres, these were generally the result of local initiative rather than of systematic planning. The Report of the Melville Committee[12] recommended that teachers should be employed in adult training centres to provide a programme of continued education, and we endorse this proposal. We are convinced that, in addition to providing training in vocational skills, to which we return in paragraphs 10.88-89, all adult training centres should provide instruction in basic educational and social skills as well as a variety of imaginative and creative activities, particularly for young people in the 16-19 age group. A similar educational programme should also be provided in day centres run by the local authority social services department or voluntary bodies. As we explain more fully in Chapter 15, it is important that arrangements for young people should be made separately from those for older people in the centres.

10.53 The need for the provision of education in its broadest sense in adult training centres was urged in a recent pamphlet by the National Development Group for the Mentally Handicapped which suggested that adult training

---

[11] E Baranyay, *A lifetime of learning: a survey of further education facilities for mentally handicapped adolescents and adults* (National Society for Mentally Handicapped Children, 1976).

[12] *The Training of Staff for Centres for the Mentally Handicapped.* Report of the Committee appointed by the Secretary of State for Scotland (HMSO, 1973).

centres might in future be known as social education centres.[13] We consider that the most effective way of ensuring a specifically educational element in adult training centres as well as day centres would be by the local education authority's assuming responsibility for its provision whilst leaving responsibility for the general management of the centre to the social services department. This should have the additional advantages of promoting continuity when young people move from a special school to a centre and making special schools more aware of the educational programme which their leavers will be offered in the centres. Moreover, it would make for closer links between adult training centres and establishments of further education. *We therefore recommend that there should be a specifically educational element in every adult training centre and day centre and that the education service should be responsible for its provision.*

10.54 The assumption by the education service of responsibility for the educational element in these centres should also help to keep the staff more closely in touch with developments in the mainstream of education. We believe that they should have access to the same range of training courses as teachers in further education establishments, and we return to this in Chapter 12. Developments on these lines would also help to increase the awareness of members of the education service of some of the long-term problems of the young people attending these centres.

10.55 A very few young people with physical disabilities or severe learning and other difficulties require long-term hospital care. They too need opportunities to continue their education, and to maintain links with the world outside hospital. Their individual needs will vary, from those of intelligent young people with very severe physical disabilities to those of young people with profound learning and other difficulties. *We recommend that local education authorities should provide programmes of continuing education to meet the individual needs of young people who require long-term hospital care.* These programmes would be made available by appropriately qualified visiting teaching staff, for example from an establishment of further education in the vicinity, or, where the young people were able to attend a local college if transport was provided, at a further education college in the vicinity.

III TRAINING, PREPARATION FOR EMPLOYMENT AND SPECIAL MEASURES FOR UNEMPLOYED YOUNG PEOPLE

10.56 Our recommendations for improved careers guidance and increased educational opportunities for young people with special needs are designed to enable them to develop their potential and to prepare them for employment suited, as far as possible, to their individual aptitudes, interests and preferences. Unemployment amongst young people has, however, been high in recent years and has risen much more rapidly than unemployment generally. The scarcity of jobs and factors such as employers' attitudes make it difficult for young people with special needs to achieve their aspirations for employment. The extent to which young people ascertained as handicapped are at a disadvantage in the

---

[13] *Day Services for Mentally Handicapped Adults.* National Development Group for the Mentally Handicapped Pamphlet Number 5 (July 1977).

labour market was indicated by the findings of the research project on the employment experiences of handicapped school leavers which was undertaken for us by the National Children's Bureau (see following table).

PERCENTAGE OF HANDICAPPED AND NON-HANDICAPPED YOUNG PEOPLE
WORKING OR NOT WORKING AT TIME OF THE INTERVIEW

Current employment status	Sample group	
	Ascertained as handicapped	Non-handicapped (control group)
Employed	47.8	66.4
Unemployed – seeking work	19.1	4.4
– not seeking work	8.0	—
Still at school or in further education	5.6	29.2
Adult training centre or sheltered workshop	14.7	—
Other (includes hospital, borstal)	4.8	—
TOTAL	100	100
NUMBER	251	113

In considering these findings it has, of course, to be recognised that the sample contained a large number of young people categorised as ESN(M) or ESN(S), as the details given in Appendix 7 indicate.

10.57 The findings of the research project also revealed that there were considerable differences between the young people ascertained as handicapped and the non-handicapped young people in the control group in the type of job held; almost 60% of the handicapped who had entered employment were in industrial jobs (including construction), compared with less than 40% of the non-handicapped. Within the industrial sector, the handicapped were more likely to work as packers, warehousemen and labourers; the non-handicapped were nearly three times as likely as the handicapped to have jobs in engineering trades. There were further differences between the handicapped and non-handicapped young people in the sample in terms of their share of unemployment. Excluding those young people categorised as ESN(S), 64% of the handicapped school leavers in the sample had experienced some unemployment compared with only 30% of the non-handicapped who had applied for jobs. Moreover, nearly one-third of the handicapped had been out of work for six months or more over a period of two years compared with only 3% of those non-handicapped young people who had left full-time education.

10.58 We recognise that with the present high level of unemployment young people with special needs, particularly those seeking unskilled jobs, will inevitably find it very difficult to get a job. Moreover, increasing demand for skilled workers and decreasing demand for the unskilled may well tend to depress the prospects of employment for young people with special needs still further. They will therefore depend increasingly on opportunities for further education and vocational training to improve their qualifications and skills for employment.

Training
10.59 Arrangements for vocational training have become increasingly complex and young people with special needs may understandably face difficulty

180

in finding their way through this complicated field. Responsibility for vocational training is now shared mainly between employers, Industrial Training Boards, the Manpower Services Commission (MSC) and its two executive arms, the Training Services Agency (TSA) and Employment Service Agency (ESA), and the education service. The education service is represented on the Industrial Training Boards and on the MSC and its agencies, and many local education authorities work closely with the Industrial Training Boards and the TSA. Co-operation between the education and training services has steadily grown, although some serious problems remain to be solved, such as the differing levels of financial allowances and awards paid by local education authorities and by the TSA respectively to young people attending courses. In the following section we identify the responsibilities of the different bodies and make suggestions for improving the opportunities for young people who need special help with work preparation or vocational training.

10.60 The principal responsibility for training both adults and young people rests with employers. We consider that many more employers in both the public and the private sectors should recognise that people with disabilities or significant difficulties can make a full contribution to the organisation in which they work, provided that they receive not only guidance about the nature of the job but also proper induction and training, sometimes for a longer period than other new employees. Employers must be prepared to invest in the training of such people in order to reap long-term economic gains.

10.61 The Industrial Training Boards, which have very close contacts with employers, are responsible for encouraging the development of training policies within industries and for devising schemes which help employers both to analyse and to meet the training needs of their employees. The provision made by employers for the induction of young people with disabilities and for their training in requisite skills leaves much to be desired. This was borne out by the evidence which we received. All too often, as a survey undertaken by one of our co-opted members of 16 companies in East Anglia showed, young people with disabilities are recruited into areas of unskilled work and have no opportunity to acquire the skills which lead to progression within the company or industry. *We recommend that Industrial Training Boards should play a much greater part in encouraging employers to provide employment and training opportunities for people with disabilities or significant difficulties.*

10.62 The Training Services Agency, which is responsible for the development of an efficient national training scheme, seeks to promote training by employers either through Industrial Training Boards where they exist or directly where industries are not covered by such boards. The TSA additionally runs the Training Opportunities Scheme (TOPS), which is designed essentially for adults who for whatever reason need training for new employment. So far as disabled people* are concerned, the TSA seeks to satisfy the needs of those who are suitable for vocational training for open employment. The arrangements whereby this policy is applied are under review but, at the present time, the TSA tries to help disabled people in the following ways.

---

* Disabled here and in this section means "disabled in relation to employment". This definition is derived from the Disabled Persons (Employment) Act 1944.

10.63 Disabled young people over school-leaving age who are considered able to take up open employment may be trained under the TOPS scheme. (Young people who are not disabled cannot enter TOPS schemes until they are aged 19.) There are over 500 different types of courses available: these are either exclusively TOPS courses (at skill centres, establishments of further education or private colleges), or are provided on an in-fill basis at colleges of further education or private colleges. Individual disabled people of any age can also be trained with TSA financial help by employers willing to provide employment after training. (This is known as the training with employers scheme.) Where residential provision is needed, young people with disabilities can take a variety of vocational courses at the four residential training colleges run by voluntary organisations, again with TSA financial and technical assistance. The colleges are: Finchale Training College, Durham; Portland Training College near Mansfield, Nottinghamshire; Queen Elizabeth's Training College, Leatherhead; and St. Loye's College, Exeter. Together, these colleges train 800 disabled people a year. The TSA also provides special courses for unemployed young people under 19 which are included in the Manpower Services Commission's new programme.

10.64 We note with approval that the TSA's services for disabled young people are currently being expanded and that several new courses are being mounted. TSA regions are being encouraged, in co-operation with the local authority careers services, to review the demand for training and to consider providing flexible and extended courses exclusively for disabled young people who are unable to benefit from normal provision. It is intended that all courses should include training in personal and social skills and, where necessary, basic English and arithmetic. Some courses will provide for students to be assessed specifically for training and employment and will lead to further courses where desirable.

10.65 TSA regions have also been asked to consider with local education authorities the joint funding of some courses so as to ensure continued education throughout training. Such courses will clearly be beneficial to many young people with disabilities or significant difficulties and we urge their early development. A major expansion of the training with employers scheme is under way and local careers services are being encouraged to exploit this form of provision with its assurance of employment at the end of training. Procedures for the entry of disabled young people to courses are under review and a campaign to publicise the courses is in progress. The TSA hopes that some courses will cater for some young people with moderate learning difficulties who at school were categorised as ESN(M).

10.66 Unfortunately the use made by young people with disabilities of the facilities provided by the TSA has so far been limited. TSA statistics show that during the twelve months ending 30 September 1976 only 273 disabled young people were trained by the TSA (although according to the TSA many disabled young people prefer not to be identified as such). Moreover, a survey conducted by one of our co-opted members in East Anglia produced very few examples of such young people receiving training in skills at about operator level under TSA auspices. The reasons for the low use of TSA facilities are complex; they probably include the geographical distribution of the facilities, lack of information about them and the educational qualifications required for entry to some courses.

10.67 We have noted that in the recently published Development Programme,[14] which was prepared by the MSC in consultation with the National Advisory Council on Employment of Disabled People, the MSC indicated that following the publication of our report it would review what, if any, additional special provision was needed in the existing vocational assessment, preparation and training provision for young people. We hope that the TSA will carefully consider ways of spreading training facilities more evenly throughout the country and *we recommend that more opportunities should be provided for young people with disabilities or significant difficulties to take locally-based TSA courses suited to their needs*. We recognise that some of these young people may require a period of continued education before entry. Much wider publicity needs to be given to TSA training facilities for disabled young people and we understand that the TSA has taken measures to achieve this.

10.68 The TSA is also currently giving special attention to certain aspects of the training of disabled people, including the contribution that it could make to the preparation for open employment of those classified as mentally handicapped, the integration of people with and without disabilities during training and the use of residential courses. We hope that this attention, particularly as it concerns young people with learning difficulties or sensory disabilities, whose requirements are inadequately met by present arrangements, will lead to substantial improvements.

10.69 The contribution of the education service to training is provided mainly by means of courses arranged in colleges of further education or in co-operation with the Industrial Training Boards and the TSA. As we explained in paragraph 10.44, there is a number of establishments of further education run by voluntary bodies which provide vocational training for young people with particular disabilities and which we consider should in time become part of their regional patterns of further education.

10.70 Among the further education and training facilities available to young people with special needs are the so-called "training schools". These include establishments run by independent bodies; the former senior approved schools, which have now generally been taken over by social services departments but continue to provide training in a variety of trades; and the nautical training schools, some administered by social services departments and others maintained by independent bodies. Some of the pupils attending these schools have previously attended residential special schools for those classified as ESN(M) or maladjusted; others have attended ordinary schools. Some are placed in the schools by local education authorities, others by social services departments. We regard it as essential that the staff of these schools should have access to the

---

[14] *Developing Employment and Training Services for Disabled People. An MSC Programme* (Manpower Services Commission, 1978).

same range of training courses and the same sources of advice and support as staff dealing with young people with special educational needs in schools or establishments of further education.

Special measures for unemployed young people

10.71 In June 1977 the government asked the MSC to introduce a new programme of opportunities for unemployed young people aged 16-18 years. The programme, which is based on the MSC Working Party Report *Young People and Work*,[15] is designed to alleviate the worst effects of unemployment among young people. The report predicted that high levels of unemployment would persist into the 1980s. We describe the new programme of special measures below and make some suggestions regarding the educational component.

10.72 The two main elements of the new programme of special measures for young people are COURSES TO PREPARE YOUNG PEOPLE FOR WORK, including employment induction courses, short industrial courses and remedial and preparatory courses; and WORK EXPERIENCE of various kinds, including work experience on employers' premises, training workshops, community service and other special projects. The programme will provide some 130,000 places for unemployed young people aged 16 to 18 and it should be possible for at least 234,000 young people to benefit from it each year. The MSC has undertaken "that sufficient places will be made available over the year to ensure that no-one leaving school at Easter or in the summer who fails to get a job by the following Easter will remain without an offer of a suitable opportunity under the programme". We hope that this means that a suitable opportunity will in practice be provided for every such person. A uniform flat rate allowance of £18 per week is payable to those taking part in the programme and this will be reviewed in April 1978. Its present level is much higher than that of most educational maintenance allowances made to parents in respect of school-children over statutory school leaving age and of most discretionary awards paid to students undertaking courses of further education. (We return to these educational allowances and awards in paragraphs 10.106-107.) Arrangements similar to those made under the MSC's new programme are in operation in Scotland, where school leaving takes place at Christmas or in the summer.

10.73 The MSC is concerned that, so far as is possible, young people taking part in the programme should not be type-cast by being channelled into particular forms of provision, since this would affect how they see themselves and are seen by others. The intention is that the programme should cater for young people with different needs and abilities, many of whom may be disadvantaged in various ways. We are impressed by the MSC's determination that its programme should be sufficiently flexible, both in its approach to recruitment and in the design of opportunities, to accommodate this wide range of young people. Some concern has been expressed about the lack of schemes specially designed for young people with particular disadvantages but we understand that the MSC proposes to review this programme in the light of our report. Moreover, special provision for young people already exists in TSA courses and in Employ-

---

[15] *Young People and Work*. Report on the feasibility of a New Programme of Opportunities for Unemployed Young People (Manpower Services Commission, 1977).

ment Rehabilitation Centres – soon to be expanded as part of the new special programme (see below paragraph 10.75): further, the MSC considers that in addition to its basic programme, certain elements such as work preparation courses and training workshops may be particularly suited to young people with disabilities.

10.74 As we pointed out in paragraph 10.33 young people tend to respond better when education courses are related to the world of work. We urge those who are designing individual schemes under the new programme to ensure, through co-operation with establishments of further education, that the education elements are related to work and that provision is made for tutors to visit young people where they are working or training. We recognise that the further education of young people, especially those of low educational attainment, and the organisation of peripatetic teaching will present many colleges with new challenges. They are challenges to be met and not avoided.

Preparation for employment

10.75 The Employment Service Agency maintains 26 Employment Rehabilitation Centres (ERCs) which offer individually tailored courses for people who, following injury, illness or prolonged unemployment, find it difficult to obtain a job. The centres have professional and technical expertise which enables them to carry out vocational assessment for all their clients and identify skills, aptitudes and interests. Their clients include young people: in 1976 2,250 out of 15,500 were aged 16 to 18. As part of the new MSC programme referred to above the assistance provided by ERCs to young people is to be substantially increased. The number of places for young people aged 16 to 18 on normal rehabilitation courses will be expanded from 1,500 in 1976 to 2,500 in 1978-79. The number of places on short assessment courses will rise from about 200 in 1976 to about 1,200 in 1978-79. Young persons' work preparation courses, which are currently available in 14 ERCs and which assist young people to grow accustomed to work, enable them to adjust to a working environment and give them the opportunity of working with other people, will have around 1,000 places in 1980-81 compared with 550 places in 1976. Those of us who visited the Sheffield ERC were impressed by the help given to handicapped young people on the young persons' work preparation course and the success of the young people who had taken the course in obtaining employment. We therefore welcome the recent decision by the MSC to extend the courses to all ERCs over the next few years and *we recommend that this development should be brought about as quickly as possible.*

IV EMPLOYMENT

10.76 We firmly believe that there is much greater scope for employing in open occupations many young people with disabilities or disorders who are at present unemployed or in some form of sheltered employment (which we consider further below). The possibility of successfully employing even those people currently described as severely mentally handicapped in open occupations has been demonstrated in a food-processing factory in East Anglia. The handicapped were originally recruited from an adult training centre at a time of acute labour shortage, when others were reluctant to do important but

185

repetitive work such as loading, unloading and packaging. They receive the same treatment as other employees and have proved that they are able to work no less effectively. Provided people with severe disabilities are not exploited through being made to work in poor conditions or for low wages, open employment even in occupations which are repetitive and low in stimulus is infinitely preferable to diversionary activities in adult training centres or day centres, both because it actually provides a basis for independent living, and because it is seen to do so by the young people themselves, and their families.

10.77 We consider that there is scope for the extension of opportunities for the employment of young people with disabilities or significant difficulties not only in routine, repetitive jobs but also in a range of other, more demanding work. At present the range is unduly restricted, principally because of stereotyped ideas about the kinds of work that people with particular disabilities can perform and the common assumption that certain jobs are intrinsically unsuitable for anyone who is disabled in whatever way or degree. In our view the public sector has a special responsibility to give a lead in widening the opportunities available to people with disabilities for employment and, where they have the requisite qualifications, for professional training and entry into the professions. *We recommend that the public service and nationalised industries should urgently review their policies with a view to opening their doors more widely to and providing more imaginative opportunities for work for people with disabilities.*

10.78 There are already sources of skilled advice for people with disabilities or significant difficulties seeking professional jobs. The Employment Service Agency's Professional and Executive Recruitment's candidate consultants, helped by Disablement Resettlement Officers as necessary, assist such people. Moreover, many local authorities employ careers officers to specialise in advising young people on the vocational opportunities available through further and higher education; and their advice may also be sought by specialist careers officers for handicapped young people. In the last analysis, however, handicapped young people will be able to start their chosen career only if suitable opportunities are made available to them by employers.

10.79 Under the Disabled Persons (Employment) Act 1944, employers of 20 or more work people are required to employ a quota (at present 3% of their total work force) of registered disabled persons. The quota system has the disadvantage that it may lead to undesirable pressure on people with disabilities to register as disabled in order to enable their employers to meet the quota. We concur, however, with the view expressed in evidence by representatives of the CBI, TUC and the Scottish TUC/CBI joint committee on the employment of the disabled that the quota has a part to play as one way of encouraging the employment of people with disabilities, but that it needs to be complemented by other, more positive measures. We have been impressed by the efforts of the Scottish TUC/CBI joint committee on the employment of disabled people to promote the creation of more opportunities in Scotland by urging employers to discuss with local Disablement Resettlement Officers the problems of the disabled and possible ways of helping them. We also welcome the Employment Service Agency's developing strategy of ensuring that employers are aware of the employment needs of disabled people and of ways of meeting them. This was brought into prominence in May 1977 by the publication of *Positive Policies*, a guide to employing disabled people.[16] It marked the beginning of a programme of visits, carried out with the support of the TUC and CBI, by ESA Managers and Disablement Resettlement Officers to employers throughout the country to bring to their notice the employment needs of those who are disabled. *We recommend that the ESA's strategy of alerting employers to the employment needs of the disabled should be further developed and that there should be more contact at local level between employers or, where the management of large companies is decentralised, local managers and both ESA officers and careers officers.*

10.80 It is sometimes argued that, since employees who are disabled take longer to train than other workers, some form of financial incentive should be offered to encourage employers to engage them. In evidence to us the suggestion was made of an employment subsidy for young people with disabilities on the lines of the various types of employment subsidy schemes which have been operated to prevent redundancies or to encourage recruitment of young people who have been unemployed for a considerable period of time. We welcome the experimental Job Introduction Scheme for disabled people, under which employers can be paid £30 a week for a total of six weeks to give a disabled person a trial period in which to show that he can do a job. We have, however, found a general lack of enthusiasm for the idea of a long-term subsidy in respect of young employees with disabilities, on the grounds that it would serve to emphasise their disability rather than their ability and could adversely influence the attitude of other employees. We agree that it would be retrograde to institute such a payment and think that resources would be better spent on rehabilitation and training and on grants to employers towards the adaptation of their premises. We welcome the scheme introduced by the Employment Service Agency under which capital grants of up to £5,000 may be paid to cover all, or part, of the costs incurred by employers in altering their premises or equipment in order to engage or retain a disabled worker.

10.81 It has been suggested in evidence by representatives of employers' organisations that the requirements imposed on employers by recent industrial legislation have among other things inhibited them from recruiting disabled young people. We urge all employers in the public and private sectors to adopt a positive attitude to the employment of young people with disabilities and not to be deterred by legislation such as the Health and Safety at Work Act 1974. This Act does not, in our view, prejudice wider employment opportunities for such people and, indeed, in some cases it provides for assistance to be given to employer and employee.

10.82 The most effective way of encouraging employers to take on more young people with disabilities or significant difficulties and to employ them in a wider range of occupations is, in our view, to give them more information about the practical implications of doing so. Those who submitted evidence to us emphasised the need for employers to be educated to accept such people as

[16] *Positive Policies* (Manpower Services Commission and National Advisory Council on Employment of Disabled People, May 1977).

employees. The enquiries of employers made in the course of the research project carried out by the National Children's Bureau revealed that many of them had little idea of the type of work which people with disabilities could successfully undertake and were unaware of the support available. We consider that both the TUC and CBI should seek to increase employers' knowledge of the needs of those with disabilities or significant difficulties and support the government's efforts to do so. The Employment Service Agency already produces leaflets for employers containing practical information about the employment of disabled people, some of which include success stories. We particularly welcome the publication of *Positive Policies* issued jointly in May 1977 by the Manpower Services Commission and the National Advisory Council on Employment of Disabled People.[17] This guide, which was sent to those employers who employ 20 or more workers (about 55,000), has the full support and encouragement of the government, the CBI and the TUC. It represents a major new initiative, intended to focus attention on the needs and aspirations of all disabled workers. The guide encourages employers to develop policies on the recruitment, training and career prospects of disabled people. More consideration needs to be given to ways of extending the opportunities for employment open to people with disabilities or disorders and *we recommend that local education authorities and their careers services should play a greater part in promoting discussions with employers' and employees' organisations about how best to persuade employers to take on young people with disabilities, in conjunction with the MSC and, where necessary, the social services.*

10.83 Other workers as well as employers need to understand the implications of disabilities for employment. We suggest that discussions should be held between employers and workers before disabled people, particularly those with severe disabilities, are employed in normal jobs, to ensure that the implications are clearly understood. These include any special arrangements to meet the disabled employees' needs and agreement on the conditions under which they are to be employed. An approach that combines compassion with a business-like attitude, rather than one grounded in sentimentality, is most likely to provide the disabled young person with the opportunity to give of his best in a job and to lead to the removal of those obstacles which arise simply from ignorance of his needs.

Sheltered employment

10.84 Sheltered employment is provided in sheltered workshops for disabled people run by Remploy, local authorities and voluntary bodies. Although some of the work provided in sheltered workshops is highly skilled, much of it is routine contract work. We regard sheltered employment as very much a second best to open employment, but we recognise that it is preferable to unemployment or inactivity. It can be constructive and satisfying, and by helping handicapped young people to develop their manual skills, social competence and self-confidence can point the way to open employment for some.

10.85 At present the provision of sheltered workshops is inadequate, especially in rural areas, and more resources and effort are required to extend the facili-

---

[17] *Ibid.*

ties. We consider that young people with disabilities or disorders should be encouraged more strongly to take advantage of the residential facilities where these are available.

10.86 We hold that the range of work in sheltered employment also needs to be extended if people with disabilities are to gain wider experience, in skilled as well as unskilled work. We support the government's policy of increasing the rehabilitative element in sheltered workshops and consider that opportunities for people to progress from sheltered provision to open employment should be increased. Some sheltered workshops actively promote this progression but others are insufficiently ambitious. The fact that earnings in a sheltered workshop can often be almost as high as in open employment is a disincentive to movement from the workshops; so too is the security which they provide. We would naturally deplore any worsening of conditions in sheltered workshops, but would point out that unless there is progression out of them, they will have no room for new entrants. *We therefore recommend that sheltered workshops should introduce progressive programmes of activities designed to enable as many people with disabilities as possible to enter open employment.*

10.87 Those of us who visited West Germany were very much impressed by a workshop for the disabled at Dusseldorf, which is one of two run by the Association for Mentally Handicapped and is jointly funded by that Association and the Association for Cerebral Palsied, the government and the municipal authority. It aims to provide work experience and training for a full range of handicapped young people and to develop their independence so that they are ultimately able to maintain themselves in the community. Following an introductory course during which their needs and abilities are assessed, entrants are allocated to a specialised training group where they learn to perform specific operations under skilled craftsmen. When ready, they join a working team. Part of each week is allocated to the development of leisure skills and social competence under the guidance of two social workers. Medical and nursing support is also provided. We consider that the approach to work, training and personal and social development in this workshop could very usefully be followed by staff in sheltered workshops in this country.

Adult training centres

10.88 Although some adult training centres for mentally handicapped people may provide routine contract work similar to that provided in sheltered workshops, too many of them offer only diversionary and social activities. Some try to inculcate basic skills and equip handicapped people for greater independence but all too often these are seen as ends in themselves rather than the means of achieving rehabilitation. For example, the staff of one adult training centre which some of us visited had rejected any form of industrial production and placed their main emphasis on craft activities. While their programme was clearly more imaginative than that of some more traditional adult training centres, there was little pressure on the trainees and the atmosphere was lethargic.

10.89 Adult training centres, like sheltered workshops, should provide progressive programmes of activities which encourage as many people as pos-

189

sible to enter open employment, and we urge their development as soon as possible. We think that consideration should be given to the development of a new course for instructors in adult training centres, on the lines recommended by the Report of the Melville Committee, possibly lasting two years with up to half consisting of supervised experience in various centres.[18] Moreover, as we have recommended in paragraph 10.53, there should be a specifically educational element in every adult training centre, and the education service should be responsible for its provision. It is important that the educational and training needs of young people attending the centres should be regularly reviewed and arrangements made for their transfer to another establishment where this is considered appropriate.

Other work centres

10.90 The experience of some of our members has revealed a growing number of young people who are too severely physically handicapped to be accepted by sheltered workshops run by Remploy or local authorities but who are intellectually unsatisfied by attendance at a day or adult training centre. They want to work and to be rewarded for their work in the usual way by receiving a weekly wage. There are also growing numbers of young people who at school were categorised as ESN(M) and who are socially and emotionally immature, and of maladjusted young people who do not fit into adult training centres and, unhappy and underchallenged, cause disturbances within them. They too would benefit from an industrially orientated but sheltered environment before proceeding to open employment. The work centres pioneered by the Spastics Society and its local groups are helping to meet the needs of some of these young people. Their main aim is to give those who are not ready for employment or who are too severely handicapped to earn a normal living an opportunity to work and receive a small wage and to gain experience before moving on wherever possible to sheltered or open employment. Day release and other educational facilities are available in some of the centres and the Society hopes to extend them. We see considerable scope in future for the development of work centres on these lines, whether by social services departments or voluntary organisations or in other ways, to help meet the needs of those handicapped young people for whom sheltered employment or an adult training centre is not for the time being appropriate.

V SUPPORTING SERVICES

10.91 If young people with special needs are to make full use of their abilities they will require support in several ways. This is true whether they are being educated or trained, are in open or sheltered employment or are not actively engaged in any work. In this section we examine the various forms of support that may be required, particularly by those with more severe or complex disabilities. We start by considering the needs of young people (or of their parents acting on their behalf) for a Named Person who, during the transition from school to adult life, will be able to help them take full advantage of the available opportunities for further or higher education, training or employment.

---

[18] *The Training of Staff for Centres for the Mentally Handicapped (op. cit.).*

A Named Person

10.92 There is a danger that, at the moment of leaving school, young people, particularly those with more severe or complex disabilities, may find themselves receiving far less support than at any time before. The Court Report, which drew attention to the need of many handicapped adolescents for psychiatric, genetic and psycho-sexual counselling to prepare them for adulthood, recommended that these services should be available through school and hospital but that, like all other adolescents, the handicapped should be able and encouraged to seek help and guidance on their own initiative.[19] We agree that handicapped young people should have direct access to professionals in the different services. At the same time we consider that someone should be designated as Named Person to whom they can turn for advice on which service or which professional to approach for help.

10.93 Moreover, at the school leaving stage, as much as at earlier stages, parents of young people with special needs require advice and practical guidance on the arrangements for their child's future. Like the young people themselves, they need a Named Person to be their point of contact and to arrange access to the professional best placed to offer them advice and support.

10.94 The careers officer or, in the case of young people with more severe or complex disabilities, the specialist careers officer, is likely to be the person best placed to provide a continuing link for young people with special needs and their parents during the transition from school to adult life. Guidelines issued by the Department of Employment suggest that the careers officer's responsibility for a young person should continue for up to two years after he has left full-time education (whether at school or in further or higher education) or longer if he left full-time education while still in his teens. There is no statutory upper limit to the age at which the careers officer may help and advise a young person, and in the case of a handicapped young person the point at which the Disablement Resettlement Officer rather than the specialist careers officer assumes the main responsibility will be decided by mutual agreement between the two officers following a period of co-operation. The careers officer or his specialist colleague should therefore be able to provide a single point of contact for a sufficient period of time to help the young person with special needs until he is settled in employment. We recognise, however, that a young person may well choose to go for advice or help to someone with whom he has developed a special rapport, such as a teacher at his old school or a social worker. *We therefore recommend that the careers officer or, in the case of young people with more severe or complex disabilities, the specialist careers officer should act as Named Person for young people with special needs and their parents or should ensure that another professional takes on the function of providing a single point of contact for them during the transition from school to adult life.*

Counselling young people

10.95 Young people with special needs may require advice on a range of personal matters including health, and personal and sexual relationships. Counselling on these subjects needs to be readily available, and it should be a

---

[19] *Fit for the future*. The Report of the Committee on Child Health Services. Cmnd 6684 (HMSO, 1976), Vol 1, pp 174-5.

function of the Named Person to make the necessary arrangements for a young person with special needs to receive appropriate counselling where this is required. Where a young person is receiving treatment from a psychologist or psychiatrist or help from a social worker, that professional should be consulted by the Named Person on the arrangements to be made. We believe that there is room for using both professionals and non-professionals in counselling. A professional may be most expert at recognising and appreciating the young person's various needs, and some social workers, health visitors and teachers make excellent counsellors provided – and this is vital – that they have time to do the job effectively. Non-professionals are generally less constrained by time, and with adequate training and supervision many of them are able to give wise and experienced counsel to handicapped young people. If they are themselves handicapped they may be particularly well-placed to offer advice and support to others with disabilities or disorders.

10.96 Young people with disabilities or significant difficulties may need counselling on various aspects of personal relationships, and we see this as a very important part of health education. Those who are in employment may need counselling on, for example, the development of good relations with their fellow workers, while those who are trying to achieve significant living without work may need counselling on personal relations with those who care for them. Health education in general needs to be improved for all young people, particularly those with disabilities or disorders, and should include aspects of personal hygiene and subjects such as the effects of alcohol, smoking and drugs. Much greater emphasis should be given to personal counselling not only for young people with special needs themselves but also for their parents. *We therefore recommend that better counselling on personal relationships should be available to young people with special needs and their parents from a variety of sources, including the health and social services and voluntary groups.*

10.97 One important aspect of personal counselling is counselling on sexual relationships. At present sex education and counselling on sexual relationships tend to be badly handled generally. This is unfortunate for all young people, but it is particularly serious in the case of young people with severe disabilities, whose opportunities for personal development through self-education are so limited compared with those of other young people, and for whom the problems of adolescence are likely to be increased by their disability. Problems of sexual relationships are compounded for them by the attitude of society, which tends not to appreciate the sexual identity of handicapped people. The general public, many professionals working with handicapped people and also the families of the handicapped people themselves often fail to recognise or to understand that young people with disabilities undergo the normal biological and psychological changes associated with sexual development and have normal needs. We consider that sexual counselling and advice on contraception should be readily available to young people with special needs and their parents. Advice on sexual relationships should be both realistic and humane and should always be planned within the broader concept of education in personal, social and moral responsibility. We see a need for the inclusion of some reference to sexual counselling in courses of training for all professionals working with adolescents with disabilities or disorders so that as many professionals as possible are able to recognise signs of personal problems and give advice on where appropriate counselling might best be sought. In particular, the careers officer or his specialist colleague should be able to advise young people or their parents on whom to approach for guidance on sexual problems as part of his function of being Named Person. In this as in other fields handicapped people can often be helped by others who are also handicapped. *We recommend that more research should be carried out into how sexual counselling can best be provided for young people with special needs, including the training of counsellors and other staff.*

10.98 Genetic counselling needs to be readily available to handicapped young people and their parents. This requires expert knowledge of the risks of transmitting different kinds of disability and disorder. Those engaged in health education should be able to refer handicapped young people to professional experts in this field, whose work needs to be more widely recognised and supported.

Health care

10.99 It is essential that continuing support from the health service should be provided for all young people who require any form of treatment or care. In the case of those with serious handicapping conditions, arrangements will need to be made for continuing care at a local hospital or, where specialist treatment and care are necessary, in regional or supra-regional centres (for example spinal units). A very small number of physically handicapped and more profoundly mentally handicapped people may require long-term hospital care. However, we welcome the change of emphasis towards care in the community which has taken place in recent years. Those concerned in providing primary health care, particularly general practitioners, district nurses and health visitors, together with social workers, have a major part to play in enabling people with severe disabilities to live in their own homes or in residential homes in the community for as long as possible.

10.100 As the Court Report indicated, the prevalence of psychiatric disorders rises in adolescence. Some forms of disorder dating from childhood or early school years may continue, while others begin to appear only after the age of about 16. For disturbed adolescents who require psychiatric treatment, a range of out-patient, day-patient and in-patient psychiatric services is provided through the National Health Service. As older adolescents become less dependent on their families, facilities such as "walk in" advisory centres, provided usually by voluntary bodies and sometimes funded by health authorities, are useful for those who seek psychiatric help for themselves. We have noted the recommendation in the Court Report that there should be a greatly increased provision of residential facilities such as hostels, schools and hospital units for severely disturbed adolescents.[20] We recognise the need for residential placement for young people over 16 who have attended boarding schools and who, on leaving school and returning home, present their families with severe behavioural or other problems. Wherever possible, however, we think that these young people would be most suitably placed in semi-independent hostels, which we consider further in paragraphs 10.111–112.

---

[20] *Ibid.*, pp 173-4 and 268-270.

10.101 The transition from school to adult life can be a period when the health of young people with disabilities or significant difficulties presents many problems and, paradoxically, it is often the case that the better the health service that they received while at school, the worse and more difficult for them is this transition. No young person with a disability should be left without any one professional taking active responsibility for co-ordinating his health care during this period of transition. Like the Court Committee, we regard it as neither possible nor desirable to draw rigid demarcation lines between the child and adult sectors of the health service. Rather, we regard it as essential that close links should be maintained between the two and that the major responsibility should at all times be clearly assigned.

10.102 At the time when a young person with a disability or significant difficulty leaves school his general practitioner, who has direct responsibility for his health, will naturally be able to provide an element of continuity. The young person may, however, need more specialist support than his general practitioner can provide. In such cases it is essential that the general practitioner should be consulted over arrangements for the allocation of major responsibility for the young person's health. Where the young person leaves school, the school health service should not relinquish responsibility for his health until he enters employment or until there is an alternative available service which is more appropriate and which will assume this responsibility. In some cases the Employment Medical Advisory Service may be the most suitable service for this purpose. In Chapter 15, where we return to this subject, we recommend that the Specialist in Community Medicine (Child Health) should ensure that arrangements are made for the transfer of responsibility for a young person's health to the appropriate branch of the health service when he leaves school or further education. We envisage that responsibility for the arrangements for his health care at area level would pass to the Specialist in Community Medicine (Social Services) when he leaves full-time education.

Financial support for young people to continue their education

10.103 Our recommendations for increased opportunities for young people with special needs to continue their education will be to little avail unless adequate financial assistance is available to attract them to stay on at school or to undertake courses of further education. Financial assistance for this purpose, however, is given at the discretion of local education authorities or, in certain circumstances, as we explain more fully below, the Supplementary Benefits Commission. We consider that this discretion should be exercised as generously as possible, particularly since the provision of financial assistance at this stage for young people with special needs may well have a long-term economic benefit by enabling them to improve their basic educational skills and so attain a greater degree of independence.

10.104 Local education authorities in England and Wales have discretionary powers to pay educational maintenance allowances in respect of pupils who stay on at school beyond the statutory leaving age. The level of notional net income at which an allowance becomes payable and the maximum value of the allowance vary between authorities. We urge local education authorities to look sympathetically on the families of pupils with special needs who remain at school beyond 16 and, where they make an allowance, to ensure that it is adequate.

10.105 Every local education authority has a duty to make an award to any person ordinarily resident in its area who is attending a first degree or comparable course, a course leading to the Diploma of Higher Education, the Higher National Diploma or an initial teacher training course. A disabled student receiving a mandatory award for one of these courses is entitled to a supplementary maintenance grant wherever the authority is satisfied that he is obliged by reason of his disability to incur additional expenditure in respect of his attendance at the course. *We recommend that local education authorities should use their discretionary powers generously in making supplementary grants to students with disabilities who are receiving mandatory awards.*

10.106 Awards for students attending full-time courses other than those mentioned above are given at the discretion of their local education authority. We have been very much concerned about the difficulty faced by handicapped students in obtaining financial assistance to take further education courses which do not attract mandatory awards, especially as the difficulty is likely to increase given the continuing financial restraint on local authorities. We considered the possibility of recommending the extension of mandatory awards to handicapped students as a group, but most of us rejected it because of the difficulties of definition that would be entailed. We also considered recommending an extension of the range of designated courses which attract mandatory awards to include other specified full-time courses, but most of us rejected this on the grounds that it would be a clumsy and costly way of directing help to certain students and would have the disadvantage of tending to move handicapped students towards certain courses. We believe that, as things now stand, the most practicable way of improving financial support for handicapped students is for local education authorities to exercise their discretionary powers more generously. *We therefore recommend that local education authorities should use their discretionary powers far more generously in making discretionary awards to students with disabilities or significant difficulties who enter further education.* We recognise that this recommendation may seem to be lacking in weight. We urge local education authorities, however, to bear in mind that support for such young people at this stage may, by enabling them to gain the skills necessary to obtain and hold down a job, reduce their dependence on supporting services and so have a long-term economic benefit. In considering whether to make an award, the local education authority should consult and take into account the views of the young person's Named Person, who will usually be the careers officer or his specialist colleague.

10.107 At present there is often considerable disparity between the level of educational maintenance allowances and that of discretionary awards for young people aged 16-19. We regard it as desirable that the respective levels and conditions of educational maintenance allowances in respect of pupils staying on at school and of discretionary awards should be harmonised in the interests of ensuring that decisions by young people as to whether to remain at school or to enter further education are taken on educational grounds and are not influenced by financial considerations. We have already commented in paragraph 10.72 on the disparity between the level of discretionary awards and that of training allowances.

10.108 In Scotland responsibility for the financial support of handicapped young people who wish to continue their education is divided between the education authorities and the Scottish Education Department. The Scottish education authorities have discretionary powers to assist persons, including handicapped pupils and students, who are ordinarily resident in their areas. There are two main kinds of assistance: higher school bursaries for pupils who remain at school beyond the age of compulsory attendance to complete their secondary education; and further education bursaries for students attending full-time courses of non-advanced further education. The authorities have complete discretion whether or not to grant a bursary in any particular case, but having exercised this discretion they are required to apply the rates of allowances and parental means test prescribed by the Secretary of State for Scotland in statutory regulations. Grants for students ordinarily resident in Scotland who are attending first degree or comparable courses are administered centrally by the Scottish Education Department under the students' allowances scheme, corresponding to the mandatory system of student awards in England and Wales. Under this scheme, a supplementary allowance may be paid to disabled students who incur expenditure on the purchase of special equipment necessary for their studies because of their disability. In addition, expenses may be reimbursed for travel by special means made necessary by disablement, for example taxi between home and the place of further or higher education.

10.109 The Supplementary Benefits Commission has discretionary powers to pay benefit in particular cases where it considers that there are exceptional circumstances. We understand that it takes the view that benefit can be paid to a young person aged 16-19, even though he may be continuing at school or in further education, if he is physically or mentally handicapped and his prospects are so poor that, were he to leave school or college, he would be unlikely to be able to enter employment within a reasonable period of time. We were concerned to learn that in 1976 only about 700 handicapped people were receiving benefit on these grounds. In practice there seems to be a considerable variation between different areas in the way in which the Commission's discretionary powers are exercised and a greater readiness to pay supplementary benefit to young people with an easily recognisable physical disability than to young people with learning difficulties, even though the employment prospects of the latter may be very poor. We recognise that to attempt to define more clearly the group of handicapped people for whose benefit the Commission may use its discretionary powers in this way could in practice restrict it even further than at present. In the interests of greater uniformity of practice, however, we urge local offices to consult the local careers officer and the Disablement Resettlement Officer as to whether or not a handicapped young person is likely to be able to enter open employment.

Accommodation
10.110 Handicapped young people, particularly those with severe disabilities, may need help with accommodation. Those with very severe disabilities may

need full residential care in residential homes. We are aware that residential units are often unpopular with those who live in them: rules have to be kept; personal choice may have to be severely restricted; invidious comparisons may be made by some residents with the way other residents are treated, for example over the grants they get or the payments they are expected to make for their accommodation; and too much power may rest in the hands of residential staff. We are sure that ways can and should be found to "humanise" such accommodation and to give individual residents more privacy and personal choice. Moreover, we welcome the increasing tendency on the part of good residential homes to encourage handicapped people to move into the community wherever possible.

10.111 We believe that a graduated range of accommodation is required, with continual encouragement for people with disabilities to move a step further along the range in the direction of full independence. In some cases, accommodation in the community with a progressive reduction in supporting services may be appropriate. In others, we believe that hostels need to be provided, where handicapped people can carry out most of the tasks of daily living themselves but can, in cases of need, seek the help of a warden who has separate accommodation close by. Semi-independent accommodation may be particularly desirable for young people with learning difficulties or emotional or behavioural disorders during the transition from school to work. There is already some hostel provision of this kind in existence but it needs to be considerably increased. The Scottish Society for the Mentally Handicapped, for example, has taken an initiative in offering interest-free loans to local authorities to build hostel units for mentally handicapped young people who are expected, wherever possible, to be able to move subsequently into independent housing in the community. Student accommodation is used to support young adults currently described as mentally handicapped in a project being carried out at University College, Cardiff, in which students and handicapped young people share accommodation and the tasks of daily living. Further, hostels for severely disturbed school leavers are provided by the Richmond Fellowship and the Society of Friends. We see a very important part for voluntary organisations, working in conjunction with social services departments and local education authorities, in developing this form of provision.

10.112 Those of us who visited Denmark had the opportunity to see a "halfway house" in Copenhagen, which is one of five financed by the Board for Provisions and Services to the Mentally Retarded, under the Ministry of Social Welfare. These are intended to be staging posts along the road to independent living. We were impressed by the arrangements made for admitting young people, for assessing their special needs and for devising a programme to cover those needs. This usually deals with the personal implications of their handicap, personal hygiene, health care, sex education, the use of leisure time and the management of money. The programme is carried out in the evenings and at weekends. It was however clearly very difficult to persuade the young people to take the final step to independent living; conditions in the hostel were so good that they had little incentive to move on. While we concur with the view that wherever possible young people with disabilities or significant difficulties should live independently, it is clear that a great deal of encouragement needs to be given to those who can do so to move from "half-way houses" of this kind into independent units.

10.113 The final stage along the road to independent living in this country is that of independent units where handicapped people can live entirely on their own, with access to outside services such as personal counselling. Units are specifically designed or adapted for those with physical disabilities. New units in the public sector may take the form of either "mobility housing", which is built to the normal standards but provides wheelchair access, or "wheelchair housing", which is special housing designed to suit the needs of disabled people. Alternatively, adaptations may be made to public or private housing (for example to eliminate steps and widen doorways for wheelchairs, or to lower the level of kitchen worktops and switches) and moveable aids and equipment such as hoists installed. At present both housing authorities and social services departments have powers and functions in relation to adaptations to both public and private housing. This overlap is clearly unsatisfactory, resulting as it does in a wide variation between areas in the division of responsibility, and we welcome the proposal by the Department of the Environment in a consultation paper issued jointly with the Department of Health and Social Security and the Welsh Office to rationalise responsibilities for adaptations for people with disabilities.[21] The accommodation needs of handicapped students in further and higher education require particular consideration and can be met only by close consultation between housing authorities and associations on the one hand and local education authorities, social services departments and educational establishments on the other, as well as between the Departments of Education and Science, Environment, and Health and Social Security and the Welsh Office at national level in England and Wales. Similarly, close consultation of this kind is required in Scotland.

10.114 We believe that more consideration needs also to be given to ways of enabling young people currently described as mentally handicapped to live as independently as possible. In Denmark it seems to be fairly generally accepted that, wherever possible, handicapped young people should leave home at 18 and that adequate facilities should be provided to enable them to do so. Mentally handicapped young people are encouraged to live independently in flats with the support of a home visitor, usually a social worker, who visits about twice a week. We hope that this practice will be adopted wherever possible in this country.

Equipment and aids

10.115 A wide range of aids and equipment is now available for use by severely physically handicapped people in their daily activities. If they are to derive maximum benefit from these aids, however, three conditions need to be fulfilled. First, since information about aids is not widespread, centres are needed where the handicapped young people and their parents, as well as the professionals advising them, can go and see the range of equipment and aids available and be fully informed by qualified and experienced staff about their suitability. At present there is only a small number of such centres but they are increasing and in some areas facilities are provided for a selection of equipment

---

[21] Department of the Environment, Department of Health and Social Security and Welsh Office Joint Consultation Paper, Adaptations to housing for people who are physically handicapped (February 1976).

to be viewed.* We should like to see this service expanded and a series of specially designed centres set up to act as regional centres. We recognise the importance of the contribution made by occupational therapists to the centres already in existence and regard them as key members of the staff. In Scotland the Scottish Information Service for the Disabled, run by the Scottish Council on Disability, plays an important part in providing information on all types of aids.

10.116 A second condition which needs to be fulfilled if handicapped people are to derive maximum benefit from the available aids is that resources should be provided to cover not only their purchase but also their installation and maintenance. At present, apart from aids provided nationally by the Department of Health and Social Security, the Scottish Home and Health Department and the Welsh Office, the main statutory sources of supply are health and social services authorities. The powers and duties of these authorities cover an over-lapping range of aids, and in practice whether or not a particular aid is provided in any one area may depend on the willingness and ability of either authority to provide the necessary funds, though social services authorities have the power to make a charge. The local variations in the current arrangements seem to us inequitable and unsatisfactory. In Scotland guidance on the division of re-sponsibility between health boards and local authorities for the provision of aids and equipment for disabled people living at home, as well as for adaptations to their homes, was issued in 1976.[22] Difficulties remain, however, over co-ordination of the provision of aids to individuals and there is a need for joint funding arrangements. *We recommend that a more rational and uniform approach to the provision of aids for handicapped people throughout the country should be developed.*

10.117 Thirdly, handicapped people and, where necessary, their relatives and others who care for or work with them must be fully trained in the use of the appropriate aids and must be confident that they can handle them. The hearing aid is the most obvious example of equipment which is often not properly used because it is not fully understood. Hoists, too, are sometimes not properly used

---

* The existing aids centres which are known to the Department of Health and Social Security or the Scottish Home and Health Department are listed below. The first seven hold joint meetings on a bi-annual basis.
1. The Aids Centre, Disabled Living Foundation, London W14
2. Disabled Living Centre, Birmingham
3. Merseyside Aids Centre, Liverpool
4. Newcastle-upon-Tyne Council for the Disabled Aids Centre, Newcastle
5. The National Demonstration Centre, Wakefield (Limited display, but professional staff available)
6. The Medical Aid Department, British Red Cross Society, Leicester (Shortly moving into new premises; it will probably be comprehensive when fully established)
7. The Spastics Society Visiting Aids Centre, London W1 (Limited range of aids on view, but this is supplemented by cards showing other aids)
8. The Spastics Society Family Services and Assessment Centre, London W1 (Children's aids only)
9. CHS Help for the Disabled, Manchester
10. Aids Centre, Industrial Education Unit, Psychiatric Rehabilitation Association, London N17 (in process of being set up)
11. Aids and Adaptations Centre, Croydon Area (in process of being set up)
12. Aids Display Centre, Lothian Region (in process of being set up)
13. Mobile Aids Centre, Scotland.

[22] Social Work Services Group Circular SW19/1976 and NHS Memorandum No 1976 (GEN)90.

because the handicapped person lacks confidence in handling them. Training in the use of aids should begin as soon as possible, since the younger the person is when he starts such training, the more likely he is to gain the necessary confidence. We believe that the main reason why some aids are not properly used, however, is that they are not very efficient. More imagination is required in the design of aids and equipment and we are pleased to know that in Scotland the Committee on Orthotics, Prosthetics and Aids for the Disabled (a committee of an advisory group of the Scottish Health Services Planning Council) assesses research applications in this field and advises the Secretary of State on the allocation of funds for research. *We recommend that more research should be carried out into the design of aids and equipment for handicapped people.*

10.118 In addition to aids provided by social services departments and area health authorities, aids can be made available by local education authorities where they are required for educational purposes. In practice, however, it is not always easy to distinguish those needs which arise from an educational course from those arising from day-to-day living. Nor is there any clear definition of the responsibilities of local education authorities and social services departments towards the provision of aids for handicapped students. Section 2 (1) (c) of the Chronically Sick and Disabled Persons Act 1970 states that a local authority in its social services capacity must provide (where it is satisfied that a need exists) "assistance to that person in taking advantage of educational facilities available to him" without, however, specifying the kind and extent of assistance that may be given. As a result of this lack of definition of the responsibilities of local education authorities and social services departments, in some areas the education authority on one side and the social services department on the other has each been reluctant to accept responsibility. We consider that a clear statement is needed from central government on the relative responsibilities of social services departments and local education authorities for the provision of help to handicapped students. This would not, however, preclude the continuing need for active co-operation at a local level between all the various authorities and bodies who might be concerned with provision for handicapped students. In particular, medical views will often be influential in determining which service should more appropriately assume responsibility for the provision of such assistance.

10.119 We welcome the initiative taken by the Rehabilitation and Engineering Movement Advisory Panels (REMAP) of the British Council for Rehabilitation of the Disabled in harnessing the voluntary services of engineers, doctors, therapists and others to the design and production of equipment needed by handicapped people to enable them to lead as normal a life as possible. There are 60 panels throughout the country and a small central organisation which provides information and advice. Individual problems are considered by the panels and designs for equipment passed on, often to a college of technology, to be made up. The cost of the materials is met by the manufacturer of the aid or by the agency which called attention to the problem, for example the social services department, or sometimes by the handicapped person himself. Examples of equipment provided in this way are a handle which opens a car door in one movement, an adjustable framework for a severely paralysed invalid and a variety of hoist installations and lifts.

10.120 Aids for employment may be issued to disabled people by the Employ-ment Service Agency. These include adapted furniture, tools or machines, special writing and reading aids, and dictation and tape recording devices. We would expect ESA officers to take account of the views of the employer and of the various professionals concerned in meeting the person's needs in determining whether to issue an aid and, if so, what sort of aid.

Mobility

10.121 Mobility is the passport today to a full and independent life for the young. Probably no age group travels more than young people aged 16-21. We regard adequate and appropriate provision for every handicapped young person throughout the country as absolutely vital if handicapped people are to lead a full social life and have easy access to facilities for further education, training, employment, recreation and entertainment.

10.122 In July 1976 the government decided to phase out provision of the invalid tricycle. We recognise that the tricycle was unsafe, unreliable and subject to mechanical failure, and we see the mobility allowance as a step forward in so far as it extends the help to severely handicapped young people equally, whether or not they can drive. We regard it as essential, however, that the level of the allowance should be such that it offers a realistic alternative to a vehicle service. We therefore welcome the announcement by the Secretary of State for Social Services on 6 December 1977 that from July 1978 the allowance will be increased from its present level of £7 to £10 per week and that there will be an annual uprating starting in November 1979. However many cases of hardship remain. We are pleased to learn of the Secretary of State for Social Services' decision to introduce new regulations governing eligibility for mobility allow-ance in order to ensure that those who have a physical condition which results in a mental disability and, as a consequence, are unable to walk, receive an allowance. We hope that this will lead to a significant extension of the scheme.

10.123 We welcome too the formation of the Motability organisation, which was announced by the Secretary of State for Social Services in his statement on 6 December 1977, to ensure that disabled people, both drivers and passengers, who want to use their mobility allowance to obtain a vehicle will get maximum value for their money in doing so. In particular, we are pleased to know that it aims to enable disabled people to have the personal use of a car by means of a leasing scheme and to negotiate discounts and other special arrangements for purchasing a car. Already the Royal Association for Disability and Rehabilita-tion has negotiated a number of discounts and other concessions for recipients of mobility allowances and Motability aims to extend these. We hope that the proposed leasing scheme will be established without delay and that further financial arrangements will be negotiated to enable those receiving mobility allowances to purchase cars on as favourable terms as possible.

10.124 The phasing out of the invalid tricycle has worked to the disadvantage of one group of people, namely 16-year olds. The minimum age for driving a car is, of course, 17 but 16-year olds may be licensed to drive invalid carriages.

Those who were eligible for help under the old scheme and received an invalid tricycle were thus able to drive from the age of 16. We attach very great import-ance to the need for adequate help for handicapped young people aged 16-19 who are attending establishments of further education and who need to be mobile in order to take a full part in the corporate life of their college. We recognise that some may receive help from their local education authorities with arrangements for or the costs of travelling. It is essential, however, that the students should be able to make arrangements which are sufficiently flexible to allow them to take part in recreational as well as academic activities. Moreover, we share the concern expressed by the National Advisory Council on Employ-ment of Disabled People about the problems faced by some young people who would previously have been entitled to a tricycle to enable them to travel to and from work and who have difficulty in meeting the cost of their transport. *We therefore recommend that further consideration should be given urgently to the needs of young people with disabilities for help with mobility, particularly those aged 16-17 and those who need special help to travel to and from work.*

Facilities for recreational and social activities

10.125 There is a danger that physically handicapped school leavers will be isolated by lack of mobility and by the loss of friends they had at school. We believe that handicapped young people should be given opportunities when they want them to share in community activities, as well as opportunities to enjoy the exclusive use of community facilities on occasions. The youth service has an important part to play in encouraging them to participate and providing social and recreational services for them. There are several examples in the evidence submitted to us of activities which are of great benefit to handicapped people, including drama, music and riding. We also welcome such initiatives as the Physically Handicapped – Able-Bodied Clubs which bring together handicapped and non-handicapped young people.

Community care

10.126 There will be some severely handicapped young people who are very heavily dependent on their parents and able to progress only a little way along the road to independence. Nevertheless, it is of crucial importance that they should be encouraged to achieve what measure of independence they can. We have heard with interest, for example, of the activities of the Linkage Community Trust in Lincolnshire, which aims to establish a network of friendship and sup-port among neighbours, workmates and employers, in order to help the families of severely handicapped young people to care for their children and to encourage them to move progressively towards greater independence. We recognise the anxiety which parents of such young people feel when the continuous support provided by special schools comes to an end, and there is no assurance that their children will be properly cared for if they themselves become unable to look after them. We have seen some small communities run by voluntary bodies which provide high standards of care and the complete assurance that the parents of very severely handicapped children seek for the future.

VI SIGNIFICANT LIVING WITHOUT WORK

10.127 The problem of how to accept the prospect of a life without employment and how to prepare for it faces people with a variety of disabilities, including some who are of the highest intelligence but very severely physically handicapped. Working gives people a sense of purpose and competence; it makes them feel needed; it provides a change of environment, so that they may appreciate their home better when they return to it in the evening; it brings them in contact with a different range of people from their friends at home and may lead to fresh interests and social activities; and it provides them with a framework for the day and a routine which may help to develop self-discipline. All these features may be absent from the lives of young people with severe disabilities who cannot go to work. The most important of them are the first two – the need for a sense of purpose and effectiveness and the need to feel wanted by other people or by the community at large. We believe that the secret of significant living without work may well lie in handicapped people doing far more to support each other, and also in giving some support to people who are lonely and vulnerable though not handicapped.

10.128 At present, few handicapped people are engaged in helping other handicapped people apart from blind people who are Blind Persons Resettlement Officers; they are trained to act as liaison officers with industry, finding suitable vacancies for blind people and then training and introducing them to new posts. With the shortage of social and welfare workers of all kinds that is likely to continue, there should be plenty of scope for handicapped people to give encouragement and unpaid help to others who are facing problems which they themselves have had to face and overcome. In addition, there should be scope for handicapped people to do things for others who are in great need of practical help (for example those who are paralysed), even if they have not been through the same experiences. An imaginative scheme has been introduced in some places for linking six to eight people with severe disabilities by telephone to form a group capable of maintaining contact with its own members and promoting their well-being.

10.129 As we have already mentioned, there are many lonely and vulnerable people who are not handicapped. We have heard of special schools for the physically handicapped where older pupils go out to help with community projects like "meals on wheels" or decorate the homes of old people. There is similarly a variety of projects with which handicapped young people who have left school could help.

10.130 Distance teaching, to which we referred in paragraph 10.46, may be a useful way in which opportunities for continued education can be made available to young people with severe disabilities who cannot work. They also need opportunity to take part in satisfying forms of recreation, including sporting activities. Part of the enjoyment of many recreations lies in the anticipation and in the struggle to master a skill even though this may never be achieved to one's satisfaction. It is important that young people with severe disabilities should be able to share these pleasures so far as is possible.

CONCLUSION

10.131 Provision for young people with special needs over 16 is a complex field. It embraces not only education but also training, employment and a wide range of supporting services. Moreover, within this field there is a very considerable diversity of special needs according to the nature and degree of the disabilities of the young people concerned. We believe that provision for these young people must be a recognised and well-respected part of all arrangements for continued education. These arrangements, like those for training, must be designed to develop the young people's potential to the full, while employers must be helped to recognise their potential and give them opportunity to fulfil it.

CHAPTER 11: SOME CURRICULAR CONSIDERATIONS

INTRODUCTION

11.1 While considering evidence and during visits to many schools we were impressed by the concern shown for individual pupils with special educational needs. But we also became aware that the quality of the education offered to them is in some respects less satisfactory. In particular, it is sometimes limited in scope and in the challenge which it presents to individuals. In this chapter we set out our views on aspects of the curriculum in special education, including its development and dissemination.

11.2 The secular curriculum in maintained schools is controlled by the local education authorities and the schools themselves. The Schools Council, which works closely with authorities and teachers, is the major agency for curriculum development and dissemination in England and Wales while in Scotland the Consultative Committee on the Curriculum is responsible for curricular guidance. Our concern in this chapter is with principles and with issues of special importance. We consider the particular needs of children and young people with different disabilities without, however, entering into a detailed discussion of specific areas of the curriculum. A considerable amount of detailed work is currently being undertaken on the curriculum for children with different disabilities which we regard as very important, and we suggest ways in which it should be promoted in future.

11.3 As we explained in Chapter 1, we believe that the general aims of education are the same for all children. We also recognise that the activities and experiences planned for children in a school are necessarily a selection from a much wider range of possibilities. The curriculum which evolves from this selection and planning implies certain more precise objectives which a school sets for its pupils. The term "curriculum" as we use it here therefore means those school activities which set out to achieve specific aims within the general aims of education as a whole. Thus the curriculum should take into account the particular needs of children with different disabilities and learning problems. A curriculum for deaf children, for example, should pay particular attention to language and communication while one for blind children should emphasise the interpretation of the environment through touch and sound.

11.4 Children normally learn through unplanned interaction with their surroundings as well as through being taught in school and many children with special needs are no exception. Some children, however, are impeded by their disability or disorder in the development of social skills and relationships, often of the simplest kind. These children may need to be taught as part of the school's curriculum many things which other children learn naturally. Whether children with special needs are in ordinary or special schools, their development should be regularly reviewed to see if any elements which for other children are self-taught should for them form a deliberate part of the curriculum. Although arrangements in ordinary schools may make some forms of incidental learning easier for children with disabilities or significant difficulties, staff in ordinary, as in special schools, must be alert to the importance of this aspect of education and to the need to take special steps to promote it wherever necessary. Equally, when young people enter further or higher education, attention needs to be paid to ensuring that they have an opportunity to acquire, if they have not already done so, the many skills necessary for successful participation in the activities of a complex educational institution.

I THE NATURE OF THE CURRICULUM

11.5 There are four interrelated elements which contribute to the development of a curriculum. They are: i. setting of objectives; ii. choice of materials and experiences; iii. choice of teaching and learning methods to attain the objectives; and iv. appraisal of the appropriateness of the objectives and the effectiveness of the means of achieving them.

11.6 The first question in planning the curriculum is frequently where to begin. One starting point is the detailed specification of each child's attributes and needs. Another is experience and knowledge of the problems faced by children with different disabilities, at home, in the neighbourhood and as young adults in achieving the maximum degree of independence. In all cases the available premises, resources and staffing will set limits to what is possible.

11.7 The objectives set for a school, class or group must be practicable, related to the particular children to whom they apply, and informed by careful analysis of what is to be learned. When the objectives have been determined it will be necessary to work out the steps by which they are to be reached. Finally there must be a means of judging when objectives have been attained. In selecting objectives every attempt should be made to offer a rich and varied range which covers not only a variety of separate subjects but also a range of goals, including emotional, social, intellectual and physical development. Where children have complex or multiple disabilities difficult decisions will have to be taken in the selection of priorities. However, every attempt should be made to see that the chosen objectives are as near in scope and quality to those of other children of the same age as is practicable, given the nature and degree of the children's disabilities.

11.8 The choice of materials, experiences and teaching and learning methods will be determined by the objectives and by the nature of the children's disabilities. Children who have difficulties with mobility or manipulation may require means of learning different from those appropriate for children with severe learning difficulties. In some fields of special education there is a pre-occupation with the choice of teaching methods which neglects consideration of the objectives or the materials or the experiences which may prepare a child for adult life. In others too little attention is given to appraisal of the planned programme and its effectiveness.

11.9 In Chapter 4 we discussed the importance of regularly reviewing individual progress, and the means of doing so. Such reviews are required for two purposes: for appraisal of the response of individual children to their education; and, taken together, for regular reconsideration of the school's curriculum as a whole. However, the response of individual children is only one element in this reconsideration. Teachers, other professionals, parents, potential employers and other agencies which may subsequently be concerned with the children's care all have a contribution to make to an assessment of the appropriateness and success of the school's work, including its curriculum.

Curriculum development in ordinary schools

11.10 The scope for developing suitable curricula for children with special needs will vary according to where their education takes place. One important factor in determining the success of special educational provision in ordinary schools is the degree to which such schools, particularly secondary schools, can modify their curriculum to accommodate different groups of children with special needs, without detriment to the quality of education offered to other children in the school. There are at least two senses in which modification may be necessary. First, modification of materials may be needed for children with physical or sensory disabilities who may be able to follow an ordinary curriculum provided that special materials are prepared in advance, for example tapes and tactile material for the blind. This requires that lessons are carefully planned and prepared and that materials are selected in good time. Secondly, modification of teaching objectives as well as materials may be needed for other children with a variety of mild or moderate learning problems. They need access to the whole range of the curriculum, not just a limited part of it. For example, there is scope for devising for them modern language courses which include a greater proportion of oral work and less written work and study of grammar. The organisation of the school will also be significant for slow learners, or children with moderate learning difficulties as we have defined them, and the curriculum for mixed ability groups will require particular attention to the selection of aims and materials if these children are to make useful progress. Ordinary schools vary widely in the degree to which they recognise and are able to cater for individual needs within their curriculum and organisation in all the ways described.

11.11 Where units or classes for children with disabilities or significant difficulties are set up in ordinary schools it may be difficult for the units or classes to develop their own distinctive curricula if they are to share activities with ordinary classes. Such activities may have to be planned within the curriculum of the ordinary classes, and in this case it will be particularly important for all the teachers concerned to co-operate closely in the choice of materials and methods. On the one hand the materials and methods in use in ordinary classes will need to be adapted or supplemented for use by children in the units or classes; and, on the other, teachers in the units or classes will need to shape their work in ways that are compatible with the activities in ordinary classes.

Curriculum development in special schools

11.12 The special school, in contrast, does not have quite the same constraints on the development of a curriculum appropriate for the particular children for whom it is intended. For those children whose disabilities are not associated with marked learning problems, it may be the methods and materials which need to be special, while the teaching aims remain the same as for other children. For children with severe learning difficulties, a careful selection of clear and simple goals is required if teaching is to be effective. However if transfer to ordinary schools is to be a possibility for some children, the curriculum must share common ground with that of ordinary schools. Special schools will need to pay particular attention to curriculum development, as we explain more fully below, if they are to become centres of expertise for children with special educational needs as we proposed in Chapter 8.

11.13 The evidence presented to us reflected a widespread belief that many special schools under-estimate their pupils' capabilities. This view was expressed in relation to all levels of ability and disability. Many people also thought that the curriculum was too narrow, in concentrating on reading and numbers and giving insufficient attention to, for example, wider aspects of English and mathematics and to science and environmental and social studies. The importance of the social training provided by special schools was generally recognised but, as one contributor put it, "a good educational programme is just as therapeutic and important to personal development". The development of language was considered to be a major requirement of the curriculum, not only for children with impaired hearing but also for maladjusted children as a means of helping them to understand and express their feelings. It was considered by many to be a first priority for children with moderate and severe learning difficulties. Music, art, drama and physical education were emphasised in evidence as being particularly important for children with special needs, as was education in the forming of relationships with others. For children whose disabilities prevented them from moving about in, or profiting from incidental contact with, their surroundings, the need for well-planned excursions and activities outside schools was also emphasised in evidence. Finally, education in the use of leisure and preparation for adulthood was considered a very important aspect of the special school's curriculum. Some people, according to the evidence, believe that aspects of education such as these are not receiving adequate attention in many schools. Our own experience does not entirely support these views. Although, in the course of our numerous visits to special schools, we found some evidence to substantiate the beliefs expressed, we also saw much evidence to the contrary. We are also aware that during the period of our enquiry there have been changes in many schools, including developments in the scope of the educational programme offered.

11.14 The main problems faced by special schools in developing a satisfactory curriculum are inherent in the fact that their pupils are relatively few in number and may span a wide age range and present many combinations of abilities and disabilities. It is essential that the curriculum should be carefully planned and that everybody in the school should work to agreed ends. The leadership of the headteacher is a vital factor in forging common policies and practices to cover all aspects of the school's work. As part of the process of curriculum development and in order to ensure that the curriculum is understood and effectively followed the headteacher should consult his staff and the other professionals who work with the school, and also parents. We have seen some good examples of such leadership. The need in all schools for careful planning of the curriculum and full consultation on its implementation was emphasised in the Green Paper *Education in Schools: A Consultative Document* published in 1977.[1]

11.15 The school's policies, aims and practices must be clear, since they provide the framework within which individual teachers and other workers can make their contribution, and within which flexible arrangements can be made for individual children. Wherever the quality of special education is high, we have found that two strands have emerged. First, well-defined guidelines for each area of the curriculum have been drawn up, which enable teachers to plan their own work and relate it to that of colleagues and other professionals. Secondly, programmes have been planned for individual children with clearly defined short-term goals within the general plan. We regard these strands as important criteria of effective special education. For, where pupils have learning difficulties, or where special methods are required, all teachers need to develop a continuity and consistency of approach to avoid confusing children. Moreover, teachers often need to work closely with other professionals, such as psychologists and physiotherapists, and to be effective all must work towards agreed goals within an agreed framework. Where programmes for individual children are carefully planned and monitored, it is possible to achieve a degree of flexibility in meeting assessed needs. This can be more difficult in a large regular class in the ordinary school, but may be possible in smaller groups. It should be a feature of the work of special schools and classes, where these are properly staffed.

11.16 Once the school's curriculum has been developed, it must be regularly reviewed. The regular monitoring of individual progress which we have already advocated, together with a systematic canvassing of the views of teachers, other professionals and parents about the work of the school, should afford the means of keeping the curriculum and its implementation under surveillance. This process is vital in order to establish whether objectives are being achieved and materials and methods are effective.

II ASPECTS OF THE CURRICULUM FOR DIFFERENT AGE GROUPS

Educational programmes for children under five
11.17 Early learning is important for all children but it need not always be deliberately planned. Young children with disabilities or significant difficulties, on the other hand, need structured programmes, and the importance of training and education before the age of five cannot be over-estimated. It is therefore necessary to ensure that early education programmes for children not yet attending school are developed in close consultation with schools, particularly those which are acting as resource centres for children with special educational needs. Collaboration between those working with young children below school age and staff in schools is essential if the starting points of a school's curriculum are to be a natural extension of early education programmes.

Transition to adult life
11.18 Within schools all members of staff should be aware of the implications of the curriculum for the future life of their pupils, particularly for their

---

[1] *Education in Schools: A Consultative Document.* Cmnd 6869 (HMSO, 1977).

prospects of employment. The implications are especially important for those with disabilities and difficulties who are receiving special education, and for whom the concluding stages of the curriculum should include significant elements of preparation for the next phase in their life. Sometimes this will require a review of the range of subject options to see that they do not unnecessarily restrict a pupil's qualifications for employment. More commonly it will require a positive approach to helping young people acquire the self-confidence and skill to manage their personal life as independently as possible and to cope with the conditions which they will find in further education or at work.

11.19 If schools are to prepare young people for adulthood as effectively as possible, they will need to accumulate knowledge about the living and working conditions which the pupils are likely to face on leaving school and their opportunities for leisure-time activities. As the Circular issued jointly by the Department of Education and Science and the Welsh Office in 1975 on the discovery and assessment of special needs stressed,[2] it is particularly important for handicapped young people that careers guidance of a high standard should be available in schools and that there should be close co-operation between teachers, careers officers, or their specialist colleagues, and parents on all matters concerning further or higher education and employment, and collaboration with those involved in further education and local industry and commerce. It is equally important that the school should be closely in touch with social and health services, voluntary agencies and the community in which the young person is to live. These links between the school and other bodies and professionals should help to guide the teaching staff in planning the school's curriculum for older pupils.

Further education

11.20 In the last chapter we set out our views on the opportunities which need to be available to young people over the age of 16 with special needs. Many of the considerations applicable to curriculum planning in schools which we have discussed in this chapter are applicable also to establishments of further education. Colleges of further education will need to consider both the modification of ordinary courses and the provision of special courses, either as links between school and college or as bridging courses to prepare young people with special needs for ordinary courses or work. A survey by Her Majesty's Inspectorate during 1976-77 revealed a steady increase in the number of courses available to students with special needs, but at the same time insufficient knowledge on the part of lecturers of the needs of young people with particular disabilities. We return to the subject of training for lecturers in establishments of further education in teaching young people with disabilities or significant difficulties in the following chapter. We recognise that some students will continue to require the facilities of the specialist establishments of further education, at present national colleges, which we recommended in the last chapter should in time become part of the regional pattern of further education for students with special needs. We hope that such establishments will develop

---

[2] DES Circular 2/75, Welsh Office Circular 21/75, The Discovery of Children Requiring Special Education and the Assessment of their Needs (17 March 1975).

as resource centres which offer support for students and lecturers in other colleges as well as special courses for those who cannot follow ordinary ones. We urge that the Further Education Review and Curriculum Development Unit should pay particular attention to the curriculum for students with special needs.

III THE PARTICULAR NEEDS OF CHILDREN WITH DIFFERENT DISABILITIES

11.21 In other chapters in this report and in the previous section of this chapter we have been concerned with general principles which we believe should apply to all children with special needs. It has not been our task to make a study of each of the major areas of disability or disorder, although we have considered each of them in forming our general views and have drawn attention to some of them to illustrate particular points. However, during our work we have identified a number of issues specific to children with different disabilities which we discuss in this section. Some of them directly concern the curriculum; others concern the organisation and other aspects of provision.

11.22 Two general considerations have been brought to our attention which make it essential that the particular needs of children with different disabilities are not too narrowly conceived. Special schools and classes now contain many children who each have a number of special needs, either because they have several handicapping conditions or because of factors such as interrupted schooling as a result of periods of medical or other treatment. This consideration has influenced many of our comments throughout this report and also needs to be borne in mind in curriculum development. The second consideration is that many children with disabilities, particularly those which are severe or complex, have associated emotional problems, especially in adolescence. The incidence of emotional and behavioural difficulties in such groups is high and there are few professionals in the fields of child psychiatry and mental health who have specialist knowledge of the problems associated with handicapping conditions, particularly when communication difficulties exist as part of the condition. We hope that in future health services will give greater attention to this area of work.

Visual disabilities

11.23 Our evidence suggests that the recommendations of the Vernon Committee[3] remain valid and widely acceptable, although some disquiet was expressed at the slow rate at which the recommendations are being implemented. Some organisations for the visually handicapped argued for a much clearer policy of integration, with the whole of special provision being based in units in ordinary schools. It was pointed out in other evidence that visually handicapped children in special schools increasingly have additional disabilities which bear upon their placement. In general, we believe that our views on integration expressed in Chapter 7 are applicable to both the blind and partially sighted, although the educational needs of the two groups should be considered separately.

---

[3] *The Education of the Visually Handicapped.* Report of the Committee of Enquiry appointed by the Secretary of State for Education and Science in October, 1968 (HMSO, 1972).

11.24 A programme of early training and education is particularly important for children with visual disabilities. For this reason we stress the importance of an educational component in multi-professional assessment, particularly for children under five. It is also vital that advisory teachers of the visually handicapped should be readily available in all areas to work with parents and children. They should ensure that the education of children under five years of age in interpreting and responding to their surroundings, and in mobility, is started as soon as possible. Moreover, they should help parents to acquire special skills and to gain confidence in rearing their children, so that the children themselves will grow as confident learners.

11.25 Children who have been ascertained as blind are not necessarily totally so. They, no less than partially sighted children, need to make maximum use of whatever vision they may have. The Schools Council Project on the training of the visual perception of children with impaired vision has been very valuable in showing how limited vision may be assessed and used in teaching.

11.26 Where visually handicapped children are being successfully educated in ordinary schools (and we gave some examples in Chapter 7), they have usually been well prepared as independent learners and have access to good supporting services and special tutoring. Even so they still depend on the curriculum being clearly planned and predictable so that special materials can be prepared. Changes at short notice can place blind children at a severe disadvantage in following normal courses. Morcover, a distinction can be drawn between different school subjects in terms of the difficulties encountered by blind children in studying them. The humanities, for example, can be studied relatively easily given good preparation and adequate resources. Sciences, on the other hand, present. particular difficulties, especially with regard to practical work and studies at an advanced level. There is therefore a danger that the choice of subjects, especially at "O" and "A" level, available to children with severe visual disabilities in ordinary schools may be very restricted. These difficulties should not be under-estimated and it is to be hoped that further progress can be made in solving them. We would urge those concerned with syllabuses and examinations where practical work is involved to take these problems into account, and we note the valuable work that has been carried out in this respect in science at the Royal Blind School in Edinburgh. We would not wish to see courses leading to different certificates for any group of pupils with disabilities but we would support the development of alternative courses suitable for all children which are not heavily based on practical work. Visually handicapped children should not be prevented from taking the same range of courses and the same examinations as other children on account of default in the planning of their practical aspects.

11.27 Children with visual disabilities who are educated in special schools, other than those for the blind and partially sighted, seldom have the services of teachers who have specialised in the education of the blind and partially sighted. We regard it as essential that the services of advisory teachers of the visually handicapped should be regularly available to all special schools with such pupils. For their part special schools for the blind and partially sighted need the services of other advisory teachers wherever they admit children with additional disabilities, particularly learning and behavioural difficulties.

11.28 We are aware that, of those children who may require some form of special educational provision at some time during their school career, a considerable number other than those in special schools or classes for the blind and partially sighted may have visual disabilities. Failure to detect these children or to ensure that prescribed spectacles are worn when necessary may lead to their developing learning problems. The present development of health surveillance procedures for children under five, including improved arrangements for testing visual acuity, should reduce the number of children entering school with undetected visual disabilities and prevent possible early learning difficulties. But continued assessment at intervals is also needed as part of health surveillance, since some conditions requiring correction manifest themselves for the first time during childhood and adolescence. Many children and their parents may be unaware that visual difficulties exist which need correction and not all teachers will know of the learning problems which may result from a failure to wear glasses. Two problems are not uncommon: the first, a failure on the part of parents and children to follow up appointments with opticians; and the second a failure on the part of the children to wear glasses regularly once prescribed. School nurses should ensure that both problems are known to the school and both tackled strenuously so far as home circumstances permit.

11.29 The majority of special schools for the blind and for the partially sighted are non-maintained schools run by voluntary organisations. Many are residential and not all are well situated to serve regional needs. Some evidence submitted to us expressed disappointment at the absence of a national plan for the visually handicapped (a recommendation of the Vernon Committee). It is essential that these schools should in future work within a planned framework of regional and local services. The services themselves should be organised on a regional basis and this should be one of the tasks of the regional conferences for special education whose functions we discuss in Chapter 16.

11.30 The provision of further education and training for the visually handicapped needs reconsidering in the light of our recommendations in the last chapter. In particular, the present national specialist centres will need to provide support and advice for students and teachers in other establishments of further education. The relatively small number of young people with special needs in this field requires that specialist advice is widely available so that opportunities are as extensive and carefully planned as possible.

Hearing disabilities

11.31 The last major enquiry in this field, which was carried out by the Lewis Committee,[4] concerned methods of educating deaf children. That Committee was set up as a result of concern about oral and other methods of instruction, an issue also raised in much of the evidence presented to us. It was frequently linked with concern about the limited levels of language and literacy achieved by many young people in schools for the deaf. The steady increase in units for partially hearing

4 *The Education of Deaf Children:* The possible place of finger spelling and signing (HMSO, 1968).

children in ordinary schools and the placement in them of children with more severe hearing losses but with reasonably well developed language have meant that the population in some special schools for the deaf is both decreasing and coming to consist increasingly of more multiply and heavily handicapped children. All these developments in our view point to the necessity of a single service for hearing impaired children to embrace special schools, units and peripatetic services. Such a service needs to be planned on a regional basis, a further important function of the regional machinery for special education proposed in Chapter 16.

11.32 The need for early diagnosis of impaired hearing is particularly important in order that advice and support for parents can go hand-in-hand with early education programmes. Peripatetic services are not yet available in all areas and there is evidence to suggest that in some localities parents are not treated as partners in their children's education. Peripatetic teachers can effectively support and encourage the activities of parents but it is essential that parents should not feel failures if their child does not progress as rapidly as they hoped. Where parents are unable to carry out early education programmes effectively, peripatetic teachers should assume responsibility and see that regular teaching is carried out. Our evidence suggests that additional training is necessary for teachers of the deaf who are to work with young children under five years of age and their parents, and we return to this in the following chapter.

11.33 The curricular needs of pupils currently termed deaf or partially hearing are different, since the deaf have greater difficulty than the partially hearing in acquiring, and learning through, language. In the education of the deaf there has often been more concern with methods than with the curriculum to be taught. Thus, the report of the Lewis Committee was concerned mainly with methodology and said very little about the curriculum. More recently the Schools Council Project "Language Development for Deaf Children" has produced guidance based on work in schools which should help in the setting of objectives and the selection of materials and methods. The current diversity in methods of teaching is not necessarily an unhealthy state of affairs, but rigid adherence to a single method may be unhelpful. The different needs of individuals should be considered and appropriate methods used. We consider it essential therefore that each school should plan its curriculum carefully to ensure that the material is stimulating for the child and that there is continuity. Schools need to ensure that the approaches of different staff so far as methodology is concerned are consistent and compatible and that teachers are properly trained in the use of any new methods that they intend to adopt. As the Lewis Committee recommended, there is a continuing need for well planned evaluative research into methodology and the teaching of language.

11.34 Units for partially hearing children have been pioneering examples of the organisation of special educational provision in ordinary schools. Many have been successful but problems still remain. It may seem self-evident that children with impaired hearing often have difficulty in learning and in mixing with other children as a result of poor command of speech, limited grasp of language or simply failure to understand or be understood by others. Yet many of these problems are not readily appreciated by teachers in ordinary schools, and the stress on individual children can be very great. Teachers in charge of units and peripatetic teachers need strong support in their efforts to help such children, particularly in creating the conditions in ordinary schools which facilitate their mixing with other children. Children with impaired hearing need to be educated in good acoustic conditions wherever they are taught within the ordinary school and not merely in their own particular base. For them, no less than for their counterparts in special schools, the supply and maintenance of effective equipment, including individual aids, are crucial. More discussion is needed between consultants and teachers about the appropriateness of aids for activities in school. Unless technicians who understand both the equipment and its use are readily available to schools and units, much equipment tends to be both mis-used and under-used.

11.35 We are aware that there are many children in ordinary schools who suffer from temporary and episodic impairments of hearing which may lead to educational difficulties if they occur frequently. Teachers need to be informed about children for whom this is a likely occurrence and where necessary to receive advice and support from specialist teachers of children with impaired hearing. Moreover, the school nurse should, in our view, be particularly attentive to such children and alert teachers to any change in their condition. Teachers in their turn should ensure that the school nurse is informed of these children's educational progress.

11.36 Provision for young people with hearing disabilities in further and higher education is currently receiving attention, for example at the Open University and the City Literary Institute and more recently at the College of St Hild and St Bede, Durham. These efforts, among others, demonstrate both the possibilities and the gaps in provision which exist in large areas of Great Britain. *We recommend that there should be at least one centre in every region to support students in further and higher education who have impaired hearing and to train those who work with them.* Such a centre might be an integral part of a special unit for students with disabilities or significant difficulties such as we recommended in the last chapter should be developed in an establishment of further education in each region.

11.37 Teacher training is considered in detail in the following chapter but there are two aspects relating to the education of the deaf which call for special mention here. The courses leading to qualification as a teacher of the deaf are at present too narrowly conceived and should be broadened to give students a wider view of special education, including an understanding of other disabilities. Secondly, there is need for special elements of additional training in aspects of education for the deaf which the one-year course or its equivalent cannot reasonably encompass. The counselling of parents, peripatetic work, particularly with children under five, and different methods of teaching are all areas where additional courses of training are required.

Physically handicapped children

11.38 Arrangements for young children with physical disabilities involve many different professions and the importance of collaboration between them cannot be over-stressed. In addition to medical and nursing care, other services such as physiotherapy, occupational therapy or speech therapy may be provided for individual children, and social services departments may support their families. Moreover, early education programmes are increasingly recognised as important. Careful planning is necessary to ensure a balanced scheme of activities and treatment which is easily understood by parents and to which they can contribute. This calls for the training of teachers and other professionals in working together in a multi-professional framework.

11.39 Many children with physical disabilities may be educated in ordinary schools if adequately supported. It should be recognised, however, as we stressed in Chapter 3, that there is no simple relationship between the degree of physical impairment and educational handicap. Sometimes very severe learning problems may be experienced by children with comparatively minor physical disabilities, and it is therefore important that the regular support of a specialist teacher knowledgeable about their difficulties should be available wherever necessary. Arrangements for physically handicapped children in ordinary schools demand careful educational planning and may also involve the planning of services provided by area health authorities including nursing, physiotherapy and speech therapy. We return to the provision of these services in Chapter 15. Ancillary helpers in schools need training in how to help children and at the same time to encourage them towards independence. In all these respects the teachers in day-to-day charge of the children need to know what supporting services are available and how best to work with the professionals in those services. The effective use of ancillary helpers should also be covered in in-service training.

11.40 There will be some children with both severe physical disabilities and severe learning difficulties whose needs can be met only by the concentration of both health services, including therapeutic services, and specialised teaching in one setting, and for whom placement in a special school will therefore be essential. Some special schools catering for such children should be designated as resource centres, as we proposed in Chapter 8, to be sources of advice for teachers and others working with physically handicapped children and centres of research. Boarding schools will continue to be needed, not only to cater for those children who cannot be looked after at home, but also to offer a much wider range of recreational and leisure opportunities than is available to severely handicapped children living at home. We hope that more short-term residential provision will be available to help children and young people with severe physical disabilities to develop their independence and to provide necessary relief for their families from the exacting daily task of looking after them.

11.41 When children of any age who have physical disabilities are receiving medical treatment that involves spending a cycle of periods in hospital, at home and at school, their education may lack continuity. Hospital and home teaching services should work closely with children's schools to ensure that education is provided when the children are not in school and that the provision made in the various settings has a unity of purpose and progression.

11.42 Opportunities for further and higher education and training for physically handicapped young people are limited and many more young people could, with adequate preparation and support, benefit from attending colleges of further education. In particular, more opportunities are needed for independent living and independent study closely linked with schools and colleges. These points and many others in this section form part of the conclusions and recommendations of the McCann Committee.[5]

Children with epilepsy

11.43 The great majority of children who have seizures experience them only for brief periods of time, or at very long intervals. Only those who have repeated seizures, or who need continuous anti-convulsants, can justifiably be described as children with epilepsy. Most such children are educated in ordinary schools, but not all are known to their teachers. This may be because society's attitudes to epilepsy make some parents reluctant to pass on or let their doctors pass to the school information which they think might be embarrassing to the children. In other cases the epilepsy may be so well controlled and so much a part of everyday life that parents and children consider it hardly worth mentioning. We consider that every effort should be made to inform staff in schools and colleges about the facts of epilepsy, how it may be controlled by drugs, what the side effects of these drugs may be and how to manage seizures should they occur, in order to create the right attitudes to children with epilepsy. Lack of full knowledge may cause a child's activities to be unduly restricted and if the school does not know about the existence of the condition the child may run unnecessary risks. This is an instance where mutual confidence and understanding between parents, doctors and teachers is particularly important.

11.44 Even where satisfactory control of seizures by anti-convulsants is achieved, many children with epilepsy may have serious problems in concentration and behaviour, which affect their learning. Recent surveys and research[6] have shown that significant numbers of children with epilepsy fall behind in their school work. Their particular difficulties are not always recognised by schools and colleges, and better arrangements for reviewing their progress are needed, as part of the general procedures which we suggested in Chapter 4, if these children are to be helped to develop their potential to the full.

11.45 Some children with epilepsy need to go to special schools either because their seizures are difficult to control or because they have additional or associated disabilities or difficulties, sometimes consequent on adverse social conditions, which make unreasonable demands on their families and on ordinary schools. There are at present six special schools for such children and their population, which has changed markedly in recent years, now includes a very high proportion of children with other problems, mainly moderate and severe learning difficulties and behavioural disorders. We think that the functions of these schools should be re-considered. We see an important task for the regional conferences for special education, which we discuss in Chapter 16, in making sure

---

[5] *The Secondary Education of Physically Handicapped Children in Scotland.* Report of the Committee appointed by the Secretary of State for Scotland (HMSO, 1975).

[6] L Holdsworth and K Whitmore, "A study of children with epilepsy attending ordinary schools. I: Their seizure patterns, progress and behaviour in school", *Developmental Medicine and Child Neurology*, 16 (1974), 746-58. A C Hackney and D C Taylor, Education and the epileptic child: A comparison of psychiatric and epileptic patients (Research project based at the Park Hospital for Children, 1975).

that members of advisory teaching services are aware of the needs of children with epilepsy and that they and the schools concerned have available specialist advice on the condition. We consider that there should be at least one residential special school in each region where expertise in the multi professional assessment and approach to the health, care and education of children with epilepsy is developed. It should be of a sufficient size to command adequate medical and nursing support. Such a school would be designated as a regional resource centre under our proposals in Chapter 8.

Children with speech and language disorders

11.46 The special educational needs of this group of children are only slowly becoming recognised and understood. The group includes children whose language development is delayed, those who have severe problems of articulation, those who are dysphasic and those who have other communication difficulties. Although speech therapy services work intensively with many of these children, the development of language and communication should be an important part of the educational programme provided for them. There has been a growth of provision in recent years but no corresponding development of teacher training. We believe that in the immediate future medical officers, speech therapists and teachers should work together more closely to develop appropriate forms both of special education and of teacher training in this field.

Children with specific learning difficulties

11.47 We have received much evidence from dyslexia associations about the needs of children with specific learning difficulties in reading, writing and spelling. The Secretary of State's Advisory Committee's Pamphlet *Children with Specific Reading Difficulties* published in 1972 discusses the issues and we generally concur with its conclusions.[7] There are many reasons for perceptual and learning difficulties in reading, writing and spelling, and careful assessment is required. We hope that our proposals for procedures for assessing children's special needs, involving a formulation of individual need, will be particularly helpful in devising programmes to meet the requirements of this group of children.

11.48 Although there are no agreed criteria for distinguishing those children with severe and long-term difficulties in reading, writing and spelling from others who may require remedial teaching in these areas, there are nevertheless children whose disabilities are marked but whose general ability is at least average and for whom distinctive arrangements are necessary. There has been an increase in clinics and centres both inside and outside the education service to meet their needs and a survey carried out by the Department of Education and Science in 1977 found that three-quarters of local education authorities in England and Wales had reading centres or clinics, or remedial centres, or both. We are of the opinion that further work is necessary to evaluate the effectiveness of the different approaches being followed. In the meantime assessment services and in-service training for teachers should pay greater attention to what is already known and make a more discriminating approach to children with reading, writing and spelling difficulties.

---

[7] *Children with Specific Reading Difficulties*. Report of the Advisory Committee on Handicapped Children (HMSO, 1972).

Children with mild learning difficulties

11.49 Children with mild learning difficulties, as we have described them, are those for whom remedial services and remedial teachers in ordinary schools usually have responsibility at present. We have argued in Chapter 3 that the distinction between remedial and special education can no longer be maintained, and we see these children as forming the largest proportion of all those who, in our view, require special educational provision. Their problems should not be under-estimated. If adequate arrangements are not made for these children when they are young, more severe difficulties in learning, motivation and behaviour may arise as the result of their failure and frustration. It is necessary in all instances to look beyond a lack of progress, for example in reading, to see whether other factors such as minor physical or sensory difficulties are contributing to learning difficulties.

11.50 In many instances children with mild learning difficulties can be helped successfully to follow the normal curriculum and, indeed, we envisage that the majority will be able to manage, with appropriate support, in ordinary classes. But some will continue to have difficulty in mastering complex ideas unless preparation is thorough, explanations are clear and tasks are well defined. Many may require persistent, personal support and encouragement if they are to make progress. The proposals for teacher training which we make in the next chapter will ensure that more teachers are aware of the difficulties in learning that children experience, and are acquainted with the means of overcoming them or at least mitigating their effects.

Children with moderate learning difficulties

11.51 Children with moderate learning difficulties is the term which we propose should be used to describe those children currently described as ESN(M), whose difficulties stem from a variety and combination of causes. These often include mild and multiple physical and sensory disabilities, an impoverished or adverse social or educational background, specific learning difficulties and limited general ability. The children showing these difficulties constitute the largest group of children at present in special schools and a large proportion of children in many ordinary schools for whom special education is needed. Much of our report is concerned with general procedures which it is hoped will prevent moderate learning difficulties from becoming severe handicaps in school and in the community.

11.52 The report of the Schools Council Project "The Curriculum for Slow Learners", which has recently been completed, will reveal a far from satisfactory situation in both ordinary and special schools. Examples of good practice were not common and much work seen was narrowly conceived and poorly planned. More research is needed into the causes of moderate learning difficulties and into the development of curricula, including methods and materials, which will be of most benefit to the children in this field of special education. *We recommend that particular attention should be given to curriculum development for children with moderate learning difficulties and that further research should be carried out into the causes of such difficulties.*

11.53 Provision in ordinary schools for these children normally takes two forms: support in ordinary or special groups by the school's remedial teachers; or units set up by local education authorities as part of their special educational provision. Our recommendations for assessment, improved supporting services and improved training for teachers, set within our wider concept of special education, should in the long run make for better and increased provision for children with moderate learning difficulties in ordinary schools. We have dis-cussed both in Chapter 7 and in earlier paragraphs of this chapter the provision to be made for them. Moreover, the organisation of schools and the allocation of resources within them are key factors in the achievement of satisfactory arrange-ments, whilst these in turn depend upon the extent to which headteachers and their senior colleagues appreciate the children's needs and know how best to meet them.

11.54 We consider that both day and boarding special schools will continue to be needed for children with moderate learning difficulties, although the numbers required may decrease as ordinary schools acquire greater expertise and ex-perience in this field. We envisage that the special schools will provide for child-ren with more complex learning problems combined with other disabilities and emotional and behavioural disorders. Increasing recognition of the complexity of the problems of such children, which are often associated with difficult home circumstances, particularly in the case of children in boarding schools, has implications for the staffing of the schools. Both the numbers and training of teachers, child care staff and ancillary helpers need to be improved as the population of the special schools changes in character. As a matter of urgency, these schools also require increased and regular support from specialist teachers, for example of the hearing impaired, and from psychiatric, medical and social services.

11.55 A notable feature of many special schools for children with moderate learning difficulties has been their programmes of preparation for work and independence. Such programmes, sometimes linked with attendance at a college of further education, have shown the value of continued education between the ages of 16 and 19 years. An increasing number of colleges of further education is developing special courses for young people with moderate learning difficulties and we see this as a valuable development and one which should be more wide-spread.

11.56 As we have already indicated, many of the children whom we describe as having mild or moderate learning difficulties may live in adverse conditions and their educational difficulties are often a result of this. Our proposals for special arrangements to meet their special educational needs, for example support from specialist teachers and small teaching groups, can be seen as measures of compensatory education. At the same time, they have to be seen alongside other measures taken in the neighbourhood and community by other agencies to alleviate social disadvantage.

Children with severe learning difficulties

11.57 Children with severe learning difficulties is our preferred description of those children who are commonly referred to as being mentally handicapped and

220

defined in statutory regulations as severely educationally sub-normal. The majority of these children are at present educated in day special schools or hospital schools, although a few units for them have been set up in ordinary primary and secondary schools. Their education has been developing in scope and purpose in recent years. Publications by the Hester Adrian Research Centre at Manchester University, the Schools Council Project on the education of severely mentally handicapped children and the Department of Education and Science's Education Pamphlet Number 60 *Educating Mentally Handicapped Children* all outline the main issues and suggest guidelines for development, with which we concur in principle. It is now recognised that the tasks and skills to be learned by these children have to be analysed precisely and that the setting of small, clearly defined incremental objectives for individual children is a necessary part of programme planning. We commend current work in curriculum development for them and hope that means may be found to disseminate successful practices more widely.

11.58 Particular attention has been directed more recently to the most profoundly and multiply handicapped children in this group. They require a form of special education which necessitates intimate collaboration between doctors, nurses, teachers, therapists of all kinds and psychologists, so that programmes can be devised which build on the slightest responses elicited from individuals. Hospital schools in particular have a very high proportion of such children. This kind of work is on the frontiers of special education and continues to demand research and development by inter-professional teams.

11.59 Our evidence suggests that many children with severe learning difficulties continue to learn useful skills well beyond the minimum school leaving age. It points to the need for continued education allied to social and vocational training between the ages of 16 and the early twenties. We believe that there should be a specifically educational element in adult training centres and in the last chapter we recommended that it should be provided by the local education authority. It is very desirable that the programmes for young adults in adult training centres and day centres should be separate and different from those for older people. Indeed, we commend this principle to all those services – health, educational and social – which have responsibility for meeting the varied needs of young people with severe disabilities.

Children with emotional and behavioural disorders

11.60 Children with emotional and behavioural disorders have few common distinguishing features. Unlike most other kinds of disability, specific characteristics of maladjustment are not always noticeable until the child has been at school for some time. Such disorders spring from many causes, including difficult home circumstances, adverse temperamental characteristics and brain dysfunction. In many cases the cause may be exceptional and may sometimes be unrecognised. Often, especially in the case of anti-social children, such disorders are accompanied by difficulties in learning. The problems underlying maladjustment may derive from or be influenced by the regime and relationships in schools and many children may simply be reacting to these. A number of research projects is currently being undertaken to investigate contributory factors to maladjustment in schools. Although the small number of children with severe emotional and

221

behavioural disorders can and should be identified as early as possible, it is unlikely that early screening procedures will be very effective in identifying the majority of children who may develop problems of adjustment. The identification of such children is more likely to be improved by increased awareness and sensitivity on the part of teachers, as a result of training and experience, and good arrangements in schools for maintaining contact with individual pupils.

11.61 The education of children with emotional and behavioural disorders and others classified as maladjusted is now receiving more attention. Much early work concentrated on treatment and the fostering of good personal relationships. Although these objectives continue to be of prime importance, they are only part of what is needed. Educational failure is now recognised as a significant factor in maladjustment and the contribution of successful learning to adjustment is more widely recognised. The Schools Council Project on the education of disturbed children has found that for this reason many more special schools and classes are placing greater emphasis on the quality of education that they provide. Areas of conflict between therapeutic and educational objectives are still evident, particularly where the latter are characterised as being formal and academic. However, relationships are often developed within well planned educational activities which are recognised by the individual as both serving his needs and being intrinsically interesting. This is particularly true of arts subjects which, if well taught, may be of great benefit in their own right, as well as being media for therapies. We are of the opinion that special education for maladjusted pupils is not complete unless it affords educational opportunities of quality which subsequently enable them to profit from further education and training on relatively equal terms with their contemporaries.

11.62 In some cases truancy or indiscipline in school is a sign of emotional or behavioural disorders as we have described them. The need to adjust the curriculum to meet the particular requirements of unruly pupils who find school boring and irrelevant was emphasised by the Pack Report on truancy and indiscipline in schools in Scotland.[8] While we see merit in the proposals made in that Report for provision for children excluded from classes in ordinary schools on grounds of indiscipline, we consider that the Report drew too sharp a distinction between such provision and special educational provision. In many cases unruliness in pupils is a symptom of special educational needs which require careful assessment in the ways we have proposed and which need to be met within our framework of special educational provision. In fact, the type of provision proposed for such children in the Pack Report could well be organised within this framework.

11.63 The complexities of the aetiology of emotional and behavioural disorders, the number of different agencies involved in dealing with children with such disorders and the range of present provision require that further attention is given to the development of services and of special educational arrangements. Various research projects are being completed, including those at the Nuffield

---

[8] *Truancy and indiscipline in schools in Scotland.* Report of a Committee of Inquiry appointed by the Secretary of State for Scotland (HMSO, 1977).

Psychiatric Unit of Newcastle University, which may yield useful information. Our limited studies lead us to believe that more work is required in assessing the needs of different sub-groups within the maladjusted group and in developing appropriate objectives and methods for their education. We also suggest that a pamphlet of guidance for teachers concerned with maladjusted children on the lines of that published by the Department of Education and Science in 1965[9] but now out of print should be issued.

11.64 Childhood autism is a disorder in which there are fundamental disabilities in both language development and the formation of personal relationships. At this early stage in our understanding of the complex educational needs of children with this disorder it is difficult to know how important it is for such children to be educated separately, though research[10] has established the importance of appropriate educational methods.

IV CURRICULUM DEVELOPMENT AND IMPLEMENTATION

11.65 Curriculum development and its implementation are related processes but each presents distinctive problems. Development may take place in a variety of settings: in a single class or teaching group, in individual schools or groups of local schools, in teachers' centres and workshops, or more generally in colleges, universities and other institutions, with local, regional or national coverage. In special education the nature of curriculum development will be influenced by many factors, but principally by the purposes it seeks to serve. It may be rooted in the programmes of ordinary schools and in such a case will include the adaptation of normal curricula for use by some groups of children with disabilities as well as the development of special curricula for others: or, it may be directed more particularly to the needs of children in special schools, units or classes; even here however it may include elements designed to promote a closer relationship between ordinary and special teaching programmes. Wherever it takes place, curriculum development should arise naturally from the work of schools and should involve the active participation of practising teachers.

11.66 The implementation of curriculum development is likewise a very varied process. It may be comparatively straightforward, as for example when a group of teachers in a local centre have been pursuing a particular theme or topic arising from their current work, and are ready to apply the results to their own teaching. At the other extreme the effective dissemination of a major national curriculum development project may call for extensive organisation and effort. Whatever the scale or complexity of the development, however, the aim of implementation is always the same – the mediation to schools of successful curriculum practices, and thereby the improvement of the teaching programmes for classes, groups and individuals.

11.67 In England and Wales since the 1960s the Schools Council and other foundations have undertaken projects in almost every area of the ordinary school

---

[9] *The Education of Maladjusted Children.* Department of Education and Science Education Pamphlet No 47 (HMSO, 1965).

[10] M Rutter and L Bartak, "Special educational treatment of autistic children: A comparative study – II. Follow-up findings and implications for services", *Journal of Child Psychology and Psychiatry*, 14 (1973), 241-70.

curriculum. Teachers in ordinary schools have been closely involved in this development work but, although the results have influenced the work of some ordinary schools, most special schools have been isolated from these initiatives. Projects such as those concerned with language development, mathematics, science and the humanities could enrich the work of special schools. Such projects may need to be modified, either by putting the material in a form in which it can be used by, for example, the blind, or by making a special selection of materials, for example for children with moderate learning difficulties. The Schools Council has been able to carry out only a very limited amount of work in modifying materials and has not made any special arrangements to disseminate and implement completed projects within special education.

11.68 In Scotland there is no body like the Schools Council. The Consultative Committee on the Curriculum is appointed by the Secretary of State to advise him on all aspects of the curriculum through its Curriculum Development Service. It is responsible for curricular guidance and for the production of materials in a wide range of subjects. As in England and Wales, special schools in Scotland have not been greatly influenced by these national developments. Initiatives at a local level are taken by groups of teachers and advisers of the education authority working with colleagues from colleges of education and universities and through this collaboration some valuable curricular materials have been produced for special schools. In many instances these developments are financed in the initial stages through research grants from the Scottish Education Department. *We strongly recommend that resources should be made available to the Schools Council, the Consultative Committee on the Curriculum and to local teachers' centres so that curriculum projects can be translated into forms useful to special schools, units and classes.*

11.69 Curriculum development specifically for groups of children with particular needs presents many problems. Not all children with the same disability can profit from the same programme and the number of children in some groups is small. Material for even smaller groups who may be Welsh or Gaelic speaking also presents problems. There is evidence that curriculum materials for these groups take time to develop and are not attractive as commercial products to educational publishers. *We recommend that funds should be allocated to subsidise the production of curriculum materials for particular small groups of children whose special needs are not commonly met by the normal process of curriculum development.*

11.70 In England and Wales the Schools Council has taken useful initiatives in curriculum developments for special groups, many of which are mentioned in the previous section. However, the funds allocated to projects have not always allowed for the dissemination of the outcomes and the development of training for teachers in new approaches once the project is complete. Although the implementation of new developments is necessarily a matter of collaboration between the Council and the local education authorities and training agencies, we think that all projects should be funded to allow members of their staff to work for 6–12 months after completion with teachers in resource centres to ensure that new methods and materials are as widely known as possible. In Chapter 8 we discussed the future of some special schools as resource centres

224

and we see the dissemination of curriculum developments as one of their important functions. There are, therefore, in our view two immediate needs: the setting up of further projects concerned with the curriculum for particular small groups and the dissemination of current special education projects to schools. *We recommend that a special section of the Schools Council should be formed and given separate resources to carry out these tasks.* We return to this in Chapter 18 where we also propose the establishment of a Special Education Research Group, with which the special section of the Schools Council would need to have close links. We are pleased to note that the Consultative Committee on the Curriculum in Scotland has adopted as one of its priorities consideration of the curricular needs of pupils requiring special education. We hope that arrangements similar to those recommended in connection with the Schools Council will be introduced in Scotland and that in the interests of economy and shared knowledge they will be co-ordinated so far as possible with those in England and Wales.

CONCLUSION

11.71 However effective the central initiatives proposed in this chapter are, the quality of special education will ultimately depend on the headteachers and teachers concerned. Their commitment to curriculum development is crucial if special education is to be of high quality. It is evident from our enquiries that the skills and knowledge required to develop the curriculum in special education are thinly spread. Accordingly we turn in the next chapter to the provision of opportunities through in-service training for the acquisition of such skills and in Chapter 13 to the organisation of advice and support for all teachers.

CHAPTER 12: TEACHER EDUCATION AND TRAINING

INTRODUCTION

12.1 Our broader concept of special education and the provisions of Section 10 of the Education Act 1976 will make extensive demands on teachers and our proposals in this chapter for increasing their knowledge of special educational needs are therefore of the utmost importance. It is imperative that every teacher should appreciate that up to one child in five is likely to require some form of special educational help at some time during his school career and that this may be provided not only in separate schools or classes but also, with suitable support, in the regular classes of ordinary schools. The procedures which we have proposed for identifying, assessing and meeting the needs of children who require special educational provision will demand insight on the part of all teachers into the special needs which many children have. They must also be aware of the importance of working closely with parents and with other professionals and non-professionals concerned with helping those children who have special needs. The positive attitudes required of teachers in recognising and securing help for children with special educational needs, and the necessary skills, must be acquired in the course of training. In this chapter we consider the developments necessary in teacher training if this is to be brought about.

12.2 It is also vital that those teachers who have a defined responsibility for children with special educational needs should have considerable expertise in special education. This will be true whether the teachers concerned are in charge of a resource centre or other supporting base within an ordinary school, in charge of a designated special class or unit, members of the staff of a special school, or peripatetic teachers. In this chapter we consider the additional training that these teachers will require, and we make proposals for a pattern of in-service training that will enable them to extend and deepen their specialised knowledge. Our proposals are directed towards improving the quality of the education provided for children with special educational needs and enhancing the status of the teachers who specialise in meeting these needs – aims which are interdependent and should be recognised as such.

12.3 The first four sections of this chapter are concerned with the training of teachers for work in schools or, in the case of children under statutory school age, in the home or in other settings such as nursery schools or classes, day nurseries or playgroups. The fifth section considers the training of teachers in the further education sector. The sixth discusses the admission of people with disabilities to teacher training courses and their subsequent employment as teachers, and the final section emphasises the need for a career structure for teachers specialising in the teaching of children or young people with special educational needs.

1 INITIAL TEACHER TRAINING

A special education element

12.4 Since the large majority of children who are likely to require special educational provision will manifest their difficulties for the first time in school they will have to be identified there. Close and continuous observation of all children by their teachers is therefore essential and for this to be effective teachers must be equipped to notice signs of special need. Moreover, having noticed such signs in a child, they must appreciate the importance of early assessment of his needs and must know when and where to refer for special help. We believe that this knowledge and appreciation should be taught to all teachers in the course of initial teacher training and during their induction into their first teaching post. In-service training will be vital if teachers are to help effectively in recognising the children who have special educational needs and in making suitable provision for them; but the groundwork should be laid in initial training.

12.5 Courses of initial teacher training already include instruction in teaching methods and forms of classroom organisation to promote effective learning. It will be increasingly important in future that this should cover the variety of learning and behavioural problems which are likely to be found in many classes. A recent survey in Scotland of the views of newly qualified teachers who had completed the primary diploma course revealed that many felt insufficiently prepared for teaching children with a range of needs: 58 % felt inadequately prepared for teaching slow learners and 6 % said the topic had not been dealt with; 28 % felt inadequately prepared for teaching handicapped children and 61 % said the topic had not been dealt with.[1] We have no reason to think that a similar survey in England and Wales would produce significantly different results. We suggest that in future courses should give more attention to the organisation and management of different learning activities by means of which the disparate educational needs of individual children may be met within the unity of the ordinary class. Moreover, teachers should be helped to understand the wide variety of reasons why individual children behave in a disruptive manner, for example tensions in the family, school or community or the frustrations of a highly gifted child whose abilities are insufficiently recognised and developed.

12.6 Initial teacher training courses already include elements in educational psychology and child development which normally devote some attention to children's individual differences in the main areas of development – physical, intellectual, emotional and social. The evidence we have received and our own observations, however, indicate that in some courses the teaching of child development is too theoretical and limited in scope. *We recommend that the teaching of child development should always take account of different patterns and rates of individual development, particularly as they affect learning, and should include the effects of common disabilities and other factors which influence development.*

12.7 The teaching of child development, orientated in the way that we have proposed, will provide a basis for promoting among teachers awareness of their part in recognising children with special needs and of the importance of taking

---

[1] J Nisbet, D Shanks and J Darling, "A survey of teachers' opinions on the primary diploma course in Scotland", *Scottish Educational Studies*, 9, 2 (November, 1977).

steps to see that such needs are met, first and foremost by seeking skilled help. A large number of contributors to our evidence proposed that an element should be included in all initial teacher training which would promote this awareness and afford a basic knowledge of special education services. We entirely support this idea and *recommend that an element, which we shall from now on describe as a "special education element", should be included in all courses of initial teacher training, including those leading to a postgraduate certificate in education. We further recommend that it should be taught within the general context of child development.* Its aims should be as follows:

(i) to develop an awareness that all school teachers, whatever the age group of their pupils or level of their work, are likely to be concerned with helping some children who have special educational needs;

(ii) to enable teachers to recognise early signs of possible special educational need;

(iii) to give teachers knowledge of the part which they can play in the assessment of a child's educational needs and in the execution of any special measures prescribed;

(iv) to give teachers knowledge of what special education is like, together with knowledge of the range of various forms of special educational provision and of specialist advisory services;

(v) to provide some acquaintance with special schools, classes and units;

(vi) to give teachers some understanding of how to communicate effectively with parents and an awareness of the importance of appreciating parents' anxieties and encouraging their continued involvement in their child's progress; and

(vii) ABOVE ALL, to give teachers knowledge in general terms of when and where to refer for special help.

12.8 The following skills, understanding and appreciation must be developed if the aims of the special education element are to be achieved:

(i) practical skills in the observation of children, both individually and in groups, to help teachers sharpen their perception of variations in children's learning and behaviour and develop their awareness of variations in children's circumstances (such as their home conditions, which may give rise to difficulties in school);

(ii) appreciation of the educational needs of children with developmental difficulties – physical, sensory, emotional, behavioural or learning – the needs of their parents and the value of the contribution which parents can make to their children's development. It will not be appropriate, nor will there be time, for students to study specific disabilities in any depth within this element of the teacher training course;

(iii) some understanding of the practical steps necessary for meeting a child's special needs, and an ability to adopt the attitudes most suited to dealing with his particular difficulties and to appreciate the need for modification of the school or classroom organisation, the curriculum

228

or teaching techniques. The special education element will not, however, be intended to equip teachers to provide specialist help themselves;

(iv) appreciation of the range of specialist services available to children with special needs and their families and of the advisory services available to teachers. This might best be developed by inviting professionals from the various services to visit the college so that, through discussion, the students can learn about the work of teachers in relation to other professions, the contributions which different specialists can make, the services to expect from them and the kind of questions to put to them; and

(v) awareness of the range of career and professional opportunities in special education, the availability of further qualifications in special education, and the fact that special education offers the teachers engaged in it an intellectual challenge of the highest order.

12.9 Micro-teaching techniques,* videotapes and other audio-visual material will be of value in helping students to acquire skills in observation and gain experience of special education in a systematic way. Such material can also serve to reduce the need for visits to schools, which can be an uneconomical use of time both for students and for the school. Some opportunities for student teachers to visit schools must be provided in order that they may gain direct experience of special education and see competent practitioners at work, but the visits should be carefully organised to ensure that students are well prepared and that the work of the schools is not unnecessarily disrupted. Adequate facilities for observing children without interfering with the class work should be provided in schools wherever possible, and the agreement of the teacher to visitors observing his pupils should always be sought. One-way windows have proved a useful way of enabling visitors to observe a class without disturbing its work.

12.10 It will be argued that it will be difficult to accommodate our proposed special education element within the time-table of existing initial teacher training courses. It is difficult to specify the exact number of hours needed to teach the skills and knowledge to be covered. We contend, however, that if they are taught within the general context of the study of child development, orientated as we have recommended, the additional demands on the time-table should be small. We regard it as essential that they should be explicitly covered in all initial teacher training courses for teachers of all subjects and age ranges, including postgraduate courses, as part of a coherent and well co-ordinated plan drawn up by each college and department of education. Every college will need to have a base for providing this special education element; where the college is also providing options in aspects of special education it may be a separate special education department. We recognise that this recommendation for a special education element will have implications for the content and order of other parts of existing teacher training courses, particularly those leading to the postgraduate certificate in education, which will need to be worked out. In our view,

---

* Techniques which focus on a small segment of a lesson in order to help teachers to improve their teaching skills; for example a teacher may be asked to spend three minutes demonstrating how he would teach a single concept (eg a plural form; a chemical formula) to a group of children. His exposition is videotaped, played back and critically discussed.

however, the need for this element is so great that it should be included in all courses of initial teacher training as soon as possible.

12.11 Our recommendation for a special education element in initial teacher training is addressed to colleges and departments of education and, in addition, to the bodies which validate teacher training courses. *We recommend that those responsible for validating teacher training courses should make the inclusion of a special education element a condition of their approval of all initial teacher training courses.*

12.12 Some 40 years will need to elapse from the time that the proposed special education element is introduced before it can be assumed that all teachers have undertaken such an element in the course of their initial training. It is therefore essential that teachers already in post should have the same opportunity as future entrants to courses of initial teacher training to gain an insight into the special needs which many children have. We regard this as a prerequisite of the progressive integration of more children with disabilities or significant difficulties in ordinary schools. *We therefore recommend that a determined effort should be made to ensure that short in-service courses which cover the same ground as the proposed special education element are provided as a matter of urgency and that the great majority of serving teachers take one of these courses within the next few years.* This proposal, though a novel one, is in our view a necessary corollary of Section 10 of the Education Act 1976 and should be implemented without delay.

12.13 The short in-service courses which we have in mind will comprise about a week's full-time study or its part-time equivalent. Ideally they should be taken full-time but in practice they will need to be organised in a variety of ways. Where they are taken on a part-time basis, however, they should be completed in as short a period as possible. We would urge the Education Departments, in collaboration with Her Majesty's Inspectorate, local education authority representatives, including members of the proposed special education advisory and support service (see the next chapter), the Open University and other academic bodies to take the initiative in devising suitable courses.

12.14 We recognise that our proposal that the great majority of serving teachers should take a short course on special educational needs within the next few years will be expensive. As we explain more fully in Chapter 19, at least 200 additional full-time lecturers or their part-time equivalent would be required if courses were to be provided for the great majority of serving teachers within a period of five years. We firmly believe, however, that such courses are urgently required if special educational provision in ordinary schools is to be both extended and improved.

Special education options

12.15 Options in aspects of special education, for example the education of slow learners, are included in a number of initial teacher training courses. These are offered either as educational or professional studies options or as main subject options. We believe that these should be more widely available and *we recommend that, wherever possible, students should have the opportunity in their initial teacher training to take an option that enables them to pursue their interest in children with special educational needs in more depth than will be possible in the proposed special education element.* Such an option should not, however, be so specialised that it restricts the breadth of the training offered. It should be closely related to and integrated with the rest of the course.

Specialist initial teacher training

12.16 In some countries very specialised initial teacher training in teaching children with different disabilities is offered, which prepares students for teaching only children with such disabilities. No such training is available in England, Wales or Scotland, although initial courses with a significant element directed to preparing newly qualified teachers to work with children currently designated as severely educationally sub-normal are available in 18 colleges or polytechnics in England and Wales. The status and qualification gained by students completing these courses, however, are the same as those of all other newly qualified teachers, and the general elements in the training are sufficient to enable the students to take up initial and subsequent appointments within a range of different kinds of school, ordinary and special. Such courses are not offered in Scotland. Teachers of severely mentally handicapped children in Scotland, like other teachers in special education, train initially as primary or secondary school teachers; the subsequent additional qualification in special education which they are required to obtain is expected to include a specialist module in the teaching of severely mentally handicapped pupils.

12.17 There is also an initial teacher training course at Manchester University's Department of Audiology and Education of the Deaf which specialises in training to teach deaf pupils. This is a four-year degree course combining academic study of audiology with a course of teacher training, and a specialist course for teaching the deaf. Successful completion of the course leads to both qualified teacher status and a recognised qualification for teaching the deaf. The one-year Certificate for Teachers of the Deaf at the same University may be taken either concurrently with a postgraduate certificate in education, or at any time after completion of an initial teacher training course.

12.18 Initial teacher training courses with a significant element directed to work with the mentally handicapped were introduced in England and Wales in 1970 in anticipation of the need to provide special training for teachers of children with severe mental disability, when responsibility for their education was transferred to the education service. Training for teachers of such children had previously been provided through diploma courses run by the Training Council for Teachers of the Mentally Handicapped. The present courses are basic general teacher training courses with a specialist bias. In some colleges, mental handicap is a main course of study, alternative to an academic subject, while in others it is a professional course of study. In most colleges offering the courses, teaching practice begins in ordinary schools and progresses towards specialisation in special schools as the course proceeds. The basic design of the combined studies course at Manchester University which specialises in teaching the deaf is different, in that audiology is studied as an academic subject additional to the teacher training elements.

12.19 There was a difference of opinion among contributors to the evidence submitted to us about the appropriateness of initial teacher training for immediate employment with children with disabilities and, among those who supported specialist initial teacher training courses, about how specific in their aims such courses should be. So far as the present courses for work with children currently designated as severely educationally sub-normal are concerned, it was argued on the one hand that the training should be more specific and place greater emphasis on the needs of severely and multiply handicapped children; and on the other, that the courses should be broader and more general, rather than being confined to one area of disability.

12.20 As a general principle we believe that it would be undesirable to afford opportunities for specialisation in special education in initial teacher training to such a degree that teachers completing their training were qualified to teach only children who required special educational provision. Moreover, we hold that a teacher can benefit very considerably from a period of wider teaching experience, normally in an ordinary school, before he begins to specialise in the teaching of children with special educational needs. We recognise, however, that general courses with a specialist bias such as those for teachers of severely educationally sub-normal children are helpful in enabling students with a high level of commitment to teaching a particular group of children to start to specialise straightaway. Moreover, these courses have been a means of attracting candidates of good intellectual and professional ability to work with severely handicapped children.

12.21 Knowledge of teaching children who, in our terminology, have severe learning difficulties and whose intellectual functioning is well below that of children with other disabilities is still in its infancy. The present initial training courses which specialise in the teaching of such children have helped to create a body of suitably qualified teaching staff and we would not wish to suggest that they should be discontinued. On the other hand, we consider that no new courses should be established and that continuation of the present courses should not preclude the development of one-year full-time courses or their equivalent which concentrate upon children with severe learning difficulties such as we propose in paragraph 12.41. We envisage that our proposed courses would be taken by teachers already working with children with severe learning difficulties, as well as by other teachers wishing to do so.

12.22 With regard to training for the teaching of deaf and partially hearing children, we recognise that the combined studies course at Manchester University offers some prospective teachers of the deaf the opportunity to study audiology in far greater depth than is at present possible in the one-year post-qualification courses which lead to a recognised qualification as a teacher of the deaf. We consider that, on this account, it should continue but that, as at present, it should be only one of several ways of obtaining a recognised qualification as a teacher of the deaf. Moreover, wherever possible, teachers completing the course should gain experience of teaching children with unimpaired hearing before taking up posts with responsibility for those with hearing disabilities. We consider the provision of one-year full-time courses or their part-time equivalent which specialise in the teaching of deaf and partially hearing children in paragraphs 12.42–45.

12.23 We believe that specialist training in the teaching of children with other kinds of disability should be carried out through one-year full-time courses or their equivalent and that the principle of specialist initial teacher training should not be extended. It is most important that candidates admitted to the initial training courses with a specialist element in the teaching of children currently described as severely educationally sub-normal should be emotionally mature and have at least some acquaintance with severely handicapped children. Moreover, wherever possible, opportunities should be available for students on such courses to transfer to ordinary courses of initial teacher training if they so wish. There should be a close inter-relationship between different elements of the course, and the specialist element should be directed to children whose learning difficulties are severe and who may have multiple disabilities. Opportunities should be provided for students to learn about the contributions of other professionals to meeting the needs of such children. *We recommend that the training provided through the existing initial teacher training courses directed to work with children currently described as severely educationally sub-normal should be closely monitored by Her Majesty's Inspectorate and its effectiveness in preparing teachers to work with such children evaluated.*

II A RECOGNISED QUALIFICATION FOR TEACHERS WITH RESPONSIBILITY FOR CHILDREN WITH SPECIAL EDUCATIONAL NEEDS

12.24 All teachers in special schools in England and Wales are, with certain exceptions, required under the Handicapped Pupils and Special Schools Regulations 1959, as amended, to have qualified teacher status. Teachers of blind, deaf or partially hearing pupils (except those engaged exclusively in teaching craft, domestic or trade subjects) in special schools are further required to have a recognised qualification in teaching such pupils and must obtain such a qualification within three years of taking up a post. Teachers of classes or units for the partially hearing in ordinary schools are required to have obtained a recognised qualification in teaching the deaf before taking up a post. Teachers of classes or units for children who are blind in addition to being deaf or partially hearing (whether in a school for the blind or in one for the deaf or partially hearing) must have, or obtain within three years, a recognised qualification in teaching the blind or deaf. In practice, about 57% of teachers in special schools for the blind, 67% of teachers in special schools for the deaf and 74% in special schools for the partially hearing (maintained and non-maintained) in England and Wales in January 1977 had such a qualification. Of the rest, some were teachers of craft, domestic or trade subjects and were not therefore required to have the qualification; the majority, however, were either taking in-service training or awaiting secondment to a full-time course. The requirement of an additional recognised qualification does not apply to teachers of children with other types of disability; and the proportion of teachers in all special schools in England and Wales in 1977 who had an additional qualification in the teaching of handicapped children was about 22%.[2]

---

[2] Department of Education and Science statistics.

12.25 In Scotland the Schools (Scotland) Code 1956 (as amended) requires that all teachers employed wholly or mainly in teaching deaf, partially deaf or mentally handicapped pupils should hold a special qualification. Teachers employed wholly or mainly in teaching blind, partially sighted or physically handicapped pupils whose initial teaching qualification is in primary education must also hold a special qualification. It has not yet been possible, however, to implement these requirements and at present the proportion of teachers in special schools in Scotland who have a special qualification is about 50 %.[3]

12.26 There was wide support from contributors to the evidence submitted to us for the view that all teachers specialising in the teaching of children with special educational needs should undertake additional training leading to a special qualification. A proposal to this effect was put forward in 1954 by the National Advisory Council on the Training and Supply of Teachers, who recommended that all teachers of handicapped pupils in special schools should be required to undergo special training and to obtain a special qualification as a teacher of handicapped children, and considered it desirable that a proportion of teachers in ordinary schools should have similar training. The Council recognised, however, that its recommendation could not be implemented until adequate training facilities were available and until a considerable proportion of teachers of handicapped children had undergone special training.[4]

12.27 In principle we believe that all teachers with defined responsibilities for children with special educational needs, wherever they are receiving education, should have an additional qualification in special education. We envisage that these would include teachers in charge of a resource centre or other supporting base in an ordinary school, teachers in charge of a designated special class or unit, members of staff of a special school, teachers in community homes with education on the premises and peripatetic teachers of children with special needs. A number of recognised qualifications is therefore needed, including not only the existing ones for teaching the blind, deaf or partially hearing but also some specific to other disabilities and others of a more general kind. *We therefore recommend that there should be a range of recognised qualifications in special education, to be obtained at the end of a one-year full-time course or its equivalent.*

12.28 The Burnham Primary and Secondary Salaries Document contains provisions for the award of extra payment to teachers who have obtained special qualifications in teaching the blind, deaf or partially hearing or other specified qualifications in the education of handicapped children, and to those who have satisfactorily completed certain one-year courses for teachers of handicapped children. Holders of some of the special qualifications within the terms of the document are allowed to receive a salary increment above the maximum of the scale provided that they are teaching in special schools or classes. *We recommend that the list of qualifications which at present entitle a qualified teacher to obtain extra payment under the terms of the Burnham Salaries Document should be extended to cover all recognised qualifications in special education in the range we have proposed.* In view of the intrinsic value of the training and the fact that

---

[3] Scottish Education Department statistics.

[4] *Training and Supply of Teachers of Handicapped Pupils.* Fourth Report of the National Advisory Council on the Training and Supply of Teachers (HMSO, 1954).

the teaching skills acquired during the training would be applicable to a considerable proportion of schoolchildren (up to one in five at some time during their school career), we regard it as important that the extra payment for a recognised qualification in special education should be made whether or not the qualification appears to be directly relevant to the teacher's current post. Moreover, in order that there should be a sufficient financial incentive to teachers to obtain the qualification *we recommend that this extra payment for a recognised qualification in special education should continue to be made after a teacher reaches the maximum of his salary scale, whether he is teaching in an ordinary or a special school.*

12.29 At present teachers in special schools in England and Wales receive an extra allowance. Teachers taking full-time charge of special classes of partially hearing or partially sighted children in ordinary schools are also entitled to the extra allowance, while teachers of classes of other pupils with disabilities may receive it at the discretion of the local education authority. We recognise that this extra allowance may have been useful as a way of attracting teachers into special schools and special classes at a time of teacher shortage; but it should not be needed on these grounds in the foreseeable future. We believe that teachers in special schools and classes should be entitled to extra payment in respect not of where they teach but of any recognised qualifications in special education which they hold. *We therefore recommend that, from a date to be announced well in advance, the extra allowance payable to teachers in special schools and special classes in England and Wales should be abolished.* The salaries of teachers already in post in special schools and special classes should, of course, be safeguarded for a specified period, to be determined by negotiation. We are not in this proposing any change in the weighting given for posts of responsibility in special schools.

12.30 In Scotland all teachers in special schools or classes are paid on the salary scale for secondary teachers with incremental credits, irrespective of whether their qualification is for primary or secondary teaching or of the age of the pupils they teach. Further, teachers of maladjusted children receive an additional allowance. Teachers who hold a special qualification to teach handicapped children receive a qualification payment while they are teaching in a special school or class. *We recommend that the present arrangements for enhanced salaries for teachers in special schools and special classes in Scotland should be discontinued from a date to be announced well in advance and that an increased qualification payment should be made to a teacher who holds a recognised qualification in special education, whether he is teaching in an ordinary or a special school.*

12.31 While a significant financial incentive will, we hope, prove a strong encouragement to teachers with responsibility for children with special educational needs to obtain a recognised qualification, a statutory requirement which is strictly enforced will be the only way of ensuring that ALL teachers with such responsibility have an additional qualification. The immediate introduction of such a requirement, however, would create a demand for courses which the present training facilities in England and Wales would be unable to meet. (The present facilities in Scotland, however, would be able to meet the demand in that country.) Moreover, the introduction of the requirement would lead to a very considerable increase in the demand by teachers for secondment with pay in order to obtain the qualification. *We therefore recommend that training facilities and local education authority support for teachers to take in-service courses should be so increased that possession of an additional recognised qualification can be made a requirement on all teachers with a defined responsibility for children with special educational needs as soon as possible.* It should be borne in mind that setting a date for the introduction of this requirement will in itself stimulate the development of courses and encourage teachers to undertake them. We consider the content and the organisation of the courses in paragraphs 12.37-50.

12.32 We envisage that teachers taking up a post involving specific responsibility for the teaching of children with special educational needs would be required to obtain an additional recognised qualification within a period of three years. We suggest that teachers already in post when the requirement is introduced, however, should be given a longer period of time in which to obtain the qualification. Moreover, a period of satisfactory experience in a teaching post with responsibility for children with special educational needs might be allowed to count towards fulfilment of the requirement so long as the teacher concerned completed some part of the additional training required for other teachers. This would be for negotiation between the Department of Education and Science, the Scottish Education Department, local education authorities and teachers' unions.

12.33 We believe that in the immediate future the present statutory requirement on teachers of children with certain kinds of disability to obtain an additional recognised qualification should be extended in three ways. First, the exception of teachers of craft, domestic or trade subjects from the requirement on other teachers of blind, deaf or partially hearing pupils in special schools in England and Wales to obtain an additional qualification seems to reflect an outdated view of the place of those subjects in education. Moreover, growing numbers of teachers of these subjects are acquiring an additional qualification. *We therefore recommend that the exception of teachers of craft, domestic or trade subjects from the present requirement on other teachers of blind, deaf or partially hearing pupils in England and Wales to have an additional recognised qualification should be removed as soon as possible.* Secondly, given the increasing move towards educating children with disabilities in ordinary schools, we consider that teachers of blind or deaf pupils in ordinary schools should be no less well qualified than those in special schools. The numbers of such pupils in ordinary schools are at present few but may be expected to increase in future. *We therefore recommend that the present requirement on teachers of blind or deaf pupils in special schools to have an additional recognised qualification should be extended to teachers of blind or deaf pupils in special classes or units.*

12.34 Thirdly, we fully support the recommendation of the Report on the Education of the Visually Handicapped (the "Vernon Report"),[5] which was accepted by the then Secretary of State for Education and Science in June 1974, that teachers (other than existing teachers of the partially sighted) who wish to specialise in teaching the partially sighted should be required to obtain further teaching qualifications through a full or part-time course. We hope that this will

---

[5] *The Education of the Visually Handicapped.* Report of the Committee of Enquiry appointed by the Secretary of State for Education and Science in October, 1968 (HMSO, 1972).

be implemented forthwith and *we therefore recommend that a requirement should be imposed on teachers of the partially sighted in special schools and special classes and units, like teachers of the partially hearing, to obtain an additional recognised qualification.* We consider below in paragraphs 12.42-45 the particular training needs of teachers of children with visual or hearing disabilities.

III IN-SERVICE TRAINING

12.35 Our proposals envisage three types of in-service course: first, short courses on special educational needs to be taken by the great majority of serving teachers within the next four years; secondly, one-year full-time courses or their part-time equivalent leading to a recognised qualification in special education; and thirdly, other, mainly short, courses on the teaching of children with special educational needs. We have already stressed in paragraphs 12.12-14 the urgency of the need for the first type of course and the desirability of its being organised wherever possible on a full-time basis. In the rest of this section we consider the content and organisation of the second and third types of course. It is important that these should be developed as part of a coherent pattern if their range is to be as comprehensive as possible and, at the same time, duplication is to be avoided. We indicate below what this pattern should be.

12.36 There are certain areas of special education which, as some of the contributors to our evidence pointed out, deserve much more attention in in-service training than they currently receive, namely working with parents and non-teaching assistants, peripatetic teaching and work with children below school age who require special help, as well as the principles of guidance and counselling. We believe that they merit consideration in all courses of the second and third types described above. *We therefore recommend that all in-service courses designed for teachers specialising in the teaching of children with special educational needs should include consideration of these areas.* The extent to which they can be covered will depend on the length and level of the individual course, but it should be possible at least to touch on some aspects of all of them. In addition, there should be separate courses or options in courses devoted to these topics. These should include courses for teachers with responsibility for children with special needs in nursery schools and classes and in diagnostic and assessment units. There is scope for the development of courses at different levels in guiding and helping parents or young people, ranging from a short course in the basic principles and skills to a one-year full-time course or its equivalent which would offer opportunity to specialise in different areas, for example the giving of advice to parents of very young children with disabilities or significant difficulties or the counselling of adolescents with special needs. Such courses, which might lead to a further qualification, might well be organised on an inter-professional basis, and we make proposals for the development of these and other inter-professional courses in Chapter 16.

One-year full-time courses or their equivalent leading to the proposed qualification in special education

12.37 If, as we have proposed, all teachers with responsibility for teaching children with special educational needs are to be encouraged and, as soon as it is practicable, required to have an additional recognised qualification, a wide range of courses leading to the qualification will need to be available. These will be one-year full-time courses or their part-time equivalent. In principle, we believe that full-time training is preferable to training carried out on a part-time basis because of the opportunity it offers for more sustained study. In practice, however, part-time training is often likely to be more practicable. This would not preclude the inclusion of a full-time element or an element of day release in some courses. We regard it as essential, however, that part-time courses should be monitored to ensure that so far as possible they are equivalent to full-time courses. We recognise that an expansion of in-service training on this scale implies additional expenditure and we consider this in Chapter 19.

12.38 We foresee that some teachers will wish to undertake a course leading to the additional recognised qualification in special education immediately after their initial teacher training course. Most teachers have a great deal to gain by doing some teaching after their initial training, and before undertaking further training in special education. Indeed, we note that in Scotland, where teachers have to complete a two-year probationary period before entering a course leading to a special qualification in the teaching of handicapped children, at least one of their probationary years must be spent in an ordinary school. However, we would not wish to rule out entirely the option of taking a course leading to the recognised qualification in special education immediately after completion of initial teacher training and we hope that local education authorities will be willing to make grants to teachers who wish to obtain the recognised qualification through this route.

Content of the courses

12.39 We consider that some of the courses leading to the proposed qualification in special education should cover a range of different types of disability in a fairly general way and that others should afford opportunity to specialise in the teaching of children with particular disabilities. Given, however, the overlap of many handicapping conditions and the frequency of multiple handicap, it is important that there should be a general component common to all courses. *We recommend that all courses leading to the recognised qualification should include a general component, which would aim to give teachers knowledge of the characteristics and signs of different types of disability and to equip them with a basic core of teaching skills appropriate to the teaching of children with a range of special educational needs.*

12.40 There is at present a number of one-year in-service courses for teachers of children variously described as backward children, slow learners and children in need of remedial education. The scope of these courses varies, some being predominantly general, others offering the opportunity for specialisation; and some confusion exists as to their aims and the groups of teachers for whom they are designed. We believe that there is a need for courses leading to the recognised qualification which are clearly defined as predominantly general and which aim to provide a broader, not a specialised, knowledge of different types of special educational need and the teaching methods appropriate to them. They will be likely to cater particularly for teachers with posts in ordinary schools which carry responsibility for children with special needs and for those teachers interested in joining the proposed special education advisory and support service. We envisage that most of the one-year courses mentioned above could serve, with some modification, as general courses leading to the recognised qualification. They will, however, need to be submitted for approval to validating bodies in England and Wales and to the Secretary of State in Scotland, to whom it will fall to judge their acceptability. We think that those teachers who already hold certificates for completing such courses should be regarded for salary purposes as having already obtained a recognised qualification.

12.41 If the academic level and quality of work with children with particular disabilities or disorders is to be improved, it is essential that some courses leading to the recognised qualification should offer teachers the opportunity to concentrate on those areas of disability. In particular, the courses should help teachers to develop the teaching skills and techniques needed in each case, including the means of adapting the curriculum to suit the abilities and disabilities of individual pupils. The different disabilities to be covered by such courses should include visual and hearing disability, physical disability, learning difficulties, emotional and behavioural disorders and speech and language disorders. We regard it as important that the needs of children with moderate learning difficulties, currently designated as ESN(M), should be covered by separate courses rather than be treated as an element of predominantly general courses. The same is obviously true of the needs of children with severe learning difficulties; and even though there are some initial teacher training courses directed to work with such children, one-year full-time courses or their equivalent which focus on their needs are specifically required.

12.42 Courses for teachers of children with visual or hearing disabilities leading to an additional recognised qualification will necessarily be of a very specialised nature. It is important, however, that they should not be too narrowly conceived. While their emphasis should be on training in the development of language, audiology and the teaching of speech in the case of the hearing impaired and in the effective use of any residual vision, teaching through braille and the development of mobility skills in the case of the visually impaired, their scope should embrace other skills such as those required for peripatetic work.

12.43 The inclusion of a general component in courses for teachers of children with visual or hearing disabilities is highly desirable in view of the acquaintance it will give them with developments in the teaching of children with other kinds of disability. Its inclusion in a one-year full-time course or its equivalent will make considerable demands on the time-table, but nevertheless we believe that with careful planning it should be possible to devise a satisfactory course which accommodates a general component. We hope that, wherever possible, courses for teachers of children with visual or hearing disabilities will be provided in the same institutions as special courses in other areas of disability so that teachers in the different fields will have opportunity to take the general component together. This will help to reduce the professional isolation which too often occurs among teachers specialising in the teaching of children with visual or hearing impairments. Moreover, it has to be remembered that children with impaired sight or hearing sometimes have other special needs as well.

12.44 We have some doubts about the effectiveness of the training leading to two of the existing recognised qualifications for the teaching of the blind, deaf or partially hearing, namely the School Teachers' Diploma of the College of Teachers of the Blind and the Teachers' Diploma of the British Association of Teachers of the Deaf (formerly of the National College of Teachers of the Deaf), which are obtained through part-time study. Although these Diplomas have been a valuable means of qualification for many years, it should be recognised that neither College provides instruction itself, or visits the schools in which teachers studying for the qualification are teaching. As a result, the onus for covering the syllabus rests on the candidates themselves and most teachers preparing for one or other of the Diplomas have to depend on the headteacher or other experienced staff of their schools for any training that they receive.

12.45 Some local education authorities have regional arrangements whereby advisory teachers or tutors are available to help and guide teachers studying for one or other of the Diplomas, and to supervise their work. This is a welcome advance but there is still room for considerable improvement in the supervision of the work of teachers studying for either of the Diplomas. To this end, we suggest that the professional bodies concerned – the College of Teachers of the Blind and the British Association of Teachers of the Deaf – should work in conjunction with an external validating body capable of ascertaining that the facilities, staffing and other resources of the schools which are acting as training centres are adequate. It would be advantageous if the training were based on existing centres with expertise in the fields of visual and hearing disabilities. We welcome the proposal which has been made to the Department of Education and Science by Birmingham University with the support of the College of Teachers of the Blind and the National Association for the Education of the Partially Sighted for a two-year part-time diploma course for the training of teachers of the visually handicapped, which would be open to teachers in special schools and units for the blind and partially sighted and would be validated by the University. We hope that this proposal will be supported and that similar schemes will be developed for the part-time training of teachers of the deaf and partially hearing. Like the scheme proposed by Birmingham University, they should be based on a specialist centre and incorporate the use of materials pre-pared in advance and practical supervision in the teachers' own schools by visiting tutors. The tutors might be specialist lecturers from an establishment of further or higher education in the vicinity or, as seems more likely with courses for teachers of the blind or partially sighted, regional-based teachers or tutors, some of whom might be advisory teachers in the special education advisory and support service proposed in the next chapter.

12.46 We see scope for the inclusion in courses leading to the proposed recog-nised qualification of options in aspects of special education for which particular skills and knowledge are required but to which too little attention tends to be paid. These include home teaching, teaching in hospital schools, teaching in community homes with education on the premises, vocational guidance and the organisation of work experience for young people with special needs. A possible option in the teaching of students with special educational needs in further education is considered later in this chapter.

240

12.47 All courses leading to the recognised qualification should contain a significant practical as well as a theoretical element, the two being closely inter-related. The practical element should involve a number of tasks or projects, for example in various aspects of the curriculum.

Organisation and validation

12.48 We have indicated that part-time training is likely to be more feasible than full-time. There is a variety of ways, however, in which courses leading to the recognised qualification might be organised. An approach to some courses based on distance teaching would be desirable, as affording opportunities for teachers who do not live near a teacher training centre to study for the special qualification. We see scope for the development of courses which include an element of distance teaching, for example through an Open University unit, as well as for courses whose theoretical element is handled almost entirely by this method. It would be important, however, that teachers taking such courses should be supervised in their studies.

12.49 If, as we have proposed, successful completion of a one-year full-time course or its equivalent leading to a qualification in special education is to carry with it an extra payment, the course will need to be validated in England and Wales by a university, the Council for National Academic Awards or any other body that would ensure its national recognition. We understand that the Council for National Academic Awards might be interested and willing to consider proposals to set up courses, and we hope that individual colleges of education and establishments with departments of education will submit schemes, on the lines we have proposed, to the Council and other recognised validating bodies. In Scotland proposals for courses will need to be submitted to the Secretary of State. In order to stimulate the development of courses we suggest that the Education Departments should take the initiative in devising prototypes.

12.50 We believe that the Open University could make a very considerable contribution to the development of complete courses leading to the recognised qualification. We suggest that the University should consider developing a course, perhaps including some of the course material already in preparation, for example on the development of language. The practical element could suit-ably be organised by the University's regional tutorial staff, in close collaboration with existing institutions. In view of the opportunities which an Open University course would give to large numbers of teachers *we recommend that the Department of Education and Science should grant-aid the preparation by the Open University of a course leading to the proposed recognised qualification in special education.*

Other courses

12.51 Given our estimate of the incidence of special educational need and the likelihood that most teachers in ordinary schools will be dealing with children who require special educational provision, it is important that a high proportion of in-service courses on the curriculum or subject specialisms should include reference to the needs of such children. Those teachers specialising in the teaching of children with special educational needs will require opportunities to pursue the study of special teaching methods and techniques in increasing depth as well as to refresh their special interests, to explore new subjects and develop new skills, to acquire the managerial as well as the professional skills required for senior posts and to obtain further qualifications. It should be possible for some of these opportunities to be provided within courses of a general nature; but special or extended courses will also be needed. The different kinds of courses that we consider should be provided are described below.

Content of the courses

12.52 Teachers specialising in the teaching of children who need special help, like other teachers, require short courses designed to deepen their knowledge of educational theory, refresh their subject specialism or examine the content of what they teach. They should have access to and join other teachers on in-service courses, for example on curriculum evaluation or record keeping, which are as important to them as to teachers who are less closely concerned with children who require special educational help.

12.53 Such teachers also require advanced short courses which are specifically directed to the special needs of the children with whom they are concerned. For example, teachers of the deaf need to know about supplementary methods of communication and subject specialists teaching academically able blind or deaf children may need to review their teaching methods and up-date their knowledge of the special equipment and other resources required by the pupils. There is also particular call for special courses in the teaching of children who are both blind and deaf. *We therefore recommend that a range of advanced short courses specifically directed to the teaching methods and techniques appropriate to children with different kinds of disability or disorder and involving study in depth of their special educational needs should be provided for teachers who have a professional commitment to teaching such children.* The different levels at which they are offered should be clearly indicated for the benefit of teachers interested in taking them.

12.54 It is important that the needs of headteachers and senior staff for training should not be overlooked. *We recommend that courses should be provided for headteachers and senior staff, whether in special or ordinary schools, in management and administrative skills, including aspects directed to children with special educational needs.* Headteachers and senior staff in special schools and senior staff in special classes attached to ordinary schools have particular need of knowledge of methods of working with members of a wide range of other professions, as well as with representatives of voluntary organisations concerned with meeting the needs of children who require special help. It is essential that training for all headteachers and senior staff should emphasise the importance of working with parents and indicate the ways of doing so.

12.55 No future pattern of in-service training for teachers specialising in the teaching of children with special educational needs would be complete without the provision of opportunities for training and research at a high level. We consider that further advanced courses leading to qualifications in aspects of special education should be provided and opportunities for teachers and other professionals to take higher degrees in this field increased. *We therefore recommend that courses leading to higher degrees in special education should be established in universities and other establishments of higher education.*

Organisation and validation

12.56 The present arrangements for the provision of short courses of in-service training are often confused; some aspects of special education are not covered at all, while courses covering other aspects are duplicated. This confusion stems largely from the diffusion of responsibility for providing in-service courses among a wide range of bodies: local education authorities, establishments of further education, university extra-mural departments and individual bodies have all built up expertise in particular fields. In order that the future development and extension of short course provision should be as coherent as possible *we recommend that local education authorities should review the provision of short courses in their own areas and ensure that a comprehensive range of courses in special education, provided under their own auspices or through other agencies, is available.* It is desirable that these courses should be provided in a variety of institutions, including schools, teachers' centres, colleges of education and establishments of further and higher education, so that they are readily accessible to teachers. The special education advisory and support service proposed in the next chapter will have a central part to play in the organisation of these courses. It will need to work in conjunction with other agencies, in particular voluntary organisations and professional associations in this field, which have made an important contribution to in-service training in special education in the past and may be expected to continue to do so. Some courses may need to be organised on a regional basis, and we consider regional co-ordination of provision below.

12.57 We envisage that some short courses of in-service training might be organised through distance teaching, for example through a course on the lines of that run by the Open University on "The handicapped person in the community". Indeed, we see considerable scope for the involvement of the Open University in the provision of short in-service courses and suggest that the University should consider whether parts of existing initial degree courses might be used for this purpose and the extent to which new short courses will be needed. There might also be scope for an approach similar to that which some of us observed in Holland, where additional training for special education is organised part-time at local centres on the basis of a model course devised centrally. Some of the training might be school-based and carried out under the supervision of teachers with additional training and experience in special education, either members of the school's staff or teachers in nearby special schools designated under our proposals as resource centres. In some cases training might be organised full-time during the school holidays.

12.58 Some short courses might be presented as modules, the accumulation of which could lead to a further qualification. Such courses would need to be validated by a university, the Council for National Academic Awards or other national body in England and Wales or in Scotland approved by the Secretary of State if the qualification were to be nationally recognised.

12.59 Some senior appointments in special education will need to be made in establishments of higher education if courses leading to higher degrees in this field are to be established. We return to this in Chapter 18. We do not think that research in special education draws sufficiently upon the experience of teachers working in schools, and we see considerable scope for more positive collaboration between establishments of higher education and other bodies which conduct research and the schools so that increasing numbers of teachers participate in projects.

Regional co-ordination of course provision

12.60 In order to ensure that there is an adequate range of courses, that the services of experienced staff are used efficiently, and that there is no wasteful duplication of provision, in-service training must be co-ordinated regionally or, in Scotland, where the regions are the equivalent of local authorities in England and Wales, on an inter-regional basis. In England and Wales the regional co-ordination of arrangements for in-service training has recently been considered by the Working Group on the Management of Higher Education in the Maintained Sector under the chairmanship of the Minister of State for Education and Science, Mr Gordon Oakes.[6] It will be important that any new regional bodies set up as a result of the proposals by the Working Group should collaborate with the regional conferences for special education to secure the co-ordination of arrangements for in-service training in special education. We argue in Chapter 16 that the regional conferences should be strengthened in the interests of more effective deployment of the various services in the region concerned with children and young people with special needs; and to enable them, as part of their functions, to co-ordinate arrangements for in-service training on an inter-professional basis. In Scotland co-ordination at this level is carried out by area co-ordinating committees.

12.61 The need for co-operation between authorities within a region will be particularly important so far as the staffing of courses in special education is concerned. The inclusion in all initial teacher training courses of a special education element and the introduction of options in special education, as well as the development of a pattern of in-service training on the lines proposed including the provision of short courses for all serving teachers on special educational needs, will be possible only if teaching staff with suitable training and practical experience are available in colleges and departments of education. Every college and department of education must ensure that some members of its academic staff have the necessary training and practical experience in the field of special education. They may need to offer posts which carry a sufficiently high grading and status to encourage present staff to undertake additional training and obtain advanced qualifications in special education; or they may need to attract new staff with training and experience in this field. We recognise, however, that not all institutions which offer teacher training courses will be able to cover all aspects of the in-service courses which we have proposed in the teaching of children with special educational needs. *We therefore recommend that the deployment of college staff with training and experience in particular*

---

[6] Report of the Working Group on the Management of Higher Education in the Maintained Sector. Cmnd 7130 (HMSO, 1978).

fields of special education should be considered on a regional (or in Scotland an inter-regional) basis. In addition, it may well be necessary for specialist resources such as audio-visual material and packaged course materials to be shared between different establishments in a region. The development of the joint use of staff and teaching materials by a number of establishments will be facilitated if courses of in-service training in special education are seen as part of a regional network.

12.62 Within any one region of the country there will, under our proposals, be a number of special schools designated as resource centres, including at least one designated as a specialist resource centre for relatively rare or particularly complex disabilities. These schools will have a very important contribution to make to in-service training in the region, and this in two ways. First, they will be expected to act as training bases for some teachers. Secondly, members of their staff, some of whom will also be members of the special education advisory and support service proposed in the next chapter, will be invited to contribute, as visiting lecturers, to courses in colleges and departments of education, both in-service courses and the proposed special education element and options in special education within initial training. We would encourage colleges to draw on members of a range of professions in the education, health and social services, who are concerned with children with special needs, to serve as visiting lecturers. We would also note the opportunities which exist for many colleges and departments of education, following the amalgamation in England and Wales of some colleges of education with other institutions, to draw upon a wide range of expertise among teaching staff in different disciplines in devising options in special education in initial teacher training.

National co-ordination of course provision

12.63 In Scotland in-service training is co-ordinated nationally by the National Commitee for the In-Service Training of Teachers, a representative body set up by the Secretary of State for Scotland. We hope that this body will give particular attention to the co-ordination of in-service training in special education. We see scope in England, Scotland and Wales for the organisation on a national basis of some short residential courses, particularly courses for senior staff in special education and for teachers of children with relatively rare and complex disabilities. These could be organised by the Special Education Staff College proposed in Chapter 18.

IV INDUCTION

12.64 Any teacher taking up for the first time a post with defined responsibility for the teaching of children with special educational needs, whatever the stage of his career, will have particular need of an induction programme which acquaints him with the range of different forms of special educational provision and specialist and advisory services available in the area. Accordingly, *we recommend that local education authorities should organise an induction programme for all teachers taking up for the first time a post with responsibility for children with special educational needs.*

12.65 The particular needs of individual teachers will vary according to their qualifications and experience, the type of school they are entering and the post to which they are appointed. *Induction programmes should therefore be shaped to meet each teacher's individual needs.* Their form, content and duration will depend largely on the individual teacher's background; a teacher experienced in special education may need only a very short programme, whereas one who is relatively inexperienced may need support and guidance over a longer period of time. We envisage that the planning and organisation of induction courses will be carried out by members of the special education advisory and support service proposed in the next chapter.

V FURTHER EDUCATION TEACHING

The existing pattern of training

12.66 There is a wide variety in the qualifications and experience of teaching staff in further education, many of whom are recruited from occupations in industry, commerce and the public service. Unlike their counterparts in schools, they are not required to have completed a course of teacher training and prospective entrants to the profession are often understandably reluctant to undertake a full-time course of initial training on a student's grant, with no guarantee that they will thereafter be successful in obtaining a teaching post. There were 76,403 full-time teachers in further education in England and Wales in 1976, of whom 45% had successfully completed full courses of initial teacher training, whether an ordinary teacher training course at a college or department of education or a one-year full-time or four-term sandwich course specifically for teaching in further education. The last two types of course are available at Bolton College of Education (Technical), Garnet College, London, Huddersfield Polytechnic, Wolverhampton Polytechnic and University College, Cardiff; two-year part-time courses are also offered at the extra-mural centres of these institutions. There are, in addition, shorter part-time courses for teachers in further education, of which the most readily available is that for the City and Guilds of London Institute's Further Education Teacher's Certificate. In Scotland all training for further education teachers is organised at the School of Further Education at Jordanhill College of Education. In-service training for further education teachers in England, Scotland and Wales is available in the form of short courses, conferences, seminars and teachers' workshops and long advanced courses leading to the award of degrees and diplomas. At present the teaching of students who have special needs is covered in very few of these courses, conferences or workshops. We welcome the introduction by the City and Guilds of London Institute of a course for further education teachers designed to provide them with a basic knowledge and appreciation of the background of and the services available to handicapped people and to enable them to identify and analyse the special educational needs of such people. This course, which is currently being offered at five colleges, is designed to comprise at least 75 hours' work in classes and about the same length of private studies elsewhere.

Training for work with students with special needs

12.67 The provision of opportunities for young people with special needs to take courses of further education is increasing and in Chapter 10 we recommended that it should be still further increased. It is therefore important that teachers in this sector should have correspondingly greater opportunity to gain knowledge of the special needs which students may have and of the teaching methods appropriate to meet them. This applies to teachers of courses of further education wherever they are provided, whether in colleges of further education, hospitals, prisons or other institutions. Although our remit does not cover educational provision for adults, our suggestions below should have the effect of improving the quality of the education provided for them as well as benefiting young people with special educational needs.

12.68 The length of the training and degree of specialisation required by individual teachers will depend upon their previous experience and the posts to which they are appointed. We believe that all further education teachers, however, must be helped to develop an awareness of special needs and the ability to recognise and respond to them. They must also learn about the different supporting services available in the area for the young people, their parents and themselves. In order to help them to develop this insight *we recommend that a special education element should be included in all initial training courses for further education teachers, both full and part-time courses, on the lines of that proposed for inclusion in all initial training courses for school teachers but orientated towards the needs of young people over 16 who require special help*. Further, in order to enable teachers already in post and new teachers who do not take a full course of initial training to acquire this knowledge *we recommend that short part-time courses should be provided which cover the same ground as the special education element*. For new teachers without previous training or experience these courses might form part of the systematic induction arrangements recommended in a report of November 1977 by the Sub-Committee on the Training of Teachers for Further Education of the Advisory Committee on the Supply and Training of Teachers.[7]

12.69 It is likely, and highly desirable, that as provision in further education for students with special needs increases, some teachers already experienced in special education in schools will choose to move to further education. The short courses proposed above will be useful to them, particularly if they have been teaching young children, since these courses will be orientated towards the special needs of students over 16. In addition, however, they will need a period of induction to acquaint them with the further education sector.

12.70 Teachers working wholly or mainly in specialist units for students with disabilities or significant difficulties or holding posts with responsibility for students who require special help need specialist training in this field. We believe that further education teachers responsible for students with special needs should, like their counterparts in school, take a one-year full-time course or its equivalent leading to a recognised qualification in special education. *We therefore recommend that a one-year full-time course or its equivalent leading to a recognised qualification should be available to teachers in further education specialising in the teaching of students with special needs and that those who obtain the recognised qualification should receive an additional payment.*

---

[7] Advisory Committee on the Supply and Training of Teachers. The Training of Teachers for Further Education: A report by the Sub-Committee on the Training of Teachers for Further Education (attached to DES Circular 11/77, The Training of Teachers for Further Education (17 November 1977)).

12.71 Teachers of young people with special educational needs will also need access to a range of short courses designed to extend and refresh their knowledge of particular subjects and skills. We envisage that some of the short courses in special education techniques which we have proposed for teachers of schoolchildren will be equally useful to teachers in further education. In addition, *we recommend that short courses should be provided in particular aspects of the teaching of young people and adults with special educational needs.*

Organisation of the provision of courses

12.72 We strongly urge those establishments which offer courses of initial training for teachers in further education and the validating bodies to ensure that a special education element is included in initial teacher training for such teachers as soon as possible. Training establishments will need to develop the capacity to do so; for example by ensuring that some members of their staff have training and experience in work with young people who have special educational needs. We envisage that one or more of these establishments would offer the proposed one-year full-time course or its part-time equivalent leading to a recognised specialist qualification in the teaching of students with special needs. In addition, there would be advantages if such a course were to be offered by one or more of the colleges and departments of education which provide courses leading to the proposed recognised qualification for teachers of schoolchildren; in particular, further education teachers might then be able to join school teachers for a large part of the general component of the course.

12.73 The provision of induction programmes and short courses for further education teachers with responsibility for young people with special needs is likely to call for regional planning. Members of the proposed special education advisory and support services in the region may be expected to have an important contribution to make to their organisation.

12.74 Teachers of further education courses in establishments such as hospitals or prisons, as well as teachers in adult training and day centres, have the same need as teachers in colleges of further education to acquire insight into the special needs which many of their students or trainees may have and, where they wish to specialise in meeting those needs, to undertake further training in this field. Moreover, it is important that they should not work in isolation from their colleagues in further education. *We therefore recommend that steps should be taken to ensure that teachers of young people and adults with special educational needs who teach outside establishments of further education have access to the same range of training courses as their colleagues in further education establishments.*

VI THE ADMISSION OF PEOPLE WITH DISABILITIES TO TEACHER TRAINING COURSES AND THEIR EMPLOYMENT AS TEACHERS

12.75 *We recommend that there should be more opportunities for people with disabilities to become teachers and obtain teaching posts in both special and ordinary schools.* A teacher with, say, a visual, hearing or physical disability may be able to contribute in a very special way to the development of pupils with the same disability by helping them, for example, to improve their self-

248

confidence. Moreover the appointment of teachers with disabilities to the staff of ordinary schools can be a very effective way of promoting more positive and sympathetic attitudes towards handicapped people among children and young people in the schools. It is important that teachers with disabilities should take on full-time duties, as indeed they will almost certainly wish to do. Although they may be unable to carry out certain duties, for example playground super-vision, or teach certain parts of the curriculum, there is likely, particularly in large schools, to be sufficient flexibility in the deployment of the teaching staff for teachers with disabilities to be able to work effectively as full members of the staff, particularly if the concept of team-work among the teaching staff has been developed.

12.76 However desirable it may be, in the last analysis the increased employ-ment of people with disabilities as teachers in schools will be possible only if colleges and departments of education are prepared to accept them for initial teacher training courses. We recognise that there will be some people, for example those who are profoundly deaf, who will be unable to satisfy the requirements of an ordinary teacher training course. We would not wish to advocate the introduction of a teaching certificate with only limited validity, say for teaching children with certain kinds of disability. Instead we hope that the flexibility already inherent in many teacher training courses will be increased to take account of the problems of some students with disabilities.

12.77 The initial responsibility for considering the fitness of a person for teaching in England and Wales falls on the college or department of education which has to take the decision whether or not to accept him for training. Since, however, the responsibility for deciding whether the person, after training, is medically fit for employment as a teacher in schools rests with the Secretary of State for Education and Science there must be close consultation about indivi-dual cases between the employing and college authorities on the one hand and the Department on the other. Candidates with a handicapping condition are sometimes rejected as unfit for teacher training without adequate reference to the notes of guidance on medical fitness issued by the Department of Education and Science.[8] We understand that when the Department's medical adviser is consulted at an early stage fewer candidates with disabilities are automatically regarded as unfit for training or for employment as teachers.

12.78 The guidance issued by the Department of Education and Science to examining medical officers indicates that in their medical reports they should classify candidates for admission to a college or department of education or for employment as teachers "A", "B" or "C". In category "C" are those whose medical condition is such as in the opinion of the medical officer to make them unfit for the teaching profession. Similar arrangements operate in Scotland where it is the General Teaching Council which has to be satisfied that candi-dates are fit to enter teaching, and this Council will not grant registration unless the college medical officer has confirmed that the candidate meets the Council's standard of medical fitness. Students in Scotland are categorised as "fit" or "unfit". The medical assessment is, however, only one factor to be taken into

---

[8] DES Circular 4/75, Medical Fitness of Teachers and of Entrants to Teacher Training (8 April 1975).

account by the college or department of education in deciding whether or not to admit a candidate, and a candidate who is classified in category "C" or, in Scotland, as "unfit" should not be refused admission on that account alone.

12.79 In Scotland a candidate who has been refused entry to a teacher training course on medical or other grounds has a right of appeal under Regulation 5(2) of the Teachers (Education, Training and Registration) (Scotland) Regulations 1967, as amended, to the governing body of the college of education. We believe that a similar procedure for appeal should be introduced in England and Wales. There is no statutory right of appeal in England, Scotland or Wales against the result of the medical examination at the end of the course, which is carried out, usually by the college medical officer, to determine whether the teacher can satisfy the Secretary of State for Education and Science as to his health and physical capacity for teaching, as required under the Schools Regulations 1959, before first employment in a maintained school. *We recommend that, in future, there should be a recognised right of appeal to the appropriate Secretary of State against classification as medically unfit for the teaching profession at the end of a teacher training course and that candidates should be told of this right when notified of their classification.*

12.80 A person's suitability for teaching can also be assessed at the stage of teaching practice, which gives institutions an opportunity to assess whether the student is likely to be a competent teacher. Moreover, the local education authority has an opportunity to assess a newly qualified teacher's competence during his probationary period, which is one year in England and Wales and two years in Scotland. In Scotland final registration is granted to teachers by the General Teaching Council on headteachers' assessment of competence. There is thus a number of different stages which a person with a disability, like any other prospective teacher, has to go through before gaining and continuing in employment as a teacher, each of which should provide an opportunity to assess his competence and suitability as a teacher.

12.81 It is also important that young people with disabilities should have more opportunity for self-assessment of their suitability for teaching and other professions before seeking to undertake the appropriate training. Improved vocational guidance and counselling, as we have recommended in Chapter 10, together with opportunities to gain experience of working conditions in particular occupations, should help them to make more informed and realistic choices of training and employment. Information should be available to those young people with disabilities who wish to enter teacher training or other forms of further or higher education about the special facilities available at different institutions, including not only modifications to premises and specialist equipment but support from advisory teachers, so that they can apply to the institutions best placed to meet their special needs. Detailed information about such facilities should be included in college prospectuses.

VII CAREER STRUCTURE

12.82 Training programmes and career structures for teachers specialising in the teaching of children or young people with special needs are closely interrelated. Unless there are good career prospects, teachers are likely to be reluctant to undertake further training; at the same time the development of training is an important element in the establishment of a good career structure. We firmly hold that specialisation in the teaching of children or young people with special educational needs should be as highly regarded as specialisation in other areas of teaching and should be equally recognised as a qualification for advancement.

12.83 We believe that the recommendations contained in this report will substantially improve the career structure for teachers specialising in the teaching of children with special educational needs. In particular, our recommendations for resource centres or other supporting bases in ordinary schools (in Chapter 7), for the development of a special education advisory and support service (in Chapter 13) and for the establishment of senior academic posts in special education in universities and other establishments of higher education (in Chapter 18) should bring them new opportunities. We are confident that the pattern of training recommended in this chapter will enable teachers to equip themselves to take advantage of these opportunities.

12.84 If the development of further education provision for students with special needs is to be effective, staff of the right quality must be attracted to it. Poor career prospects, however, can deter trained and experienced staff from entering further education to work with students with special needs. We believe that the expansion of opportunities in further education for students with special needs which we have recommended will improve the career prospects of their teachers. We hope that, in making their staffing arrangements, establishments of further education will give due weight to the considerable experience and specialist knowledge required to teach such students. Employment in the special education advisory and support service proposed in the next chapter should also be seen as part of the career structure for further education teachers specialising in this field.

CONCLUSION

12.85 The procedures which we have recommended elsewhere in this report for recognising and meeting the needs of children who require special educational help will be of no avail unless all teachers have an insight into the special needs which many children have and unless teachers with defined responsibilities for such children have the specialist expertise required to meet those needs. The necessary skills and expertise must be acquired through training. Our proposals for the future development of teacher training are therefore central to our report and should be acted on as quickly as possible.

CHAPTER 13: ADVICE AND SUPPORT IN SPECIAL EDUCATION

INTRODUCTION

13.1 Throughout this report we have stressed the importance of adequate support and help for the considerable proportion – up to one in five – of children who may have special educational needs, the majority of whom will be attending ordinary schools. In the last chapter we urged that all teachers should be helped through training to recognise and understand those special needs and that teachers with defined responsibilities for such children should undertake additional training. In addition, it is essential that all teachers should have ready access to advice, support and the expertise of specialist teachers to supplement and complement their own efforts to meet the special needs presented by individual children. A teacher who has a child with a physical disability in his class, for example, may need information about the educational implications of the child's disability; another teacher may be worried in a more general way about the progress of a particular child. In such cases, teachers need to know to whom they can turn for advice and support. In this chapter we consider how the provision of advice and support in special education should be organised to meet the needs of teachers as effectively as possible.

13.2 The evidence we have received strongly supports the view that ordinary schools need better and more comprehensive advice and support if they are to make efficient provision for children with special educational needs. Over 85% of the teachers in ordinary schools who replied to a question about specialist support in the survey of teachers' views conducted for us by the Department of Education and Science[1] claimed that they had received no visits in the past year from an adviser in special education, or from an advisory or peripatetic teacher. Regular, specialist advice will be necessary if teachers are to cater effectively for children with disabilities or significant difficulties who are already in ordinary schools, including those with emotional or behavioural disorders, and for increased numbers of children with disabilities, sometimes severe or complex, who may in future be educated in ordinary schools. We regard the proposals in this chapter for the provision of advice and support as an indispensable condition for effective special educational provision in ordinary schools.

13.3 Much valuable work is already being carried out by advisers in special education, advisory and peripatetic teachers working with children with particular disabilities, and home visiting teachers, working mostly with young children. Moreover, advisers and peripatetic teachers concerned with remedial education are helping many children at present in remedial groups who, in line with our broader concept of special education, should in future be regarded as having special educational needs. However, we have become aware, both from the

---

[1] For details of this survey see Appendix 8.

evidence received, and from our own observations, that the various educational advisory services for children with special educational needs are fragmented. Individual advisory or peripatetic teachers may work directly to different administrative officers, and there is often little contact between those concerned with the various arrangements which may be made for education otherwise than at school. We consider that the provision of advice to schools on children with special educational needs, wherever they are being educated, should be co-ordinated and *we therefore recommend that every local education authority should re-structure and, if necessary, supplement its existing advisory staff and resources to provide effective advice and support to teachers concerned with children with special educational needs through a unified service.* As we explain later in this chapter, the school psychological service, which also has an extremely important advisory function, would remain a separate, though complementary, service.

13.4 We would emphasise before proceeding that we are not recommending that there should spring into existence a new set of people to advise the teacher. We are fully aware of the danger of multiplying "experts", who are removed from the actual teaching of children in the classroom. The support service which we propose would be made up substantially of existing advisers, advisory teachers and other specialist remedial teachers, reinforced by a number of practising teachers, many of whom would spend part of their time in the classroom, or might be seconded to the service for a limited period. More staff will be needed, particularly in areas of the country where elements of our proposed service do not already exist, but, for many local education authorities, the formation of an advisory and support service will entail in the first instance the reorganisation and retraining of existing staff rather than the employment of large numbers of new staff. Moreover, if the school population continues to decrease, and if the number of children in special schools contracts, there should be scope for the redeployment of senior and experienced teachers in special schools as full or part-time members of the advisory and support service.

13.5 We therefore see the advisory and support service as a means of deploying as effectively as possible special education teaching skills and expertise in support of children with special needs, wherever they are being educated; of ensuring that the progress of individual children is regularly reviewed; and of co-ordinating and improving existing advisory services in this field. At the same time the service will be part of a network of other services for children, including health and psychological services. In case it may be thought that our recommendation makes excessive demands for new resources, we stress that the principal function of the proposed service will be the co-ordination of present efforts to help teachers meet the special needs of children. Substantially, therefore, we are proposing the reorganisation of present staff and resources rather than the creation of new demands.

13.6 Although we apply the term "service" to the collective body of people who will be responsible in each local education authority area for providing advice and support to teachers concerned with children with special educational needs, we use the term in a functional rather than an institutional sense. As we explain in paragraph 13.29, any attempt to set out a blue-print for the service would be unrealistic, given the diversity in the character and size of individual authorities. Within the general guidelines offered in this chapter, which are designed to achieve effective co-ordination of advice and support, we accept that each authority must be able to re-structure and, if necessary, supplement its existing advisory staff and resources in the way that it considers most suited to its own circumstances. We are therefore more concerned with the range and quality of help that a local service provides than with the particular organisational form that it takes.

I FUNCTIONS OF THE ADVISORY AND SUPPORT SERVICE

13.7 We have identified the functions of the special education advisory and support service in relation to ordinary and special schools, to the local education authority and to parents. We start by considering its functions in relation to children with special educational needs attending ordinary schools, and to the staff of those schools.

Ordinary schools

13.8 The aims of the advisory and support service in ordinary schools should be two-fold: first to maintain and raise the standards of special education generally; and secondly to help with the teaching of individual children. The two aims clearly interact. The first entails helping teachers to improve the quality of their teaching through the mediation of specialist advice and support; the second requires that members of the service visit schools to work with teachers in helping particular children to master the difficulties, whether of learning or of behaviour, which they have.

13.9 The service should be responsible, as we proposed in the last chapter, for the planning and organisation of induction programmes for teachers taking up for the first time a post with responsibility for children with special educational needs. It should also be prominent in the organisation of short courses of in-service training for teachers, ancillary workers and other members of staff who come into contact with children with special educational needs. We recommended in the last chapter that courses dealing with special needs should be arranged as a matter of urgency for all serving teachers, whatever their main commitment in the school. Moreover, aspects of the education of children with special needs should be included in a high proportion of courses on the curriculum or subject specialisms. In addition to contributing to the courses themselves, members of the service should arrange for other professionals in their area, including specialists of all kinds concerned with children with special needs and teachers in ordinary and special schools, to participate in workshops, discussions and courses.

13.10 We envisage that the advisory and support service will also be a source of information for ordinary schools on local procedures for the assessment of special educational needs and on the help available to meet them. We have already recommended in Chapter 4 that responsibility for monitoring and developing the effectiveness of school-based assessment should rest with the service and that responsibility within the local education authority for the SE Forms procedure, which will be initiated when a child is referred for multi-professional assessment at Stage 4 or 5 of our proposed assessment procedure,

254

should normally be delegated to a member of the service. Advisers in the service will thus be well placed to ensure that ordinary schools are knowledgeable about assessment procedures. Further, they should ensure that special aids are available for those children in ordinary schools who require them and that they are properly serviced.

Special schools

13.11 The functions of the advisory and support service in relation to special schools will be rather different, although they too will include responsibility for the quality of education provided. Senior members of the staff of special schools, particularly those which are designated as resource centres, may themselves be part-time specialist advisory teachers. While staff in special schools will not normally be in need of specialist advice about the requirements of the children for whom they make provision, they may need guidance on aspects of multiple disability which may not be familiar to them. The advisory and support service should provide or point them to it and should also offer them personal support in their work.

13.12 If members of the service are to be able to exploit the expertise available to them from specialist teachers they will need to be conversant with the special schools, units and classes in their area and have some knowledge of other schools in the region which cater for particular types of special educational need. We hope that they will also help to break down the isolation experienced by staff in some special schools by bringing together subject advisers and teachers in ordinary schools on the one hand and teachers in special schools on the other to discuss materials and methods likely to be useful in both kinds of school. The development of some special schools as training bases, which we envisaged in the last chapter, should also help to increase the opportunities for staff in special schools to take courses of in-service training and so further reduce their professional isolation.

The local education authority

13.13 We have already emphasised in previous chapters the need for the local education authority to be informed about the special educational needs of children assessed at one of the school-based stages of our proposed assessment procedure as requiring special educational provision. This will be essential if the authority is to arrange for additional staff or resources to be provided. In practice this information will be collected by members of the special education advisory and support service, who will also be responsible for informing the authority about the quality of special educational provision made in ordinary as well as special schools. Moreover the service should be influential in ensuring that standards in special education are maintained by carrying out such responsibilities as the local education authority assigns to it to inspect as well as to advise on different forms of special educational provision.

13.14 In order to carry out the task of monitoring the development and conduct of school-based assessment, as well as to see that the individual needs of children requiring special educational provision are met and that continuity of support for them is maintained (particularly if they move to a different school), the members of the service will need to work closely with professionals in the health, psychological and social services. Their consultations with colleagues in those services should help them to formulate policies for the development of special educational provision and to offer informed advice to the local education authority on current provision and future needs, including the suitability and planning of premises, and the evaluation and selection of materials, apparatus and equipment for use with children with special needs.

13.15 The ultimate responsibility for providing a child with special education rests with the authority itself, and the administrative procedures must be conducted through the chief education officer's administrative staff. We consider that, in the case of children recorded as requiring special educational provision, no arrangements for placement should be made without members of the advisory service being involved. They should also be consulted about the placement of children with special educational needs in hostels or boarding accommodation for other than educational reasons. Indeed, where the child is in care and it is proposed to place him in an independent school, the placement should be made only with the agreement of both the local education authority and the social services department, as we recommended in Chapter 8. The movement of children with special educational needs in and out of hospital should also, wherever possible, be discussed with members of the service. Such placements have to be made in circumstances in which educational considerations may not be paramount, but all placements have educational repercussions, and it is important that those who place the child should at least be aware of them.

13.16 The advisory and support service should not, however, be responsible for the administrative implementation of decisions about the placement of individual children. The primary consideration in every case must be what course of action is best for the child. The service should therefore be in a position to give independent advice from that standpoint. This does not mean that administrative difficulties can be ignored, for no authority can provide facilities that exactly match the needs of every child. It does however imply that advisers should from their knowledge of the range of special facilities available (both in the area and, more widely, in the region) be free to suggest which of them is best for a particular child, or, if none is suitable, what new or different provision is required.

Parents

13.17 The advisory and support service will be a very important source of help and guidance to parents of children with special educational needs. In the case of some children who are recorded as requiring special educational provision, a member of the service may be the person nominated by the multi-professional team to act as Named Person for the parents, as proposed in Chapters 5 and 9. The service should however be readily accessible to all parents of children with special educational needs who are seeking advice on their children's progress.

13.18 Advisory teachers who specialise in working with young children with special needs will be involved in planning early teaching programmes with parents, and they will have particular need of training in counselling. All advisers, however, should help parents to understand and co-operate in any special programmes drawn up for their children. Moreover, they should be responsible for seeing that parents are generally helped to contribute as effectively as possible to their children's education.

13.19 Where placement in a special school or class is recommended, parents need to be able to visit the school and discuss the recommendation. It will be an important function of the advisers to facilitate visits by parents to special schools and classes and contacts with the staff.

II THE PERSONNEL AND ORGANISATION OF THE SERVICE

13.20 In the following section we identify the different members of the service and their duties. First, there should be special education advisory teachers who will each be responsible for providing advice and support to a small group of ordinary schools. Secondly, there should be peripatetic specialist teachers whose work with particular disabilities may cover a wider geographical area. Thirdly, many authorities will require advisers with responsibility for co-ordinating the work of a group of advisory teachers in a sub-division of the authority's area and the work of peripatetic specialist teachers in a particular field of disability. Fourthly, each local education authority should have a senior adviser in special education responsible for providing services to schools. We consider these different sorts of adviser in turn below.

Advisory teachers

13.21 If the needs of children attending ordinary schools who require special educational provision are to be suitably met and the teachers responsible for them are to be adequately supported, the schools will require ready access to teachers with a greater breadth and depth of knowledge about special education than will normally exist among the school's own staff. We therefore see a need for special education advisory teachers who will be members not of the staff of any one school but of the advisory and support service. Each of these advisory teachers should work in a group of schools. It will usually include one or more secondary schools, which may have their own resource centre or other supporting base for children with special needs, together with their contributory primary schools, which in some cases may have only two or three teachers. The number of schools in the group, however, should be small enough to allow the advisory teacher to spend an appreciable amount of time in each one and gain personal knowledge of the individual children in need of special educational provision.

13.22 The work of the advisory teachers should, as their description implies, be mainly advisory, but they should be concerned also with facilitating the contributions of other services to school-based assessment of special educational needs. We envisage advisory teachers helping teachers in the schools in their area to identify signs of special needs in children and to devise special methods and programmes to meet them. They will also, in particular cases, advise on the need for other professionals to be consulted at Stage 3 of our proposed assessment procedure, for example a doctor, an educational psychologist, a speech therapist or a physiotherapist, a social worker, a careers officer or a peripatetic specialist teacher, say, of the visually handicapped, and will facilitate the participation of these experts in the assessment procedure. It will thus be important that they should work closely with the individual professionals in the various services in their area who may be called upon.

13.23 Another function of the special education advisory teachers will be to help smooth the transition of children with special needs from a primary to a secondary school, or from an ordinary to a special school or vice versa, or from school to an establishment of further education or other institution. Further, they should be readily accessible to parents of children with special needs who wish to discuss their child's education with a professional in the education service other than the headteacher of the school, who will, in most cases, be their Named Person.

13.24 In practice the duties of the advisory teachers will vary according to the size and character of the local authority. Where there are many small schools, which may not have their own resource centre or supporting base, the advisory teachers will have increased responsibilities for work with individual children and it will be particularly important that they should be frequent visitors to the schools and know the children well. The number of special education advisory teachers required may appear to be very large. In practice, however, peripatetic remedial teachers are already employed by some local education authorities on the basis of a ratio of one to 3–4,000 schoolchildren or less and such teachers might, with additional training where necessary, become special education advisory teachers. Thus the staffing implications, at least in some areas, will be less significant than would appear at first sight.

Peripatetic specialist teachers

13.25 Specialist advisory teachers are already familiar to many schools, particularly peripatetic teachers of children with impaired hearing. Teachers may also require help in meeting the educational needs of other children with significant disabilities, including visual impairment, physical disability, speech and language disorders, specific learning difficulties and emotional and behavioural problems. The special education advisory and support service for any local authority should be able to provide peripatetic specialist teachers in such fields when required. For the more common disabilities, most authorities should be able to provide them from within their own service, particularly where special schools are designated and developed as resource centres, as we proposed in Chapter 8. For some of the less common disabilities it will be necessary for local education authorities to draw on a regional service, based on those special schools which, under our proposals in the same chapter, would be developed by groups of authorities as specialist centres. The satisfactory education of some children with more marked disabilities in ordinary schools will be impossible without the regular attention of peripatetic specialist teachers and it will be a task of the senior special education adviser mentioned below to ensure that they are available.

13.26 We stressed in Chapter 5 the contribution which peripatetic teachers can make to the development of young children with special needs, and the support which they can offer to parents. We see a very important place in the advisory and support service for teachers who specialise in work with children whose special needs are discovered in early childhood, and with their parents, and who have close links with nursery schools and other forms of provision for young children. In addition to working with individual children and their families, these teachers should be available to advise staff in playgroups, opportunity groups and day nurseries as well as nursery schools and classes. We suggested in Chapter 5 that they should be attached in most cases to assessment centres. It is vital that all the teachers concerned should be trained to work with young children and that the advisory teachers in the service (see paragraphs 13.21–24) should not be automatically assumed to be competent to deal with children under five years of age.

Advisers with senior responsibilities

13.27 In large authorities there will be a need for advisers in special education with either specialist or general duties who have responsibility for groups of other advisers. Some advisers will be required to take responsibility for co-ordinating the work of special education advisory teachers in one sub-division of the local authority's area and for the development of special educational provision in that area. They may also be responsible for all the peripatetic specialist teachers for one disability in the local education authority, for example those specialising in the education of children with impaired hearing. Given the frequency of multiple disability, we hope that most special education advisers will have a combination of such duties, since narrow specialisation in one disability may limit the quality of advice available to the authority and schools. In addition, there will be a need in each local education authority for a senior adviser in special education who will be in charge of the proposed advisory and support service.

The structure of the service

13.28 The organisation of the service must be a matter for local decision in the light of the circumstances which exist in each local education authority's area. Our proposals regarding its different functions have been made on the assumption that all secondary and middle schools and all large primary schools will have as a full-time member of staff at least one teacher with additional training who can understand and deal with the more common learning and behavioural problems which children present and help other teachers to appreciate the educational implications of the less serious physical and sensory disabilities. We would expect this teacher to have undertaken the one-year or part-time equivalent general course leading to a recognised qualification which we outlined in the previous chapter. We recognise that there are at present some trained remedial teachers who are carrying out these functions successfully, but we believe that many of them should have further training if they are to ensure that effective help is provided for the wide range of needs of up to one in five children who may require special educational provision at some time during their school career.

13.29 We recognise that any attempt to set out a blue-print for the advisory and support service would be unrealistic, since local education authorities vary considerably in character and size; for example, in England and Wales two are responsible for fewer than 25,000 children, while five or six have more than 200,000 children in their areas. Similar variations exist in Scotland. Moreover, some authorities are almost entirely urban while others cover extensive rural areas with a sparse population. Nevertheless one basic principle is clear: the special education advisory and support service must be both a unified service and closely integrated with the local education authority's other educational advisory services. It must not be a series of unconnected individual units each operating in a limited field of special education. Nor should the service as a whole operate in isolation from other advisory services to schools; rather it should be closely co-ordinated with them.

III ADMINISTRATION: THE SERVICE IN A LOCAL AUTHORITY CONTEXT

The local education authority

13.30 Administrative responsibility for special education is delegated by chief education officers in different authorities in a variety of ways. In many authorities there is an education officer responsible for special education who often has additional responsibility for other assorted services including transport and school meals. Sometimes the education officer concerned is responsible only for special schools, and arrangements for remedial services and other provision in ordinary schools are the concern of education officers for primary and secondary education. It follows from our broader concept of special education and our proposal for a co-ordinated advisory and support service that the education officer responsible for special education should have wide terms of reference which embrace special educational provision wherever it is made. *We therefore recommend that every local education authority should have an education officer responsible for all arrangements for children with special educational needs, wherever these needs are being met.* He will naturally need to work very closely with colleagues responsible for primary, secondary and further education.

13.31 The changes in approach and attitude recommended in this report also have implications for the structure of local authority education committees. In some authorities there is, within this structure, a separate special services committee but in many others special education is included within the terms of reference of the schools committee. We recognise that there are disadvantages in having a separate committee for special education; in particular, the risk of its becoming isolated from other sub-committees. However the importance of having a group of elected members who can focus on the special needs of children wherever they are being met cannot be overestimated. *We therefore recommend that every local education authority should have a separate committee or a sub-committee of the schools committee responsible for the provision for children and young people with special educational needs of all ages, that is children under five, children of school age, whether they are in ordinary schools, special schools or other establishments, and young people attending establishments of further education or other institutions. We further recommend that members of this committee or sub-committee should represent the local education authority on the Joint Consultative Committee (or in Scotland the Joint Liaison Committee).*

The school psychological service

13.32 Some local education authorities have tended to regard their school psychological service as providing a special education advisory service. We hold, however, that there is a need for two separate services to carry out two distinct but overlapping areas of work, both of which are vital to effective special education. Our proposed advisory and support service for special education will have a clear responsibility for the quality of special education wherever it takes place and will be concerned with the whole curriculum, the professional development of special education teachers, and the progress of individual children. The school psychological service, for its part, will be primarily involved in work with individual children, including assessing their special needs and making recommendations for individual programmes for them within the curriculum, and in providing support for schools and parents. The work of educational psychologists is discussed more fully in Chapter 14. The services are in many respects complementary but they should not in our view be combined into one service. The senior adviser in special education and the chief educational psychologist should work closely together and both should work to the same administrative officer.

Other services

13.33 The effectiveness of the special education advisory and support service will depend to a large extent upon its ability to build up good relationships with the other services that are involved with children with special educational needs and their parents. Those advisers specialising in work with young children, for example, must have particularly close links with health visitors. All advisers should develop close working relations with members of the health, psychological and social services, and those working with older children should work closely with careers officers and their specialist colleagues in the careers service. In their turn, the members of those services should be aware of the functions of the advisory and support service. The fact that there will be a co-ordinated service with responsibility for providing advice on the special educational needs of children wherever they are receiving education should in itself make communication easier, for communication often breaks down, not because anyone is unwilling to communicate, but because no-one is sure with whom to communicate or where to reach that person. Assessment centres, to which we have proposed that members of the service who specialise in work with young children with special needs should in most cases be attached, can provide an effective point of contact for all those professionals concerned with children with special needs below school age. It should be a prime duty of the members of the advisory and support service to take the initiative in establishing communication between the schools and other services, so that doctors, psychologists, health visitors, social workers, careers officers and other professionals become well known personally in the schools.

13.34 The maintenance of extremely close links between the advisory and support service and other services concerned with children with special educational needs will also be an essential condition for the effectiveness of our proposed assessment procedure. The senior special education adviser should be responsible for informing the chief education officer about the working of multi-professional teams at Stages 4 and 5 of our proposed procedure so that the latter, through his elected members on the appropriate Joint Consultative Committee, can ensure that inter-professional arrangements in the locality continue to be developed and improved.

IV IMPLICATIONS FOR STAFFING AND TRAINING

13.35 At present only about two in every three local education authorities have an adviser in special education, although a number of authorities has developed small but effective teams under the leadership of a senior inspector or adviser. Some training arrangements will be necessary to prepare advisers for senior posts. The arrangements we suggested in the last chapter on teacher training, together with an increase in the number of senior posts in special education in universities and polytechnics, should provide the means of offering the necessary training. The Special Education Staff College will also have an important part in high level training. Moreover, we envisage that members of Her Majesty's Inspectorate concerned with special education will continue their very valuable contribution to the development of expertise amongst advisers through the organisation of conferences and courses.

13.36 We think it important to repeat that we are not proposing the development of an entirely new service. We recognise that in some areas many more advisory teachers will be needed if an effective service is to be provided, but initially the service will be drawn from existing experts in special education, with additional training where necessary. These will include senior teachers in special schools, particularly those designated as resource centres, and peripatetic and other advisory teachers. The single framework that our proposed service provides will enable all those within it to work confidently together to the greater benefit of children and young people with special educational needs.

CONCLUSION

13.37 In this chapter we have outlined our concept of a special education advisory and support service. We consider this to be among the most important developments which will be necessary if up to one in five children are to receive adequate special education when they need it. We recognise that it will not be possible to staff such a service fully in all areas immediately but we see no reason why its structure should not be set up straightaway. Once this has been established, it should be possible, as resources become available, and as the numbers of children in special schools decrease, progressively to build up the service we have in mind over a period of years.

CHAPTER 14: OTHER STAFF EMPLOYED IN THE EDUCATION SERVICE

INTRODUCTION

14.1 The different professions whose members are employed by local education authorities to provide services to teachers, pupils and parents all make an important contribution to services for children with special needs. Our concept of special education has significant implications for their pattern of work, their initial and in-service training and their numbers. In this chapter we examine these implications so far as they concern educational psychologists, careers officers, education welfare officers, nursery nurses, classroom ancillaries and, in Scotland, instructors*. We also comment on those aspects of the work of school counsellors, careers teachers, guidance teachers and home-school liaison teachers which involve the provision of guidance and support for children and young people with special needs, and for their parents.

14.2 The broader view of special education adopted in this report will require an awareness on the part of all the professionals mentioned in this chapter, no less than teachers, that up to one in five children may need special educational provision at some time during their school career. Since all these workers have direct contact with children, they must know how to recognise signs of special needs and must be aware of the range of services available to meet these needs. Moreover, in the light of our recommendations for increased opportunities for early educational provision for young children with special needs and for further education for young people with such needs, they will need to appreciate the importance of continuity of concern from early childhood to early adulthood. Further, the increased and improved arrangements for inter-professional working which we have proposed will call for the development of close relationships between them and teachers and other professionals in local authority and health services. Our recommendations will thus have significant implications for the training of these various professionals, the supply of trained personnel in each field of work and organisational arrangements within each profession. They will also call for some reconsideration of the priorities accorded to different aspects of work within each professional area.

14.3 We deal first with educational psychologists and careers officers, who provide services to all schools as part of their work and who have important concerns in common with the special education advisory and support service outlined in the last chapter. We then turn to those teachers and members of other professions who are concerned with establishing links between home and school. Teaching apart, these various professions are all based outside schools, but each is effective to the extent that its members are known in schools and

---

* References to instructors in this chapter are confined to instructors in special schools for severely mentally handicapped children in Scotland.

work with teachers and pupils as well as with parents. Finally, we consider a different group of workers who are part of the staff of ordinary and special schools and who collaborate with teachers in the day to day care of children with special needs.

I EDUCATIONAL PSYCHOLOGISTS

14.4 The first appointment of a psychologist by a local education authority was made in 1913 when Cyril Burt was appointed by the London County Council. The numbers of educational psychologists have steadily increased over time and at a quickening pace in the last 15 years. Their work and training have been influenced by the Kilbrandon Report in Scotland and by the Summerfield Report in England and Wales.[1] The former contributed to an extension of the functions of educational psychologists in the Education (Scotland) Act 1969. There is no corresponding statutory definition of the functions of educational psychologists in England and Wales but in view of our recommended procedures for assessment and for recording certain children as in need of special educational provision it may be desirable that educational psychologists should, in future, have a statutory status.

14.5 In England and Wales almost all local education authorities employ educational psychologists and many have a well developed school psychological service. In Scotland, where the Education (Scotland) Act 1969 requires every education authority to establish a child guidance service, the local psychological services are also well developed, and educational psychologists are employed by all authorities. The present ratio of psychologists to the school population is on average one to 11,000 in England and Wales and one to 4,000 in Scotland. These averages cover a wide range from a psychologist working single-handed in one English authority to a ratio of one to 2,000 in a Scottish authority.

Demands on educational psychologists

14.6 The Summerfield Report in 1968 recommended a ratio of one educational psychologist to 10,000 schoolchildren. Since then a number of additional demands has been made on educational psychologists in England and Wales. These have arisen from the transfer of responsibility for mentally handicapped children to the education service in 1971, increased provision for children below statutory school age, the reorganisation of secondary education, the raising of the school leaving age in 1972–73, an increased incidence of disturbed and disturbing behaviour in schools and the new procedures for the assessment of children with special needs advocated in Circular 2/75.[2] In the following paragraphs we consider a number of these demands in more detail and identify the further demands which will arise from our recommendations.

14.7 The procedures for the discovery and assessment of special needs outlined in Chapter 4 call for three kinds of contribution by psychologists. First

---

[1] *Children and Young Persons, Scotland.* Report by the Committee appointed by the Secretary of State for Scotland. Cmnd 2306 (HMSO, 1964). *Psychologists in Education Services.* The Report of a Working Party appointed by the Secretary of State for Education and Science: the Summerfield Report (HMSO, 1968).

[2] DES Circular 2/75, Welsh Office Circular 21/75, The Discovery of Children Requiring Special Education and the Assessment of their Needs (17 March 1975).

their specialised knowledge of observation techniques and assessment procedures will be needed to help headteachers and teachers develop school-based assessment at Stages 1 to 3 and to help teachers and other staff who are working with children below statutory school age. Secondly they will generally be involved in the assessment of the special educational needs of individual children at Stage 3 in school or as members of multi-professional teams at Stages 4 and 5. Thirdly our proposals for monitoring whole age groups of children at different stages during their school life will require their professional skills. Involvement in assessment, either directly or indirectly through their work with teachers, will therefore be a continuing and increasing demand on psychologists' time. It will also be the foundation of their many other and varied contributions to local authority services for children and young people with special needs.

14.8 Educational psychologists have been concerned increasingly with children with emotional or behavioural disorders. They now play a central part in the discovery of such children, in helping them and their teachers in schools and in working with individual children out of school. We generally endorse the conclusions reached in Chapter 15 of the Court Report[3] on the services needed for children and adolescents with a marked abnormality of behaviour, emotional development or personal or social relationships, but we regard the term "children with psychiatric disorder", which is used in the Court Report, as less satisfactory than "children with emotional and behavioural disorders" or "maladjusted children". We think it undesirable to draw a sharp distinction between psychiatric disorders and other emotional or behavioural difficulties; further, the term "children with psychiatric disorder" may lead to the conclusion that all such children should be treated by psychiatrists. In our view psychologists, working where necessary with psychiatrists and social workers, should remain foremost in helping teachers to deal with emotional and behavioural problems when they occur in school. We discuss the contribution of psychiatrists in more detail in the next chapter (paragraph 15.25).

14.9 Our recommendations for better and more extensive early education programmes for children under five with special needs will call for increasing help from educational psychologists, particularly in the planning and development of programmes carried out by parents, teachers and others. At a later stage the psychologist's expertise will often be needed in the planning of programmes within the curriculum for pupils who require special educational provision, whether in ordinary or special schools. Further, educational psychologists may be expected to contribute significantly to the provision of continuing and further education for young people over 16 with special needs by working with them and their teachers in schools and colleges, by developing programmes for individual pupils or students and by providing information to careers officers and contributing to vocational guidance for individual young people with special needs.

---

[3] *Fit for the future.* The Report of the Committee on Child Health Services. Cmnd 6684 (HMSO, 1976). The Report concluded that the aim should be to provide a staffing level of at least one child psychiatrist per 35,000 children over the next decade; child guidance clinics and psychiatric hospital services should be recognised as an integrated child and adolescent psychiatry service; greater attention should in future be paid to the provision of psychiatric services for children of pre-school age; there should be a greatly increased provision of residential facilities such as hostels, schools and hospital units.

14.10 We proposed in Chapters 5 and 9 that parents should have a Named Person to whom they can turn for advice on the different services available and for guidance as they follow their child's progress at school. In certain circumstances the educational psychologist may be the most suitable person to act as Named Person for the parents of some children whose special needs are assessed at Stage 4 or 5 and, in the light of that assessment, are recorded as requiring special educational provision.

14.11 We outlined in Chapter 12 a pattern of courses of in-service training for teachers with responsibility for children with special educational needs. Although many of these courses will be primarily in the hands of the proposed special education advisory and support service, their quality will be enhanced by the special expertise which educational psychologists can contribute. This includes an understanding on the part of most educational psychologists of research methodology, which should enable them to appraise and communicate to teachers the results of relevant research and development. We hope that psychologists working in the education service will themselves have time to carry out locally-based research in collaboration with establishments of higher education and with teachers in schools, and we return to this in Chapter 18.

Staffing levels

14.12 The staffing levels of psychological services for children need to be considered in relation both to the functions of the services and to the supporting services which complement and supplement their work. Research being undertaken for the Department of Education and Science[4] and a recent inquiry carried out by the Division of Educational and Child Psychology of the British Psychological Society[5] as well as a report by the Principal Psychologists of Scotland[6] suggest that the additional demands which have been made on educational psychologists in recent years cannot be met by the present establishments in most areas. Both the British Psychological Society and the Association of Educational Psychologists have recommended that staffing levels in England and Wales should be based on a ratio of one educational psychologist to 5,000 children (not confined to pupils in schools). This does not, however, take into account the additional demands which will arise from certain of our own proposals. In Scotland a ratio of one educational psychologist to 3,000 children is generally accepted as a reasonable basis for the development of local services, given the additional demands which have been made in recent years, including those arising from the transfer of responsibility for mentally handicapped children to the education service in 1975, and the statutory duties laid on the child guidance service by the Education (Scotland) Act 1969. These include the psychological examination of children, the giving of advice to parents as to appropriate methods of education and training, in suitable cases the provision of special education for such children in child guidance clinics, and the giving

[4] H J Wright, Evaluation of a School Psychological Service (Research Project started in September 1975 by Hampshire LEA).

[5] "Psychological services for children: DECP Inquiry into psychological services for children in England and Wales – Preliminary summary of findings", Bulletin of the British Psychological Society, 31 (January 1978), 11-15.

[6] Child Guidance Services – The Future. A Report by the Principal Psychologists of Scotland (September 1972).

of advice to a local authority regarding the assessment of the needs of any child for the purposes of any of the provisions of the Social Work (Scotland) Act 1968. In addition, the requirement on education authorities under Section 66 of the Education (Scotland) Act 1969 to keep generally under consideration the cases of children ascertained as requiring special education has important implications for the work load of educational psychologists. Since educational psychologists in Scotland have a number of statutory duties which do not exist in England and Wales, it cannot be assumed that the staffing levels of psychological services for children in Scotland would also be appropriate in England and Wales. At the same time, however, we regard a ratio of one psychologist to 5,000 children as recommended by the British Psychological Society and the Association of Educational Psychologists as the minimum that is likely to be adequate. *We therefore recommend that initial training arrangements for educational psychologists should be increased so as to allow local education authorities in England and Wales to attain a target of at least one psychologist to 5,000 children and young people up to the age of 19.*

The relationship between educational psychologists and advisers in special education

14.13 In the previous chapter we outlined the different contributions of the proposed special education advisory and support service and the psychological service to schools. The former will be concerned with the quality of special education, curriculum development and the professional development of teachers working in special education, and its members may also supply some specialist teaching for children with special needs. The psychological service, for its part, will be primarily concerned with the needs of individual children, and also with providing support for schools and parents to prevent the development of significant learning and behavioural difficulties. Work with children will entail both the assessment of their special educational needs, followed by the formulation of recommendations for individual programmes within the curriculum, and the development of proposals for ways of helping individual children to achieve satisfying personal relationships. We consider that the two services have distinct sets of functions which, although they overlap, need to be carried out by different people. Educational psychologists may wish to become advisers in special education where their training and experience are suitable. However, we are strongly of the opinion that the posts of adviser in special education and educational psychologist should not be combined. As we indicated in the last chapter, the senior adviser in special education and the chief educational psychologist should nevertheless work closely together and both should work to the same administrative officer of the local education authority.

The relationship between educational and clinical psychologists

14.14 Educational psychologists, who have nearly all had teaching experience and professional training, generally work in the education service. Clinical psychologists work in the health service, most of them with adults, but some with children. There is therefore some overlap in the functions of educational and clinical psychologists in respect of work with children and young people. This was brought to our attention in evidence and in the reports of the Trethowan and Court Committees.[7] We have not given this issue detailed consideration but

---

[7] Consultation Document from the Sub-Committee reporting on the Role of Psychologists in the Health Services (DHSS, 1974); *Fit for the future, op. cit.*

were interested to note that the recent inquiry by the Division of Educational and Child Psychology of the British Psychological Society revealed a considerable degree of local co-operation between psychologists working in the education and health services. In our view there is a need for much further discussion on the development of psychological services for children, given the waste of skill and work that can result where arrangements are duplicated because of lack of co-ordination between the services. We regard it as essential that better co-ordinated working arrangements should be planned in future. This would be facilitated by the sharing of experience between educational and clinical psychologists through common elements of training. *We therefore recommend that course modules common to the training of educational and clinical psychologists should be developed.*

Training

14.15 The training of educational psychologists needs further development. In initial training more attention should be given to the needs of children under five and of children with emotional or behavioural disorders or multiple and complex disabilities, and a broader range of experience should be provided during courses. We recognise that the usual one-year course may have to be lengthened to include these elements and we acknowledge the value of those two-year courses which have been established. But we particularly wish to stress the need for more post-qualification courses for educational psychologists. These courses, which could be held jointly for educational and clinical psychologists and other professionals working in special education, should provide training in specialised areas of work and should up-date knowledge and skills. Attendance at such courses should in our view be an essential qualification for senior posts concerned with specialised responsibilities and posts with general responsibility for services in the local education authority. *We therefore recommend that existing training centres for educational psychologists and other establishments and organisations should institute a range of in-service courses, varying in both length and content.*

II CAREERS OFFICERS

14.16 As we pointed out in Chapters 10 and 11, members of the local authority careers service can play an important part in helping careers and guidance teachers in schools to develop programmes which inform pupils about career opportunities and prepare them for the world of work. Our broader concept of special education means that all careers officers, generalists as well as those who specialise in helping young people with disabilities, will come into contact with young people with special needs in the course of their work. They will therefore all need to be aware of the implications of special needs for further and higher education, training and work. We start by considering the extra demands on the careers service which are likely to arise from our recommendations.

Demands on careers officers

14.17 Careers officers and their specialist colleagues will be closely involved in providing school leavers with special needs with information, advice and guidance about further and higher education, training and employment and in helping in more specialist assessment specifically directed to employment. Our recommendation in Chapter 10 that careers officers should always be involved in the re-assessment of special needs at least two years before young people are due to leave school will make additional demands on them and increase the need for training in this field, to which we return below.

14.18 We recommended in Chapter 10 that the careers officer or, in the case of young people with more severe or complex disabilities, the specialist careers officer, should be the Named Person for young people with special needs and their parents during the transition from school to adult life or should ensure that another professional takes on the function of Named Person. This would be an extension of the careers officer's present concern to see young people settled in suitable employment wherever possible. Every young person with a disability or significant difficulty should have a Named Person to whom to turn in the first few years after he has completed full-time education and training. The careers officer or his specialist colleague should carry out this function until satisfied that the young person no longer requires a Named Person or that the function has been assumed by another professional. Careers officers and their specialist colleagues will need to maintain close links with Disablement Resettlement Officers and other professionals so that they can ensure that responsibility for being Named Person is assigned to the most suitable professional in each particular case.

Training
14.19 The initial training of careers officers already includes an element designed to develop their awareness of special needs in young people. Our evidence suggests, however, that when pupils with disabilities or significant difficulties are educated in ordinary schools the need for specialised careers advice is not always understood and that, even where it is, such advice is not readily available. Greater emphasis may therefore need to be placed on this element of initial training and particularly on helping careers officers to recognise when specialist careers advice is needed. In addition, careers officers already in post should have the same opportunity as future entrants to the profession to develop an awareness of special needs. This will require the provision of short in-service courses dealing with the transition from school to work of young people with special needs. We understand that the content of initial training courses for careers officers is currently being reviewed by the Local Government Training Board. *We therefore recommend that the Local Government Training Board should review the element in the initial training of careers officers which is concerned with young people with special needs and should develop in-service courses on special needs for all careers officers in post who have not already taken this element.* Some in-service courses for careers officers as well as for careers teachers could be organised by the regional conferences for special education to which we refer in more detail in Chapter 16. There will continue, however, to be a need for central provision by the Local Government Training Board of opportunities for the study by careers officers of the problems associated with specific disabilities.

14.20 We envisage that specialist careers officers will work directly with young people with special needs in special schools and in association with their non-specialist colleagues when they are consulted about individual pupils in ordinary schools. Experience as a careers officer working with young people in ordinary schools should precede appointment as a specialist officer. *We recommend that careers officers wishing to specialise in work with young people with disabilities or significant difficulties should undertake training on lines similar to that of Disablement Resettlement Officers.* (This begins with a seven-week course based on the National Training Centre for Disablement Resettlement Officers at Leeds and is supplemented later by further in-service training courses, seminars and conferences.) We expect that courses for specialist careers officers will generally be organised by the Local Government Training Board. The Special Education Staff College proposed in Chapter 18 will however play an important part, particularly in the organisation of courses with other professionals concerned with young people with special needs.

Staffing and career structure

14.21 We pointed out in Chapter 10 that if the careers officer or his specialist colleague is to work closely with individual young people both before and after they leave school, it will be necessary for the careers service to be considerably strengthened. Accordingly we recommended that, as a general guide and on the understanding that adequate support would be provided, one full-time specialist careers officer should be appointed for every 50,000 of the school population (or for a substantial proportion of 50,000). It is essential that there should be a recognised career structure for careers officers with specialist training and that specialist work should be regarded as a valuable asset for promotion to posts at a higher level in the careers service with general responsibilities. Further, *we recommend that some senior posts in local education authority careers services should be made available to careers officers specialising in work with young people with disabilities or significant difficulties.*

III PROFESSIONALS WHO LINK HOME AND SCHOOL

14.22 Good links between home and school are essential if effective support is to be provided for parents and their co-operation is to be encouraged and maintained. Further, such links are required if teachers are to learn about children's home circumstances where appropriate and so understand and take account of individual needs. Throughout this report we have stressed that teachers and parents of children with disabilities and difficulties should work closely together. In ordinary schools some teachers may be specially appointed as teacher-counsellors, guidance teachers or home-school liaison teachers with responsibilities for work with parents of children with special needs and for maintaining links with other services and agencies outside school. We consider it important that they should have special training for the purpose which gives them a deeper knowledge of the special needs of such children. In special schools many more teachers may work closely with parents, particularly when parents take part in educational programmes for their children. Many special schools will also need the services of social workers. Some, particularly those for children with emotional and behavioural disorders, and especially those providing residential education, will require a school-based social worker able to maintain links with families and with social services in the child's home neighbourhood. Some such appointments have already been made. The primary concern of a social worker attached to a special school must be the children in the school, and a person so employed should obviously be in sympathy with the aims and ethos of the school if his or her work is to be effective.

Social workers

14.23 Both ordinary and special schools need to work closely with social services departments and with social workers in respect of individual children with special needs and their families. There is much overlap in the work of social workers, education welfare officers, school counsellors, guidance teachers and home-school liaison teachers, and their separate functions need clarification. Since the Seebohm Report[8] social services departments have had responsibilities for the care and welfare of handicapped children and young people and for the support of their families. However, scarcity of resources, particularly of trained manpower, has meant that the contribution of social workers has often been limited to intervention in crises. Even with a continuing increase in the number of social workers who are qualified, it is unlikely, in the foreseeable future, that social services departments will be able to work with all the families of the children who may have special educational needs. In practice their concern in the educational context is likely to be limited usually to those children whose needs are recorded by the local education authority. Regular interaction between school counsellors, social workers in schools, guidance teachers, home-school liaison teachers and education welfare officers will therefore be particularly important in ensuring that children and their families receive appropriate help. We see the need for social workers and education welfare officers to work closely together in each area; the former engaged on social case work with particular families and also working directly in some special schools where disturbed family relationships affect a child's education; and the latter, among other duties, facilitating good home-school links for all other children with special needs. A flexible administrative structure is needed both in social work and in schools if links between schools and the homes of children with special needs are to be forged and patterns of contact established which will help define the particular contributions of each professional. Whatever pattern of working is developed in each area the need for school-based welfare services of one kind or another is in our view essential, particularly for children with special needs. *We therefore recommend that local authorities should ensure, through co-operation between their education and social services departments, that adequate social work services are available to meet the needs of children who require special help in all schools in their area, that the social workers are clearly linked to individual schools or groups of schools and that, where appropriate, the social workers are school-based.*

14.24 For some parents of children whose special needs are asssessed at Stage 4 or 5 of our proposed assessment procedure and who are recorded as requiring special educational provision, the Named Person may most appropriately be a social worker. As with other professionals acting as Named Person, the social worker should be familiar with the education and health services for children with special needs and should know to whom to turn for special help when necessary.

---

[8] Report of the Committee on Local Authority and Allied Personal Social Services. Cmnd 3703 (HMSO, 1968).

Education welfare officers

14.25 Local education authorities need "field officers" to carry out a variety of important non-teaching functions such as checking on and enforcing school attendance, arranging school transport, providing information to individual families about entitlement to free school meals, educational maintenance allowances, grants for school uniforms and other matters, conducting censuses particularly of children under five and providing escorts for children to and from schools. In England and Wales these functions are carried out by education welfare officers and in Scotland some of them are performed by school attendance officers. In the course of their work these officers inevitably come into contact with children with special educational needs and their families and, indeed, they may well be able to detect special needs in children and mobilise help for them. They thus have an indispensable part to play in the support of children with special needs.

14.26 The close concern of education welfare officers in identifying and arranging help for children with special educational needs emerged clearly from a recent survey of their work by Keith MacMillan.[9] 67% of officers in his survey had duties with handicapped children; 45% were concerned with finding places and arranging admission to special schools; and 40% with making arrangements for home teaching under Section 56 of the Education Act 1944 (as amended). Almost all officers were involved at some time or other in transporting and escorting children to and from residential schools. The survey also revealed that in the course of their various contacts with families education welfare officers often discovered children under five with special educational needs. Additionally, their specific enquiries and visits in connection with the enforcement of school attendance gave opportunity for the discovery of special educational needs amongst children of school age.

14.27 We recognise that there are still uncertainties about the way in which education welfare services should be developed and about the interrelationship of education welfare and social work. But we are quite clear that the education welfare service is an essential practical arm of the local education authority and has a very important part to play in providing support for children with special educational needs and their families. *We recommend that further studies should be undertaken to determine the best way of providing the essential though in some respects overlapping services carried out by education welfare officers and social workers.*

Training

14.28 The training of education welfare officers was the subject of a report by a Local Government Training Board working party chaired by Sir Lincoln Ralphs, which recommended a number of improvements.[10] We consider that education welfare officers need an understanding not only of the education system generally but also of the special educational needs which many children have. *We therefore recommend that education welfare officers should be helped in initial and in-service training to recognise signs of special educational needs and to*

---

[9] K MacMillan, *Education welfare: strategy and structure* (1977).

[10] The Training of Education Welfare Officers. The Report of the Working Party (Local Government Training Board, 1973).

be aware of the ways in which the education and other services can meet such needs.

IV OTHER IMPORTANT WORKERS IN SCHOOLS

14.29 In this section we deal with four groups of people whose work with teachers with responsibility for children with special needs has a significant influence on the quality of special education provided. These are nursery nurses, ancillary workers in classrooms, residential child care workers and instructors in schools for the severely mentally handicapped in Scotland. All will benefit from training related to their work with children with disabilities and difficulties. Equally, most teachers need in-service training to work with these staff more effectively.

Nursery nurses

14.30 Nursery nurses work in a variety of settings with children with special needs, including day nurseries, nursery schools and classes and residential homes for young children. Sometimes they take responsibility for the care of groups of children and sometimes they participate with teachers in the early education of children. Their training is recognised as very effective in developing an awareness of child development and the knowledge and skills necessary for young children in day and residential settings.

14.31 As we noted in Chapter 5, many children in ordinary day nurseries, playgroups and nursery schools or classes may have special needs. It is therefore important that nursery nurses employed in these establishments or groups should be able to recognise signs of such needs and assist in meeting them. We recognise the value of their training and are aware that many nursery nurses are already skilled in detecting special needs. Those nursery nurses who are employed in special nursery classes, opportunity groups and other types of provision intended for children with more severe disabilities or difficulties, including older children with a very low developmental age, will need more specialist knowledge. We have already welcomed in Chapter 5 the development of pilot courses leading to the advanced certificate of the National Nursery Examination Board and the Scottish NNEB, which are designed to give nursery nurses a deeper knowledge of children with special needs. We hope that at least one such course will be developed in each region. Moreover, as we recommended in that chapter, nursery nurses need opportunities to attend in-service courses organised on an inter-professional basis. The career prospects of nursery nurses are often limited, particularly within the education service, and ways need to be found to recognise the responsibilities of more senior nursery nurses where a number of nursery nurses is employed in any one school. As a step towards this *we recommend that the possession by nursery nurses working in day nurseries, playgroups, nursery schools or classes of the advanced certificate of the National Nursery Examination Board or the Scottish NNEB should carry an increase in salary.*

Ancillary workers

14.32 In the course of our visits to schools we became aware of the important contribution made by ancillary staff, sometimes called non-teaching assistants, to the work of classes and groups of handicapped children, and our evidence

273

suggests that this is particularly the case where there are young children, children with severe disabilities and emotionally disturbed children. Not only do they provide care for the children but they enable teachers to concentrate their attention on individuals and small groups. Moreover, they themselves carry out important educational work with children under the direction of the teacher. As we pointed out in Chapter 8, the staff-pupil ratios suggested in the Circular on the staffing of special schools issued in 1973[11] are based on the assumption that adequate numbers of suitable ancillary staff are available. We have found that local education authorities have very different ideas of the strength of ancillary support required in schools, and we therefore recommended in Chapter 8 that guidance should be issued in a further Circular on the numbers of ancillary staff that should be regarded as adequate. We considered recommending particular staffing ratios but were aware that local circumstances vary. However we would suggest that where children are immobile and need regular training in feeding and looking after themselves there should probably be one ancillary worker for every four or five children. *We recommend that special classes for children of primary school age, whether in special schools or units or attached to ordinary schools, and special classes for children of secondary school age with physical disabilities, severe learning difficulties or emotional or behavioural disorders should each have at least one ancillary worker*. Further, the help of an ancillary worker is often crucial to the effective placement of an individual child with a disability or disorder in an ordinary class. An ancillary worker should be provided for each child who needs such support, but it should be possible in many cases for him to be employed in this capacity on a part-time basis and often to combine this work with other necessary tasks within the school.

14.33 Ancillary workers are usually chosen for their sympathetic attitude to children and their experience as parents. Indeed, the care, extra understanding and affection they offer can be very important to some children. They have little training, except where school-based in-service training is well developed, and they rely on the teachers with whom they work for guidance as to their duties. We think that courses for ancillary workers are needed which include particular attention to child development and we would urge that such staff should be encouraged to take advantage of them.

Child care staff in residential special schools

14.34 Child care workers and teachers who undertake residential care act in many ways as parents, and in special schools they are often seen as such by the children. The importance of close collaboration between teachers and child care workers in these circumstances should be self-evident. Their work overlaps and both groups contribute to and facilitate the personal development of children, as we pointed out in Chapter 8. We have noted that a survey carried out by Her Majesty's Inspectorate in 1970 revealed that only 9% of child care staff in special schools were trained residential child care workers. Although courses of different kinds have been introduced since that time the percentage of trained staff is still low. The contribution of child care staff is vital to the effectiveness of

---

[11] DES Circular 4/73, Welsh Office Circular 47/73, Staffing of Special Schools and Classes (6 March 1973). Scottish Education Department Memorandum, Revision of Schools (Scotland) Code 1956 (October 1973).

boarding special schools and in the following paragraphs we consider their functions, their training and the staffing levels necessary for them to carry out their duties well.

14.35 Although child care work includes some domestic duties, these should not be so extensive as to limit the time which the staff can spend in personal contact with the pupils in the school. It should be recognised that child care staff have a responsibility for establishing close personal relationships with the children which supplement family experiences, and that in many cases they may act as substitute parents. This is a facet of their work which has been adequately appreciated only in recent years and there is scope for its further development. Trained and experienced staff can create patterns of living which reduce the institutional effects of boarding schools and encourage individual development, and their independent contribution to children's development needs to be more fully recognised. The staffing levels required obviously depend on the nature of the premises, the nature and severity of the children's disabilities and the methods of care and treatment chosen. Nevertheless we regard it as important that the Education Departments should give general guidance on desirable staffing levels. As a general principle we suggest that the teaching staff ratios outlined in Circular 4/73 and the Scottish Education Department's Consultative Document[12] should be used as a guide to the number of child care staff required; thus the younger the children and the more severe their disabilities the better the staffing ratio should be. The ratios should also take into account the need for intimate groupings of children in day-to-day living and for a stable and enduring relationship between individual staff and children.

14.36 Working with handicapped children in residence, particularly those with sensory and physical disabilities, requires special training. For this reason all child care staff should have an induction course when they first take up work in residential special schools. We are aware that the Certificate in Social Service now being developed gives scope for covering in a course of professional training some aspects of the work of child care staff in boarding special schools. However, the Certificate may not give sufficient weight to the problems of working with children with some types of disability, for example deaf children or children with severe learning difficulties. Further thought therefore needs to be given to the provision of in-service training for child care staff in boarding schools. *We recommend that special training leading to a recognised qualification should be available for child care staff in residential special schools, whatever their previous qualifications, along lines compatible with that for staff in community homes.* We hope that the regional conferences for special education, whose functions we discuss further in Chapter 16, will give particular attention to the development of such training. Teachers working in residential special schools also need training in aspects of residential child care and they should be given opportunities to take courses in this field along with other professionals concerned with meeting the needs of children who require residential special education.

14.37 A career structure is needed for child care staff, not confined solely to special schools but extending to community homes run by social services

---

[12] *Ibid.*

departments. Indeed, we would welcome an interchange of child care staff between education and social services departments. *We recommend that there should be one post in boarding special schools at deputy head level, carrying responsibility for all arrangements for residential care, and that this should be open to trained child care staff.*

Instructors in special schools in Scotland

14.38 From 1947 to 1975 schools for severely mentally handicapped children in Scotland were known as junior occupational centres and were staffed in the main by instructors who completed a short in-service course at Jordanhill College of Education. The Report of the Melville Committee[13] recommended that such centres should be known as schools and that teachers should be employed in all of them. It also recommended the introduction of two-year courses for instructors designed to prepare them to work alongside teachers with the following main responsibilities: i. encourage children to develop independence in basic social functions such as feeding, toileting and dressing; ii. stimulate the social and emotional development of the child by encouraging co-operation in groups; iii. promote the child's development by skilful use of play; iv. co-operate with parents in promoting the full development of the child; and v. advise the teaching staff about individual children and the need for links with social and health services and voluntary agencies. Because of financial constraints the training courses for instructors have been restricted to one year. *We recommend that training courses for instructors in Scotland should be extended to two years and that education authorities should consider providing posts of responsibility for instructors where a number is employed in any one school.* This would be in line with the recommendations of the Melville Committee.

CONCLUSION

14.39 In this chapter we have considered the work and training of a number of different people who make an important contribution to provision for children with special needs in ordinary and special schools and elsewhere. The main needs are for improved training, increased staffing and better developed patterns of working between different professionals to eliminate duplication of effort and to ensure the best use of limited resources. We urge the regional conferences for special education and individual local education authorities to put into practice the suggestions made in this chapter for staffing levels and training. In particular we hope that every opportunity will be taken to provide post-qualification training on an inter-professional basis so that mutual understanding and co-operative patterns of working can be fostered between teachers, other members of the education service, and professionals in the health and social services.

---

[13] *The Training of Staff for Centres for the Mentally Handicapped.* Report of the Committee appointed by the Secretary of State for Scotland (HMSO, 1973).

CHAPTER 15: THE HEALTH SERVICE AND THE SOCIAL SERVICES

INTRODUCTION

15.1 The health service and the personal social services make an essential contribution to meeting the educational needs of children with disabilities or significant difficulties. The evidence presented to us and our own visits underlined the importance of close collaboration between these services and the education service in providing help for children with special needs and their families. The need for an awareness on the part of the members of all these services of the nature of each other's contribution also emerged very clearly. It has not been our purpose to comment in detail on the work of the health and social services. In the course of our report, however, we have identified areas of interest and responsibility common to the education, health and social services and have made proposals for the development of collaboration between them in particular ways. We cannot stress too strongly that the effective development of special education along the lines we have proposed requires wholehearted co-operation between the health, social and education services.

15.2 We do not think that it is any part of our brief to comment on the wisdom or otherwise of the re-organisation of the health services and of local government (in England and Wales in 1974 and in Scotland in 1974 and 1975), except to say that in some very important respects re-organisation made co-operation at local level, which we seek to promote, more rather than less difficult. However, given the present structures and systems, we turn to aspects of health and social services which are particularly important to the special educational arrangements proposed in this report. We also consider the contributions of some of the different professionals working within these services. Many issues have been discussed in the context in which they arose, for example in the context of assessment in Chapter 4 and of the needs of young people with disabilities in Chapter 10, and we do not propose to repeat our views on these matters in this chapter.

15.3 The provision of help and support for children with special educational needs and for their families in their own homes, in schools and in the neighbourhood is a task which health and social services share with education. We welcome the statement by the Secretary of State for Social Services on the Court Report on 27 January 1978 in which he said: "I am asking health authorities to examine each component part of their child health services – primary care, community services and specialist services to see how best to produce the integration of services to which the Court Committee rightly attached such importance. But in this field, as in so many others, the health services must work in tandem with local authority services which reach out to children and their families. Special effort by all those services is needed to find those families

277

who most need help and are least likely to seek it out".[1] We regard the task of discovering, assessing and providing for children with special educational needs as a shared one which merits very high priority, particularly in areas (mainly, but not exclusively, inner city areas) where there are adverse social conditions.

I THE HEALTH SERVICE

15.4 Public concern about ill health, malnutrition and disabilities in school-children led to the appointment of school doctors at the beginning of this century. The school health service was established in 1908 and its development in England and Wales up to the re-organisation of the national health service in 1974 is described in a recent publication.[2] Over that period many changes have taken place in the incidence and nature of health problems in children. Infectious diseases have been largely controlled and better nutrition, public health and housing have helped to reduce the incidence of illness and disability. Advances in medical diagnosis and treatment have also led to changes in the pattern of handicapping conditions. Congenital malformations, disorders arising in the new-born and problems arising from the social and emotional climate in which children grow up now account for a much greater proportion of child health problems.

15.5 The re-organisation of the health service in 1974 resulted in the transfer of responsibility for the school health service from local education authorities to area health authorities and of that for community child health services from local health authorities to area health authorities. The re-organisation was intended to result in a comprehensive service in which the school health service was integrated with other child health services and with hospital and specialist services which, together with general practitioner services, would cover all health services for children. This goal has not yet been achieved. Whilst the re-organisation was in the planning stage the report *Towards an Integrated Child Health Service*[3] described the possible development of the child health service in Scotland. Since re-organisation the future of health services for children in England and Wales has been studied by the Court Committee which reported in 1976.[4] We entirely agree with that Committee's view that "the child health service and education services must see themselves as engaged, to a large extent, upon different aspects of a common task". During the period when the Committee was sitting many initiatives awaited its recommendations. Now that the government has announced its conclusions on the Committee's recommenda- tions[5] we hope that no time will be lost in strengthening health services to schools. We regard a properly structured school health service as essential for all children and particularly for those with special educational needs.

---

[1] DHSS Health Circular HC(78)5 Local Authority Circular LAC(78)2, Welsh Office Circular WHC(78)4, Health Services Development (January 1978), Annex A.

[2] *The School Health Service 1908-1974* (HMSO, 1975).

[3] *Towards an Integrated Child Health Service.* Joint Working Party on the Integration of Medical Work. Report of a Sub-Group on the Child Health Service (HMSO, 1973).

[4] *Fit for the Future.* The Report of the Committee on Child Health Services. Cmnd 6684 (HMSO, 1976).

[5] DHSS Health Circular HC(78) 5 Local Authority Circular LAC (78)2, Welsh Office Circular WHC(78)4, *op. cit.*

Delivery of health services

15.6 There are four essential features of good health services for children with special educational needs: professional skill; availability; continuity; and adequate understanding and experience of education. We review below the delivery of health care to children with special needs, bearing in mind the importance of these four features. A detailed account of the organisation of the health service in England, Scotland and Wales is given in Appendix 4.

15.7 School health services in England and Wales are provided by area health authorities to matching local education authorities. The Area Specialist in Community Medicine (Child Health) and the Area Nurse (Child Health) in England and Wales have dual responsibilities to, and are appointed with the agreement of, both the area health authority and the local education authority. They work particularly closely with local education authorities, and their functions are crucial to good health services for special education. The services to be provided, which are described in detail in a Circular issued by the Department of Health and Social Security on the re-organisation of the health service,[6] include the provision of medical staff, nurses and therapists to ordinary and special schools; arrangements for medical examinations and immunisation; and the oversight of health care in schools. Particularly important among these services, in view of our recommendations elsewhere in this report, are advice to parents, teachers and local education authorities on the nature and extent of handicapping conditions or other medical conditions significant for a child's education, participation in health education and the provision of counselling services for pupils and others.

Primary health care

15.8 General practitioners have traditionally been the first point of contact for children and their families seeking medical advice and treatment. Although independent contractors, they need to maintain close links with colleagues in other parts of the health service and in other services and agencies, such as social services. In recent years some general practitioners have accepted the concept of team work, with the attachment of health visitors, district nurses and social workers to general practice. This team approach is a developing one, but we recognise that for many different reasons the establishment of such teams may be difficult.

15.9 General practitioners and clinical medical officers share responsibility for the health surveillance of children and advice to their parents. Collaboration and communication between these doctors are essential for the provision of an effective service. Moreover, they have a responsibility to ensure that local authorities are aware at the earliest opportunity of children's special needs so that appropriate steps can be taken to meet them. Health visitors, whose main duties include visiting homes where there are babies and young children, may be the first members of the health service with whom some families come into

---

[6] Department of Health and Social Security Circular HRC(74)5, Welsh Office Circular WHRC(74)7, Operation and Development of Services: Child Health Services (including School Health Services) (January 1974) Annex 3.

contact after the child's neonatal period. They work closely with general practitioners and clinical medical officers in the health surveillance of children and therefore in the early identification of those with problems.

Child health services in schools

15.10 We endorse the aims of child and school health services in relation to education which were identified in the Court Report, namely: i. to promote the understanding and practice of child health and paediatrics in relation to the process of learning; ii. to provide a continuing service of health surveillance and medical protection throughout the years of childhood and adolescence; iii. to recognise and ensure the proper management of what may broadly be described as medical, surgical and neurodevelopmental disorders, insofar as they may influence, directly or indirectly, the child's learning and social development, particularly in school, but also at home; iv. to ensure that parents and teachers are aware of the presence of such disorders and their significance for the child's education and care; and v. to give advice and services to the local education authority as required by the Education Act 1944 and the National Health Service Reorganisation Act 1973. We have been concerned that these aims may not receive sufficient priority in the health service. However, we are encouraged by the Secretary of State for Social Services' response to the Court Report, in particular his wish to see improved child health services especially in areas of greatest social need. The importance of such services to schools cannot be over-emphasised if children with special educational needs are to receive effective help. *We therefore recommend that health authorities should make adequate resources available to promote effective child health services in ordinary and special schools.*

15.11 We regard the functions of Specialists in Community Medicine (Child Health) as particularly important to the development of effective special educational provision. Being in the special position in England and Wales of working for both the area health authority and the local education authority, they are able to provide valuable links between the two. Their responsibilities include ensuring that information about special needs discovered by primary care services, community health and hospital services is conveyed to the education authority; arranging for the medical aspects of assessment which we described in Chapter 4; ensuring that necessary medical services and the services of other professionals in the health service are made available to educational institutions; and generally advising the education authority on all matters concerned with child health and educational medicine.

15.12 It has been put to us that there is likely to be a shortage of Specialists in Community Medicine with training and knowledge of educational and school health problems. We believe that this potential problem is receiving far too little attention. *We therefore recommend that as a matter of urgency high priority should be given to the recruitment and appropriate training of doctors for this field of work.* We urge local education authorities in England and Wales, whose agreement to the appointment of Specialists in Community Medicine (Child Health) is required, not to consent to the appointment of doctors without adequate clinical and educational experience. Similarly, in giving their agreement to the appointment of Area Nurses (Child Health) local education authorities should ensure that those appointed have relevant experience.

Discovery, assessment and support

15.13 In Chapter 2, where we reviewed the history of special education, we explained that the Education Act 1944 introduced the requirement of a medical examination to determine whether a child was handicapped. This provision was a logical outcome of the concern shown by school medical officers for handicapped children since the inception of the school health service. Since that time the importance of psychological, educational and social as well as medical assessment has been recognised. The Sheldon Working Party[7] recognised the importance of multi-professional assessment in hospitals and elsewhere and Circular 2/75 emphasised the inter-professional character of discovery, diagnosis and assessment,[8] as did the Education (Scotland) Act 1969 and the Brotherston Report.[9] In supporting this trend and in recommending new procedures for assessment (see Chapter 4) we in no way wish to diminish the importance of medical examinations of all kinds for children with special needs. We wish only to emphasise the need for these to be carried out in association with members of other professions if a complete picture of an individual's needs and the means of meeting them is to be compiled.

15.14 Our recommendations for procedures for discovering, assessing and meeting special educational needs impinge upon many aspects of the health service. Those professionals, doctors and others, concerned with primary and community health care will be in contact with many of the children who are likely to require special educational provision at some time during their school career. Professionals in a wide range of hospital and specialist services, including ophthalmic, orthopaedic, Ear, Nose and Throat, paediatric and child psychiatric specialists, may also be in contact with children with special educational needs, and will have responsibilities for those with more complex problems.

15.15 We stressed in Chapter 4 the importance of health surveillance and screening procedures for young children, particularly in order to identify children for whom early education is vital, such as those with impaired hearing. In the case of children under five, members of the health service responsible for primary care or community health care will often be the first professionals to notice disabilities and significant delays in development, as we indicated in paragraphs 15.8-9. They may also be the first to whom parents turn for advice and guidance when they are worried about their child's development. It is therefore important that all the professionals concerned should be well informed of the possible educational implications of the problems that they recognise. They should also be aware of the services available to meet the needs of such children, including special education services, and should recognise the need to keep the education service informed through the Specialist in Community Medicine (Child Health) about children with special needs. They may also play an important part in helping children when they first enter school by supporting parents and working closely with teachers. Where the health visitor is acting as

---

[7] The Report of the Working Party under the chairmanship of Sir Wilfred Sheldon was not formally published but was circulated to regional hospital boards and local health authorities in 1968. It was subsequently referred to in DHSS HM(71)22, Hospital Facilities for Children.

[8] DES Circular 2/75 ,Welsh Office Circular 21/75, The Discovery of Children Requiring Special Education and the Assessment of their Needs (17 March 1975).

[9] *Towards an Integrated Child Health Service, op. cit.*

the Named Person for a family she should continue to act in this capacity until the parents are informed of the Named Person who will succeed her.

15.16 Procedures for assessment, for the communication of medical information and for medical and nursing support in schools will, in our view, develop to the full only if there are opportunities for regular discussion between members of the health service and teachers who are known to each other. Regular contact between doctors, nurses and class teachers about individual children is essential to the development of health education and counselling as well as to the discovery of special needs. The staff of each school must know the names of members of the health service to whom they can turn for advice and help.

15.17 We see the need for a nominated doctor and nurse for every school. The doctor will in most cases be a clinical medical officer (child health). The doctor and nurse will play a very important part in health surveillance in school, which may be the only contact that some children have with health services. They may also be instrumental in the discovery of special educational needs, which can arise at any time during a child's school career. We envisage that their contribution to the help and support of children with disabilities in ordinary schools will increase as the progressive implementation of Section 10 takes place. In those areas, for example in inner cities, where social disadvantage is most manifest, the work of the school doctor and nurse will be especially important. *We therefore recommend that there should be a named doctor and nurse for every school.*

15.18 The Court Report recommended that, as a way of improving links between health services and special education, each special school should have a consultant community paediatrician as its doctor. Although the creation of this new specialist has not been accepted, we consider that the idea should be the subject of experiment and discussion at area health level, as suggested by the Secretary of State for Social Services in his statement on the Court Report on 27 January 1978. Where children with disabilities are educated in ordinary schools, it is important that the doctors concerned with their health should gain direct experience of educational settings in ordinary schools. Moreover, paediatricians working in hospitals and other hospital specialists should have more contact with children in schools. As we emphasised in Chapter 7, the quality of health care and its continuity and availability will be an important factor in deciding whether a particular school is appropriate for an individual child with special needs.

15.19 Health services to non-maintained special schools may be provided by area health authorities on request, and when resources permit. Independent schools catering wholly or mainly for handicapped pupils, however, are not in receipt of national health services, but they may provide adequate health services themselves. We believe that health services to both types of school should be similar in scope and scale to those available in maintained special schools. Non-maintained special schools should ask area health authorities for specialist health services and authorities should supply them. Independent schools catering wholly or mainly for handicapped pupils should request and pay for such services. The availability and level of such services should be important criteria for decisions by local education authorities as to whether to use a particular school for an individual child. *We recommend that local education authorities, in consultation with area health authorities, should satisfy themselves that adequate health care is available before placing children in non-maintained special schools or independent schools catering wholly or mainly for handicapped pupils.*

15.20 Our enquiries about arrangements for young people over 16 with special needs suggest that health services do not always cover satisfactorily the transition from school to further or higher education and training, or the discovery and assessment of special educational needs which may arise at this stage. The transfer to work from school is also not normally accompanied by continued medical surveillance although, as we indicated in Chapter 10 (paragraph 10.102), one of the functions of the Employment Medical Advisory Service is to provide occupational health guidance during this period and thereafter. We believe, as we indicated in that chapter, that the Specialist in Community Medicine (Child Health) should ensure that major responsibility for the health of young people with special needs, particularly those with more severe disabilities, during the transition to early adulthood is clearly assigned before the end of their formal education. *We therefore recommend that the Specialist in Community Medicine (Child Health) should ensure that arrangements are made for the transfer of responsibility for the medical surveillance of a young person with special educational needs to an appropriate branch of the health service when that young person leaves school or further education.* We make this recommendation in the knowledge that the Court Committee referred consideration of this matter to us, and that the recommendation will have resource implications. We recognise that district handicap teams may also play an important part in these transitional arrangements.

15.21 Local education authorities and educational institutions have been urged to consult area health authorities and family practitioner committees about arrangements to assist students to use national health service facilities if they need them.[10] Clearly students with more severe or complex disabilities or disorders will continue to need health service support, and it is important that it should be readily available. *We therefore recommend that health services comparable to those provided for special schools should be made available to establishments of further or higher education which cater for students with more severe disabilities or disorders.*

15.22 We now turn to arrangements for the assessment of the special needs of those children with particularly rare or complex disabilities and for their support. We are pleased to note that the principle of the establishment of district handicap teams has been accepted by the Secretary of State for Social Services. The Circular advising health authorities of the government's conclusions on the recommendations of the Court Report indicates that such teams should provide a framework within which all the needs of the relatively few children with severe disabilities, physical, sensory and mental, can be met, including their

---

[10] DES FECL 5/76, DHSS HN(76)173, Health services for students on full-time and sandwich courses (30 September 1976).

needs for psychological and psychiatric help.[11] There are already in existence child guidance and child psychiatric teams concerned with the assessment and treatment of a wide range of learning, emotional and behavioural disorders. These operate in parallel with district handicap teams. The membership of these different teams as well as some of their functions often overlap, as we indicated in Chapter 4 (paragraph 4.44). There is therefore a need for discussion at local level regarding the interaction and relationship between the various assessment teams, and the way in which the needs of the children with more severe disabilities or disorders seen by the child guidance team can be met.

The role of different specialisms and professions

15.23 We turn now to the work of different members of the health service. Our list is not exhaustive, nor is it intended to diminish the contribution of those not mentioned, some of whose functions have been discussed earlier in this report. Physiotherapists, speech therapists, occupational therapists and nurses may all contribute with doctors and teachers to a programme of treatment and education. Where each profession works in isolation programmes will be unco-ordinated, ineffective and uneconomical in the use of professional time. We have observed in special schools and elsewhere the importance of well-planned teamwork within which each specialist contribution is enhanced by co-operation with and reinforcement from others. We hope that these patterns of working will become more common.

Paediatricians and clinical medical officers

15.24 The former school medical officers were transferred to the national health service, on reorganisation of the health service, as clinical medical officers and senior clinical medical officers. They have always had a vital role to play in the identification, assessment and follow-up of children with special needs; and in giving advice to parents, teachers and others about such children. We therefore welcome the assurance of the Secretary of State for Social Services in his statement on 27 January 1978 that there is an important long-term future for these doctors as an integral part of child health services. We also welcome his endorsement of the need to increase the extension of specialist paediatric services into the community, as an essential contribution to the successful development of services for ordinary and special schools and for district handicap teams. These doctors must work closely together, and with other members of their own profession as well as those of other disciplines, in order to ensure the effective delivery of services.

Child and adolescent psychiatrists

15.25 Although we suggested in Chapter 14 that educational psychologists should remain foremost in the assessment and management of behavioural and emotional problems which present themselves in schools, the child psychiatrist will have a vitally important part to play when such difficulties arise. Severe problems, especially when they may indicate some form of mental illness or

[11] DHSS Health Circular HC(78)5. Local Authority Circular LAC(78)2, Welsh Office Circular WHC(78)4, op. cit.

unusually serious emotional disturbance in the child or his parents, will need to be referred to psychiatric services for further investigation. The psychiatrist's medical background will be of particular value when physical symptoms arise that are not organically determined and essential when the use of drugs in treatment is under consideration. His contribution however will by no means be limited to such cases. He will often need to consult the school when he is dealing with children initially referred by general practitioners because of problems arising within the home. Indeed it is desirable that at least some members of child guidance teams apart from psychologists should have regular contact with teachers, if possible in the school setting. Such contacts already exist in many cases and are particularly necessary in special schools for maladjusted children or schools taking a high proportion of such children. It would be desirable for this practice to be extended to ordinary schools. In some schools for maladjusted children the staff feel a need for regular discussion with someone less intimately involved in the school of the feelings aroused in them by particular children and of techniques for managing the pupils' behaviour. A psychiatrist, social worker or psychologist may be a suitable person for this task, but whoever undertakes it will need special skills for the purpose.

15.26 The skills of the child and adolescent psychiatrist will often be required for the multi-professional assessment of special needs. For this reason the psychiatrist, if not a member of the district handicap team, should be readily available to participate in assessment. Special expertise is required for the psychiatric assessment and management of children currently described as mentally handicapped. In some areas the child psychiatrist will be trained and experienced to deal with children of all ranges of ability, whereas in others a psychiatric specialist in mental handicap, including mental handicap in children, will have this responsibility. Finally, we have been made aware of the current dearth of psychiatric services in many respects, in particular the lack of facilities for adolescents, especially hospital units for very disturbed young people. We hope that these services will be increased as soon as possible.

Dental services

15.27 Children with disabilities may have special dental needs which call for special dental arrangements. Moreover, orthodontic treatment may have educational implications. The Area Dental Officer is responsible for seeing that the necessary professional advice and arrangements for treatment are available. As with other branches of the health service, not every practitioner will have knowledge and experience of children with disabilities and the Area Dental Officer will need to ensure that the necessary provision is made to meet special needs. Dental services for children with disabilities and significant difficulties in ordinary and special schools need to be further developed.

Nurses

15.28 The Area Nurse (Child Health) has responsibility for ensuring, in consultation with the local education authority, that nursing services are provided for ordinary and special schools within the area. We are aware that the wide-ranging duties of the Area Nurse (Child Health) are difficult to carry out in the existing management structure of the area nursing services. The contribution of health visitors was discussed at length in Chapters 4 and 5. We outlined in Chapter 5 an important function which we consider health visitors should assume, namely that of acting as the Named Person to whom parents of children with special needs below school age can turn for information and advice. We welcome the increase in health visitors for England proposed by the government in the period up to 1980–81[12] and urge that the issues raised in this report should be given due weight in the future development of the health visiting service. The health visitor, with additional training in the needs of children with disabilities and significant delays in development, has a crucial part to play in ensuring that early special help is available to parents and children, and by so doing limiting the effects of such disabilities on the child's subsequent development. Close relationships with the local education authority will clearly be very important in ensuring that all the necessary elements of that special help are provided.

15.29 We now turn to the contribution of the school nurses who will normally work with health visitors. The school nurse in both ordinary and special schools can play a very important part in the discovery and support of children with special needs. In ordinary schools, part of the school nurse's task is both to inform the health service of needs detected by the school and to ensure that teachers have the necessary information about individual children. Her function in providing health care for children in ordinary schools is particularly important as far as those children with special needs are concerned, and will assume increased importance as Section 10 of the Education Act 1976 is progressively implemented. Similarly her contribution to health education may be expected to increase in future. For these reasons we see the provision of adequate nursing services to ordinary schools as essential. As we mentioned in Chapter 8, a recent survey of nursing care in special schools found wide variations in the service provided from one area health authority to another.[13] We consider that in day special schools the level of staffing required should normally be determined by the nature and degree of the children's special needs rather than the particular disability or disabilities for which the school caters. In boarding special schools, particularly for children with physical disabilities, nursing arrangements need to be very closely co-ordinated with those for child care. We foresee that the proportion of pupils in special schools with severe and complex disabilities will increase, and for this reason we regard it as essential that adequate numbers of appropriately trained and experienced nurses should be available to work in special schools. We welcome the recognition by the Secretary of State for Social Services in his statement on 27 January 1978 of the need to establish a national training scheme for school nurses.

15.30 Hospital schools and other educational arrangements in hospitals also bring nurses and teachers into partnership in meeting children's needs. In hospitals for the mentally handicapped programmes for individual children are most successful when nurses and teachers adopt a common approach and reinforce each other's efforts. In units for children who are disturbed or who have psychiatric disorders, too, the work of nurses and teachers needs to be complementary. We recognise that both nurses and teachers need additional training

---

[12] *Priorities in the Health and Social Services. The Way Forward* (HMSO, 1977), p.10.

[13] DHSS Circular CNO(78)1, Provision of Nursing Care in Special Schools (9 January 1978).

to work in such units and it is our view that shared arrangements for in-service training should be developed.

Speech therapists

15.31 The work and training of speech therapists have recently been reviewed by the Quirk Committee.[14] We have observed their work only in the context of assessment services and special schools but we recognise the valuable contribution which they make to the speech and language development of many children with different disabilities and difficulties. We have been particularly impressed by the very considerable contribution made by speech therapists in recent years to the teaching of non-communicating children, in the course of which they have used supplementary forms of communication. The survey undertaken for us of teachers' views and attitudes in both ordinary and special schools revealed the strong need felt by many teachers for more contact with speech therapists.[15] There is an urgent need for more speech therapists and in particular for better speech therapy services to ordinary schools. We would welcome the development of courses which lead to the dual qualification of teacher and speech therapist. The contribution of speech therapists is enhanced when they work closely with teachers and child care workers as well as parents so that their special help is supplemented by regular practice in everyday settings. We also commend those arrangements in which speech therapists in special schools and units contribute to programmes worked out by a multi-professional team.

Physiotherapists

15.32 The contribution made by physiotherapists to the assessment and development of the physical skills and mobility of children with special educational needs is widely acknowledged. In special schools and in ordinary schools where there are groups of children with physical disabilities, their services are needed to provide treatment and to assist in the development of physical education programmes and work with individual children. We have visited schools where physiotherapists have carried out successful work in classrooms with teachers and where teachers and aides have been enabled to supplement and complement their work. The way in which the professional skills of physitherapists, remedial gymnasts, teachers and others are shared in the interests of promoting the development of children including those who are physically handicapped, those currently described as mentally handicapped and others with motor and spatial problems seems to us a highly valuable development.

Occupational therapists

15.33 Some occupational therapists who work with children and young people with disabilities are employed by the health service and others by local authority social services departments. Their work with children under five, with pupils in special schools and with young people over 16 has commonly taken the form of giving advice to the professionals engaged in meeting their needs and

---

[14] *Speech Therapy Services*. Report of the Committee appointed by the Secretaries of State for Education and Science, for the Social Services, for Scotland and for Wales in July 1969 (HMSO, 1972).

[15] For details of the survey see Appendix 8.

of training the children and young people to overcome physical disabilities in the activities of daily living and in recreational pursuits. In these and some other fields, for example work with the mentally handicapped and the emotionally disturbed, their contribution in collaboration with teachers, health visitors, nurses and child care staff can be significant. We see the need for an increasing use of their services to enable young people with disabilities or significant difficulties to lead as independent a life as possible.

The training of members of the health service concerned with children with special needs

15.34 It is not within our remit to comment in detail on the supply and training of members of the health service. In a number of chapters in this report, however, we have drawn attention to the additional training required to work with children with special needs. A considerable amount of attention is currently being given to the training of doctors, health visitors and school nurses as a consequence of the Court Report. We hope that our findings will be taken into account. We consider that training for work with children with special needs should be conducted through post-qualification in-service courses organised wherever possible on an inter-professional basis. These should be of a general nature for some professionals and of specific relevance to different areas of disability for others, particularly doctors, nurses and therapists working in special schools and units of different kinds. Post-graduate medical centres throughout the country could, in our view, make an important contribution to the post-qualification training of doctors, nurses and other professionals in this field. *We therefore recommend that more opportunities for post-qualification training on an inter-professional basis should be made available to members of the health service concerned with children with disabilities and significant difficulties.*

Future developments

15.35 The increasing trend towards the provision of special education for children with more complex and severe disabilities in ordinary classes and in special units in ordinary schools will have significant implications for the provision of health services to ordinary schools. It is essential that the health services provided should be of the same quality as those available to special schools and that there should be scope for a multi-professional approach to work with children. We recognise the danger of dispersing scarce health service resources and, as we pointed out in Chapter 7, envisage that it will in some cases be necessary to concentrate certain special classes and the related provision of therapy and treatment at particular schools. Nevertheless, a wider delivery of health services will be essential to the extension of special educational provision in ordinary schools. Area health authorities and local education authorities must jointly plan arrangements for special educational provision in ordinary schools which will guarantee that adequate health services beyond those which would normally be available will be provided. Later in this chapter we recommend that they should be advised by the Joint Consultative Committees on the services that will be required.

15.36 The decrease in the school population which will occur in the next few years may encourage some area health authorities to consider a reduction in the resources devoted to child health services. There are however many aspects of the services which need strengthening and we would emphasise that the opportunity provided by the falling school population should be used to secure the developments proposed in this report.

II THE PERSONAL SOCIAL SERVICES

15.37 Local authority departments of social services (social work departments in Scotland) are of comparatively recent origin, although the concern of local authorities for the social problems of handicapped children and young people has a much longer history. The Kilbrandon Report in 1964 laid the foundation for the formation of social work departments in 1968.[16] The Seebohm Report in 1968 led to broadly similar arrangements in England and Wales in 1970,[17] (though the two reports were acted on differently in their respective countries). The powers of local authorities in relation to handicapped children are defined in the National Assistance Act 1948, the Health and Public Services Act 1968, the Social Work (Scotland) Act 1968 and the Chronically Sick and Disabled Persons Act 1970. The Children Acts of 1948, 1963 and 1975 and the Children and Young Persons Act of 1969 also have a bearing on their duties in this respect. Social services departments now carry out the social service duties of local authorities in respect of families and most children with disabilities or significant difficulties, especially those living in a seriously deprived environment.

15.38 Social services departments now provide a wide range of facilities and specialist staff. Since the National Health Service Reorganisation Act in 1973, which brought hospital-based social workers into social services departments, all social workers employed by health and social services have been based in the same department. In the last chapter we discussed some duties of social workers with regard to school-based work. The contribution of some social workers was also considered in Chapter 10 in the context of services for young people with disabilities and significant difficulties over the age of 16. Many of the services discussed in that chapter are equally important for younger children with disabilities and for their families, particularly those children living in circumstances that may be disadvantageous to their development. In this chapter we deal with various aspects of the work of social services departments and with the contributions of some of those who work in them as they relate to the special educational needs of the children and young people who are our concern.

15.39 There is almost certainly family and social stress where children with special educational needs are living at home. Indeed the problems of such children and their families may have far-reaching social implications. We are in no doubt that the support and advice provided by social services departments in a variety of ways is an essential component of the services we wish to see developed for children with special educational needs. Ideally social services departments should be able to work with all the families of the children who, in our view, are likely to require some form of special educational provision. In practice, however, they will normally be concerned, in the educational

---

[16] *Children and Young Persons, Scotland.* Report by the Committee appointed by the Secretary of State for Scotland. Cmnd 2306 (HMSO, 1964).

[17] Report of the Committee on Local Authority and Allied Personal Social Services. Cmnd 3703 (HMSO, 1968).

context, with those children who are recorded by the local education authority as requiring such provision, but any parents of children with special educational needs should be able to seek and receive their help and support should they wish to do so.

15.40 Throughout this report we have had regard to the contribution of social services departments to assessment, support for families and provision for children and young adults with special needs. We have discussed in Chapters 8 and 10 the educational component of the work of community homes and adult training centres. We also recognise the contribution of the staffs of day nurseries, residential homes and day centres, in collaboration with social workers specialising in work with different disabilities and other specialists, to meeting the needs of the children with whom we are concerned and of their families. In the following paragraphs we consider a number of particular issues concerning the work of social services departments in relation to education departments, without attempting a comprehensive review of social services for children and young people with disabilities.

Discovery, assessment and support

15.41 The staffs of day nurseries, those running playgroups and child minders may be the first people outside the family to see signs of special educational needs in children. As we explained in Chapter 5 their awareness of special needs may be vital if children are to receive the help they need, and our comments in the last chapter on the need for training opportunities for nursery nurses apply equally to these staff. The staff of social services departments responsible for the registration of child minders and playgroups and those who work with them from the education, health and social services should ensure that appropriate advice and support is available. We are aware that there are many problems in achieving this aim at present. As the research undertaken for us by Dr Clark indicated, a significant proportion of children in playgroups and day nurseries have recognisable special needs which are not being met by the normal programmes.[18] Staff in playgroups and day nurseries thus need knowledge and understanding of special educational needs and the services available to meet them as we stressed in the last chapter. So, too, do any social workers designated by the multi-professional team to act as Named Person for the parents of young children assessed by the team as requiring special educational provision. We consider their need for training further in a later section of this chapter.

15.42 When children or young people at any stage of their education are thought to have special needs which require assessment, the contribution of social workers will in many instances be of considerable importance. We hope that the ordinary school will have a sufficiently close relationship with the locally based social work team for any necessary information about a child's social background to be readily available to the school for the purposes of school-based assessment, though we recognise that this is not always the case at present. We discussed the need for close links between social workers and schools

---

[18] For details of the research project see Appendix 6.

in Chapter 14. The school should look to the social worker for help at Stage 3 where this is appropriate. We recommended in Chapter 4 that social services departments should always be informed of the referral of children for assessment at Stage 4 or 5 so that they can make a contribution if they wish to do so. They should also be informed of the decision by a local education authority to record a child as requiring special educational provision, so that they can make social service support available if required by the family.

15.43 In our view social services departments should accept that they have a major responsibility for providing support at the stage when young people with special needs move from school to further education, work or other arrangements within the community. Unless the continuing support of social services departments is available, the future development of some young people with disabilities may be in jeopardy and those with more profound disabilities may have no alternative to placement in hospital. We discussed these matters more fully in Chapter 10. The involvement of social workers in the process of re-assessment, to be carried out under our proposals at least two years before a young person with special needs is due to leave school, should result in an early intimation of the young person's future needs for social service support. These may include the provision of occupational therapy, of special aids and equipment and adaptations to living arrangements. Close collaboration between social workers and specialist careers officers is also, in our view, essential. *We recommend that social services departments should nominate a senior social worker to act as a liaison officer with the careers service and the specialist careers officer.*

Children in care

15.44 We recognise that the circumstances which may lead to children being taken into care by local authorities are also likely in many instances to give rise to learning and behavioural difficulties. Any assessment made under the aegis of social services departments should therefore in our view always include consideration of special educational needs and, where necessary, arrangements should be made for the children to be recorded by the local education authority as requiring special educational provision. We regard it as essential that when children with special educational needs are placed in foster homes or community homes or moved from one home to another, account should always be taken of the availability of suitable educational provision in the vicinity and there should be close collaboration between education and social services departments. It is equally important that any special educational arrangements made in independent boarding schools should be known to be appropriate and that such schools should not be used by social services departments without the agreement of the local education authority, as we recommended in Chapter 8.

15.45 In Chapter 8 we mentioned the needs of children with disabilities who spend long periods in hospital. The trend to make more provision in the community for these and other children who require long-term residential care is one which we support, provided that adequate resources are made available. Such care may be provided in a variety of ways, for example in foster homes. Some hospitals provide short-term residential care to relieve parents from stress and we emphasised the need for this form of help in Chapter 9. We consider however that it is preferable for such short-term residential arrangements to be made in the community without interrupting the child's normal pattern of schooling and that social services departments should assume responsibility for making such arrangements.

15.46 The planning and running of community homes without education on the premises (children's homes in Scotland) should be discussed regularly with local education authorities to ensure that suitable provision is available in local schools for children in the homes who have special educational needs. Moreover, good relations should be fostered between residential social work staff in the homes and teachers in the schools which the children attend. Without good relations between community homes and schools there is a very real danger that the social and educational needs of the children concerned will be considered in isolation from each other and inadequately met. For some children, child care staff may be substitute parents and in our view all that has been said elsewhere in this report about the needs and contribution of parents applies equally to them. The provision of education in community homes with education on the premises was discussed in Chapter 8, where we recommended that teachers working in such homes should be employed by local education authorities and seconded to social services departments.

Adult training centres for the mentally handicapped and day centres for the physically disabled

15.47 The staffing of adult training centres and day centres, to which many young people with severe disabilities proceed on leaving special schools, forms a major part of the responsibilities of social services departments. In our view those staff working with handicapped young people in adult training centres and day centres need specific training for the purpose. We recognise the initiatives taken by the National Development Group for the Mentally Handicapped as outlined in their recent pamphlet,[19] in which they proposed that education in its broadest sense should be provided in adult training centres and that these should in future be known as social education centres. The developments in Scotland have been influenced by the Melville Report.[20] The evidence submitted to us and our own visits suggest that it is important that arrangements for the education and training of young adults in adult training centres and day centres should be separate from those for older people, since it may be possible for the young people to make considerable progress if a special programme is developed for them. It is undesirable in our view that young people entering adult training centres or day centres should be admitted to and retained in age groups ranging from 16 to 60 plus. *We therefore recommend that separate provision and a differentiated programme of education and other activities including training should be available for young people in adult training centres and day centres or elsewhere.* We have already recommended in Chapter 10 that the educational element in any programme should be provided by local education authorities. The staff of adult training centres and day centres where young people are admitted direct from

[19] *Day Services for Mentally Handicapped Adults.* National Development Group for the Mentally Handicapped Pamphlet Number 5 (July 1977).

[20] *The Training of Staff for Centres for the Mentally Handicapped.* Report of the Committee appointed by the Secretary of State for Scotland (HMSO, 1973).

school need to be familiar with the special schools in the area. They should be encouraged by social services departments to visit the schools and take part in discussions with the staff in order to facilitate the transition of the young people from the school to the centre. For their part, teachers in special schools should be encouraged to visit the training or day centres.

Training

15.48 Training in dealing with the particular problems of children and young people with special educational needs is as necessary for workers in social services departments as for members of other services. *We therefore recommend that an element should be included in the initial training of all social workers and residential child care staff which acquaints them not only with the social work aspects of different disabilities but with the special education services available to children and parents.* Further training is also needed for some social workers to deal with the problems associated with particular disabilities, for example deafness or psychiatric disorders, and we hope that the Central Council for Education and Training in Social Work will take steps to see that such training is provided. Misunderstandings sometimes occur between teachers and social workers simply because of a lack of knowledge of each other's work, and inter-professional training is one way of overcoming them. We urge local authority education and social services departments to place much greater emphasis on the provision of joint in-service training for teachers and social workers.

III JOINT CONSULTATIVE COMMITTEES

15.49 As we have already indicated, the needs of children and young people with disabilities and significant difficulties are the common concern of health, education and social services, which have overlapping responsibilities. The National Health Service Reorganisation Act 1973 set up statutory bodies, known as Joint Consultative Committees, to consider and advise the three services on the planning, provision and co-ordination of arrangements in their areas. Membership of these Committees is drawn from the appointed members of the area health authority and elected members of the local authority, some of whom are members of education and social services committees. Some Committees now include officers of health, education and social services, while others appoint sub-committees of officers to study specific problems. Where the boundary of the area health authority is not co-terminous with that of the local authority, it is of course necessary for the latter to have relations with more than one Joint Consultative Committee, with the result that there may be variations in the recommendations made for different parts of a local authority's area. Notwith-standing this problem, we regard the work of Joint Consultative Committees as vital for the co-ordination and development of services for children and young people with disabilities or significant difficulties, and in the next chapter we consider how their influence might be increased. We welcome and endorse the point made by the Secretary of State for Social Services in his statement on the Court Report on 27 January 1978 that Joint Consultative Committees should be the forum in which concentrated local effort should be planned.

15.50 The National Health Service (Scotland) Act 1972, while laying on health boards, local authorities and education authorities a duty to co-operate with one another, did not provide for the establishment of statutory joint committees. The recent Report of the Working Party on relationships between health boards and local authorities,[21] however, recommended the establishment of Joint Liaison Committees. Health boards and local authorities have been urged to implement this recommendation wherever arrangements for such committees do not already exist.

15.51 There is one aspect of the work of Joint Consultative Committees which we wish to emphasise in this chapter. The provision of health and social services to ordinary and special schools is, as we have indicated, central to the development of special education, particularly when increased provision is to be made for children with disabilities in ordinary schools. We regard the Joint Consultative Committees as having a crucial part to play in advising their constituent authorities on the degree of dispersal of health and social services compatible with effective support for children with special needs in ordinary schools. Thus they will be one important influence in determining the rate at which it will be practicable to implement Section 10 of the Education Act 1976. *We recommend that Joint Consultative Committees should be asked to advise health, education and social services authorities as soon as possible on the health and social services which will be needed by and can be provided for ordinary schools to meet the needs of increasing numbers of children with disabilities or significant difficulties, and what priority their provision should be accorded.* We hope that when Joint Liaison Committees are set up in Scotland they will give priority to this task.

CONCLUSION

15.52 In this chapter we have discussed some aspects of the work of health and social services in relation to educational provision for children and young people with special needs. It is, we believe, evident throughout our report that children with special educational needs are often the concern of other services besides education and that a co-ordinated approach to their problems is essential at all levels. Where they are effective, Joint Consultative Committees (and in Scotland Joint Liaison Committees) can play a significant part in influencing the provision of different services within a local authority area. They can also stimulate arrangements for in-service training on an inter-professional basis. However, it is at the level of the individual doctor, teacher, nurse, social worker or other professional that the ideas of collaboration and joint working advanced in this report must be put into practice. The effectiveness of joint working arrangements for children with disabilities and difficulties will depend on all concerned being well informed and aware of each other's work and able to develop the means to deal with common problems.

---

[21] Working Party on Relationships between Health Boards and Local Authorities – Report (HMSO, 1977).

CHAPTER 16: RELATIONS BETWEEN PROFESSIONALS, CONFIDENTIALITY AND CO-ORDINATION OF SERVICES

INTRODUCTION

16.1 The development of close working relations between professionals in the different services concerned with children and young people with special needs is central to many of the recommendations in this report. In particular, it is a prerequisite of the effectiveness of our proposed procedures for assessment and of provision for children with special educational needs whether in ordinary or special schools. We recognise that the development of such relations is necessarily a slow process, depending as it does on the establishment of trust between different professionals and understanding of each other's functions. This process can, however, be facilitated in various ways, particularly by the development of good practice in the sharing of information and by the provision of opportunities for members of different professions to take courses of training together. In this chapter we consider aspects of the communication of information and of inter-professional training. We also make proposals for formal machinery for co-ordinating services at different levels, since such machinery, though not sufficient in itself, can help to provide a framework within which relations between different professions can develop effectively.

I THE DISSEMINATION OF INFORMATION

16.2 It was widely argued in the evidence submitted to us that information is often not shared between doctors, nurses, psychologists, teachers and social workers, and that in the interests of individual children it should be. The inadequate communication of information both between and within different professions and between professionals and parents also emerged very clearly from the report of the research project on services for parents of handicapped children under five which was undertaken on our behalf by a team under the co-direction of Professor Chazan and Dr Laing of the University College of Swansea.[1]

16.3 We concur with the view expressed in evidence that information should be shared between those professionals concerned with meeting the special needs of a particular child. We emphasised in Chapter 4 that information about any special needs that a child may have should be passed to community health and other professional community services, including the education service where appropriate, as quickly as possible after his birth so that suitable provision can be made for him without delay. We also stressed the need for all pertinent information that is available from educational, medical, social and other sources including, wherever possible, the parents to be taken into account in assessing special educational needs at all of the stages of our proposed assess-

---

[1] For details of the research project see Appendix 5.

ment procedure. Further, we have urged that information about a child's special educational needs should be given to the headteacher when the child starts school and that it should subsequently be passed on when he moves from one school to another or from school to an establishment of further or higher education or a training centre.

16.4 We recognise that in practice, however, professionals are faced by many difficulties in deciding what information should be passed and to whom, not least those arising from considerations of confidentiality. The issue of confidentiality has become increasingly sensitive in recent years as more personal records have been put on computers and have thus become capable of almost instantaneous retrieval. Many professionals therefore feel very cautious about passing on information given to them both in confidence and in the belief that they would act responsibly in making use of it. At the same time, however, as the findings of the research project referred to in paragraph 16.2 showed, confidentiality is often used as an excuse for failure to communicate. Moreover, concern was expressed in evidence submitted to us by handicapped young people and parents of handicapped children that confidentiality was tending to inhibit the development of a wider understanding of the problems and needs of children and young people with disabilities. Clearly, therefore, there is an increasing need for the establishment of general principles to guide professionals in deciding what information should be passed to others.

16.5 Some professions already have or are in the process of developing codes of practice which cover the sharing of confidential information. Doctors, in particular, are bound by a strict ethical code of practice. The Health Visitors' Association has issued guidelines to its members which include advice on the communication of confidential information and the British Psychological Society has drawn up a statement on personal privacy. Both the Association of Educational Psychologists and the British Association of Social Workers have produced codes of practice for their members which cover this subject, while the Institute of Careers Officers is currently engaged on preliminary work which may lead to the production of a professional code of practice. We welcome the development of such codes provided that they are drawn up in close consultation with other professions. Teachers also are likely in future to be in increasing need of guidelines on the sharing of confidential information, given the move towards educating more children with disabilities, including some with severe or complex disabilities, in ordinary schools. At the same time, through the close contacts they have with parents, teachers may obtain information likely to be useful to other professionals concerned with meeting a child's needs. *We therefore recommend that teachers' associations, in consultation with local authority associations and representatives of other professions, should draw up guidelines for teachers on the handling of confidential information as well as the sharing of information with members of other professions.*

16.6 There are already certain general principles which are followed by many professionals in deciding what information should be passed on. We identify them below, though we stress here that their application in individual cases always calls for professional judgement. Observance of these principles can, by enabling professionals in the different services to demonstrate their ability to handle sensitive information with care, be a very effective way of developing inter-professional trust.

General principles

16.7 We start with the basic general principle that relevant information should be shared between professionals concerned with meeting an individual child's needs whenever that is in the best interests of the child and his parents. In the majority of cases these interests will coincide but where they diverge the child's interests must take precedence. In every case, however, it must be a matter for professional judgement on the part of the person in possession of the information whether or not it is in the child's interests that it should be passed on and, if it is in his interests, to which professional or professionals it should be passed.

16.8 In some cases it may be in the child's interests that a particular piece of information should be treated as confidential. This is particularly likely to be so where the child or his parents would regard the information as being in some sense "shameful" or embarrassing. This type of sensitive information may be medical information, information about home circumstances or family relationships, or information about behaviour which could be regarded as undesirable or anti-social. We proposed in Chapter 4 that sensitive information given in confidence about a pupil's social background or family relationships as well as the results of professional consultations concerning his special needs should be kept in a confidential folder to which access would be restricted.

16.9 The fact that information is confidential should be an important consideration, but not an overriding one, in determining whether it should be communicated and in what degree of detail. Where confidential information of a particularly sensitive kind is judged to relate to another professional's work it may be possible to provide that professional with a useful insight into a child's background without providing details. This could be done in general terms which are implicit, rather than explicit, and morally neutral but nevertheless convey a message. The degree of detail in which information should be provided can be determined only by the professional judgement of those in possession of the information, taking account of the needs and responsibilities of the person to whom it is to be passed. We believe that it should be unnecessary to convey sensitive information in a way that reveals that the information is "shameful" except in rare cases where this is essential to the safety or welfare of a child, for example where there are grounds for suspecting that he has been subjected to physical violence.

16.10 Where professionals in different services are working in a team, questions of confidentiality are less likely to constrain communication because certain basic principles are implicitly if not explicitly accepted by the team. In these circumstances, and particularly where common records are kept, it is possible for members of the team to develop the idea of "extended confidentiality" so that information given to one member of the team can be shared by the group and, at the same time, remain confidential to the group. A case conference about the problems of a sick or ill-treated child, for example, or discussion in

297

an assessment centre is, in fact, a procedure for the sharing of information which is widely practised.

16.11 Whether or not information that is communicated from one person to another is confidential, it must be intelligible to the recipient. There is no point in passing on information that is so highly technical in expression or so obscure as to be bewildering to the person for whom it is intended. We commend the development of Form 10bM, which is designed to provide for educational use a summary by school doctors of medical findings and recommendations for individual children. The equivalent in Scotland is the Health Record Section of pupils' progress records. When properly used, Form 10bM can provide the school with an up-to-date and comprehensible record of medical conditions with significance for a child's education or care, practical recommendations for his management and notification of any drugs or appliances required. We recognise that not all local education authorities use Forms 10bM and that, where they are used, the manner and degree of detail in which they are completed vary considerably. We believe, however, that the maintenance of a short medical record of this kind designed for retention in schools is essential for the efficient education of children, especially those children with disabilities or significant difficulties who attend ordinary schools. *We therefore recommend that Form 10bM or its equivalent should be used properly and consistently for all schoolchildren.*

16.12 It is inherent in all that we have said that members of different professions must regard each other as partners so far as the exchange of information is concerned. Similarly, parents too should be treated as partners in this process wherever possible. They should be the most important source of information about their child and, as we have emphasised, should be consulted as part of our proposed assessment procedure. In their turn they should be able to see most of the factual information about their child. They should, as a matter of course, be able to see their child's folder containing records of his progress and other facts about him, which we proposed in Chapter 4 should be maintained in school for every pupil. The results of professional consultations, however, would be maintained in a separate, confidential folder as we recommended in that chapter. Whether or not parents are shown the actual reports on their children must be a matter for the judgement of the professional concerned. Some professionals may be ready to show parents their actual reports on children; but for others the knowledge that parents would be able to see their reports could lead to the production of less detailed reports. The overriding consideration should always be whether or not it is in the child's best interests that the parents see the reports on him. Where a child is recorded by the local education authority as requiring special educational provision, the parents should, as we recommended in Chapter 4, have ready access to the documents comprising his record, namely the completed Form SE4 with a profile of the child's needs and a recommendation for the provision of special help, as well as a separate note on how that recommendation is being met in practice and the name of their Named Person.

16.13 Wherever possible, parental consent should be obtained to the passing of information about a child from community physicians to professionals outside the health service. Parental consent should also be sought to the passing of information between services other than the health service, though we would expect this to be done in a very informal way. As we have already emphasised, however, the child's interests must be regarded as overriding. Where the parent's consent cannot be obtained or is withheld and the child's welfare is considered to be at risk information available to one service about any factors which suggest the need for special help should be passed to others as may be necessary in the interests of the child.

16.14 Where parents are asked to consent to the transmission of information about their child, they should be helped to understand to whom and for what purposes the information is to be passed. This may be done by suitable explanations on any forms the parents are asked to complete or, wherever possible, by a personal interview. Where parents have given explicit consent to the passing of information about their child from one professional to another, it cannot be assumed that they have thereby consented to that information being subsequently forwarded to a third party. For example, where a parent has consented to medical information about his child being passed by a school doctor to a careers officer, it does not follow that he has thereby consented to the careers officer forwarding that information to an employer. Nor, when parents have given consent to the passing of information on one occasion, can it be assumed that their consent holds for its transmission at a later date. The recipients of information must consider whether they need to go back to the parents or, in the case of young people over 16, the young people themselves to obtain their consent to its further transmission or to its transmission at a later date than was originally envisaged.

16.15 The methods of transmitting and storing information must be determined by the professional judgement of those concerned. All methods of communicating confidential information carry with them the risk of improper disclosure. The communication of highly sensitive information by word of mouth involves the risk that the information may be misunderstood and the recipient may make an incorrect or unbalanced record of it; moreover there can be no check on the nature of the information passed in the event of subsequent complaint about breach of confidentiality. On the other hand, the communication of such information in writing carries with it the serious risk that the information could fall into the wrong hands. Each professional must decide which method of communication carries least risk of improper disclosure. Clearly his task will be facilitated if his relations with professional colleagues are founded on mutual trust.

16.16 Records and reports must obviously be stored securely and access to them carefully controlled. The most effective way of keeping records secure will vary according to circumstances but, as a general rule, they should be kept in an area to which access is restricted. They should always be kept locked when unattended. The clerical and support staff who handle the records should be made aware of the need for discretion in handling them. All school health records (except Forms 10bM) should be centrally controlled by the school health service, which is responsible for their production, but should not necessarily be centrally stored. In large ordinary schools or in special schools which have their own health service staff and a designated room for health purposes, complete health records may be held in the school under the control of the school doctor or nurse. It is an important but easily overlooked requirement that the source of any information contained in records and the date on which it was obtained should be noted and the information regularly reviewed and up-dated.

16.17 Finally, it should be recognised that the production of guidelines and of codes of practice on the sharing of information cannot be a substitute for personal knowledge on the part of individuals of their professional colleagues who are also concerned with meeting a particular child's needs and appreciation of their colleagues' professional expertise. Indeed, without such personal knowledge and trust it is unlikely that any exchange of information will be as useful as is possible. In the following section we turn to ways of developing the insight of different professionals into each other's work through inter-professional training.

II INTER-PROFESSIONAL TRAINING

16.18 Courses organised on an inter-professional basis provide an invaluable opportunity for members of different professions to get to know each other and learn about each other's work. As the evidence which we received on this subject stressed, such courses can be an extremely effective way of promoting understanding between members of different professions concerned with meeting the needs of children and young people who require special educational provision.

16.19 Inter-professional training can take two forms: joint initial training courses leading to a dual qualification and post-qualification courses organised on an in-service basis. Joint initial training courses for a dual qualification in teaching and librarianship have been developed but there are no comparable courses, for example courses leading to a dual qualification as a teacher and a social worker or as a teacher and a health visitor, in our field of enquiry. There is a range of post-qualification courses in our field which have developed in a piecemeal fashion. In the following section we consider the scope for developing both forms of inter-professional training for professionals engaged in meeting the needs of children and young people who require special educational provision and their parents.

Joint initial training courses leading to a dual qualification

16.20 We recognise that there are already professionals who are qualified in more than one field as a result in most cases of having taken consecutive courses of training. We are aware from our own experience and visits that the possession by teachers of a second professional qualification, for example as a social worker or speech therapist, combined with practical experience in a second field, can considerably enhance their contribution to the work of a school. We believe, however, that there is a need for the development of some joint courses of training for two professions. This might enable people to gain two professional qualifications in a shorter period of time than would be possible by consecutive

300

studies and, in addition, would be a particularly effective way of furthering co-operation between different professions.

16.21 There are, however, objections to concurrent training for two qualifications, not least the very understandable fear that it might lead to lower professional standards, and the undoubted difficulty of organising and staffing a single programme, possibly lasting four years, which would bring together theory and practice in separate, if related, fields. Nevertheless, whilst appreciating the difficulties, we think they can be overcome, and we are swayed by the advantages to which we have referred. *We therefore recommend that establishments of further and higher education as well as the bodies responsible for the training of members of the health, psychological and social services should explore the possibility of developing initial training courses leading to a dual qualification. We further recommend that a limited number of such courses should be introduced on an experimental basis as soon as possible (with the students receiving mandatory awards for the whole period of the course) and that their benefits should be evaluated with a view to their further development if the results are favourable.*

16.22 Whether or not it proves possible to develop joint initial training, we hope that the amalgamation of colleges of education with other institutions and the diversification of courses in establishments of further and higher education will increase the scope for shared elements in training courses for members of different professions, for example teachers, health visitors and social workers.

Post-qualification courses of inter-professional training

16.23 Post-qualification courses of inter-professional training have a dual function: first, to enable members of different professions to gain an insight into the contribution each can make to meeting the needs of children and young people who require special help and into each other's patterns of working; and secondly, to extend and improve skills and practice in areas of common concern to the participants. We consider that there is scope for the development of such courses in three ways: through lectures by workers drawn from different professions; through short courses; and through longer advanced courses. We examine these in turn below.

16.24 Lectures can be an effective way of improving understanding between members of different professions, particularly if adequate time is allowed for discussion. It is desirable that, wherever possible, lectures should be organised over a weekend so that the participants have sufficient opportunity to get to know each other and discuss each other's work.

16.25 The most practicable and effective means of developing inter-professional training in the near future is likely to be through short courses of one to three weeks' full-time study or their part-time equivalent. Such courses are already run successfully by a number of organisations. Part-time courses might be organised on the basis of one evening's study a week for a term or a number of weekend workshops. *We recommend that there should be an expansion of the provision of short courses of inter-professional training which focus on subjects of common concern to members of different professions engaged in*

301

meeting the needs of children and young people who require special educational provision. We have identified three areas in which we believe such courses are particularly needed: first the early development of children, which would be of interest to teachers and other professionals in the education service, particularly peripatetic teachers and those in nursery schools and classes, as well as to the staff of playgroups and day nurseries and to members of the health and social services; secondly the needs of children in residential special schools, which would be of particular concern to teachers, nursing and child care staff, educational psychologists and social workers; and thirdly the problems of adolescence, which is an area of common concern to many professionals, including teachers, careers officers and members of the health and social services.

16.26 Wherever possible short courses on the lines proposed should be provided jointly by two or more services. There would clearly be advantages in their provision being planned on an area or regional basis: the Joint Consultative Committees and regional conferences on special education, to which we turn in the following section, might well be instrumental in co-ordinating the arrangements. *We recommend that initiatives to develop courses on the lines suggested should be taken by the colleges and departments of education and the special education advisory and support service as well as by those bodies responsible for the organisation of post-experience training for professionals in the health, psychological and social services.*

16.27 Finally, we see scope for the development of one-year full-time or equivalent advanced level courses of inter-professional training on subjects of common concern to professionals working with children or young people who require special educational provision. We envisage that some might lead to a higher degree or diploma, for example in fields such as the education and training of young children with special needs, or counselling.

III CO-ORDINATION OF SERVICES

16.28 Contact at working level between members of different services is, as we have already emphasised, essential to the effective delivery of those services. We consider that it can be encouraged, though never replaced, by formal machinery for the co-ordination of services. In this section we examine machinery for co-ordination of services at different levels.

Joint Consultative Committees

16.29 We referred in the last chapter to Joint Consultative Committees (JCCs), which were set up by each area health authority and the matching local authority (or authorities where the area health authority is not co-terminous with a single local authority) in England and Wales under the National Health Service Reorganisation Act 1973. The Committee's functions are first to advise the two sets of constituent authorities on the performance of their statutory duties to co-operate, for example in the field of school health, and secondly to further the collaborative planning and operation of services of common concern. No provision was made in Scotland for the formation of statutory bodies analogous to the Joint Consultative Committees but, where they do not already exist,

Joint Liaison Committees are being established in accordance with the recommendations of a recent report.[2]

16.30 We believe that the JCCs could be in a key position to promote the effective co-ordination of services for children and young people with special needs and, as we suggested in paragraph 16.26 above and in Chapter 12, the development of courses of inter-professional training. At present, however, they have the disadvantage that they do not cover the employment service. Moreover, they vary considerably in effectiveness and some lack the status and prestige necessary to exert a major influence.

16.31 Despite these disadvantages, we consider that the existing structure of the JCCs should be utilised to promote the co-ordination of services for children and young people with special needs. We have noted the suggestion in the Court Report[3] that JCCs may wish to appoint a sub-committee of members of health and local authorities to advise on the development of services for children, including children who are mentally or physically handicapped. We believe, however, that there is a need for the establishment under the auspices of the JCCs of working groups on the lines of the Area Review Committees for Non-Accidental Injury, with a wide membership extending beyond the two constituent authorities of the JCCs and adequate supporting staff. These groups should have a clearly defined remit concerned with the co-ordination of services for children and young people with special needs. Such groups could not only be instrumental in achieving better co-ordination of the services with which we are concerned, but could also have the desirable effect of increasing the influence and prestige of the JCCs themselves. *We therefore recommend that working groups should be set up under the auspices of the JCCs to review the provision and operation of services for children and young people up to the age of, say, 25 with disabilities or significant difficulties, with a view to identifying deficiencies in provision and practice, developing strategies and programmes to meet those deficiencies and, as necessary, recommending policies for improving the effectiveness of the separate services and of their co-operation with each other.*

16.32 The composition of the working groups should be large enough to include officers from the education, employment, social and health services, and representatives of voluntary bodies and of employers' and employees' organisations, but not so large as to be unwieldy. We suggest that the groups should have about a dozen members. Although the membership will be for decision by the individual JCC, we envisage that it should include as a minimum the following: two or three officers designated by the local education authority, probably the assistant education officer for special education or the senior adviser in special education or both, together with the specialist careers officer; one or two representatives of the employment and training services, designated by the regional offices of the Department of Employment, with special knowledge of the problems of young people with special needs; one officer designated by the local authority social services department, probably a deputy or assistant

---

[2] Working Party on Relationships between Health Boards and Local Authorities – Report (HMSO, 1977).

[3] *Fit for the future.* The Report of the Committee on Child Health Services. Cmnd 6684 (HMSO, 1976), Vol 1, p 348.

director with special knowledge in this field; one or two officers designated by the area health authority, probably the Specialist in Community Medicine (Child Health) and the Area Nurse (Child Health) or their representatives; people designated by the voluntary organisations in the area, including at least one parent of a young person with special needs and a handicapped person himself; and one representative designated by each of the local representative employers' and trade union organisations. The chairman should be appointed by the working group. The need for the groups to be adequately serviced should be taken into account in determining the work loads of those officers expected to service them as part of their official duties.

16.33 The working groups should report annually through the JCCs to the two constituent authorities and the employment and training services. Their reports might include statements on work completed or put in hand as well as plans for the future. Although, like the JCCs, the groups would not be executive bodies, we suggest that consideration should be given to the possibility of some measure of joint funding which would enable them to support schemes designed to promote the co-ordination of services. We hope that their activities would be seen as sufficiently important to engage the interest and secure the co-operation of the chairmen of the vital local authority committees, namely the education, social services, policy and finance committees, the chairman of the area health authority and the key people in other agencies, whose support is essential if their recommendations are to be accepted and implemented by the constituent authorities of the JCCs as well as the employment and training services. At least for an initial period the progress of the working groups should be regularly reviewed by the National Advisory Committee proposed below.

Local co-ordination

16.34 In addition to the JCCs, we see a need for various forms of local machinery to co-ordinate the provision of services for particular groups of children or young people. The need for the local co-ordination of services for children under five is widely recognised. A number of examples of effective co-ordinating machinery for the purpose established by different authorities was given in the annex to a circular letter issued jointly by the Departments of Education and Science and Health and Social Security in March 1976.[4] These included a standing committee made up of members from the social services and education committees and also from voluntary bodies; a panel made up of elected members and officers from the local authority social services and education departments, with observers from the area health authority and various voluntary organisations; and a liaison committee composed of elected members from the social services and education committees and officers from the area health authority and the social services and education departments. Without wishing to prescribe any particular form of arrangement, we would urge those authorities which have not already set up machinery for the co-ordination of services for children under five to do so. Such machinery should include representatives of voluntary bodies engaged in making provision for children under five. The very valuable contribution of voluntary bodies and the

[4] Local Authority Social Services Letter LASSL(76)5 DHSS, Reference No S21/47/05 DES, Co-ordination of local authority services for children under five (9 March 1976).

importance of their inclusion at every stage in the planning of such provision were stressed in a more recent circular letter issued by the two Departments.[5] We return to the contribution of voluntary organisations in the next chapter.

16.35 We believe that the same need for local co-ordination of services applies to provision for young people with special educational needs during and for some time after the transition from school to further or higher education, training or employment. In addition to the social services and education departments, the local authority housing department is concerned with this group of young people, and liaison with health authorities, employment and training services and voluntary bodies is also important. *We therefore recommend that local authorities should set up local machinery for the co-ordination of services for young people with special educational needs during and for some time after the transition from school to further or higher education, training or employment.*

Regional conferences for special education

16.36 Co-ordination of services at regional level is usually taken to mean co-ordination of the services provided in one field, say education or health, by a number of authorities in a particular part of the country. There already exist in England regional advisory councils for further education, regional conferences for special education, regional health authorities, regional machinery for the co-ordination of social services for children and regional offices of the Department of Employment, the Training Services Agency and the Employment Service Agency. Regrettably, their boundaries often do not coincide.

16.37 We indicated in Chapters 7 and 8 the strong desirability of effective co-operation between local education authorities in the planning of special educational provision, including the development of some special schools as specialist centres for relatively rare and particularly complex disabilities. It is important, therefore, that there should be some kind of regional machinery for co-ordinating education services for children and young people with special needs: and it should be so constituted as to be able to promote the co-ordination of education and other services for this group of children and young people.

16.38 It would seem sensible to build on the existing regional machinery, namely the regional conferences for special education, particularly as the series of meetings held in 1975 on the initiative of the Department of Education and Science appears to have been successful in reviving their activity. These conferences, which consist of nine separate groups of local education authorities, provide a forum for a systematic review of special educational provision in each region. They are advisory bodies, with no effective powers, and their membership varies widely from one region to another.

16.39 While we would not wish to see any change in their status as advisory bodies, we believe that the regional conferences will need to become more

[5] Local Authority Social Services Letter LASSL(78)1, Health Notice HN(78)5 DHSS, Reference No S47/24/013 DES, Co-ordination of services for children under five (25 January 1978).

effective if they are to promote co-ordination of services in the way we have suggested. *We therefore recommend that the functions of the regional conferences for special education should be extended to include considering the annual reports of the working groups set up under the auspices of the JCCs; reviewing the existing facilities for special educational provision in the region (including those provided by voluntary organisations) and planning for the maximum possible degree of regional self-sufficiency; facilitating inter-authority arrangements for in-service training on an inter-professional basis; and identifying the requirements of young people with special needs for further education and promoting the provision of suitable courses for them.* As part of their function of planning for the maximum degree of regional self-sufficiency in special educational provision they would be particularly concerned with those schemes which require joint funding by local education authorities, for example the development of some special schools as specialist resource centres for the region. In promoting the provision of suitable courses of further education they will need to work in collaboration with the regional advisory councils for further education. Similarly, in co-ordinating arrangements for in-service training on an inter-professional basis they will need to collaborate with any new regional machinery set up as a result of the proposals in the report of the Working Group on the Management of Higher Education in the Maintained Sector under the chairmanship of the Minister of State for Education and Science, Mr Gordon Oakes.[6]

16.40 If the regional conferences for special education are to influence the effective co-ordination of the various services in the region concerned with children and young people with special needs, not just the education service, they must include in their membership representatives of those services. *We recommend that the composition of the regional conferences for special education should include local education authority elected members and officers, representatives of employment, health and social services, of employers' and employees' organisations and of voluntary organisations, and teachers with responsibility for children with special educational needs.* We recognise that the regional conferences will require adequate support if they are to carry out effectively the functions proposed. The local education authority responsible for servicing each regional conference must therefore have some additional administrative and clerical support specifically for regional conference work.

16.41 In Scotland the need for inter-regional provision for disabilities of infrequent incidence is particularly likely to arise, given the geographical nature of the country. Any national conference of education authorities may therefore have to be supplemented by inter-regional conferences in certain parts of the country.

16.42 In Wales the Welsh Joint Education Committee (WJEC) has responsibility for co-ordinating the provision by local education authorities of special education, particularly those aspects which have implications for the country as a whole. In parallel with the revival by the Department of Education and Science of the regional conferences for special education, arrangements were made by the Welsh Office for a conference of local education authority admini-

---

[6] Report of the Working Group on the Management of Higher Education in the Maintained Sector. Cmnd 7130 (HMSO, 1978).

strators and advisers concerned with special education. This was attended by representatives of all the Welsh authorities. It has been recommended that such conferences should be held in future on a biennial basis. *We recommend that the WJEC should continue its responsibility for co-ordinating the provision of special education by local education authorities in Wales. We also recommend that conferences on special education should be organised on the basis of arrangements agreed between the Welsh Office and the WJEC and that these conferences should reflect the wider range of membership we have recommended for the regional conferences in England. Further, the Welsh Office should consider, in consultation with the WJEC, what arrangements might be made in Wales for the receipt and review of the annual reports of the proposed working groups to be set up under the auspices of the JCCs.*

A National Advisory Committee on Children with Special Educational Needs

16.43 The area and regional co-ordination of services for children and young people with special educational needs requires to be matched by effective national machinery. Throughout this chapter we have used the term co-ordination in the sense of broad concern with the quality and efficiency of the different services, working together. Thus the area and regional co-ordinating bodies will variously review, advise, plan, monitor, promote and develop. The Joint Consultative Committees, and their working groups, and the regional conferences for special education, which we have recommended should form the co-ordinating bodies, are well placed to carry out the variety of functions which we have assigned to them. Although not themselves executive bodies, their membership consists mainly of those with direct responsibility for the provision and operation of local services and who in that capacity can be influential in translating precept into practice.

16.44 At national level this machinery has its counterpart in the formal and informal arrangements whereby Ministers, officials and professional staff in the education, health and social services and employment departments collaborate in the development of joint policies and practices. In furtherance of their work government departments are able to draw upon advice and information from many sources and have their own network of contacts with the local and regional arms of their respective services and with professional and voluntary bodies of all kinds.

16.45 These arrangements are indispensable to informed and effective national administration of special services for children and young people. But they are not in our view wholly sufficient. Much of the interchange between departments takes place under the stress of day to day events and is constrained by immediate requirements: whilst departmental contacts with outside organisations tend to be concerned with particular aspects of the services as distinct from their operation as a whole. There is in our view a need for arrangements whereby knowledgeable and experienced people, drawn from a variety of specialisms, who are conversant with the services for children and young people with special needs and able to take a synoptic view of what is going on, can offer informed, objective and coherent advice to Ministers on the co-ordination and future development of the services, and, in turn, provide an authoritative viewpoint on any matters on which Ministers themselves might wish to have collective advice.

16.46 The need for advisory machinery of this kind has been recognised by the government in its decision, which we warmly welcome, to accept the recommendation in the Court Report that the Central Health Services Council and Personal Social Services Council should establish a joint committee concerned with children. The committee will advise the Secretary of State for Social Services and Secretary of State for Wales on the co-ordination and development of health and personal social services as they relate to children and families with children. Although the joint committee will not be concerned with the education service we would expect it to devote considerable attention to the provision of health and personal social services for children with special educational needs and their families, and we are pleased to note that two of the members will be appointed on the advice of the Secretary of State for Education and Science.

16.47 We see the need for a similar committee to advise Ministers on the provision of educational services for children with special educational needs with particular regard to their co-ordination with other services. The work of this committee would thus be complementary in many respects to that of the joint committee concerned with children, and close links between the two committees would be essential. Like the Advisory Committee on Handicapped Children, which was suspended on our establishment, it would report to the Secretaries of State for Education and Science and for Wales. *We therefore recommend that a National Advisory Committee on Children with Special Educational Needs should be established to advise the Secretaries of State for Education and Science and for Wales on the provision of educational services for children and young people with special educational needs and their co-ordination with other services. A separate advisory committee should be appointed for Scotland.*

16.48 We envisage that the proposed advisory committees would consist of people with a special knowledge of the educational services for children and young people with special educational needs together with a small number of people with a special knowledge of the health, social, employment and training services in this field, who would be appointed in England and Wales on the advice of the Secretaries of States for Social Services and for Employment. Each committee should be as compact as possible and should not in our view have more than twenty members. The committee for England and Wales might wish to appoint a standing advisory sub-committee to advise it on matters pertaining to Wales.

CONCLUSION

16.49 Good practice in the sharing of information together with the development of inter-professional training on the lines proposed in this chapter will, we hope, serve to foster goodwill among members of different professions and confidence in each other's professionalism. Moreover, the machinery which we have proposed for the co-ordination of services at different levels should provide a framework which will facilitate day to day contact between members of different professions at working level on matters of common concern, make for greater efficiency, extend horizons and promote development. We hope that by these means good relations between different professions, on which so many of our recommendations depend, will be promoted and consolidated.

CHAPTER 17: VOLUNTARY ORGANISATIONS

INTRODUCTION

17.1 Special education has been greatly stimulated and enriched by the work of voluntary organisations, and their contribution to the lives of the children with whom we are concerned continues to be very substantial. As we indicated in Chapter 2 the early history of special education is largely a record of voluntary effort. In many of the fields of work discussed in this report voluntary organisations have taken the lead and marked out paths which public services have followed and broadened. The last thirty years have seen an increase in the number of organisations and in the range of their activities. Although in many cases the nature of the work undertaken has changed, voluntary bodies still often reveal new and unmet special educational needs. We are in no doubt that such organisations will continue to make a vital contribution to the lives of children with disabilities and to those of their families.

17.2 The future of voluntary organisations in the United Kingdom has recently been the subject of an inquiry by the Wolfenden Committee.[1] Although education was excluded from the Committee's terms of reference, many of the organisations studied were concerned with children with special needs. In the view of the Committee "What is generally known as 'the voluntary movement' is a living thing. New organisations are formed to meet newly-discerned needs. Others die. Yet others change their emphasis or venture into fresh fields. Relations with statutory authorities constantly change with new legislation or changes in administration. There is nothing static about the scene". The valuable and detailed evidence which we have received from a large number of organisations confirms this view of the voluntary sector's changing response to needs. At the same time the multiplicity of voluntary organisations concerned with disability makes it difficult to generalise about the part they play. In this chapter we consider the development of voluntary organisations in our field, their present work and how it is likely to be influenced by the proposals in our report.

17.3 The organisations referred to in this chapter are those which include among their activities help for children and young people with disabilities, work with their families and the provision of special education. These organisations vary widely in the scale of their resources and in the nature and scope of their activities. Some are old established charities offering a comprehensive range of services and provision for handicapped or disadvantaged individuals while others are small local groups providing a single service such as a playgroup for handicapped children. Many older organisations have become national institutions working for those in need, while more recently formed groups of parents or disabled people are often involved in self-help activities and in influencing

---

[1] *The Future of Voluntary Organisations.* Report of the Wolfenden Committee (Croom Helm London, 1978).

local and national policies and practices. Among the many hundreds of existing organisations those concerned with sensory and physical disabilities are more numerous and often more assured of public sympathy and support than those for other kinds of disabilities. In particular children with moderate learning difficulties and those with emotional and behavioural problems, who together form the largest group of children with special educational needs, are not supported by as many voluntary organisations, nor in general do they so readily arouse sympathy as children with other sorts of disability, though the existing organisations for them play an important part in promoting their interests.

17.4 Many national organisations work through local groups and branches. Their coverage in any area depends on the existence and effectiveness of local groups, the best of which are very active and influential. Voluntary effort for and by those with disabilities and significant difficulties has special significance in a number of ways. It may be a refreshing challenge to the ethos and standards of maintained services and of existing arrangements. It may also be the means of enhancing the quality of life and of promoting the well-being of those with special needs, when it complements and supplements maintained provision. It is particularly important when it facilitates the participation of handicapped young people in the community in which they live and their contribution to it.

I VOLUNTARY ORGANISATIONS UP TO THE PRESENT

17.5 Three trends may be discerned in the development of voluntary organisations concerned with disability up to the present time. One trend which started in the 1930s and which has become more evident in recent years is the increasing specialisation of voluntary organisations in line with advances in diagnosis, assessment and treatment. Where once they were concerned with a general area of handicap, many voluntary organisations have tended to focus their attention on a single handicapping condition, and new bodies have been set up to promote services for a particular condition. For example Societies for Cripples have been followed by organisations such as the Spastics Society, the Brittle Bone Society and the Association for Spina Bifida and Hydrocephalus. Some organisations concentrate on specialised aspects of help for a particular disability such as the production of talking books for the blind. Yet others concentrate on research or on social work. The move towards specialisation is very clear.

17.6 A second trend is the pioneering of provision and services, including schools, to meet new needs. In many cases the needs identified by voluntary bodies have in due course received public recognition, and responsibility for making provision for meeting them on a widespread basis has been assumed by local authorities. The voluntary organisations concerned have then turned their attention to securing the organisation of adequate arrangements by all local authorities. Thereafter they have often proceeded to identify new needs and to pioneer other services. Thus the Education Acts of 1918 and 1944, which increased the responsibilities of local education authorities for handicapped pupils, were followed by a decrease in the provision of special schools by voluntary organisations. Similarly, the setting up of the national health service in 1948 and of local authority social services departments in 1971, which increased the range of provision and services made by national and local authorities for

310

children with disabilities, led some voluntary organisations to change their objectives to meet new needs which in their view were covered inadequately by statutory services.

17.7 A third trend in the development of voluntary organisations is their increasing tendency to act as pressure groups. Most of the specialised voluntary bodies aim to secure a better public understanding by advertising the problems and needs associated with a particular disability. In many cases they exert pressure on central and local government for better public provision. For example, the needs of mentally handicapped children and young people are now better understood because of the activities of organisations which work on their behalf, while public awareness of dyslexia and autism is due largely to voluntary effort.

II THE DEVELOPMENT OF VOLUNTARY ORGANISATIONS IN THE FUTURE

17.8 It is difficult to predict the direction of the future development of voluntary organisations, since many of them, as we have shown, evolve by identifying and reacting to new needs. In broad terms, however, we envisage that the three trends in their general development identified above will continue. In addition, we foresee that voluntary organisations will seek increasingly to facilitate the communication of information to parents about their children's special needs and to improve arrangements for self-help and community support for parents. In the following section we consider in more detail the likely pattern of development of voluntary organisations in the light of our proposals for future arrangements for special educational provision.

Increasing specialisation

17.9 First, we believe that the move towards specialisation will continue and increase. It is impossible to foresee in detail in what directions voluntary organisations will become more specialised in the future. We believe, however, that increasingly they will be engaged in identifying and concentrating on quite narrowly specialised areas of need which become apparent with the progressive increase in knowledge of and concern for different disabilities.

The pioneering of services

17.10 Secondly, the pioneering of services by voluntary organisations has been and is likely to continue to be important for parents and for children and young people of all ages. In Chapter 5 we discussed provision for children under five and acknowledged the work of voluntary organisations in providing help for parents in the early years. At this stage in particular parents can benefit greatly from sharing their experiences with others with similar problems. The work of some voluntary groups has been directed towards meeting the needs of parents of young children, for example through the organisation of opportunity groups, which bring children with and without disabilities together and enable their mothers to meet each other. We regard such groups as an important element in the range of special educational provision which we consider should be available in all areas.

17.11 The provision by voluntary organisations of non-maintained special schools, many of them residential schools, has a long history, as we indicated in Chapters 2 and 8. Such schools still provide a high proportion of all the available places for children of school age with certain disabilities. Although their running costs are met almost entirely (or in Scotland substantially) from the fees paid by local education authorities, the schools are often cut off from the rest of the special and other educational services provided by local authorities, and we made proposals in Chapter 8 for developing and strengthening their links with local education authorities. The provision of a wide range of special educational arrangements, particularly in ordinary schools, which we advocated in Chapter 6, holds a challenge for those voluntary organisations whose efforts have been centred on special schools and should lead to a re-appraisal of the work of such organisations in the field of education. As we indicated in Chapter 8, some non-maintained special schools may wish to explore the possibility of making provision for children with kinds of disability different from those of the children for whom they currently cater. It will be important that, wherever possible, they should retain their freedom to innovate and experiment. The future of individual schools should be discussed against a long-term plan for special educational provision drawn up by local education authorities in conjunction with the voluntary bodies which provide non-maintained special schools. The regional conferences for special education should provide a useful forum for discussion of such plans. *We therefore recommend that the future of individual non-maintained special schools should be determined through consultation between local education authorities in the region and those voluntary organisations which provide the schools. Further, the schools themselves should be kept informed of any local authority plans which may affect their continued existence.*

17.12 Some of the newer, more specialised voluntary organisations have chosen to set up independent schools for handicapped children. Many of these cater for children with emotional and behavioural disorders but some have also pioneered special education for particular groups of children, for example autistic children. We recommended in Chapter 8 that where special school provision in the maintained sector is inadequate it should be increased to the point of sufficiency. Nevertheless, we recognise that there will always be a place for well devised arrangements made by voluntary organisations for groups of children whose special educational needs may not yet be widely recognised or met or which may become apparent in future.

17.13 We referred in Chapter 10 to the provision of opportunities for assessment of a specifically vocational kind and for continuing and further education and training in specialist centres run by voluntary organisations. In the course of our enquiries we have become aware of the valuable work being developed by voluntary organisations in villages for the mentally handicapped, in centres for young people with sensory and physical disabilities and in hostels and other forms of accommodation which encourage handicapped young people to live on a semi-independent basis and which facilitate their attendance at colleges and training centres of all kinds. We see a need for an increase in provision for young people with disabilities or significant difficulties within the maintained sector of further education. Nevertheless, we recognise that those voluntary organisations which have pioneered services in this field will have gained much valuable experience which could be of great help to those charged with the task of increasing statutory provision. *We recommend that collaboration between voluntary organisations and further education establishments should be developed and improved with a view to an increase in the opportunities available to young people with special needs after they have left school.*

17.14 Several organisations have pioneered arrangements for children and young people with disabilities to enjoy recreational activities. Other organisations, which embrace all children and young people whether or not they have disabilities, make special arrangements for particular groups. Some youth organisations specialise in providing clubs where physically handicapped young people can join with others in a wide range of activities or where mentally handicapped young people can continue to develop social and recreational skills and interests. All these efforts are in our view in need of support and further development, as we suggested in Chapter 10. Organisations such as the Scouts and Guides and the Duke of Edinburgh's Award Scheme, which have sought to accommodate special groups, inevitably face difficulties in making allowances for disabilities without accepting low standards of achievement in the interests of a superficial appearance of equality. In these areas of activity we hope it will be possible for the children with whom we are concerned to join with their contemporaries as often as possible in shared arrangements. Careful adaptation of schemes where necessary should enable many children with disabilities to achieve the same goals as their contemporaries without the need for any lowering in the standards of performance expected of them. As we indicated in Chapter 10, leisure and recreational activities assume particular importance for those young people with very severe and complex disabilities who need to achieve significant living without work.

17.15 In addition to pioneering new approaches to educational and recreational provision, voluntary organisations complement and supplement existing services, particularly those for families of children with disabilities. For example, they provide specialised social work for such families, as well as day care, holiday schemes and short-term residential facilities for the children. In all these fields, educational, recreational and social, voluntary organisations are already making a very valuable contribution. There is still considerable scope, however, for pioneering new and improved arrangements.

17.16 The need for new forms of provision or services has emerged in some cases from the research and enquiry sponsored by many voluntary organisations, especially the more recently formed highly specialised societies. Some can marshal more expertise in their field than is readily available elsewhere. We hope that the voluntary organisations will supply information about their research interests and activities to the Special Education Research Group proposed in the next chapter. In its turn the Research Group should consult appropriate voluntary organisations when considering research priorities in their fields of interest.

313

Pressure groups

17.17 Thirdly, it has long been a function of voluntary organisations to bring pressure to bear on national and local government in two ways: first by seeking to ensure that authorities are fulfilling their existing responsibilities for those with disabilities and secondly by identifying the need for new forms of provision and mobilising public opinion to demand them. Both these activities will continue in the future. For example, as more children with disabilities and significant difficulties are educated in ordinary schools voluntary organisations may need to be increasingly vigilant to see that adequate special arrangements are made for them.

17.18 We would expect voluntary organisations to exert pressure on behalf of individuals who cannot easily undertake the task of seeing that statutory duties are carried out and on behalf of groups of parents and children who are seeking to ensure that authorities provide efficiently for the children's special educational needs. It is inevitable that tension between voluntary and statutory bodies will occur on some occasions when the special pleading of voluntary organisations is set against what statutory bodies see as more general considerations. This tension, however, need not be harmful and, indeed, may result in fruitful collaboration.

17.19 We recognise that, given the large number of voluntary bodies concerned with promoting the interests of those with disabilities, the recommendations made by such bodies may be diverse and sometimes incompatible. Independent views are vital but it is also desirable that the voluntary organisations in this field should be kept informed of each other's activities. The Voluntary Council for Handicapped Children provides a forum for shared opinions about common issues, and local councils for voluntary service may also play a part in co-ordinating activities. In addition, as we recommended in the last chapter, the membership of the regional conferences for special education should include representatives of voluntary organisations which operate in the region. It would hardly be feasible for any one body to be responsible for the communication of information between the different organisations concerned; rather it should be for all the co-ordinating bodies mentioned to give a high priority to this aspect of their work. Only in this way can future policies be properly determined and available resources used effectively.

17.20 National voluntary organisations have played a significant part in shaping government policies for disabled persons. The Wolfenden Report recognised the need for co-ordinated action between statutory and voluntary bodies and this is no less necessary in the field of special education. For this reason we see one of the future tasks of the National Advisory Committee on Children with Special Educational Needs proposed in the last chapter as being to receive and co-ordinate the views of national voluntary organisations concerned with handicapped children and to take account of their opinions in making any recommendations to the Secretaries of State for Education and Science and for Wales.

The facilitating of communication

17.21 Fourthly, we envisage that voluntary organisations will play an increas-ingly important part in future in informing parents, professionals and other members of the public about children's or young people's special needs. Almost all voluntary organisations aim to create a better public understanding of and a more favourable attitude towards handicapped people. Our proposals for special education, in particular those concerned with effective provision in ordinary schools, with recreational facilities and with increased opportunities for employ-ment for young people with disabilities will depend on the informed opinions of parents, teachers and other professionals and we hope that voluntary organisa-tions will be instrumental in creating the better understanding necessary for the effective implementation of the changes recommended in this report.

17.22 Among the many activities of national organisations, work with pro-fessionals in the health, education and social services is an increasingly important function. Representatives of voluntary bodies contribute a great deal to national and local courses of training for members of different professions. We are aware of one college established by a major organisation whose work is in our view outstanding in providing well organised opportunities for the consideration of specific problems and developments on an inter-professional basis. Many other organisations provide courses and workshops for workers in the field and for administrators. We see an increasing and important function for national voluntary organisations in contributing specialised knowledge and experience about particular disabilities and difficulties to initial and in-service training for a range of different professions.

17.23 In Chapters 4, 5 and 9 we pointed to the role of parents as partners in the education of their children and suggested that they should be informed of voluntary organisations which may be helpful to them. Many organisations provide information for parents about their child's condition, about the services which exist to help them and about the experiences of other parents of children with similar disabilities. Some also arrange lectures, discussions and workshops not only to inform parents but also to help them to make the best use of the information at their disposal and to apply it to their own circumstances. It is very important that parents should know where they can obtain information, even if they choose not to obtain it or to make use of it. The leaflet published by the Voluntary Council for Handicapped Children[2] is a useful example of a way in which parents may be provided with starting points for their enquiries.

17.24 It emerged very clearly from the research carried out by the York University Social Policy Research Unit for the Family Fund[3] that many parents of handicapped children have very little contact with either statutory or voluntary organisations. While we would urge local authority services to take increasing responsibility for working with parents, voluntary organisations will, in our

---

[2] *Help Starts Here* (National Children's Bureau for the Voluntary Council for Handicapped Children, 1976).

[3] D Hitch, "What help can parents get? A Family Fund Analysis", *Concern* (Journal of the National Children's Bureau) No 23 (Spring 1977), 6-12.

view, continue to have a vital contribution to make. Indeed, voluntary organisations may be better placed than statutory services to establish contact with parents, many of whom are initially very suspicious of approaches from official representatives of public authorities and may reject offers of help. Support from voluntary bodies may be welcomed more readily than that from statutory bodies, even where the voluntary organisation receives financial assistance from a public authority.

Self-help and community support for parents

17.25 A developing trend in recent years has been the formation of groups of parents or disabled people to provide self-help. This trend seems likely to continue and increase in the future. As we indicated in Chapters 5 and 9, voluntary bodies, particularly those local groups which are effective, can be of great help to parents when handicapping conditions are first discovered in their children. We attach very great importance to the work of parents' groups in providing support and in making shared arrangements for their children's care and education. We welcomed in the last chapter (paragraph 16.34) the development by a number of authorities of local machinery to co-ordinate the provision of services for children under five. *We recommend that voluntary bodies and local authorities should collaborate to see that advisory and support services are available to groups of parents of young children with special needs and that no parents of such children are unaware of them.*

17.26 Some of the evidence we received on the support provided by voluntary organisations for parents sounded a note of caution, suggesting that not all voluntary organisations can rely on having advisers with training and experience, including a knowledge of the range of services available. It is essential that all organisations should ensure, so far as possible, that the advice and counselling offered to parents are of a high quality. Moreover, if the best interests of the children and families concerned are to be promoted, close co-operation is necessary between voluntary and statutory bodies in their support for parents. It is important that parents should not be presented unnecessarily with conflicting advice.

17.27 We are aware that local voluntary organisations are capable of inspiring and harnessing local interest and effort in a way that no statutory body can emulate. They can provide an effective point of contact and understanding between local communities and those of their members with disabilities or the families of those with special needs. They can help, too, to promote voluntary effort on an individual basis, for example through the "Good Neighbour Scheme", in which people are encouraged to offer practical help to those of their neighbours with special needs.

CONCLUSION

17.28 The recommendations of this chapter are directed towards an increase in collaboration at national, regional and local level between voluntary organisations and statutory services in the interests of children with special educational needs and their families. Such collaboration does not always occur at present and our evidence suggests that by no means all local authorities appreciate the contribution which voluntary organisations can make. At the same time, it is equally important that the independence of voluntary organisations should be preserved. We have pointed to several functions, particularly facilitating communication with parents and stimulating community support, which voluntary organisations are often better placed than statutory bodies to perform. There is scope for local authorities to assist voluntary organisations to carry out their work, for example by making premises available or offering financial support, without however detracting from their independence. Increasing collaboration between statutory and voluntary bodies should go hand in hand with continuing respect for the independence of the voluntary sector.

17.29 We envisage no decrease in the importance of voluntary groups and organisations in the future; rather we see an increased need for effort particularly on behalf of children with moderate learning difficulties and emotional and behavioural difficulties who, though numerically the largest groups of children with disabilities or disorders, are supported by relatively few voluntary organisations. It is inevitable that from time to time some groups will lose influence or change direction, while other new groups will emerge. This changing pattern brings new life to special education. In our opinion the very considerable contribution of voluntary organisations will continue to be needed as far ahead as anyone can see.

CHAPTER 18: RESEARCH AND DEVELOPMENT IN SPECIAL EDUCATION

INTRODUCTION

18.1 Many different disciplines and many organisations are at present engaged in research into the needs of children who suffer from disabilities or significant difficulties of various kinds. Through their work they contribute in a number of ways to the development of special education. But the very richness and variety of these different initiatives is often a source of confusion to those who work directly with children with special educational needs. During our work we have been made aware of the need to co-ordinate the knowledge and experience of many different specialists so that special education may be improved not only by research but by the dissemination of successful experience. In this chapter we discuss the promotion and co-ordination of research and development in special education, and identify the areas which we think should have priority in future. We also consider the translation of the results into successful practice. Finally we discuss how senior administrators and professionals in special education may be helped to develop their own skills and knowledge in research and development and to apply them in practice.

18.2 There are three main sources of research and development in special education, each of which gives rise to different considerations. The first is basic research in a number of areas, such as psychology, education, medicine and social science. Such research may need translation and modification before being of use to those working directly with children with special needs. The second is new methods and approaches developed by different people working with the same children, which may need to be related to each other; for example new techniques in speech therapy may have implications for the teaching of language. Thirdly, there is work by professional groups or organisations concerned primarily with one disability. This may need to be developed in relation to other forms of disability or even over the whole range of special needs. For example, research into how deaf children acquire language may shed light on the teaching of hearing children with severe learning difficulties. We are mainly concerned in this chapter with that research and development which bears directly on the teaching of children with special needs, wherever this takes place.

I PROMOTION AND CO-ORDINATION OF RESEARCH IN SPECIAL EDUCATION

Universities and other establishments of higher education

18.3 We indicated at the beginning of this chapter that it is important to co-ordinate research. It is also necessary to bring rigour and informed judgement to bear on many developments in special education. To this end, and in order to provide the advanced courses and opportunities for research recommended in Chapter 12, more high level academic posts must be established in special education. Very few such posts exist at present and there is only one chair in special education (at the University of Birmingham) in the whole of England, Scotland and Wales. *We therefore recommend that priority should be given within universities, polytechnics and other establishments of higher education to the allocation of senior academic posts to special education and that there should be at least one university department of special education in each region of the country.*

18.4 In medical education many of those concerned with teaching and research have joint university and national health service appointments which enable academic work to be informed by practical experience: we should like to see similar dual appointments made within special education. *We therefore recommend that some of the senior academic posts in special education proposed above should be linked to part-time work with children with special needs from an educational, a medical, a psychological or a social standpoint.* Such appointments would facilitate the development of research in special education and help to overcome the reluctance of some practitioners to undertake their own research.

18.5 It is important that lecturers in departments of education in establishments of higher education, particularly departments concerned with special education, should have enough time to fulfil their obligation to carry out research. In order to increase their opportunities to do so, we urge establishments of higher education to allot to those departments particularly concerned with special education a small number of extra posts, which could be used to release members of staff from their teaching duties for periods of full or part-time research. In addition, we hope that consideration will be given to the establishment of visiting lectureships in special education, which could be used to enable experienced teachers, advisers and administrators to contribute to research activities. The visiting lecturers might also offer lectures as part of the special education element which we have proposed should be included in all courses of initial teacher training, and might lecture too to teachers taking courses of in-service training.

18.6 There is also scope for the much closer involvement of members of the school psychological service in research in special education. Educational psychologists usually study research methods in their degree courses and their postgraduate training, but they seldom have sufficient time to carry out research in the course of their day to day work. We believe that opportunities for them to develop and to apply their skills in research must be increased. We therefore welcome the growth of appointments shared between local education authorities and interested departments in universities and other establishments of higher education. In Chapter 14 we recommended that post-qualification courses of varying length and content should be developed for educational psychologists in a number of centres. *We recommend that some of these courses should offer opportunities for experienced educational psychologists to develop their skills in research and that consideration should be given by validating bodies to the award of a higher degree for satisfactory completion of such a research-orientated course.*

Resource centres and research

18.7 We hope that those special schools which, under our proposals in Chapter 8, are designated as resource centres will be centres not only of support for teachers and for parents, but also of research in special education. One of their main functions will be to provide opportunities for practising teachers to undertake research. The part which teachers can play in research and development is often under-valued and far more encouragement and support needs to be given to them to carry out systematic research. We welcome the initiatives in this direction taken by departments of education in a number of universities, including Oxford and Sussex, and we hope that the development of some special schools as resource centres will continue and increase this trend.

18.8 As centres of research, those special schools designated as resource centres should provide opportunities for members of a number of professions to work together on projects in which a range of skills is required. These might include teachers, educational psychologists, social workers, nurses and members of the proposed special education advisory and support service.

18.9 It is highly desirable that there should be close links between those special schools which are designated as resource centres and departments of education in establishments of higher education. Staff in such departments can assist in the organisation of teachers' workshops,* often the first step in the development of collaborative research, and will benefit from the expertise available in the resource centres.

A Special Education Research Group

18.10 As we have said, research into different aspects of special education and into handicapping conditions in children is initiated and supported by a wide range of different bodies, including government departments, the Social Science Research Council, the Science Research Council, the Medical Research Council, bodies such as the National Children's Bureau, the National Foundation for Educational Research, the Schools Council, the Scottish Council for Research in Education, voluntary organisations and foundations, and trusts. Applicants for research grants can apply to the various councils and bodies listed above, each of which determines its own priorities, often in consultation with government departments. For some of these bodies special education may in many instances be a peripheral field of interest. The total amount awarded by the Social Science Research Council for projects in special education over the last ten years was of the order of only £300,000.

18.11 Responsibility for determining priorities for research in special education is widely diffused. The research liaison groups of the Department of Health and Social Security and the Chief Scientist Organisation of the Scottish Home and Health Department are concerned with determining priorities so far as their research into the health and social needs of children is concerned. Before we started work, the Secretary of State for Education and Science's Advisory Committee on Handicapped Children was influential in determining priorities for that part of the Department of Education and Science's research budget which was devoted to special education. Since 1974, the major part of the Department's allocation has been devoted to projects recommended by us, of which details are

---

* Teachers' workshops combine opportunities for practical work with academic lectures. They have been used successfully in, for example, the development of the New Mathematics and in the Schools Council project on the education of severely mentally handicapped children.

given in Appendices 5–8. At present individual proposals for research into aspects of handicap in children are considered by separate agencies, often in isolation and with insufficient regard to other work in related fields. There is no co-ordinating body able to take a synoptic view of what is going on and offer guidance on priorities for future research. We have reached the conclusion that there should be such a co-ordinating body and *we therefore recommend that a Special Education Research Group (SERG) should be set up with responsibility for indicating priorities for research in special education, for identifying programmes and projects to be initiated, for awarding some research grants and for commenting if requested to do so on applications for research central to its concerns which are submitted to other bodies.* It would thus need to have its own budget and *we recommend that it should have at its disposal sufficient funds to enable it at any time to support one or two large programmes or projects together with several smaller ones.*

18.12 The members of the proposed Special Education Research Group would be drawn from the proposed National Advisory Committee on Children with Special Educational Needs and its Scottish counterpart (see Chapter 16), the Department of Education and Science, the Scottish Education Department, the Welsh Office and Her Majesty's Inspectorate. We see the group as having responsibilities in England, Scotland and Wales as a whole, but we recognise that it might need to set up sub-groups to give particular attention to Scottish and Welsh matters. The group should have links with other research liaison groups, particularly those in the Department of Health and Social Security. In addition, there should be some cross-membership between this research group and the special section of the Schools Council which we recommended in Chapter 11 should be formed to deal with matters of curriculum in special education. The Scottish Consultative Committee on the Curriculum should have a similar relationship with SERG. Cross-membership between these bodies would help to avoid duplication in areas of common interest.

18.13 The Special Education Research Group would be responsible directly to the Department of Education and Science, the Scottish Education Department and the Welsh Office and would produce reports at regular intervals giving details of the projects funded and the practical consequences of completed projects. It should also work with voluntary organisations and foundations to produce a record of all research in special education that was in progress. The priorities indicated by the group as a result of its deliberations should be publicised so that researchers could be pointed to areas of greatest need.

18.14 The Special Education Research Group would naturally need to relate its activities to those of other research bodies, who would continue their important support for research in special education. We believe that it should concentrate upon the educational implications of disabilities and upon possible educational methods designed to mitigate or overcome their effects. We would expect it to hold conferences from time to time on research in special education, in collaboration with the senior staff training college which later in this chapter we propose should be established.

II AREAS IN WHICH RESEARCH IS NEEDED

18.15 Our enquiry has led us to conclude that further research is needed in a number of areas. People will have their own ideas about the particular areas to be tackled, but we list below, though not in any order of priority, those topics which should, in our view, receive attention as soon as possible.

(i) The updating of epidemiological studies such as the Isle of Wight Study[1] in order to obtain information about changes in the prevalence of different handicapping conditions, including regional differences.

(ii) Procedures for the identification of significant difficulties and developmental delays in young children below school age.

(iii) The study of those factors in school, particularly in secondary schools, which can reduce the occurrence of learning and behavioural difficulties.

(iv) Forms of school organisation for maladjusted children in ordinary schools and elsewhere.

(v) The slow learner in the ordinary school – effective forms of organisation, curriculum and methods for children with mild or moderate learning difficulties.

(vi) The assessment and education of children with specific learning difficulties in reading, writing and spelling, and the evaluation of different approaches.

(vii) The monitoring and evaluation of changes following the implementation of Section 10 of the Education Act 1976 (including further studies of forms of integration).

(viii) Residential special education. The criteria for determining the need for boarding placement, the value of residential special education and the factors which make for effective boarding education for children with different special needs.

(ix) The problems of children with special educational needs whose first language is not English.

(x) The educational and personal needs of young people over 16 with disabilities and significant difficulties.

(xi) Techniques of guiding parents.

(xii) The administration and organisation of special education services.

(xiii) The provision of services for children with special needs and their parents in isolated areas.

III THE TRANSLATION OF RESEARCH INTO PRACTICE

18.16 A number of other arrangements is needed to translate research into successful practice and to ensure that successful methods are more widely known and used in special education. One way of achieving these results is through joint appointments of the kind proposed in paragraph 18.4. Another is through

---

[1] See M Rutter, J Tizard and K Whitmore, *Education, Health and Behaviour* (1970).

school-based in-service training. The courses for senior staff proposed in Chapter 12 should therefore include attention to the techniques of school-based training, and the advisory and support service proposed in Chapter 13 should be prominent in organising it. In this way the work of special schools can be regularly influenced by new developments. In their turn, those special schools which are developed as resource centres might well act as bases for in-service training for teachers in ordinary schools. In this capacity they should keep teachers in ordinary schools in touch with relevant research and with new methods and materials.

18.17 The work of teachers' centres has normally included attention to children with special needs and we hope that their programmes will give increasing attention to this subject in future. Some local education authorities have also set up special education teachers' centres, which have made a very effective contribution to increasing teachers' understanding of children's special needs, particularly by involving teachers in workshops and research at a local level. It must be for local judgement whether such centres should be developed or whether these activities would best be undertaken at special schools or ordinary teachers' centres. *However, we recommend that each local education authority should have a centre where research, development and in-service training in special education are based and to which all the teachers in the area with responsibility for children with special needs can turn for help with their professional development.*

A Special Education Staff College

18.18 Our proposals in this and other chapters, particularly for the development of in-service training, for research into the needs of children who require special educational provision and for a special education advisory and support service are all of them designed to enhance the quality of special education. There remains the question of how the competence of experienced administrators, advisers and teachers in special education can be further enhanced. They must be helped, through multi-professional conferences and courses, to develop approaches consonant with those of other professionals, particularly psychologists, doctors, nurses, social workers and careers officers. We know of no existing body able to co-ordinate and develop high level conferences and courses in this complex field. Such conferences and courses will not, however, be developed spontaneously. They will have to be carefully organised. *We therefore recommend that a body responsible for the further training of senior staff, which might be known as the Special Education Staff College, should be established.* We hope that the facilities of the college would be available to senior staff in special education in Scotland and Wales as well as England.

18.19 The proposed Special Education Staff College might embody some of the features of the Further Education Staff College. which was established in 1962 as a result of a proposal made in the Willis Jackson Report.[2] The general aims of that college are to provide opportunities for senior staff in establishments of further education, people from industry and commerce, educational administration and the universities to meet together for residential study con-

---

[2] *The Supply and Training of Teachers for Technical Colleges.* Report of a Special Committee appointed by the Minister of Education in September, 1956 (HMSO, 1957).

ferences, normally lasting one or two weeks. However, we have reservations about the wisdom of a staff training cadre having to administer residential facilities and about the cost of setting up a residential college, although we see the provision of a residential element as a desirable long-term aim. We regard it as more urgent and important to set up a senior staff training cadre with finance and powers to organise what should in the main be self-supporting courses and conferences. For the present we envisage that such a staff college would use the variety of existing facilities for conferences and courses in different parts of the country.

18.20 The permanent staff of the college would initially be fairly small, consisting perhaps of a Director, a Deputy Director, an Information Officer and secretarial staff. Funding would be provided by both central and local government. It would be desirable that, as with the Further Education Staff College, the Special Education Staff College should receive an initial "pump-priming" grant from the Department of Education and Science. The college should have an independent governing body, which might have some common membership with the National Advisory Committee proposed in Chapter 16. We suggest that the college should be set up for a period of five years, after which its form and work would be reviewed and the question of residential accommodation reconsidered.

18.21 As well as organising courses and conferences, the college should have responsibilities for collecting and disseminating information about new research and developments. It should collaborate with the proposed Special Education Research Group and the proposed Schools Council section on special education in ensuring that senior staff working in special education are able to know about and comment on the results of research and development in special education and are helped to apply them in their every day work.

CONCLUSION

18.22 In this chapter we have stressed the importance of research and development in special education and the need for high level academic posts which combine research with teacher training and with continued work with children with special needs. We have recommended that two organisations be set up: a Special Education Research Group and a Special Education Staff College. These two, together with the special section of the Schools Council recommended in Chapter 11, should be major centres of influence in relation to the development of national policies and the training of senior staff. The centres should work closely with departments of special education in establishments of higher education, with regional and local centres, with the special education advisory and support service and with special school resource centres to create a network in which priorities for research are identified, the results of research disseminated and practices which have been proved effective made widely known in schools.

CHAPTER 19: PRIORITIES AND RESOURCES

INTRODUCTION

19.1 We were appointed in 1974 to review the full range of educational provision in Great Britain for handicapped children and young people. We started this report by pointing out that there had been no other comparable enquiry this century. The basic framework of provision that we were to review had stood for thirty years.

19.2 Against this background we saw our work as having two main features. We were to look at the present arrangements for special educational provision; and we were to point the direction of their future development. The first exercise was a necessary condition of the second. It seemed reasonable to think that there would not be another enquiry such as ours for many years to come and that we would therefore be looking well ahead in formulating our proposals. Our perspective therefore reaches to the end of the century and possibly beyond. With some important exceptions we have not set our proposals against a time-scale for their fulfilment. Rather we have tried to produce a new framework within which the changes we recommend can take place progressively in step with resources.

19.3 We have throughout our work been acutely aware of the financial constraints on central and local government. Indeed, our terms of reference required us "to consider the most effective use of resources". We would stress that some of our proposals can be substantially achieved by redeployment of existing resources. Others are in line with present government policies for expansion, for example policies for an increase in nursery and further education provision. Further, many of the developments recommended in our report stem from Section 10 of the Education Act 1976, which Parliament enacted midway through our review. We assume that adequate resources will be made available for the implementation of present policies for expansion and of Section 10 itself. Nevertheless, we recognise that some of our key proposals will require substantial additional expenditure over the next few years and beyond.

19.4 We have not attempted to identify elements of net additional cost attaching to our different recommendations. Nor would it have been possible to do so. As we have made clear, the incidence of cost will be spread over future years, which will inevitably bring major changes in the commitment of educational resources. Moreover, any quantification of our recommendations in terms of their assumed additional cost over a selected period of time would have been entirely theoretical both in construction and result for two main reasons. First, information about the actual current cost of providing special education is incomplete. The difficulty of obtaining figures for the cost of special educational provision in special classes and units emerged very clearly from the survey conducted for us by the Department of Education and Science of the cost per place in different types of special schools, classes and units in nine local education authorities in England and Wales. Moreover, the figures obtained for special schools revealed a very wide range of costs in different schools.* Secondly, we have proposed a much broader framework of special education; and the cost of making provision within this framework is not known. In the circumstances we have thought it more helpful to pick out those of our recommendations which appear to us to have significant implications for resources.

19.5 We naturally believe that the objectives set out in our report are important and should be pursued with all possible speed. The period since 1944 has been one of increasing educational expectations on the part of parents, children and young people. There have been major developments in all three stages of education – primary, secondary and further. The two-stage raising of the school leaving age, the elimination of all-age schools, the reorganisation of secondary education on comprehensive lines, the development of middle schools and tertiary colleges, the vast expansion and diversification of further and higher education have all consumed resources. We believe that the time is ripe for a comparable outlay on innovation in special education, in line with the growing demand from parents of children with special educational needs.

19.6 In another sense as well the time is favourable. Educational aspirations will undoubtedly remain high and, indeed, will continue to rise. We expect our report to contribute to this trend. While, however, the developments referred to above took place during a period when the school population was increasing, school rolls are at present falling and are likely to continue to do so for some years. The effects are largely concentrated at present in primary education, but they will in time pass on to secondary education, where the *per capita* savings will be greater, and then to further and higher education. These trends afford a unique opportunity for improvements in the quality and range of education services within the total funds devoted to them. We firmly hold, for all the reasons given in this report, that adequate resources can and should be made available for the improvements we have proposed in provision for children with special needs. Thus we see considerable scope for the early achievement of many of our objectives.

19.7 With this in mind we proceed to identify those of our recommendations which we think come first in order of priority; to comment on the time-scale for the implementation of Section 10 of the Education Act 1976; and then to

---

* Of the six authorities who returned information on the costs of placing children in special classes or units, five were unable to separate all the costs of the special classes or units from those of the ordinary schools to which they were attached. No conclusions could therefore be drawn about the cost of special classes or units. Information was returned by nine authorities about pupil costs in 152 maintained special schools. The costs in schools catering for pupils with the same type of disability differed enormously. For example, pupil costs in day schools ranged from £1,055 to £2,115 in schools for the physically handicapped, £568 to £1,343 in schools for the ESN(M) and £757 to £1,728 in schools for the ESN(S). Pupil costs in boarding special schools ranged, for example, from £1,946 to £5,117 in schools for the physically handicapped and from £1,399 to £3,015 in schools for the ESN(M). In some cases there was a wide range of pupil costs in special schools of the same type within the same authority. For example, in one authority the pupil costs in day schools for the ESN(M) ranged from £606 to £1,154 and in two others the costs in day schools for the ESN(S) ranged from £757 to £1,293 and from £880 to £1,728 respectively.

examine aspects of our main recommendations as they affect r
Education Act 1976 does not apply to Scotland: our main recor
and the order of priority in which we place them below, however,
for England, Scotland and Wales.

1 PRIORITIES

19.8 We proposed in Chapter 3 a new conceptual framework within which special educational provision should be made. This entails a continuum of special educational need rather than discrete categories of handicap. It embraces children with significant learning difficulties and emotional or behavioural disorders as well as those with disabilities of mind or body. It is within this framework that our key proposals for the discovery, assessment and recording of special educational needs, the associated duties of local education authorities and the role of parents are set. This conceptual framework must be reflected in legislation. We urge that the necessary legislation should be introduced without delay and certainly within 18 months of the publication of our report. Even before legislation is enacted, however, there is a number of practical steps that can be taken to improve provision for children and young people with special educational needs.

19.9 Our report stresses the importance of early education for children with disabilities or significant difficulties and of increased opportunities for young people with these problems to continue their education after 16 at school or in further education. It is at these two ends of the age range that we believe improved provision to be most urgently required and it is here that our priorities begin.

19.10 If a close and, so far as possible, equal relationship between parents of children with special educational needs and professionals is established and if prompt and effective educational help for such children is provided as soon as their special needs become apparent, the whole of the children's subsequent education will benefit. The education service will also benefit, since early intervention will mean that many children will be less dependent upon support in later years and will be able to take their place in ordinary schools. In Chapter 5 we suggested a variety of ways of extending early educational opportunities for children with disabilities and educational difficulties including not only a substantial expansion of nursery education but also the encouragement of voluntary provision for young children below school age.

19.11 Provision for young people over 16 with special needs has in our view been badly neglected in the past. Many special schools do not cater for pupils over 16, and although in some areas there are increasing opportunities for them to continue their education in further education establishments, the present facilities are in general manifestly inadequate. As part of the implementation of Section 10 of the Education Act 1976 ordinary secondary schools will need to ensure that they provide a full range of opportunities for senior pupils who have special educational needs. Unless opportunities are available to young people to continue their education in special or ordinary schools, in colleges of further education or in other establishments in the range described in Chapter 10, all the earlier efforts made on their behalf may, as we indicated in that chapter, come to nothing. Conversely, good provision will pay dividends by enabling many of these young people to achieve much greater independence in adult life, with correspondingly less dependence on support from their families, statutory services or voluntary organisations.

19.12 These improvements in special educational provision for children under five and young people over 16 will not be achieved without the advances in teacher training which we have proposed. Advances in teacher training are equally essential to the progressive integration in ordinary schools of more children with disabilities, including some with severe and complex disablement, in accordance with Section 10, and to continuing effective provision in special schools. Thus we regard our proposals for the improved training of teachers as no less urgent than those for improved provision for children and young people.

19.13 We therefore urge that equal priority should be accorded to the three sets of our recommendations covering respectively provision for children under five with special educational needs, provision for young people over 16 with special educational needs and developments in teacher education and training. These are listed in more detail at the end of this chapter.

19.14 Although for present purposes we have marked out these three sets of recommendations as having priority over others, they cannot be entirely isolated. Their implementation is unlikely to be successful without the organisation by each local education authority of a unified special education advisory and support service to carry out the functions we have assigned to it. For this reason, and bearing in mind that in many cases the establishment of this service can be achieved substantially by the retraining and redeployment of existing staff, we look for the early appearance of the new service in all areas. Again, the early establishment of our proposed Special Education Staff College will be required to provide opportunities for those advisers who will be members of the local advisory and support service to improve their capabilities and meet colleagues in other professions. Equally important, the successful implementation of our three most pressing sets of recommendations demands increased recognition of special education as a challenging and intellectually satisfying activity for those engaged in it. In order to promote this recognition and thus enhance the quality of the provision we consider that no time should be lost in the development of research in special education along the lines we have suggested. We therefore urge universities and other establishments of higher education to take the initiative in promoting such research as quickly as possible.

19.15 As we have said, our three areas of first priority have additional significance in the light of Section 10 of the Education Act 1976, which is to come into force on a day to be appointed by the Secretary of State. In particular our proposed developments in teacher training are vital to the successful implementation of the principle of integrated educational provision. Our proposal for the organisation of advice and support in special education as a unified service was conceived substantially from the point of view of Section 10, and a great many of our other recommendations may be seen as different aspects of extending the capacity of ordinary schools to meet the special educational needs of children on an expanding scale.

19.16 It would be totally unrealistic to think that authorities will on the appointed day be ready to introduce immediate radical changes in the pattern of their provision for special education, and we do not think that this was ever the intention. We see the implementation of Section 10 taking place progressively over time, in step with the fulfilment of those conditions which we identified in Chapter 7 as being necessary. For this reason we do not attach undue significance to the appointment of any particular day for the introduction of Section 10. We have stated our view that it should not be introduced without comprehensive guidance to local education authorities by the Secretary of State. Given that Section 10 would be incorporated into the new legislative provisions that are needed to establish our new framework of special education we think it reasonable to expect that it would come into force within that framework. We are however convinced of the need for all authorities, in the light of Departmental guidance and in consultation with other local education authorities in their region and with health authorities, to draw up a long-term plan for special educational provision within which arrangements for individual schools, ordinary and special, will take their place. We think it important that the plans should be publicised locally so that parents and others affected by them may have opportunity to comment.

II RESOURCES

19.17 We have explained why we are not attempting to price our different recommendations, and we have stated our expectation that demographic trends will make it possible to do many things at no extra cost which in other circumstances would have required additional funds. There is one other factor which seems to us to bear directly upon the financial implications of our proposals. Many of our recommendations are as we have said directly related to implementation of the provisions of Section 10 of the Education Act 1976, which was enacted two years after we started our enquiry and confirmed the direction of much of the content of our report. In Chapter 7 we voiced our strong conviction that the necessary resources must be provided with which to implement the new provisions without detriment to the quality of special education. Parliament having willed the ends, we would expect the government to will the means.

19.18 On the basis of this approach we concentrate in the rest of this chapter on indicating the relationship of our main proposals to present government policy and in very broad terms the timing of their implementation. We first consider our recommendations for increased provision for children under five and young people over 16 and for a special education advisory and support service. We then proceed to deal in rather more detail with the resource implications of our recommendations for improved teacher training.

Provision for children under five with special needs

19.19 Our proposals for increased provision for children under five with special needs have four main components: greater recognition and involvement of parents as educators; a substantial extension of nursery education for all children, since this would have the consequence that opportunities for nursery education for those with special needs would be correspondingly increased;

an extension of peripatetic teaching services to cover all types of disability or disorder in young children; and the provision of professional help and advice from members of the various supporting services, including the proposed special education advisory and support service, to playgroups, opportunity groups, day nurseries and, above all, parents. (See recommendations 1, 10, 8, 14, 15 and 7 of Chapter 5.*)

19.20 The government is committed to a continuing expansion of nursery education, particularly in areas of social and educational disadvantage. We welcome the attention given by the Department of Education and Science to the needs of handicapped children in allocating resources for nursery education in the 1978–79 building programme. We also strongly support the government's intention that because of declining numbers of pupils of school age provision for under-fives in school will cater for increasing proportions of three and four year olds, within a steady total number of places.[1] It is most important that accommodation which becomes available in primary schools as a result of the declining school population should be used for the purpose of nursery education. It follows that, assuming that the present system of local government financing continues, central government's calculations of relevant expenditure for the rate support grant settlements and the distribution formulae in future years should enable all authorities to use spare accommodation in this way.

19.21 Peripatetic teaching services will need to be considerably expanded and improved if they are to cover the range of handicapping conditions in children. These teachers will form part of the proposed special education advisory and support service. We envisage that many of them will be drawn from the staff of special schools. Some will be seconded to the advisory and support service for a limited period; others will be assigned to the service for varying proportions of their time. With the probable decline in the number of pupils in special schools, it should be possible to expand peripatetic teaching services for young children in most fields of disability and in most parts of the country through a redeployment of teaching staff rather than an increase in their numbers.

19.22 Playgroups, opportunity groups and day nurseries will continue to be an important form of provision for young children with special educational needs. We are supported in this view by a recent joint circular letter to local authorities and local health authorities from the Department of Health and Social Security and the Department of Education and Science.[2] The provision of support to these groups should be part of the work of peripatetic teachers as well as that of professionals in the health and social services. The expansion of the health visiting service planned by the government during the period up to 1980–81[3] should make it possible for support for such groups by health visitors to be increased. We hope that members of other services will similarly be able to give more help in future, and we note with satisfaction the suggestion in the joint

---

* The recommendations of each chapter are listed in the summary of recommendations which follows this chapter.

[1] *The Government's Expenditure Plans.* Cmnd 6721 (HMSO, 1977).

[2] Local Authority Social Services Letter LASSL(78)1, Health Notice HN(78)5 DHSS, Reference No S47/24/013 DES, Co-ordination of services for children under five (25 January 1978).

[3] *Priorities in the Health and Social Services. The Way Forward* (HMSO, 1977), p 10.

circular letter mentioned above that social services departments should consider designating a member of their staff to examine with local voluntary groups how support and guidance for playgroups would best be provided. We believe that the local education authority should also be involved in such discussions with voluntary groups.

Provision for young people over 16 with special needs

19.23 The main improvements proposed in this report in the provision for young people over 16 with special educational needs are as follows: more opportunities for such young people to continue their education at school or in further education and to receive careers guidance; a variety of forms of further education provision to meet their needs, including support to enable them to take ordinary courses and, for those with more severe disabilities, special courses and facilities in a special unit in each region; a specifically educational element in adult training centres and other day centres; and the necessary financial support to enable them to undertake courses of further or higher education. (See recommendations 2–3, 5–6, 7–10, 15 and 27–28 of Chapter 10.)

19.24 The expansion of further education provision planned by the government over the next few years should afford considerable scope for improvements in provision for young people with special educational needs. As part of the education service's contribution to provision for unemployed young people, 10,000 non-advanced further education places are to be provided in England, Scotland and Wales by 1981–82, in addition to the increase in the number of students on such courses which is already included in the Education Departments' latest projections of student numbers. Moreover, it has been suggested to authorities that it would be particularly appropriate for them to improve their provision for the handicapped and to develop provision directed towards helping school leavers of low educational achievement and social competence, many of them deficient in the basic skills of literacy and numeracy.[4]

19.25 A number of the conditions identified in Chapter 10 for the effective development of further education provision for young people with special needs could be fulfilled without significant demands on resources. In particular, the co-ordinated approach by the local education authorities within each region which was advocated in that chapter calls for attention to planning rather than further expenditure. We recognise, however, that the effective support of students with special needs admitted to courses of further or higher education, whether ordinary, modified or special ones, will require substantial additional provision by the education, health and social services. In view of the high priority that we give to the development of special educational opportunities for young people we urge that the necessary resources in the form particularly of special equipment and professional help and advice should be made available to them without delay. (See recommendations 7–12 of Chapter 10.)

[4] DES Circular 10/77, Welsh Office Circular 165/77, Unemployed Young People: The Contribution of the Education Service (30 September 1977) and Scottish Education Department Circular 996 (7 October 1977).

Special education advisory and support service

19.26 The special education advisory and support service recommended in Chapter 13 is an integral part of the arrangements proposed in this report for children and young people with special needs. It might appear at first sight that the establishment of such a service will be an expensive undertaking. In practice, however, as we explained in Chapter 13, it would in most areas be made up substantially of existing advisers, advisory teachers and other specialist remedial teachers, reinforced by a number of practising teachers. We see no reason why the structure of the service should not be set up straight away and at a minimum cost through the reorganisation and, where necessary, retraining of existing staff. The service can thereafter be developed and improved over a period of years. Given the prospect of a continuing decline in the numbers of pupils in both special and ordinary schools and the consequent opportunities for redeployment of teaching staff, the resource implications of developing the service should be small.

Teacher training

19.27 In addition to the inclusion of a special education element in all courses of initial teacher training, we proposed in Chapter 12 the development of three main types of in-service courses of teacher training: short courses on special educational needs of about one week's full-time study or its part-time equivalent to be taken by the great majority of serving teachers within the next few years; one-year full-time courses or their part-time equivalent leading to a recognised qualification in special education for teachers with a defined responsibility for children with special educational needs; and other short courses of varying length on different aspects of special education. (See recommendations 2, 4, 7, 12, 19–20 and 22 of Chapter 12.)

19.28 There are about 500,000 full-time teachers in regular service in primary and secondary schools in Great Britain. Not all of them would be expected to take a short in-service course on children's special educational needs. For example, some will be approaching retirement or will have recently completed an initial or in-service course which contained a special education element. We may therefore assume that our concentrated programme of in-service training would be applicable to about four-fifths of the teaching force in schools, or about 400,000 teachers. If the programme were spread over five years and took the form of one week's full-time study or its part-time equivalent we estimate that at least 200 additional lecturers would be required working full-time. If, as we propose, the courses were to be also available to teachers in establishments of further education, the number of lecturers required would rise to some 220. For a variety of reasons this is unlikely to be an exact figure but it provides an indication of the order of magnitude. Suitable accommodation would of course also need to be available. We would foresee no difficulty in using the services of these lecturers once the programme had been completed. For example, there should be wide scope for their absorption into the local advisory and support service or for their employment on other courses in special education.

19.29 The proposed one-year or part-time equivalent courses leading to a recognised qualification in special education would be taken by those teachers in special schools who had not already completed an additional year of special training and other teachers with a defined responsibility for children or young people with special educational needs, including teachers in charge of designated special classes or units, or resource centres or supporting bases in ordinary schools, peripatetic teachers of children with special needs and teachers in charge of special units in establishments of further education. We recommended in Chapter 12 that the provision of suitable courses and support from local education authorities for teachers to attend them should be so increased that possession of an additional recognised qualification can be made a requirement on teachers with a defined responsibility for teaching children with special educational needs as soon as possible. We hope that in practice all such teachers will have undertaken training leading to a recognised qualification within a decade. Whether this training is carried out on a full or part-time basis, it is clear that a very considerable increase in lecturing staff and in accommodation for courses in special education will be required particularly in England and Wales. We estimate that if the necessary number of teachers with an additional recognised qualification is to be achieved within ten years, the staff and resources devoted to the present one-year or part-time equivalent courses in special education will need to be at least quadrupled.

19.30 The other short courses for teachers proposed in Chapter 12 will vary very considerably in length and content. We would expect them to be organised largely by members of the special education advisory and support service and to make use of existing facilities. They should not, therefore, require the provision of a substantial number of additional lecturing staff or a significant increase in accommodation.

19.31 The fulfilment of our proposals for the development of teacher training, particularly for one-year or part-time equivalent courses leading to a recognised qualification in special education, will be frustrated unless local education authorities are willing to second those teachers who wish to study full-time and to support and encourage those who wish to do so part-time. Authorities for their part will need encouragement to do this. There may, of course, be major changes in future in the system of financing local government expenditure. Assuming, however, that the present system continues, we are convinced that a nation-wide advance in teacher training on the lines we have proposed is unlikely to be achieved merely by including the costs in the calculation of relevant expenditure for rate support grant purposes. One possible solution might be to bring all this expenditure within the arrangements for inter-authority pooling; this might not however commend itself to authorities generally and we are not clear that it would be effective. Another possibility might be "joint funding" with specific central government grants available to match local education authority approved expenditure in this area. However, most of us think that the only certain way of ensuring the release of teachers on the scale required would be through the payment of specifically earmarked central government grants to cover the whole costs. We recognise that this would be regarded by local authorities as a most unwelcome infringement of their powers to make local decisions according to local needs and circumstances within a broad national system of general grant. Nevertheless, given that the provision of opportunities for teachers with responsibility for children with

333

special educational needs to take one-year or part-time equivalent courses leading to a recognised qualification is an essential part of our proposals for improving the quality of special education, we believe that very serious consideration must be given to the payment of 100% specific grants to authorities for the secondment of such teachers to take courses leading to this qualification.

19.32 We accept that the requirements for additional lecturing staff, accommodation and secondment of teachers which our proposals for teacher training entail, and which existing Regulations in Scotland require, are very substantial and in other times might have seemed beyond attainment. Today, however, the availability of lecturers owing to the contraction of teacher training, the availability of spare accommodation and the availability of teachers all provide an opportunity to be seized. As we pointed out in Chapter 2 the government accepted over twenty years ago a recommendation of the National Advisory Council on the Training and Supply of Teachers that all intending teachers of handicapped children should take a full-time course of additional training. Our present proposals pick up this theme in the context of a new framework of special educational provision. Unless the present favourable opportunity is taken to improve the professional qualifications of teachers in special education and hence the quality of special education itself, we fear that the next twenty years may yet again be a period of unfulfilled hope.

Research and development

19.33 Three of our main proposals for the promotion and co-ordination of research and development in special education call for direct or indirect government funding: the proposal that there should be at least one university department of special education in each region of the country; the proposed formation of a Special Education Research Group; and the proposed establishment of a Special Education Staff College. (See recommendations 1, 4 and 6 of Chapter 18.) The Special Education Staff College might in due course be funded jointly by central government and local education authorities. We firmly hold that government grants for the establishment and continuing support of these bodies could produce very considerable benefits not only for the staff engaged in special education but for the children receiving it.

CONCLUSION

19.34 We have discussed the financial and other implications of our different proposals and indicated those which seem to us to command particular priority. In urging that priority should be given to certain of our recommendations, however, we earnestly hope that none of the others will be overlooked or indefinitely postponed. We believe that they are all necessary for the development of the new concept of special education which we outlined in Chapter 1.

19.35 In concluding our report we must emphasise that organisational changes and additional resources will not be sufficient in themselves to achieve our aims. They must be accompanied by changes in attitudes. Special education must be seen as a form of educational activity no less important, no less demanding and no less rewarding than any other, and teachers, administrators and other professionals engaged in it must have the same commitment to children with special needs as they have to all other children. Nor will it be enough if these changes in attitudes are confined to people engaged in special education. Changes in attitude are also necessary on the part of the public at large. There must be a general acceptance of the idea that special education involves as much skill and professional expertise as any other form of education, and that, in human terms, the returns on resources invested in it are just as great. With these thoughts in mind we submit our report. We believe that it not only contains important practical proposals for improving the education of children and young people with special needs but will also, in itself, contribute to those changes in attitude which are essential if our aims are to be fully realised.

THREE AREAS OF FIRST PRIORITY

1. PROVISION FOR CHILDREN UNDER FIVE WITH SPECIAL
   EDUCATIONAL NEEDS

   (i) Greater recognition and involvement of parents, wherever possible, as
   the main educators of their children during the earliest years (Chapter
   5, recommendation 1).

   (ii) A substantial extension of nursery education for all children (Chapter
   5, recommendation 10).

   (iii) An extension of peripatetic teaching services to cover all types of
   disability or disorder in young children (Chapter 5, recommendation
   8).

   (iv) The provision of professional help and advice from members of the
   various supporting services, including the proposed special education
   advisory and support service, to playgroups, opportunity groups, day
   nurseries and, above all, parents (Chapter 5, recommendations 14,
   15 and 7).

2. PROVISION FOR YOUNG PEOPLE OVER 16 WITH SPECIAL
   NEEDS

   (i) More opportunities for young people over 16 with special needs to
   continue their education at school or in further education and to receive
   careers guidance (Chapter 10, recommendations 5–6, 9 and 2–3).

   (ii) A variety of forms of further education provision to meet their needs,
   including support to enable them to take ordinary courses and, for
   those with more severe disabilities, special courses and facilities in a
   special unit in each region (Chapter 10, recommendations 7–10).

   (iii) A specifically educational element in adult training centres and day
   centres (Chapter 10, recommendation 15).

   (iv) The necessary financial support to enable young people with special
   needs to undertake courses of further or higher education (Chapter 10,
   recommendations 27–28).

3. TEACHER TRAINING

   (i) The inclusion of a special education element in all courses of initial
   teacher training (Chapter 12, recommendation 2).

   (ii) Short courses on special educational needs of about one week's
   full-time study or its part-time equivalent to be taken by the great
   majority of serving teachers within the next few years (Chapter 12,
   recommendation 4).

(iii) One-year full-time courses or their part-time equivalent leading to a recognised qualification in special education for teachers with a defined responsibility for children with special educational needs (Chapter 12, recommendations 7 and 12).

(iv) Other short courses of varying length on different aspects of special education (Chapter 12, recommendations 19–20 and 22).

 (v) The promotion of research and development to increase knowledge and understanding of different aspects of special education (Chapter 18, recommendations 1, 2, 4 and 5).

SUMMARY OF RECOMMENDATIONS

CHAPTER 3: THE SCOPE OF SPECIAL EDUCATION

1. The planning of services for children and young people should be based on the assumption that about one in six children at any time and up to one in five children at some time during their school career will require some form of special educational provision (paragraph 3.17).

2. Statutory categorisation of handicapped pupils should be abolished (paragraph 3.25).

3. The term "children with learning difficulties" should be used in future to describe both those children who are currently categorised as educationally sub-normal and those with educational difficulties who are often at present the concern of remedial services (paragraph 3.26).

4. In order to safeguard the interests of children with severe, complex and long-term disabilities, there should be a system of recording as in need of special educational provision those children who, on the basis of a detailed profile of their needs prepared by a multi-professional team, are judged by their local education authority to require special educational provision not generally available in ordinary schools (paragraph 3.31).

5. Section 8(2)(c) of the Education Act 1944 and Section 5(1) of the Education (Scotland) Act 1962 (as amended), which define the duties of local education authorities in relation to the provision of special educational treatment and special education respectively, should be amended to embody a broader concept of special education related to a child's individual needs as distinct from his disability and a wider description of children which includes those with significant difficulties in learning, or with emotional or behavioural disorders, as well as those with disabilities of mind or body (paragraph 3.42).

CHAPTER 4: DISCOVERY, ASSESSMENT AND RECORDING

Discovery

1. Information about child development and sources of expert advice on this subject should be still more widely disseminated to parents and prospective parents, fathers as well as mothers (paragraph 4.4).

2. A basic programme of health surveillance should be provided for all children as recommended in the Court Report (paragraph 4.6).

3. The practice of giving health visitors additional training to enable them to add an understanding of young children with special needs to their existing knowledge of child development and to make the best possible use of the developmental information acquired in the course of their visits should be extended (paragraph 4.10).

4. Area health authorities should seek to ensure that all paediatricians and other hospital consultants send copy letters about handicapped children, exercising their discretion over content, to appropriate community physicians as a matter of course (paragraph 4.15).

Record keeping

5. A personal folder, containing records of his progress and other factual information about him, should be maintained in school for every pupil and should be readily available for consultation (paragraph 4.19).

6. The results of professional consultations and sensitive information given in confidence about a child's social background or family relationships should be recorded in a separate, confidential folder. The folder should be kept in the school and access to it controlled by the headteacher (paragraph 4.23).

Monitoring of whole age groups

7. Local education authorities should operate procedures for monitoring whole age groups of children at least three or four times during their school life (paragraph 4.24).

Assessment

8. Section 34 of the Education Act 1944 and Section 63 of the Education (Scotland) Act 1962 (as amended) should be amended to give local education authorities the power to require the multi-professional assessment of children of any age (after due notice to parents) and to impose on them a duty to comply with a parental request for such assessment (paragraph 4.28).

9. There should be five stages of assessment and a child's special needs should be assessed at one or more of these stages as appropriate (paragraph 4.35).

10. Where a district handicap team exists, it should be augmented as necessary so that it can carry out among its functions the assessment of children with special educational needs (paragraph 4.43).

11. Multi-professional assessment at Stage 5 should usually take place at a centre within the community other than a hospital (paragraph 4.48).

12. Regional multi-professional centres for children with relatively rare or particularly complex disabilities should be established in university hospitals and the education service should be fully represented in these cnetres (paragraph 4.48).

Review of progress

13. The progress of a child with special educational needs should be reviewed at least annually and the headteacher of his school, whether an ordinary or a special school, should be responsible for initiating the review (paragraph 4.53).

14. Responsibility for the oversight of reviews of progress should rest with the special education advisory and support service (paragraph 4.53).

15. Arrangements for any change of placement should always be carefully planned and the change subject to confirmation after a period during which the child's progress should be carefully watched by the headteacher, in consultation with the headteacher of the child's former school where the new placement involves a change of school (paragraph 4.56).

SE Forms procedure

16. The SE Forms procedure should be initiated when a child is referred for multi-professional assessment at Stage 4 or 5 (paragraph 4.57).

17. The person who refers the child for multi-professional assessment should inform the parents as soon as the SE procedure is initiated and should give them a form on which to make their own statement about their child's needs (paragraph 4.60).

18. The completed SE Form whi'ch initiates the SE procedure should be sent to the education officer of the local education authority with responsibility for special education. Responsibility for the SE procedure should normally be delegated to a member of the special education advisory and support service (paragraph 4.62).

19. Forms SE2 and SE3 should be revised, after due consultation with the appropriate professionals (paragraph 4.65).

20. A document on lines similar to the revised Forms SE2 and SE3 should be drawn up for completion by professionals in social services departments (paragraph 4.65).

21. The Specialist in Community Medicine (Child Health) or a medical colleague designated by him should be responsible for co-ordinating contributions to Form SE2 by members of the health service (paragraph 4.64).

22. Form SE4 should be introduced in Scotland (paragraph 4.66).

23. Completion of Form SE4 should remain the responsibility of an officer of the local education authority, either an adviser in special education or an educational psychologist (paragraph 4.66).

24. The completed Form SE4 should be forwarded to the officer of the local education authority with responsibility for the SE Forms procedure, who should

ensure that copies are sent to the local authority social services department, the area health authority and, where the child is of school age or attending a nursery school, the headteacher of his school (paragraph 4.66).

25. Use of the SE Forms by local education authorities in England, Wales and Scotland in a form to be determined jointly by the Secretaries of State should be mandatory (paragraph 4.67).

Recording as in need of special educational provision

26. A duty should be imposed on local education authorities to maintain a record of children whom they judge to require special educational provision not normally available in the ordinary school, subject to the proviso that no child should be recorded without prior assessment by a multi-professional team (paragraph 4.69).

27. The Secretaries of State should be required to make regulations as to the resources deemed to be not generally available in county and voluntary schools, as to the composition of the multi-professional teams and as to the form of the record (paragraph 4.69).

28. Parents should have ready access to the documents comprising the record of their own child, namely the completed Form SE4 with a profile of the child's needs and a recommendation for the provision of special help, as well as a separate note on how that recommendation is being met in practice and the name of their Named Person who will provide a point of contact for them (paragraph 4.70).

29. On the introduction of the new system, all children currently ascertained as requiring special educational treatment and also those who, though not so ascertained, are attending special schools or designated special classes or units should be recorded as requiring special educational provision (paragraph 4.71).

30. A copy of the documents comprising the record of a child who has been recorded as requiring special educational provision by one local education authority and who moves to another area should be passed to the new authority and he should be automatically recorded by that authority (paragraph 4.71).

31. Parents should have the right of appeal to the appropriate Secretary of State against a decision by a local education authority to record or not to record their child as in need of special educational provision (paragraph 4.74).

Statistical returns

32. A feasibility study on the use of a grid for the purpose of statistical returns should be carried out in a sample of local education authorities and, if it is found to be practicable, a grid should be introduced as a basis in future for such returns. The statistical returns to government departments based on the grid should be of those children recorded as in need of special educational provision (paragraphs 4.76–77).

33. Local education authorities should devise their own framework, which might be a simplified version of the grid, for collecting information from schools about pupils assessed at Stage 1, 2 or 3 as being in need of special educational provision (paragraph 4.78).

CHAPTER 5: CHILDREN UNDER FIVE

1. The education of children with disabilities or significant difficulties must start as early as possible without any minimum age limit. In the earliest years parents rather than teachers should be regarded, wherever possible, as the main educators of their children (paragraphs 5.2–3).

Information for parents about available facilities

2. At the time of disclosure of their child's handicapping condition to them, parents should be given information about available facilities and supporting services (paragraph 5.9).

3. A handbook should be available for each area giving information about local facilities for children with special needs and their parents, and where such a handbook is not already available it should be produced under the aegis of the appropriate Joint Consultative Committee (or in Scotland the appropriate Joint Liaison Committee) (paragraph 5.10).

A Named Person for parents

4. One person should be designated as Named Person to provide a point of contact for the parents of every child who has been discovered to have a disability or who is showing signs of special needs or problems. In most cases the health visitor should be the Named Person in the early years (paragraphs 5.13–14).

5. Where a child's special needs have been assessed by a multi-professional team, the team should designate someone to serve as Named Person for the parents. This might be the health visitor or it might be a social worker, educcationist or other professional with particular expertise or interest in the area of the child's disability. The parents should be given the office telephone number of an officer of the local education authority who will have been provided with information about their child and, if the arrangement for their Named Person proves unsatisfactory, will put them in touch with another professional better parents similarly placed (paragraph 5.19).

6. Parents of children with disabilities or significant difficulties should be informed at an early stage about voluntary organisations and associations of parents similarly place (paragraph 5.19).

7. Reinforcement and skilled support should be provided for parents of children with disabilities or significant difficulties in the earliest years. A range of different forms of such support should be available in every area (paragraphs 5.31–32).

Peripatetic teaching service

8. There should be a comprehensive peripatetic teaching service which would cater, wherever possible, exclusively for children with disabilities or significant difficulties below school age and cover every type of disability or disorder. There should be scope for specialisation within the service; in particular, in view of the specific skills required for their teaching, children with sensory disabilities should be visited by teachers with related expertise (paragraph 5.37).

9. Training for peripatetic teachers should be organised on an in-service basis. Training programmes should include inter-professional courses (paragraph 5.42).

Nursery education

10. Nursery education provision for all children should be substantially increased as soon as possible, since this would have the consequence that opportunities for nursery education for young children with special needs could be correspondingly extended (paragraph 5.51).

11. Special nursery classes and units should be provided for young children with more severe or complex disabilities (paragraph 5.55).

12. Parents should be involved as closely as possible in the work of nursery schools and classes (paragraph 5.58).

Playgroups and opportunity groups

13. Playgroups should be prepared to accept young children with disabilities or significant difficulties wherever possible and much greater use should be made of opportunity groups as a form of provision for such children. Their staff should receive suitable training in helping to meet the special needs of such children (paragraphs 5.62–66).

14. Professional help and advice from members of the various supporting services should be readily available to playgroups and opportunity groups, and members of the proposed special education advisory and support service, including peripatetic advisory teachers, should be in close touch with the groups and help their staff to devise suitable programmes for those children with special educational needs (paragraph 5.66).

Day nurseries

15. The provision of combined day nurseries and nursery schools should be increased (paragraph 5.70).

16. More educational opportunities should be provided for children attending day nurseries, particularly those with special needs, and the staff should have opportunities to attend in-service courses organised on an inter-professional basis at which they would learn to recognise in children signs of special need and know when and where to refer for special help (paragraphs 5.69–71).

CHAPTER 6: SCHOOLCHILDREN WITH SPECIAL NEEDS: AN INTRODUCTION

1. The lists of special schools published by the Department of Education and Science and Scottish Education Department should, at least in the case of residential special schools, in future include details of the types of special educational need catered for (paragraph 6.14).

2. Each local education authority should produce and keep up-to-date a handbook containing details of special educational provision in its area for children recorded as requiring such provision. This handbook should include information about the types of special educational need catered for in individual schools as well as the names, office addresses and telephone numbers of officers of the local education authority concerned with the provision of special education (paragraph 6.15).

CHAPTER 7: SPECIAL EDUCATION IN ORDINARY SCHOOLS

The staff

1. Before a child with a disability or severe difficulty enters an ordinary school the teaching staff should discuss among themselves and agree a plan for securing the maximum educational and social interaction between him and others in the school, and should strive collectively thereafter to implement the plan (paragraph 7.21).

The governing body

2. Where a special class or unit established by a local education authority is attached to an ordinary school, a member of the managing or governing body should be specifically concerned with that class or unit (paragraph 7.25).

Organisation of the school

3. The headteacher should normally delegate day-to-day responsibility for making arrangements for children with special needs to a designated specialist teacher or head of department (paragraph 7.28).

School-based resource centres

4. Where one does not already exist, some form of resource centre or other supporting base should be established in large schools to promote the effectiveness of special educational provision (paragraph 7.32).

5. Where a resource centre, special class or base is organised internally by the headteacher, the local education authority should arrange for the necessary staff and other resources to be made available to the school and should ensure that they are used for that purpose (paragraph 7.33).

Designated special classes and units

6. Special classes and units should wherever possible be attached to and function as part of ordinary schools rather than be organised separately or attached to another kind of establishment such as a child guidance centre (paragraph 7.35).

7. Local education authorities should ensure that a school with a special class or unit is allotted an extra specialist teacher to its staffing complement (paragraph 7.36).

8. Children in special classes or units, whether attending full or part-time, should not form such a high proportion of the school roll or present such a range of needs as would substantially change the nature of the school (paragraph 7.38).

Future planning

9. Each local education authority should have a comprehensive and long-term plan for special educational provision within which the arrangements for individual schools will take their place (paragraph 7.48).

10. Before Section 10 of the Education Act 1976 comes into force, the Secretary of State for Education and Science should issue comprehensive guidance to local education authorities on the framing of their future arrangements for special educational provision (paragraph 7.59).

CHAPTER 8: SPECIAL EDUCATION IN SPECIAL SCHOOLS

Role of special schools

1. The facilities and expertise of special schools should be more widely available to provide intensive specialised help on a short-term basis and sometimes at short notice (paragraph 8.9).

2. Firm links should be established between special and ordinary schools in the same vicinity (paragraph 8.10).

3. Within each local authority area some special schools should be designated and developed as resource centres, that is centres of specialist expertise and of research in special education (paragraph 8.13).

4. A number of special schools should be designated as specialist centres for relatively rare or particularly complex disabilities and should be developed as such by groups of local education authorities (paragraph 8.14).

Residential special schools

5. A range of different types of boarding special school should be available, which would include not only residential special schools of the traditional type but also schools which cater for children with varying needs for residential accommodation and education on or off the premises, including schools of the hostel type (paragraph 8.17).

6. Boarding special schools should be prepared to accept children and young people with disabilities or significant difficulties for short periods wherever this meets a need (paragraph 8.18).

Non-maintained special schools

7. The standards of educational provision in non-maintained special schools should be closely monitored both by Her Majesty's Inspectorate and increasingly by the proposed special education advisory and support service (paragraph 8.25).

8. Much closer links should be established, to the benefit of both sides, between non-maintained special schools and local education authorities (paragraph 8.25).

9. Every non-maintained special school should have its own governing body and this should include at least one representative of the local education authority in whose area it is situated, or of one of the authorities making particular use of it (paragraph 8.26).

Organisation of special schools

10. Separate special schools should be provided, wherever possible, for senior and junior pupils or, failing that, an all-age school should be organised in separate departments, with a clear difference in the approach to children of secondary school age (paragraphs 8.33–34).

11. So far as is possible, the length of the school day in special schools should be the same as that in ordinary schools, with scope for variation according to the age and needs of the pupils (paragraph 8.35).

12. Residential special schools should be organised on as flexible a basis as possible, and should retain the capacity to remain open at weekends so that there is a genuine choice as to whether or not the children return home at weekends (paragraph 8.39).

13. Where the multi-professional team which assesses a child's needs at Stage 4 or 5 of our proposed assessment procedure concludes that he should return home or that his parents should visit him at weekends or other regular intervals, the local education authority should meet all or a substantial part of the cost. Even where no such recommendation has been made by the multi-professional team, the local education authority should be prepared to meet all or part of the cost if subsequent review of a child's progress suggests that he would benefit from weekend visits home or visits by his parents (paragraph 8.40).

14. The staff-pupil ratios suggested in DES Circular 4/73 (Welsh Office Circular 47/73) and the Consultative Document issued by the Scottish Education Department in 1973 should be regarded as a minimum requirement (paragraph 8.41).

15. Guidance should be issued in a Circular on the numbers of ancillary staff in special schools that should be regarded as adequate (paragraph 8.42).

Specialist support

16. Local education and area health authorities should provide the necessary space, equipment, nursing and secretarial help to enable medical specialists to hold their clinics in special schools (paragraph 8.46).

17. Area health authorities should ensure that continuity of treatment and, where necessary, nursing support is provided for children during the school holidays (paragraphs 8.47–48).

Governing bodies

18. As a general rule, every special school should have its own governing body (paragraph 8.50).

19. Special arrangements should be made to ensure that the governing bodies of those special schools which have catchment areas extending beyond the locality reflect the wider communities that they serve (paragraph 8.51).

20. Wherever appropriate, the governing body of a special school should include a handicapped person (paragraph 8.52).

Independent schools catering wholly or mainly for handicapped pupils

21. Where special school provision in the maintained sector is inadequate, as it is particularly for children with emotional or behavioural disorders and those with severe learning difficulties, it should be increased to the point of sufficiency (paragraph 8.58).

22. The Department of Education and Science and the Welsh Office should maintain and publish a list of independent schools which are accepted by the Secretaries of State for the purposes of Section 33(2) of the Education Act 1944 as it will be amended by Section 10 of the Education Act 1976 (paragraph 8.61).

23. Responsibility for following up the placement of a child in an independent school catering for handicapped pupils and, where necessary, for initiating a new placement should rest with the person designated by the multi-professional team which assessed the child's needs to act as Named Person for his parents (paragraph 8.62).

24. Part of the conditions for acceptance of the use of an independent school catering for handicapped pupils under Section 33(2) of the 1944 Act as it will be amended should be that the Secretary of State is satisfied that the school will offer access to officers of both the sending authority and the authority in whose area the school is situated (paragraph 8.63).

25. All independent schools which cater for handicapped pupils and are accepted by the Secretaries of State for the purposes of Section 33(2) of the Education Act 1944 (as it will be amended) should have governing bodies and the membership of those bodies should include a representative of the authority in whose area they are situated (paragraph 8.64).

26. The Secretary of State for Scotland should make the inclusion in List G of independent schools catering for handicapped pupils conditional on their proprietors agreeing to allow officers of both the sending authority and the authority in whose area the school is situated access to the school (paragraph 8.65).

27. No child with special educational needs who is in care should be placed in an independent school without agreement between the local education authority and the social services department (paragraph 8.66).

Community homes

28. As a first and major step in improving the quality of educational provision in community homes with education on the premises and observation and assessment centres, teachers in those establishments should be in the service of local education authorities (paragraph 8.71).

29. Opportunities for teachers in community homes to undertake courses of in-service training should be improved and regular support provided for them by members of the proposed special education advisory and support service (paragraph 8.72).

30. The educational representation should be strengthened on the managing bodies of community homes with education on the premises and observation and assessment centres, where such bodies exist (paragraph 8.73).

Education in hospital

31. For administrative purposes all education in hospital should be regarded as special educational provision (paragraph 8.78).

32. Arrangements should be made for all children to receive education as soon as possible after their admission to hospital (paragraph 8.80).

33. Wherever possible, educational premises should be specially provided in hospital for children who are unable to leave the hospital to attend school (paragraph 8.82).

34. A comprehensive review of a child's need for services should take place as soon as it becomes clear that he needs long-term hospital treatment, without waiting for any fixed period of time (paragraph 8.83).

35. Within the special education advisory and support service there should be advisers who specialise in education in hospital (paragraph 8.87).

36. The arrangements which currently exist for joint financing of health and personal social services should apply also to health and education services (paragraph 8.88).

Home tuition

37. Home teachers should have close links with individual schools, particularly special schools designated as resource centres, and with centres such as tuition and diagnostic centres (paragraph 8.90).

38. Within the special education advisory and support service there should be advisers who specialise in home tuition (paragraph 8.90).

CHAPTER 9: PARENTS AS PARTNERS*

A Named Person for parents

1. The headteacher of the child's current school should be the Named Person for most parents of schoolchildren with special educational needs (paragraph 9.27).

2. Parents of children with special educational needs should have direct access to the special education advisory and support service to discuss the suitability of the provision being made by the school for their child (paragraph 9.29).

3. The Named Person for the parents of a child recorded as requiring special educational provision should be someone designated by the multi-professional team which assessed the child's needs (paragraph 9.31).

4. Parents of children recorded as requiring special educational provision should be given the office telephone number and address of the officer who completed their child's Form SE4, that is either the adviser in special education or the educational psychologist so that they can contact him if the arrangements for a Named Person prove unsatisfactory (paragraph 9.33).

Relief for the family

5. A variety of forms of short-term relief should be available for parents of children with severe disabilities who are living at home (paragraph 9.35).

6. Ways of enabling the premises of some special schools to remain open during the school holidays should be further considered by the local authorities' and teachers' associations and, where appropriate, school governors (paragraph 9.38).

---

* See also the recommendations of Chapter 5.

CHAPTER 10: THE TRANSITION FROM SCHOOL TO ADULT LIFE

Re-assessment of special needs

1. A pupil's special needs should be re-assessed with future prospects in mind at least two years before he is due to leave school. The process of re-assessment at this stage should always involve a careers officer and should usually include other professionals in the education, health and social services (paragraph 10.7).

Careers guidance

2. A teacher with special responsibility for careers guidance should be appointed in every special school which caters for older pupils. In every ordinary secondary school there should be at least one careers teacher with additional training or expertise in understanding the careers implications of different types of disability or disorder (paragraph 10.14).

3. As a general guide and on the understanding that adequate support will be provided, at least one full-time specialist careers officer should be appointed for every 50,000 of the school population (or for a substantial proportion of 50,000) (paragraph 10.15).

Preparation at school for the transition to adult life

4. Both ordinary and special schools should give pupils with special educational needs more help to acquire the basic skills and to develop social competence and vocational interests (paragraph 10.19).

Provision in school for young people over 16

5. Where it is in their interests, pupils with special educational needs should be enabled to stay at school beyond the statutory school leaving age (paragraph 10.30).

6. Where it is in their interests and possible to arrange, pupils with special educational needs should have access to sixth forms or sixth form colleges (paragraph 10.32).

Further education

7. Wherever possible young people with special needs should be given the necessary support to enable them to attend ordinary courses of further education (paragraph 10.37).

8. Some establishments of further education should experiment with modified versions of ordinary further education courses for young people with special needs (paragraph 10.38).

9. Some establishments of further education should provide special vocational courses at operative level for students with special needs and special courses of training in social competence and independence (paragraph 10.39).

10. Within each region there should be at least one special unit providing special courses for young people with more severe disabilities or difficulties which would be based in an establishment of further education (paragraph 10.40).

11. Every establishment of further education should designate a member of staff as responsible for the welfare of students with special needs in the college and for briefing other members of staff on their special needs (paragraph 10.42).

12. A co-ordinated approach to further education provision for young people with special needs should be adopted and publicised by the local education authorities within each region against a long-term plan within which arrangements for individual institutions will take their place. The institutions themselves should publicise their policy on the admission of students with special needs as well as the courses and special facilities which they provide for them (paragraph 10.43).

13. The national colleges which currently provide further education or training for young people with disabilities should in time all become part of their regional patterns of further education for students with special needs (paragraph 10.44).

Higher education

14. All universities and polytechnics as well as other establishments of higher education should formulate and publicise a policy on the admission of students with disabilities or significant difficulties and should make systematic arrangements to meet the welfare and special needs, including careers counselling, of those who are admitted (paragraph 10.49).

Adult training centres and day centres

15. There should be a specifically educational element in every adult training centre and day centre and the education service should be responsible for its provision (paragraph 10.53).

Hospitals

16. Local education authorities should provide programmes of continuing education to meet the individual needs of young people who require long-term hospital care (paragraph 10.55).

Training and preparation for employment

17. Industrial Training Boards should play a much greater part in encouraging employers to provide employment and training opportunities for people with disabilities or significant difficulties (paragraph 10.61).

18. More opportunities should be provided for young people with disabilities or significant difficulties to take locally-based TSA courses suited to their needs (paragraph 10.67).

19. The extension of young persons' work preparation courses to all ERCs over the next few years should be brought about as quickly as possible (paragraph 10.75).

Employment

20. The public service and nationalised industries should urgently review their employment policies with a view to opening their doors more widely to and providing more imaginative opportunities for work for people with disabilities (paragraph 10.77).

21. The ESA's strategy of alerting employers to the employment needs of the disabled should be further developed and there should be more contact at local level between employers or, where the management of large companies is decentralised, local managers and both ESA officers and careers officers (paragraph 10.79).

22. Local education authorities and their careers services should play a greater part in promoting discussions with employers' and employees' organisations about how best to persuade employers to take on young people with disabilities, in conjunction with the MSC and, where necessary, the social services (paragraph 10.82).

Sheltered workshops

23. Sheltered workshops should introduce progressive programmes of activities designed to enable as many people with disabilities as possible to enter open employment (paragraph 10.86).

Named Person

24. The careers officer or, in the case of young people with more severe or complex disabilities, the specialist careers officer should act as Named Person for young people with special needs and their parents or should ensure that another professional takes on the function of providing a single point of contact for them during the transition from school to adult life (paragraph 10.94).

Personal counselling

25. Better counselling on personal relationships should be available to young people with special needs and their parents from a variety of sources, including the health and social services and voluntary groups (paragraph 10.96).

26. More research should be carried out into how sexual counselling can best be provided for young people with special needs, including the training of counsellors and other staff (paragraph 10.97).

Financial support

27. Local education authorities should use their discretionary powers generously in making supplementary grants to students with disabilities who are receiving mandatory awards (paragraph 10.105).

28. Local education authorities should use their discretionary powers far more generously in making discretionary awards to students with disabilities or significant difficulties who enter further education (paragraph 10.106).

Aids and equipment

29. A more rational and uniform approach to the provision of aids for handicapped people throughout the country should be developed (paragraph 10.116).

30. More research should be carried out into the design of aids and equipment for handicapped people (paragraph 10.117).

Mobility

31. Further consideration should be given urgently to the needs of young people with disabilities for help with mobility, particularly those aged 16–17 and those who need special help to travel to and from work (paragraph 10.124).

CHAPTER 11: SOME CURRICULAR CONSIDERATIONS

1. There should be at least one centre in every region to support students in further and higher education who have impaired hearing and to train those who work with them (paragraph 11.36).

2. Particular attention should be given to curriculum development for children with moderate learning difficulties and further research should be carried out into the causes of such difficulties (paragraph 11.52).

3. Resources should be made available to the Schools Council, the Consultative Committee on the Curriculum and to local teachers' centres so that curriculum projects can be translated into forms useful to special schools, units and classes (paragraph 11.68).

4. Funds should be allocated to subsidise the production of curriculum materials for particular small groups of children whose special needs are not commonly met by the normal process of curriculum development (paragraph 11.69).

5. A special section of the Schools Council should be formed and given separate resources to set up projects concerned with the curriculum for particular small groups of children with special needs and the dissemination of current special education projects within the special education service (paragraph 11.70).

CHAPTER 12: TEACHER EDUCATION AND TRAINING

Initial teacher training

1. The teaching of child development in initial teacher training should always take account of different patterns and rates of individual development, particularly as they affect learning, and should include the effects of common disabilities and other factors which influence development (paragraph 12.6).

A special education element

2. A special education element should be included in all courses of initial teacher training, including those leading to a postgraduate certificate in education. It should be taught within the general context of child development (paragraph 12.7).

3. Those responsible for validating teacher training courses should make the inclusion of a special education element a condition of their approval of all initial teacher training courses (paragraph 12.11).

4. A determined effort should be made to ensure that short in-service courses which cover the same ground as the proposed special education element are provided as a matter of urgency and that the great majority of serving teachers take one of these courses within the next few years (paragraph 12.12).

Special education options

5. Wherever possible, students should have the opportunity in their initial teacher training to take an option that enables them to pursue their interest in children with special educational needs in more depth than will be possible in the proposed special education element (paragraph 12.15).

Specialist initial teacher training

6. The training provided through the existing initial teacher training courses directed to work with children currently described as severely educationally subnormal should be closely monitored by Her Majesty's Inspectorate and its effectiveness in preparing teachers to work with such children evaluated (paragraph 12.23).

A recognised qualification for teachers with responsibility for children with special educational needs

7. There should be a range of recognised qualifications in special education, to be obtained at the end of a one-year full-time course or its equivalent (paragraph 12.27).

8. The list of qualifications which at present entitle a qualified teacher to obtain extra payment under the terms of the Burnham Salaries Document should be extended to cover all recognised qualifications in special education in the range proposed in 7 above (paragraph 12.28).

9. This extra payment for a recognised qualification in special education should continue to be made after a teacher reaches the maximum of his salary scale, whether he is teaching in an ordinary or a special school (paragraph 12.28).

10. From a date to be announced well in advance, the extra allowance payable to teachers in special schools and special classes in England and Wales should be abolished (paragraph 12.29).

11. The present arrangements for enhanced salaries for teachers in special schools and special classes in Scotland should be discontinued from a date to be announced well in advance and an increased qualification payment should be made to a teacher who holds a recognised qualification in special education, whether he is teaching in an ordinary or a special school (paragraph 12.30).

12. Training facilities and local education authority support for teachers to take in-service courses should be so increased that possession of an additional recognised qualification can be made a requirement on all teachers with a defined responsibility for children with special educational needs as soon as possible (paragraph 12.31).

13. The exception of teachers of craft, domestic or trade subjects from the present requirement on other teachers of blind, deaf or partially hearing pupils in England and Wales to have an additional recognised qualification should be removed as soon as possible (paragraph 12.33).

14. The present requirement on teachers of blind or deaf pupils in special schools to have an additional recognised qualification should be extended to teachers of blind or deaf pupils in special classes or units (paragraph 12.33).

15. A requirement should be imposed on teachers of the partially sighted in special schools and special classes and units, like teachers of the partially hearing, to obtain an additional recognised qualification (paragraph 12.34).

In-service training

16. All in-service courses designed for teachers who are specialising in the teaching of children with special educational needs should include consideration of working with parents and non-teaching assistants, peripatetic teaching and work with children below school age who require special help, as well as the principles of guidance and counselling (paragraph 12.36).

One-year full-time courses or their equivalent leading to the proposed qualification in special education

17. All courses leading to the recognised qualification should include a general component, which would aim to give teachers knowledge of the characteristics and signs of different types of disability and to equip them with a basic core of teaching skills appropriate to the teaching of children with a range of special educational needs (paragraph 12.39).

18. The Department of Education and Science should grant-aid the preparation by the Open University of a course leading to the proposed recognised qualification in special education (paragraph 12.50).

Other courses

19. A range of advanced short courses specifically directed to the teaching methods and techniques appropriate to children with different kinds of disability

or disorder and involving study in depth of their special educational needs should be provided for teachers who have a professional commitment to teaching such children (paragraph 12.53).

20. Courses should be provided for headteachers and senior staff, whether in special or ordinary schools, in management and administrative skills, including aspects directed to children with special educational needs (paragraph 12.54).

21. Courses leading to higher degrees in special education should be established in universities and other establishments of higher education (paragraph 12.55).

22. Local education authorities should review the provision of short courses in their own areas and ensure that a comprehensive range of courses in special education, provided under their own auspices or through other agencies, is available (paragraph 12.56).

Regional co-ordination of course provision

23. The deployment of college staff with training and experience in particular fields of special education should be considered on a regional (or in Scotland an inter-regional) basis (paragraph 12.61).

Induction

24. Local education authorities should organise an induction programme for all teachers taking up for the first time a post with responsibility for children with special educational needs. Induction programmes should be shaped to meet each teacher's individual needs (paragraphs 12.64–65).

Training for further education teaching

25. A special education element should be included in all initial training courses for further education teachers, both full and part-time courses, on the lines of that proposed for inclusion in all initial training courses for school teachers but orientated towards the needs of young people over 16 who require special help. Short part-time courses which cover the same ground as the special education element should also be provided (paragraph 12.68).

26. A one-year full-time course or its equivalent leading to a recognised qualification should be available to teachers in further education specialising in the teaching of students with special needs. Teachers who obtain the recognised qualification should receive an additional payment (paragraph 12.70).

27. Short courses should be provided in particular aspects of the teaching of young people and adults with special educational needs (paragraph 12.71).

28. Steps should be taken to ensure that teachers of young people and adults with special educational needs who teach outside establishments of further education have access to the same range of training courses as their colleagues in further education establishments (paragraph 12.74).

The admission of people with disabilities to teacher training courses and their employment as teachers

29. There should be more opportunities for people with disabilities to become teachers and obtain teaching posts in both special and ordinary schools (paragraph 12.75).

30. In future there should be a recognised right of appeal to the appropriate Secretary of State against classification as medically unfit for the teaching profession at the end of a teacher training course and candidates should be told of this right when notified of their classification (paragraph 12.79).

CHAPTER 13: ADVICE AND SUPPORT IN SPECIAL EDUCATION

1. Every local education authority should re-structure and, if necessary, supplement its existing advisory staff and resources to provide effective advice and support to teachers concerned with children with special educational needs through a unified service (paragraph 13.3).

2. Every local education authority should have an education officer responsible for all arrangements for children with special educational needs, wherever these needs are being met (paragraph 13.30).

3. Every local education authority should have a separate committee or a sub-committee of the schools committee responsible for the provision for children and young people with special educational needs of all ages, that is children under five, children of school age, whether they are in ordinary schools, special schools or other establishments, and young people attending establishments of further education or other institutions (paragraph 13.31).

4. Members of the special education committee or sub-committee should represent the local education authority on the Joint Consultative Committee or in Scotland the Joint Liaison Committee (paragraph 13.31).

CHAPTER 14: OTHER STAFF EMPLOYED IN THE EDUCATION SERVICE

Educational psychologists

1. Initial training arrangements for educational psychologists should be increased so as to allow local education authorities in England and Wales to attain a target of at least one psychologist to 5,000 children and young people up to the age of 19 (paragraph 14.12).

2. Course modules common to the training of educational and clinical psychologists should be developed (paragraph 14.14).

3. Existing training centres for educational psychologists and other establishments and organisations should institute a range of in-service courses for educational psychologists, varying in both length and content (paragraph 14.15).

Careers officers

4. The Local Government Training Board should review the element in the initial training of careers officers which is concerned with young people with special needs and should develop in-service courses on special needs for all careers officers in post who have not already taken this element (paragraph 14.19).

5. Careers officers wishing to specialise in work with young people with disabilities or significant difficulties should undertake training on lines similar to that of Disablement Resettlement Officers (paragraph 14.20).

6. Some senior posts in local education authority careers services should be made available to careers officers specialising in work with young people with disabilities or significant difficulties (paragraph 14.21).

Links between home and school

7. Local authorities should ensure, through co-operation between their education and social services departments, that adequate social work services are available to meet the needs of children who require special help in all schools in their area, that the social workers are clearly linked to individual schools or groups of schools and that, where appropriate, the social workers are school-based (paragraph 14.23).

Education welfare officers

8. Further studies should be undertaken to determine the best way of providing the essential though in some respects overlapping services carried out by education welfare officers and social workers (paragraph 14.27).

9. Education welfare officers should be helped in initial and in-service training to recognise signs of special educational needs and to be aware of the ways in which the education and other services can meet such needs (paragraph 14.28).

Nursery nurses

10. The possession by nursery nurses working in day nurseries, playgroups, nursery schools or classes of the advanced certificate of the National Nursery Examination Board or the Scottish NNEB should carry an increase in salary (paragraph 14.31).

Ancillary workers

11. Special classes for children of primary school age, whether in special schools or units or attached to ordinary schools, and special classes for children of secondary school age with physical disabilities, severe learning difficulties or emotional or behavioural disorders should each have at least one ancillary worker (paragraph 14.32).

Child care staff

12. Special training leading to a recognised qualification should be available for child care staff in residential special schools, whatever their previous qualifications, along lines compatible with that for staff in community homes (paragraph 14.36).

13. There should be one post in boarding special schools at deputy head level, carrying responsibility for all arrangements for residential care, and this should be open to trained child care staff (paragraph 14.37).

Instructors in special schools in Scotland

14. Training courses for instructors in Scotland should be extended to two years and education authorities should consider providing posts of responsibility for instructors where a number is employed in any one school (paragraph 14.38).

CHAPTER 15: THE HEALTH SERVICE AND THE SOCIAL SERVICES

The health service

1. Health authorities should make adequate resources available to promote effective child health services in ordinary and special schools (paragraph 15.10).

2. As a matter of urgency high priority should be given to the recruitment and appropriate training of doctors for work related to school health in the field of community medicine (paragraph 15.12).

3. There should be a named doctor and nurse for every school (paragraph 15.17).

4. Local education authorities, in consultation with area health authorities, should satisfy themselves that adequate health care is available before placing children in non-maintained special schools or independent schools catering wholly or mainly for handicapped pupils (paragraph 15.19).

5. The Specialist in Community Medicine (Child Health) should ensure that arrangements are made for the transfer of responsibility for the medical surveillance of a young person with special educational needs to an appropriate branch of the health service when that young person leaves school or further education (paragraph 15.20).

6. Health services comparable to those provided for special schools should be made available to establishments of further or higher education which cater for students with more severe disabilities or disorders (paragraph 15.21).

7. More opportunities for post-qualification training on an inter-professional basis should be made available to members of the health service concerned with children with disabilities and significant difficulties (paragraph 15.34).

The personal social services

8. Social services departments should nominate a senior social worker to act as a liaison officer with the careers service and the specialist careers officer (paragraph 15.43).

9. Separate provision and a differentiated programme of education and other activities including training should be available for handicapped young people in adult training centres and day centres or elsewhere (paragraph 15.47).

10. An element should be included in the initial training of all social workers and residential child care staff which acquaints them not only with the social work aspects of different disabilities but with the special education services available to children and parents (paragraph 15.48).

Joint Consultative Committees

11. Joint Consultative Committees should be asked to advise health, education and social services authorities as soon as possible on the health and social services which will be needed by and can be provided for ordinary schools to meet the needs of children with disabilities or significant difficulties, and what priority their provision should be accorded (paragraph 15.51).

CHAPTER 16: RELATIONS BETWEEN PROFESSIONALS, CONFIDENTIALITY AND CO-ORDINATION OF SERVICES

The dissemination of information

1. Teachers' associations, in consultation with local authority associations and representatives of other professions, should draw up guidelines for teachers on the handling of confidential information as well as the sharing of information with members of other professions (paragraph 16.5).

2. Form 10bM or its equivalent (which provides an appropriate summary by school doctors of medical findings for educational use) should be used properly and consistently for all schoolchildren (paragraph 16.11).

Inter-professional training

3. Establishments of further and higher education as well as the bodies responsible for the training of members of the health, psychological and social services should explore the possibility of developing initial training courses leading to a dual qualification (paragraph 16.21).

4. A limited number of initial training courses leading to a dual qualification should be introduced on an experimental basis as soon as possible (with the students receiving mandatory awards for the whole period of the course) and their benefits should be evaluated with a view to their further development if the results are favourable (paragraph 16.21).

5. There should be an expansion of the provision of short courses of inter-professional training which focus on subjects of common concern to members of different professions engaged in meeting the needs of children and young people who require special educational provision. Initiatives to develop such courses should be taken by the colleges and departments of education and the special education advisory and support service as well as by those bodies responsible for the organisation of post-experience training for professionals in the health, psychological and social services (paragraphs 16.25–26).

Co-ordination of services

6. Working groups should be set up under the auspices of the Joint Consultative Committees (JCCs) to review the provision and operation of services for children and young people up to the age of, say, 25 with disabilities or significant difficulties, with a view to identifying deficiencies in provision and practice, developing strategies and programmes to meet those deficiencies and, as necessary, recommending policies for improving the effectiveness of the separate services and of their co-operation with each other (paragraph 16.31).

7. Local authorities should set up local machinery for the co-ordination of services for young people with special educational needs during and for some time after the transition from school to further or higher education, training or employment (paragraph 16.35).

8. The functions of the regional conferences for special education should be extended to include considering the annual reports of the working groups set up

under the auspices of the JCCs; reviewing the existing facilities for special educational provision in the region (including those provided by voluntary organisations) and planning for the maximum degree of regional self-sufficiency; facilitating inter-authority arrangements for in-service training on an inter-professional basis; and identifying the requirements of young people with special needs for further education and promoting the provision of suitable courses for them (paragraph 16.39).

9. The composition of the regional conferences for special education should include local education authority elected members and officers, representatives of employment, health and social services, of employers' and employees' organisations and of voluntary organisations, and teachers with responsibility for children with special educational needs (paragraph 16.40).

10. The Welsh Joint Education Committee (WJEC) should continue its responsibility for co-ordinating the provision of special education by local education authorities in Wales. Conferences on special education should be organised on the basis of arrangements agreed between the Welsh Office and the WJEC and these conferences should reflect the wider range of membership recommended for the regional conferences in England. The Welsh Office should consider, in consultation with the WJEC, what arrangements might be made in Wales for the receipt and review of the annual reports of the proposed working groups to be set up under the auspices of the Joint Consultative Committees (paragraph 16.42).

11. A National Advisory Committee on Children with Special Educational Needs should be established to advise the Secretaries of State for Education and Science and for Wales on the provision of educational services for children and young people with special educational needs and their co-ordination with other services. A separate advisory committee should be appointed for Scotland (paragraph 16.47).

CHAPTER 17: VOLUNTARY ORGANISATIONS

1. The future of individual non-maintained special schools should be determined through consultation between local education authorities in the region and those voluntary organisations which provide the schools. The schools themselves should be kept informed of any local authority plans which may affect their continued existence (paragraph 17.11).

2. Collaboration between voluntary organisations and further education establishments should be developed and improved with a view to an increase in the opportunities available to young people with special needs after they have left school (paragraph 17.13).

3. Voluntary bodies and local authorities should collaborate to see that advisory and support services are available to groups of parents of young children with special needs and that no parents of such children are unaware of them (paragraph 17.25).

CHAPTER 18: RESEARCH AND DEVELOPMENT IN SPECIAL EDUCATION

Promotion and co-ordination of research in special education

1. Priority should be given within universities, polytechnics and other establishments of higher education to the allocation of senior academic posts to special education and there should be at least one university department of special education in each region of the country (paragraph 18.3).

2. Some senior academic posts in special education in universities, polytechnics and other establishments of higher education should be linked to part-time work with children with special needs from an educational, a medical, a psychological or a social standpoint (paragraph 18.4).

3. Some post-qualification courses should offer opportunities for experienced educational psychologists to develop their skills in research, and consideration should be given by validating bodies to the award of a higher degree for satisfactory completion of such a research-orientated course (paragraph 18.6).

4. A Special Education Research Group (SERG) should be set up with responsibility for indicating priorities for research in special education, for identifying programmes and projects to be initiated, for awarding some research grants and for commenting if requested to do so on applications for research central to its concerns which are submitted to other research bodies. It should have at its disposal sufficient funds to enable it at any time to support one or two large programmes or projects, together with several smaller ones (paragraph 18.11).

Translation of research into practice

5. Each local education authority should have a centre where research, development and in-service training in special education are based and to which all the teachers in the area with responsibility for children with special needs can turn for help with their professional development (paragraph 18.17).

6. A body responsible for the further training of senior staff, which might be known as the Special Education Staff College, should be established (paragraph 18.18).

APPENDIX 1

LIST OF ORGANISATIONS AND INDIVIDUALS WHO GAVE EVIDENCE TO THE MAIN COMMITTEE, ITS SUB-COMMITTEES OR SUB-GROUPS

I LOCAL AUTHORITY ASSOCIATIONS AND INDIVIDUAL AUTHORITIES

a. Local authority associations
Association of County Councils
Association of Education Committees
Association of Metropolitan Authorities
Convention of Scottish Local Authorities
Welsh Joint Education Committee

b. Regional groups of local authorities (including regional conferences on special education)
East Midland Regional Advisory Committee on Special Education
Northern Council of Education Committees (jointly with the North Regional Society of Education Officers)
North West Associated Education Authorities
Regional Conference of Assistant Education Officers (Special Education) for London and the Home Counties
Southern Region Standing Conference on Special Education
South West Regional Conference on Special Education
West Midlands Advisory Council for Special Education
Yorkshire and Humberside Regional Conference on Special Education

c. Individual local authorities
Coventry Local Education Authority
Gwent County Council Education Department
Inner London Education Authority
London Borough of Havering School Psychological Service
Manchester Metropolitan District Education Committee
Nottinghamshire County Council Education Committee
Sheffield Education Department, Psychological Service

II TEACHERS' AND OTHER EDUCATIONAL ASSOCIATIONS OR ORGANISATIONS

a. National associations
Assistant Masters' Association
Association for Therapeutic Education

Association of Assistant Mistresses
Association of Blind and Partially Sighted Teachers and Students (jointly with the National Federation of the Blind)
Association of Career Teachers
Association of Community Home Schools
Association of Directors of Education in Scotland
Association of Head Mistresses (now the Secondary Heads Association)
Association of Principals of Colleges (formerly the Association of Principals of Technical Institutions)
Association of Tutors to Courses for Staff Working with the Handicapped (Disabled)

British Association of Teachers of the Deaf (formerly the National College of Teachers of the Deaf and the Society of Teachers of the Deaf)
British Association for Early Childhood Education

Catholic Education Council
College of Teachers of the Blind
Committee of Directors of Polytechnics
Committee of Principals of Colleges of Education in Scotland
Committee of Vice-Chancellors and Principals of the Universities of the United Kingdom
Confederation for the Advancement of State Education
Council for Educational Advance
Council for Educational Technology
Council for National Academic Awards

Educational Institute of Scotland

Headmasters' Association (now the Secondary Heads Association)
Headteachers' Association of Scotland

National Association for the Education of the Partially Sighted
National Association for Remedial Education
National Association of Careers and Guidance Teachers
National Association of Governors and Managers
National Association of Head Teachers
National Association of Schoolmasters/Union of Women Teachers
National Association of the Teachers of Wales (Undeb Cenedlaethol Athrawon Cymru)
National Association of Teachers of the Mentally Handicapped
National Association of Welsh Medium Nursery Schools and Playgroups (Mudiad Ysgolion Meithrin)
National College of Teachers of the Deaf (now the British Association of Teachers of the Deaf)
National Confederation of Parent-Teacher Associations
National Council for Special Education (and Scottish Division)
National Union of Students
National Union of Teachers

Physical Education Association[2] of Great Britain and Northern Ireland (Working Party on Physical Education for Handicapped Children)

Pre-School Playgroups Association
Professional Association of Teachers

School Broadcasting Council for the United Kingdom
Schools Council
Scottish Central Committee on Physical Education
Scottish Secondary Teachers' Association
Society of Education Officers
Society of Teachers of the Deaf (now the British Association of Teachers of the Deaf)

University Grants Committee

b. Regional or local associations or groups

East Anglia, East Midlands and Essex: Group of teachers of the deaf representative of services for hearing impaired children in Bedfordshire, Cambridgeshire, Essex, Hertfordshire, Norfolk and Suffolk

Gloucestershire Education Authority: Heads of Special Schools (Mr Bladon, Miss Burling, Mr Eggleston, Mr Maltby, Mr Spiers, Mr Tunstall)
Greater London Maladjusted Schools' Action Committee

Inner London Education Authority:
Consultative Sub-Committee of Head Teachers of Schools for the Delicate
Head Teachers of ILEA Schools for Physically Handicapped Children (Miss Arden, Mrs Battersby, Mr Bond, Miss Cowing, Mrs Dawson, Mr Down, Miss Hubbard, Mr J P Hughes, Mr T A Hughes, Mr Irons, Miss Land, Miss Maxwell, Miss Schulen, Mrs Sprague, Miss Suckling)
Head Teachers of ILEA Schools for Visually Handicapped Children (Mr Bignell, Miss Horne, Mr Matthews, Mr Pope and Mr Wood)

London Head Teachers Association
Leeds:
Heads of Leeds Special Schools for the ESN(M)
Heads of Leeds Special Schools for the ESN(S)
Heads of Schools for Maladjusted Children in the Leeds area (Mr Benson, Mr Patterson and Mr Rigby together with Mrs Valley, Teacher in charge, Allverton Assessment and Observation Unit, Leeds)

North Regional Society of Education Officers (jointly with the Northern Council of Education Committees)
North West Regional Association for Heads of Physically Handicapped and Hospital Schools (Section of the National Council for Special Education)

Oxfordshire teachers and headteachers (Mr Brodie, Mr Davidson, Mr Finch, Miss Hall, Mr Jarman, Mrs Sperring and Mrs Warren)

Wakefield District Special School Heads Association

III OTHER PROFESSIONAL BODIES

a. National bodies

Association of British Paediatric Nurses

Association of Child Psychotherapists
Association of Educational Psychologists
Association of Nurse Administrators (formerly the Association of Hospital Matrons)
Association of Professions for the Mentally Handicapped
Association of Workers for Maladjusted Children (and Scottish Division)

British Association of Art Therapists
British Association of Occupational Therapists
British Association of Otolaryngologists
British Association of Social Workers (NE Scotland Branch)
British Medical Association
British Orthopaedic Association
British Paediatric Association
British Psychological Society

Chartered Society of Physiotherapy (and Scottish Board)
College of Speech Therapists

Faculty of Ophthalmologists

Health Visitors' Association

Institute of Careers Officers

Joint Council for the Education of Handicapped Children

Medical Defence Union
Medical Protection Society

National Association of Nursery Matrons
National Association of Youth and Community Education Officers
National Council of Social Workers with the Deaf

Royal College of General Practitioners
Royal College of Obstetricians and Gynaecologists
Royal College of Physicians of London
Royal College of Physicians and Surgeons of Glasgow
Royal College of Psychiatrists
Royal College of Psychiatrists (Child Psychiatry and Mental Deficiency Sections), Scottish Division

Scottish Occupational Centres Association
Scottish Otolaryngological Society
Scottish Principal Educational Psychologists
Society of Community Medicine (formerly The Society of Medical Officers of Health)

b. Local groups

Avon: group of educational psychologists based on the County of Avon Child Guidance Clinic

London group of careers officers for the handicapped

IV VOLUNTARY ORGANISATIONS

a. National

Association for All Speech Impaired Children
Association for Spina Bifida and Hydrocephalus
Association of Disabled Professionals

Breakthrough Trust, Deaf-Hearing Group
British Council for Rehabilitation of the Disabled
British Deaf Association
British Dyslexia Association
British Red Cross Society (Scottish Branch)

Camphill Village Trust
Church of England Children's Society
Cystic Fibrosis Research Trust

Deaf Education Action Forum
Disabled Living Foundation
Dr Barnardo's
Down's Babies' Association

Institute for Research into Mental and Multiple Handicap
Invalid Children's Aid Association

KIDS National Centre for Cued Speech
Kith and Kids

MIND (National Association for Mental Health)
Muscular Dystrophy Group of Great Britain (Welfare Committee)

National Association for Deaf/Blind and Rubella Handicapped
National Association for the Welfare of Children in Hospital
National Children's Home
National Deaf Children's Society
National Deaf Children's Society, Scottish Regions, in association with the
    Scottish Association for the Deaf and the Scottish Centre for the Education
    of the Deaf Advisory Committee
National Elfrida Rathbone Society
National Federation of Gateway Clubs
National Federation of the Blind (jointly with the Association of Blind and
    Partially-Sighted Teachers and Students)
National Society for Mentally Handicapped Children
Non-Maintained Schools Association for Deaf Children

Partially Sighted Society

Queen Elizabeth's Foundation for the Disabled

Riding for the Disabled Association
Royal National Institute for the Blind
Royal National Institute for the Deaf

Scottish Association for the Deaf (in association with the Scottish Regions of the

371

National Deaf Children's Society and the Scottish Centre for the Education of the Deaf Advisory Committee)

Scottish Centre for the Education of the Deaf Advisory Committee (in association with the Scottish Regions of the NDCS and the Scottish Association for the Deaf)

Scottish Committee for the Welfare of the Disabled

Scottish Paraplegic (Spinal Injury) Association

Scottish Society for the Mentally Handicapped

Shaftesbury Society

Society for the Aid of Thalidomide Children

Society of Friends of Camphill (Southern Link)

Spastics Society

Wales Council for the Disabled

Wingfield Trust

b. Local

Aberystwyth Remedial Unit Parent-Teachers' Association

Bath Association for the Study of Dyslexia

Birmingham Society for Mentally Handicapped Children

City of Westminster Society for Mentally Handicapped Children

Derby Dyslexia Association

Elfrida Rathbone Committee (Islington and Camden)

Enfield Association for Education (Special Education Study Group)

Hackney and Islington Association for Parents of ESN Children

Hatfield and Welwyn Garden City Society for the Welfare of the Mentally Handicapped

Lakeside School Parent-Teacher Association, Welwyn Garden City

Leicestershire Standing Conference of Voluntary Organisations for the Physically Handicapped

Lincolnshire Society for the Physically Handicapped

Linkage Community Trust

London Borough of Bromley Parents and Friends of the Educationally Sub Normal

National Deaf Children's Society, Northamptonshire Region

North London Dyslexia Association (now London Dyslexia Association)

Nottingham and District Society for Mentally Handicapped Children and Adults

Oxford and District Dyslexia Association

Slough Council for Voluntary Service

Staffordshire Society for Mentally Handicapped Children

Stevenage Opportunity Class

Tavistock and District Mentally Handicapped Society

Tayside Dyslexia Association

Tower Hamlets Elfrida Rathbone Association

West Surrey Dyslexic Aid Association

Yorkshire Branch of the Partially Sighted Society

V OTHER ORGANISATIONS

Arts Research Society

Confederation of British Industry (Education and Training Committee)

Department of Employment Group (Department of Employment, Office of the Manpower Services Commission, Employment Service Agency, Training Services Agency, Health and Safety Executive)

Fabian Society
Family Fund Research Project

Girl Guides Association

Hester Adrian Research Centre, University of Manchester (Professor P Mittler, Dr P Berry, Mr M Beveridge, Mr P Conn, Miss D M Jeffree, Dr R McConkey, Mr D Mitchell, Miss E Tomlinson, Dr E Whelan)

Independent Broadcasting Authority (Education Staff and Advisers)
Inner London Juvenile Court Panel

Liberal Party Education Panel

National Bureau for Handicapped Students
National Drama Conference
National Youth Bureau

Order of the Sacred Hearts of Jesus and Mary (Chigwell Convent)

Scottish Sports Council
Scottish Trades Union Congress/CBI Joint Committee on the Employment of the Disabled
Standing Conference for Amateur Music

Trades Union Congress

VI EDUCATIONAL ESTABLISHMENTS

Bexley Tutorial Unit, London Borough of Bexley

Cambridge Institute of Education
Camphill Rudolf Steiner Schools
Castle Priory College, Wallingford
Chorleywood College for Girls with Little or No Sight
City of Birmingham College of Education (Members of College staff and members of advanced courses for teachers of handicapped children)
City of Leeds and Carnegie College
Culham College, Abingdon

Dunfermline College of Physical Education
Dyslexia Institute

Elizabeth Gaskell College of Education, Manchester

Glamorgan Polytechnic/National Association of the Teachers of Wales

Highfield School

Ida Darwin Hospital School, Governors Working Party

King Alfred's College, Winchester

Lingfield Hospital School
Lord Mayor Treloar Trust

Matlock College of Education (tutors to courses in special education at the College)
Mayfield School, Birmingham
Middle Park School, Havant

National Star Centre for Disabled Youth

Oxford College of Further Education

Rochelle Primary School, London E2
Royal Eastern Counties Schools
Royal Normal College for the Blind

St Christopher's School, Bristol
St John's School for the Deaf, Boston Spa
St Loye's College for Training the Disabled for Commerce and Industry, Exeter
St Vincent's School for Blind and Partially Sighted Children, Liverpool
Sheffield City College of Education

Trinity and All Saints Colleges, Leeds

University College of Swansea, Department of Education
University of Birmingham School of Education
University of Leeds, Institute of Education
University of Newcastle upon Tyne, School of Education (Sub-Department of Speech)
University of Sussex

Westhill College of Education, Birmingham
Whitebrook School for the Deaf, Manchester
Worcester College for the Blind

VII HOSPITALS

Social Work Department, Hospital for Sick Children, Great Ormond Street (Camden Social Services)
Whittingham Hospital, Preston, Department of Psychiatry for the Deaf

VIII INDIVIDUALS

(Positions shown are those held at the time when evidence was submitted)

Mrs A Gilvray Adamson	(Consultant Sociologist)
Dr M Agerholm	(Consultant in Rehabilitation, Inner London Education Authority)

Dr J M Aitkenhead	(Headmaster, Kilquhanity House, Castle-Douglas)
Mr F D Alderman	(Parent of a handicapped son)
Dr E M Anderson	(Research Officer, Thomas Coram Research Unit, University of London Institute of Education)
Mr J Ballantyne	(Handicapped young person)
Professor P J Barber	(Post Experience Unit, Open University)
Mr A Bates	(Teacher of hearing impaired children)
Mr B Benjamin	(Headmaster of a special school)
Dr G A Bland	(Headmaster, Brockhall Hospital School, Blackburn)
Mrs H J Block	(Education Welfare Officer)
Mr E T Briggs	(Headmaster, Yewcroft School, Birmingham)
Professor R Brown	(Parent of a handicapped son)
Mr C J Buxton	(Senior Schools Adviser, Metropolitan District of Sefton)
Mrs M Caltieri	(Teacher in a Senior ESN(M) School, Leeds)
Mr M W C Campbell	(Headmaster, Drummond School, Inverness)
Mrs M Carr	(Handicapped young person)
Dr V Carver	(Chairman, Co-ordinating Committee for Disabled Students, The Open University)
Mr G Chilvers	(Research Fellow, Westhill College of Education, Birmingham)
Mr N C Clegg	(Principal, North Nottinghamshire College of Further Education)
Dr J M Cockburn	(Regional Principal Educational Psychologist, Tayside Region)
Mr D Cohen	(Rushworth Primary School, London SE1)
Miss C S Collins	(Head of the Remedial Department at George Watson's College, Edinburgh and Adviser to the Scottish Association for the Study of Dyslexia)
Mrs C L Cooper	(Parent of a handicapped young person)
Miss G C Cotterell	(Remedial advisory teacher, Suffolk Psychological Service)
Mr P M Cummings	(Senior Educational Psychologist, Pre-School and Handicapped Children, City of Birmingham Psychological Service)
Dr D M C Dale	(Senior Lecturer in Education of the Deaf, University of London Institute of Education)

Dr K Dalzell and Miss V Reeves	(Senior Medical Officer, Clwyd Area Health Authority; Audiologist, Clwyd AHA)
Mr J Norman Davies	(Education Officer, Special Services, Gwynedd)
Mr E Daynes	(Head of the Department of Special Education, West London Institute of Higher Education)
Dr W B Dockrell	(Director of the Scottish Council for Research in Education)
Mrs J Dodds	(Audiologist, Hants Area Health Authority)
Mr J R Douthwaite	(Headmaster, Moston School, Chester)
Mr T Doyle	(Principal Educational Psychologist, Mid-Glamorgan LEA)
Mr P E Dunn	(Teacher-in-Charge, Horsham Remedial Unit, Sussex)
Mr P East	(Adviser in Special Education, Coventry)
Mr J A Edwards	(Assistant Director, Social Science, Leicester Polytechnic)
Mrs J Edwards	(Parent of a handicapped son)
Mr G R Eustance	(Education Guidance Officer, City of Liverpool)
Mrs A Feldman	(Parent of a handicapped son and founder of the Hackney and Islington Association for Parents of ESN Children)
Mr B C Fraser	
Dr W I Fraser	(Physician Superintendent, Lynebank Hospital, Dunfermline)
Miss C A Goodwin	(Educational Psychologist, City of Sheffield)
Mr and Mrs A D Goff	(Parents of a handicapped daughter)
Miss B Gray	(Teacher)
Mr E J Griffiths	(Staff Inspector, Special Education, Birmingham)
Mr D H Grossman	(County Adviser for Special Education, Hertfordshire)
Mr S Hamer	(Headmaster, Royal Liverpool Children's Hospital School)
Dr M I Heatley	(Psychiatrist, Oxfordshire Child Guidance Clinic)
Mrs M C Hockenhull	(Matron, Yorkshire Residential School for the Deaf, Doncaster)
Mr F P Holden	(Special Education Department, King Alfred's College, Winchester)
Mrs B Hornsby	(Head of Dyslexia Clinic, Department of Psychological Medicine, St Bartholomew's Hospital)

Mr L A Ives	(Educational Psychologist, The Royal Schools for the Deaf (Manchester))
Dr A D M Jackson	(Consultant Paediatrician, The London Hospital) in association with Mrs M Ellis and Miss S Eden (Occupational Therapy Department, The London Hospital)
Dr B S Jackson	(Parent of a handicapped son)
Dr R Jackson	(Lecturer in Education, Aberdeen College of Education)
Mrs S Jones	(Headteacher, Ysgol Delyn, Mold, Clwyd)
Mr L Juliac	(Handicapped young person)
Mr and Mrs I L Keiller	(Parents of two handicapped children)
Mr G C Lambert	(Tutor and Organiser, Course for Physically Handicapped Young Adults, Airedale and Wharfedale College of Further Education)
Miss L Lawson	(Handicapped young person)
Mr R Leach	(Headmaster, Torfield School, Hastings)
Mrs A Loring	(Secretary, International Cerebral Palsy Society)
Miss A E McCormack	(Gogarburn Hospital School, Edinburgh)
Dr D F Macgregor	(Consultant Psychiatrist, Prudhoe Hospital, Northumberland)
Mr G F MacKay	(Senior Educational Psychologist, Metropolitan Borough of Bury)
Mr K Mackenzie	(Principal Officer, Children's Day Care, Lambeth Social Services Department)
Dr M I Mair	(School Health Department, Argyll and Clyde Health Board (Renfrew District))
Mr W D Major	(Special Education Department, Westhill College of Education, Birmingham)
Dr A Martin	(Chairman of Governors of two hospital schools for handicapped children in Plumstead)
Mr J McAdam	(Handicapped young person)
Mr and Mrs R Meldon Smith	(Parents of a handicapped daughter)
Professor T R Miles and Mrs E Miles	(Professor of Psychology, University College of North Wales, Bangor; Tutor and Organiser, Bangor Dyslexia Unit)
Mr P K C Millins	(Director, Edge Hill College of Higher Education, Ormskirk)
Professor P Mittler	(Hester Adrian Research Centre, University of Manchester)
Rev G Monteith	(Handicapped person)

Mr G W C Montgomery	(Research Unit, Donaldson's School for the Deaf, Edinburgh)
Mrs K E Myers	(Parent of a handicapped son)
Dr M Newton	(Senior Lecturer in Developmental and Applied Psychology, University of Aston in Birmingham)
Mr R H Nicholls	(Headmaster, Tesdale and Bennett House Schools, Abingdon)
Professor J Nisbet and Mrs J Welsh	(The Head of the Department of Education, and a member of the Department, University of Aberdeen)
Mr and Mrs J Oliver	(Foster parents of a handicapped child)
Dr M O'Moore	(Lecturer in Educational Psychology, University of Dublin)
Mr C L Parkin	(Adviser in Special Education, Humberside)
Miss B Z Perman	(Researcher into the role of management in the education of hearing impaired children)
Councillor D Pettitt	(Counsellor, Nottinghamshire)
Mrs M Polack	(Parent of a handicapped daughter)
Miss J Powell	(Adviser in Special Education, Warwickshire)
Mr P D Pumfrey	(Department of Education, University of Manchester)
Mr R A Radley	(Headteacher, Sedgwick House School, Kendal)
Mrs R Ray	(Parent of a handicapped daughter)
Dr B Rigby	(Committee for use of science of creative intelligence in special education)
Mr L Rigley	(Department of Child Development and Educational Psychology, University of London Institute of Education)
Dr D P W Roberts	(Specialist in Community Medicine, Gwynedd Health Authority)
Mr D Robertson	(Handicapped young person)
Mrs S Sandow	(Research Assistant, University of Hull)
Mr C R Senneck	(Parent of a handicapped son)
Mrs M Skeffington	(Lecturer in the Education of Handicapped Children, University of Manchester)
Mr and Mrs A H K Slater	(Parents of a handicapped son)
Miss B Somerset	(Examiner of the English Speaking Board)
Mr A W E Speed	(Headmaster and parent of a handicapped child)
Mr D E Spinks	(Handicapped young person)

Mrs M Stevens	(Special Lecturer (part-time), Department of Education, University of Manchester, and Peripatetic Lecturer in Special Education)
Mrs J Taylor	(Parent of a handicapped son)
Mr and Mrs A Thomas	(Parents of a handicapped son)
Mrs M Turton	(Parent of a handicapped son)
Dr J H Walker	(Head of Department of Family and Community Medicine, University of Newcastle upon Tyne)
Mr P D Waters	(Psychologist; Director of Possum Controls Ltd)
Mrs T M Watson	(Parent of a handicapped son)
Miss T Watts	(Co-ordinator of Special Services, Lambeth Social Services Department)
Mr A Wellings	(Lecturer in Psychology, Department of Extramural Studies, University of Sheffield) on behalf of a group of six parents of handicapped children in Sheffield
Mr T Wells	(Handicapped young person)
Dr R Wigglesworth	(Senior Consultant Paediatrician, Kettering District General Hospital)
Mr P Wildblood	(Headmaster, The Calthorpe School, Birmingham)
Mrs C A Williams	(Parent of two handicapped children and a remedial teacher)
Dr C E Williams	(Consultant Child Psychiatrist, Borocourt Hospital, Berkshire)
Mr D C Williamson	(Lecturer in Physical Education on The Handicapped, Trent Polytechnic)
Mr N Winter	(Handicapped young person)
Miss D Wright	(Handicapped young person)
Mr A Zimmer	(Adviser in Special Education, Strathclyde)

APPENDIX 2

CATEGORIES OF HANDICAPPED PUPILS

ENGLAND AND WALES

1. The categories of pupils requiring special educational treatment in England and Wales are defined in the Handicapped Pupils and Special Schools Regulations 1959, as amended. The definitions are as follows:

"(a) blind pupils, that is to say, pupils who have no sight or whose sight is or is likely to become so defective that they require education by methods not involving the use of sight;

(b) partially sighted pupils, that is to say, pupils who by reason of defective vision cannot follow the normal regime of ordinary schools without detriment to their sight or to their educational development, but can be educated by special methods involving the use of sight;

(c) deaf pupils, that is to say, pupils with impaired hearing who require education by methods suitable for pupils with little or no naturally acquired speech or language;

(d) partially hearing pupils, that is to say, pupils with impaired hearing whose development of speech and language, even if retarded, is following a normal pattern, and who require for their education special arrangements or facilities though not necessarily all the educational methods used for deaf pupils;

(e) educationally sub-normal pupils, that is to say, pupils who, by reason of limited ability or other conditions resulting in educational retardation, require some specialised form of education wholly or partly in substitution for the education normally given in ordinary schools;

(f) epileptic pupils, that is to say, pupils who by reason of epilepsy cannot be educated under the normal regime of ordinary schools without detriment to themselves or other pupils;

(g) maladjusted pupils, that is to say, pupils who show evidence of emotional instability or psychological disturbance and require special educational treatment in order to effect their personal, social or educational readjustment;

(h) physically handicapped pupils, that is to say, pupils not suffering solely from a defect of sight or hearing who by reason of disease or crippling defect cannot, without detriment to their health or educational development, be satisfactorily educated under the normal regime of ordinary schools;

(i) pupils suffering from speech defect, that is to say, pupils who on account of defect or lack of speech not due to deafness require special educational treatment; and

(j) delicate pupils, that is to say, pupils not falling under any other category in this regulation, who by reason of impaired physical condition need a change of environment or cannot, without risk to their health or educational development, be educated under the normal regime of ordinary schools."

SCOTLAND

2. In Scotland the categories of pupils requiring special educational treatment are defined in the Special Educational Treatment (Scotland) Regulations, 1954 as follows:

"(1) deaf pupils, that is to say pupils who, because of defective hearing, are without naturally acquired speech or language;

(2) partially deaf pupils, that is to say pupils whose sense of hearing is defective but who possess naturally acquired speech or language;

(3) blind pupils, that is to say pupils who have no sense of sight or whose sense of sight is, or is likely to become, so defective as to be of no practical value for reading or writing;

(4) partially sighted pupils, that is to say pupils whose sense of sight is, or is likely to become, defective but is, and is likely to remain, of practical value for reading or writing;

(5) mentally handicapped pupils, that is to say pupils who have little natural ability;

(6) epileptic pupils, that is to say pupils who suffer from severe or frequent epileptic seizures or who, by reason of epilepsy, behave in such a way as to make it inexpedient that they should be associated with other children;

(7) pupils suffering from speech defect, that is to say pupils who suffer from defect or lack of speech not due to deafness or mental handicap;

(8) maladjusted pupils, that is to say pupils who suffer from emotional instability or psychological disturbance;

(9) physically handicapped pupils, that is to say pupils who suffer from a physical disability which is, or is likely to be, permanent or protracted and which does not bring them within any of the foregoing categories."

APPENDIX 3

A POSSIBLE GRID AS A BASIS FOR STATISTICAL RETURNS

1. We indicated in Chapter 4 (paragraphs 4.76–7) the need for a grid as a basis for statistical returns to the Department of Education and Science, Scottish Education Department and Welsh Office of children recorded as in need of special educational provision. We suggested that one of its axes should list a number of different areas of functioning under which any impairment could be shown and the other should take the form of a scale on which the degree of impairment could be indicated.

2. A possible grid is shown on the following page. The headings comprise a list of various areas of functioning – vision, hearing, mobility (sub-divided into upper and lower limb), intellectual functioning and language (sub-divided into expressive language and language comprehension) – as well as social and emotional behaviour and the general condition of physical health. The heading "specific learning" is designed to accommodate children with specific learning difficulties. The grid would allow the degree of any impairment in each of these areas to be recorded on a five-point scale. We envisage that the column for "specific learning" would be ruled off in the absence of a specific learning problem. All other columns would be completed and the degree of impairment indicated on the scale.

3. Instructions for completion would need to be provided defining more clearly the different headings, particularly "specific learning", and giving guidance on the use of the scale. A feasibility study on the use of such a grid would be essential, as we recommended in Chapter 4.

DEGREE OF IMPAIRMENT	VISION	HEARING	MOBILITY UPPER LIMB	MOBILITY LOWER LIMB	PHYSICAL HEALTH	EXPRESSIVE LANGUAGE	LANGUAGE COMPREHENSION	SPECIFIC LEARNING (IF ANY)	CURRENT INTELLECTUAL FUNCTIONING	SOCIAL AND EMOTIONAL BEHAVIOUR
NO IMPAIRMENT										
SLIGHT IMPAIRMENT										
MODERATE IMPAIRMENT										
SEVERE IMPAIRMENT										
TOTAL IMPAIRMENT										

INITIAL PLACEMENT	
1. Ordinary school: ordinary class with special help	
2. Ordinary school: special class or unit	
3. Day special school	
4. Boarding special school	
5. Hospital special school	
6. Independent school a. catering for non-handicapped pupils	
b. catering wholly or mainly for handicapped pupils	
7. Section 56: at home	
8. Section 56: elsewhere	
9. Other placements, specify:	
10. Awaiting placement	

Changes in placement

eg	
3 to 1	8.7.76

383

APPENDIX 4

THE ORGANISATION OF THE HEALTH SERVICE

1. The new administrative structure for the health services in England, Wales and Scotland became effective on 1 April 1974. It is based on the establishment of health authorities, which are statutory agencies of central government responsible for all health services within defined geographical areas. These services include hospital and specialist services, the primary health care (including general practitioner) services, the community services previously administered in England and Wales by local health authorities and the school health service, which was previously administered by local education authorities in England and Wales and provided on an agency basis by local health authorities in Scotland. The new health authorities also have a general responsibility for preventive health measures. They co-operate with local, port and water authorities, which have certain defined responsibilities and powers in relation to environmental health. The Employment Medical Advisory Service, however, with its limited defined objectives in relation to occupational health, is part of the Health and Safety Executive and remains outside the responsibility of the health authorities.

2. In England there is a three-tier structure for planning and control under the Secretary of State for Social Services. This comprises the Department of Health and Social Security, which has a central strategic planning role and a responsibility for monitoring the working of the service as a whole; the regional health authorities, which are responsible for regional planning, for the allocation of resources to area health authorities and for monitoring their activities; and area health authorities, which are responsible for operational management of health services and for planning within their areas.

3. There are 14 regional health authorities, each with one or more university medical schools within its boundaries. Each region comprises between three and 11 areas. The regional health authorities form part of a chain of responsibility running from the Secretary of State to area authorities, to which they delegate operational functions. They retain some direct executive functions which are more economically organised in this way than by individual area authorities. It is at regional level that the approval of specialist regional centres takes place, although these are then developed by area health authorities by agreement with the regional authority to serve a wider area. The boundaries of the regional health authorities are not co-terminous with those of the regional conferences for special education.

4. There are 90 area health authorities in England. Their boundaries generally match those of the new non-metropolitan counties and metropolitan districts of local government. In London the boundaries of the health authorities correspond in four cases to those of individual London boroughs and, in the remaining 12 cases, to those of two or three or in one case four boroughs grouped together. The area health authority is the operational authority in the national health service responsible for assessing health needs in its area and for planning, organising and administering area health services to meet them, including the necessary supportive services. It is responsible for providing school health services to the matching local education authority. These services include the

provision of medical staff, nurses and therapists to ordinary and special schools; arrangements for medical examinations, immunisation and the oversight of health care in schools; the provision of advice to parents, teachers and local education authorities on the nature and extent of handicapping conditions or other medical conditions significant for a child's education; participation in health education; and the provision of counselling services for pupils and others.

5. Each area health authority is served by an area team of officers consisting of the Area Administrator, the Area Medical Officer, the Area Nursing Officer and the Area Treasurer. This team carries out the planning and evaluation work for the area health authority. It draws up planning guidelines for each health district and reviews and monitors the performance of districts. The Area Medical Officer reviews the needs of the area for health care and advises the area team of officers and the area health authority on policies for health care. He is responsible for co-ordinating preventive and other services as well as for the work of Specialists in Community Medicine on the authority's staff. The Specialist in Community Medicine (Child Health) in England and Wales has dual responsibilities to and is appointed with the agreement of both the area health authority and the local education authority. His responsibilities include the organisation of the school health service provided for the local education authority. The Area Nursing Officer provides nursing advice to the area health authority, to the area team of officers and to individual officers at area level; monitors and co-ordinates the work of District Nursing Officers and manages his or her own staff based at area level including the Area Nurse (Child Health); and participates in the formulation of policies and plans in conjunction with other members of the area team of officers. The Area Nurse (Child Health), who is appointed in agreement with the local education authority, is responsible for the provision of nursing services in schools and provides nursing advice on child health (including school health) to the Area Nursing Officer and similar advice on child health, including health education in schools, to the local authority. The Area Nurse (Child Health) collaborates with District Nursing Officers, who have day to day responsibility for the management of school nursing services, and works closely with the Specialist in Community Medicine (Child Health) to provide a comprehensive school health service.

6. The day to day running of the services for which an area health authority is responsible is based on health districts. These always contain a district general hospital, and each district covers a population of between 100,000 and 400,000. About a quarter of the 90 area health authorities consist of one health district only; they thus fulfil the role of both an area health authority and a health district. The remainder consist of between two and six districts. The execution of health policies in a district is in the charge of the district management team, again consisting of four officers of the area health authority: a District Administrator, a District Finance Officer, a District Nursing Officer and a District Community Physician, together with two doctors elected by the district medical committee which represents doctors working in all parts of the national health service. Hospital staff and general practitioners can thus influence planning and decision making at this local level through the representative system. To assist district management teams area health authorities should establish district planning teams, which can include local authority staff where services are of concern to both health and local authorities. Their purpose is to conduct detailed planning

of the health care of particular groups of patients, for example expectant and nursing mothers, children, the elderly, the mentally ill and the mentally and physically handicapped. Under the re-organised national health service the status of general and dental practitioners, ophthalmic medical practitioners, opticians and pharmacists as independent contractors has remained. Each area health authority has set up a Family Practitioner Committee to administer their contracts and this Committee deals with the Department of Health and Social Security on contractual matters.

7. Health services in Wales are established in accordance with the same legislation as in England, with some significant differences to meet the special circumstances and needs of Wales. The Secretary of State for Wales is responsible for health services in Wales, and the eight health authorities, which are co-terminous with the new counties, report direct to the Welsh Office, which supplies central guidance.

8. In Scotland the Scottish Home and Health Department is the central authority responsible for providing and allocating resources to 15 health boards, and for monitoring their performance. These health boards broadly combine the responsibilities of the regional and area health authorities in England. The boundaries of 11 health boards coincide exactly with the corresponding regional and island councils. The remaining four health boards relate to subdivisions of the largest region, Strathclyde, and co-incide with local authority districts. The formulation of policy on health and the planning of all health services including child and school health are area responsibilities. The health board collaborates with local authority regional councils, which have among their responsibilities social work, education and strategic planning, and district councils, which are concerned with land use planning and environmental health. Each health board is serviced by an Area Executive Group, consisting of the Secretary, the Chief Administrative Medical Officer, the Chief Area Nursing Officer and the Treasurer. Their individual responsibilities in general correspond with those of their counterparts on the area team of officers in England. The day to day running of the services in Scotland, like that in England, is based on health districts. These tend to be smaller than those in England. The five smallest health boards are single district authorities. Otherwise the number of districts in a health board varies between two and five. Health board districts have an executive function and policies are carried out by an executive group consisting of four officers from the main disciplines as in England but without any elected clinicians. As in England and Wales, general and dental practitioners, ophthalmic medical practitioners, opticians and pharmacists have remained independent contractors. However, there are no statutory committees such as the Family Practitioner Committee, the functions of which are undertaken by sub-committees of the health board.

9. In Scotland the responsibilities of the Community Medicine Specialist (Child Health) and the Area Nursing Officer (Child Health) are non-clinical and advisory. These officers are not responsible for the deployment of staff or for clinical management within the service, nor do they undertake clinical duties. Community Medicine Specialists are not employed by the education authority.

They do, however, provide links between the education authority and the health board and assist with the determination of needs, the provision required to meet these needs and the formulation of policies and priorities. The clinical medical staff are accountable to the Chief Administrative Medical Officer, the nursing staff to the Chief Area Nursing Officer.

APPENDIX 5

RESEARCH PROJECT ON SERVICES FOR PARENTS OF HANDICAPPED CHILDREN UNDER FIVE

1. The research project on services for parents of children under five, commissioned by the Department of Education and Science at our request, was carried out under the co-direction of Professor M Chazan and Dr A F Laing of the University College of Swansea. Dr M Shackleton-Bailey was appointed as senior research officer and other research officers were Mrs G E Holmes, Miss G E Jones, Mrs S Threlfall and Dr J A Ward. The project began on 1 December 1975 and final reports were produced in December 1976.

2. The main aims of the project were:
   (i) to obtain from a sample of parents factual information and personal opinions about the services they were receiving or would have liked to receive; and
   (ii) to obtain from administrators, organisers and other professional workers concerned detailed information on the services being provided, their assessment of these services and future planning.

3. The survey was carried out in five areas: Hampshire, Sheffield, Suffolk, West Glamorgan and the Lothian Region. Interviews were held with 30 parents in Hampshire, Sheffield and Suffolk, 29 in West Glamorgan and 26 in the Lothian Region. Interviews were also held in each area with members of the health, education and social services and representatives of voluntary organisations.

4. The sample of parents in each area was selected to include those with handicapped children in three age groups – 0–24 months, 24–36 months and 36–60 months – and, within each age group, with different types of handicap. The children were identified through handicap registers, advisory teachers, nursery headteachers and voluntary organisations. Care was taken to ensure that, so far as possible, different types of socio-economic background were represented in the sample.

5. References to, and illustrations from, the survey are to be included in an occasional publication planned by Professor Chazan and Dr Laing on "Young Handicapped Children".

APPENDIX 6

RESEARCH PROJECT ON PRE-SCHOOL EDUCATION AND HANDICAPPED AND EXCEPTIONAL CHILDREN

1. This research project, commissioned at our request, commenced in March 1976 and lasted one year. It was directed by Dr Margaret M Clark, Reader in Educational Psychology, University of Strathclyde, with Mrs J Riach as research fellow and Dr W Cheyne as statistical consultant.

2. The study had two related aims:–

   (i) To investigate the perceptions of staffs in nursery schools and classes, and in the related primary schools, of handicapped and exceptional children and the incidence of such children in the nursery schools and classes. The research was extended to include all day nurseries organised by the social work department and a selection of community and private pre-school playgroups.

   (ii) To undertake observational studies in selected schools and units in which there were handicapped children in order to observe the extent and type of attention they received from staff in relation to other children not so perceived.

3. The pilot study was carried out in the Central Region and the main study in the Grampian Region of Scotland.

4. In the initial stage of the investigation nursery schools and classes were visited and the teachers in charge were interviewed to obtain information on the following issues:–

   (i) number of handicapped and exceptional children (as defined and described by the research worker) attending the unit;

   (ii) numbers of such children whom the headteacher thought could be accommodated and reasons for these views;

   (iii) admissions procedure for such children;

   (iv) details of any special provision for any of these children in the unit – visiting specialists, spatial layout, equipment, activities, special hours of attendance; and

   (v) links with primary schools.

These interviews were followed by a similar investigation of a sample of pre-school playgroups, selected from those registered with the social work department, two nursery classes attached to private schools, and all day nurseries (now known as pre-school day centres) in Grampian Region.

5. In the second stage of the study detailed observations were carried out in selected nursery schools and pre-school playgroups to obtain some insight into the advantages and problems of integrating handicapped children in pre-school units. Interviews were also held with primary schools receiving handicapped children who had attended nursery school or classes.

6. Close links were maintained with the regional officials in Grampian Region and regular meetings were held with a committee which was chosen to be

representative of the various agencies co-operating in the study. Plans were discussed with this group and progress reported. It was at the request of this committee that the original title of the research which referred to "deviant" children to cover handicapped and gifted children was changed to "handicapped and exceptional children".

7. For the purpose of the project handicapped children were regarded as children with a sensory handicap, a speech defect, difference or difficulty, a physical/neurological impairment, mental handicap, emotional disturbance, social maladjustment or multiple disabilities.

8. A report on the project has been published by the University of Strathclyde and is available from that University.

APPENDIX 7

RESEARCH PROJECT ON THE EMPLOYMENT OF HANDICAPPED SCHOOL-LEAVERS

1. This research project was commissioned at our request from the National Children's Bureau. It began in October 1975 and lasted two years. The senior research officer was Mr A Walker (now at the Department of Sociological Studies, University of Sheffield) and the research assistant Miss P Lewis.

2. The aims of the project were:

   (i) to explore the reasons for the success or failure of handicapped young people to get or keep a job; and

   (ii) to obtain some indication of the extent of unused capacity for employment up to the age of about 18 years, together with a consideration of further education, training and of family and other support.

3. The sample of eighteen-year-olds was drawn from the National Child Development Study (NCDS), which has studied the progress of all the children in Britain born in one week in March 1958. Information had been obtained on over 17,000 babies. There were subsequent follow-ups at ages 7, 11 and 16.[1] The third and most recent follow-up was carried out in 1974 when the young people were in their last year of compulsory education.

4. For the purposes of the selection of the sample "handicap" was defined as the need for special educational treatment. Four groups of young people were distinguished:–

   (i) The handicapped group

      Those young people formally ascertained as needing special education. A preliminary analysis of the data from the 16-year-old follow-up revealed a total of 596 young people who had been ascertained as handicapped at some time during their life. The final sample for this research project excluded those who had been ascertained as handicapped and had previously received special education but were no longer receiving it at 16 (234). The largest number in the handicapped group was that of the ESN(M), reflecting their numerical preponderance in the total population of handicapped young people.* The majority of the handicapped (nearly two-thirds) had been in special schools or units at 16.

   (ii) The "special help" group
      Those receiving help for educational backwardness but who were not formally ascertained. According to their teachers this group received special help within the school because of educational or mental backwardness.

---

[1] N R Butler and E D Alberman, *Perinatal Problems* (E and S Livingstone, 1969); R Davie, N R Butler and H Goldstein, *From Birth to Seven* (Longman, 1972); K Fogelman (ed), *Britain's Sixteen-Year-Olds* (National Children's Bureau, 1976).

* The sample included a small group of young people ascertained as ESN(M) on whom information had been collected in the follow-up at 11 years but on whom no information had been obtained in the subsequent follow-up.

(iii) The "would benefit" group

Those not formally ascertained, nor receiving any special educational help at 16, but who in the opinion of their teachers would have benefited from such provision.

(iv) The non-handicapped group

A control group of those not ascertained, not receiving and not needing any special help for educational backwardness, behaviour difficulties, physical or sensory disability at 16 years.

The sample was stratified disproportionately in relation to these four groups. All the groups except that of the handicapped were sampled randomly.

5. The research was based on a structured interview carried out with each young person in which details were obtained of his employment status, his previous employment, his education and training and the careers advice which he had received. The interview schedules were tested and revised on the basis of two small pilot studies carried out in London and Northumberland and the main survey interviews were conducted in the summer and autumn of 1976.

6. Just over one-fifth of the original sample refused to take part in the survey and the final response rate was 64%. There was a relatively high response rate of 82% at the field-work stage. The numbers of young people in each group with whom interviews were completed are shown below.

	Sample size Interview completed	Percentage of total
ESN(S)	43	8.5
Physically handicapped	36	7.1
ESN(M)	125	24.6
Maladjusted	34	6.7
ESN(M) at 11 years	27	5.3
"Special help" group	72	14.2
"Would benefit" group	56	11.0
Control group	115	22.6
Total	508	100

7. Parents were interviewed where the young person was living at home and one parent was available to be interviewed. A questionnaire was also sent to a small sample of headteachers of selected special and ordinary schools seeking information about contact with parents, careers advice and preparation for the world of work. A further questionnaire was sent to 156 employers selected from the employers of the young people in the sample.

8. A report on the research project is to be published later in 1978.

APPENDIX 8

SURVEY OF THE VIEWS OF TEACHERS IN SPECIAL AND ORDINARY SCHOOLS ON SPECIAL EDUCATION

1. At our request the Department of Education and Science conducted a survey of the views of teachers in ordinary and special schools in England, Scotland and Wales on various aspects of provision for children with special educational needs. The main aim was to discover what resources, what supporting services and specialist advice and what kinds of additional training were considered by teachers to be most likely to improve their effectiveness in dealing with children with special educational needs. It was hoped that the survey would also shed light on the reasons for the apparent failure of much educational research significantly to influence teaching practice.

2. Following pilot surveys in England Wales, questionnaires were issued in May 1976 to a total of 5,240 teachers and headteachers in all the special schools and classes in Scotland and in a sample of special schools, classes and units in England and Wales, stratified by type of school. The following month questionnaires were sent to the headteacher and one other teacher in each of 1,088 ordinary maintained primary and secondary schools in England, Wales and Scotland. The probability of the headteachers being selected was proportionate to the size of their school.

3. The questionnaires to teachers and headteachers in special schools covered the following topics: changes in the curriculum or in teaching methods in their class or school and the factors contributing to such changes; areas in the work of the school where changes were considered necessary; the ways in which parents were involved in the activities of the school; the impact of different sources of information about new ideas, good practice and research in special education, as well as the effects of different forms of educational research on teaching practice; difficulties faced by teachers in applying examples of good practice and research; the availability of advice and support from members of different professions; the value of courses of in-service training taken by the teachers, reasons for not applying for or not taking courses of in-service training, and areas in which the teachers felt a need for in-service education.

4. The questionnaires to teachers and headteachers in ordinary schools included questions about the number of children in their school ascertained as handicapped and, separately, the number considered by them to have special educational problems; the nature of those problems and the ways in which special educational help was provided; the availability and usefulness of support and advice from members of different professions; the factors contributing to the successful integration of handicapped children in the regular classes of ordinary schools; the advantages of such integration; and any training or previous experience in the teaching of children with special educational problems.

5. Both sets of questionnaires contained some questions to which answers could be selected from a given list and other open-ended questions. The answers to the open-ended questions were coded by Mrs K O'Hagan.

6. The response rates to the questionnaires were disappointingly low. The response rate to the survey in special schools was 56%, that to the survey in

ordinary schools 49%. The low response rates can be attributed mainly to the issue of the questionnaires late in the summer term when many teachers were preparing to depart for their summer holidays. The timing was unavoidable, given the need to carry out the survey before the end of the academic year. A comparison in respect of age and sex, however, between the teachers in special schools, classes and units who responded to the survey and the total population of teachers in special schools, classes and units in England, Scotland and Wales suggests that the respondents were reasonably representative of the total population of teachers in this sector.

Index

The index excludes individual authorities, establishments, organisations and people referred to only in Chapter 2. Terms used frequently throughout the report, which consist of more than one word, for example "educational psychologists", "peripatetic teachers", "special schools", are listed under the initial letter of the first word. Chapter and paragraph numbers are shown, the former in bold print.

395

Assessment
    Legal position   4. 25–8
    Of children under five   4. 34; 5. 21–7, 39, 49
    Of children whose first language is not English   4. 50–1
    Of young people   7. 41; 10. 6–10
    Procedures for   2. 73–4; 4. 35–47; 7. 16; 13. 10; 14. 7; 15. 13, 22, 26, 42
    Re-assessment   4. 54, 71–2; 8. 26; 10. 7; 14. 17; 15. 43
    Regional-based   4. 48–9
    Requirements of effective   4. 29–33; 9. 19; 13. 34; 15. 16
    Residential   4. 41, 47; 5. 25; 8. 14, 18
    Specifically vocational   10. 8–9, 64, 67, 75; 14. 17; 17. 13

Assessment Centres/Units   4. 46, 47; 5. 25, 36, 41, 43, 68; 10. 9; 12. 36; 13. 33

Association for Spina Bifida and Hydrocephalus   17. 5

Association of Educational Psychologists   14. 12; 16. 5

Association of Municipal Authorities   8. 29

Asthma, Children with   2. 53

At Risk Registers   4. 3, 7

Attendance Allowance   9. 25

Audiology   12. 17, 18, 22, 42

Audio-Visual Materials   8. 13; 12. 9, 61

Autistic Children   2. 83; 8. 33, 43, 57; 11. 64; 17. 7, 12

Behavioural Disorders, Children with (see also Maladjusted Children)
    Discovery and assessment of   4. 24, 33, 44; 11. 60; 15. 22, 44
    Organisations for   17. 3, 12, 29
    Prevalence of   3. 12, 15; 7. 5; 11. 22
    Provision for   2. 62; 3. 8, 38; 6. 10; 7. 12(iii), 30, 31; 8. 8, 12, 13, 14, 16, 33, 58, 74;
        11. 27, 45, 54, 61–3; 13. 2; 14. 32; 15. 25
    Use of the term   3. 27, 41; 14. 8
    Young people   10. 4, 100, 111

Bicester and Cooper Schools, Bicester   7. 12(iii), 30

Birmingham University   12. 45; 18. 3

Blind Children (see also Visual Disabilities, Children with)
    Category of blind pupils   2. 37, 45; 3. 23; App. 2
    Education for   2. 1, 2–3, 8, 10–15, 25, 32–3, 38, 46, 50; 7. 12(i), 51; 8. 22; 11. 3,
        10, 23, 25–9
    Organisations for   17. 5
    Teachers of   2. 8, 75–6; 12. 24, 25, 28, 33, 44–5, 53

Blind Persons Resettlement Officers   10. 128

Board of Education   2. 29, 35, 37, 71, 75

Boarding Homes for Children   2. 49, 61, 64; 3. 7; 4. 75; 14. 30; 15. 40

Bolton College of Education (Technical)   12. 66

British Association of Social Workers   16. 5

British Association of Teachers of the Deaf   12. 44, 45

British Council for Rehabilitation of the Disabled   10. 119

British Psychological Society   14. 12, 14; 16. 5

Brittle Bone Society   17. 5

Broadcasting **4.** 4; **10.** 46
 Local radio **5.** 47, 63
Brotherston Report (*Towards an Integrated Child Health Service*) **15.** 5, 13
Bullock Report (*A language for life*) **4.** 24
Burnham Primary and Secondary Salaries Document **12.** 28
Burt, Dr C **2.** 36; **14.** 4

Canada, Intro.7; **5.** 67; **7.** 1
Cardiff, University College **10.** 111; **12.** 66
Care, Children in **2.** 70; **3.** 15; **5.** 29; **8.** 19, 66, 68–77; **13.** 15; **15.** 44–6
Careers Guidance **10.** 7, 11–17, 33, 49, 56; **11.** 19; **14.** 9; **19.** 23
Careers Officers
 Advising young people and their parents **4.** 22; **10.** 7, 15–17, 21, 33, 78; **11.** 19;
  14. 16–17
 As Named Person **9.** 17, 34; **10.** 17, 94, 97, 106; **14.** 18
 In assessment and re-assessment **4.** 54; **7.** 41; **10.** 6, 7
 Links with other services **10.** 14, 24, 64; **13.** 33; **16.** 14
 Specialist careers officers **4.** 78; **10.** 15, 16, 17, 78, 94; **14.** 16–21; **15.** 43; **16.** 32
 Supply and training of **10.** 15; **14.** 19–21; **16.** 25
Careers Teachers **10.** 12–15, 17; **14.** 1, 16, 19
Case Conference **10.** 10
Categorisation of Handicapped Pupils **2.** 37, 42, 45–8, 58, 80; **3.** 21–32, 37; **4.** 51, 75–6;
 6. 2; App. 2
Cave, Cyril
 Review of recent research by Intro. 5; **5.** 1n
Central Council for Education and Training in Social Work **2.** 64; **15.** 48
 Certificate in Residential Social Work **2.** 64
 Certificate in Social Service **2.** 64; **14.** 36
 Certificate in the Residential Care of Children and Young People **2.** 64
 Certificate of Qualification in Social Work **2.** 64
Central Health Services Council **16.** 46
Cerebral Palsy, Children with **2.** 51
Chazan, Professor M
 Research project on services for parents of handicapped children by Intro. 5;
 4. 5; **5.** 6, 7, 12, 14; **9.** 13; **16.** 2, 4; App. 5
Child and Adolescent Psychiatric Services **2.** 62; **5.** 46; **10.** 100; **11.** 22, 54; **14.** 8;
 15. 25–6
 Child psychiatric teams **4.** 44; **15.** 22
Child and Adolescent Psychiatrists **2.** 55, 60; **4.** 64; **8.** 46; **10.** 95; **15.** 14, 25–6
Child Care Staff **2.** 64; **3.** 20; **8.** 44, 47; **14.** 34–7; **15.** 29, 31, 33, 46, 48; **16.** 25
Child Guidance
 Clinics **2.** 36, 44, 55, 57, 60–2; **7.** 34–5; **14.** 12
 Developments in **2.** 36, 46, 60–3; **8.** 73
 Service in Scotland **2.** 44, 63; **14.** 5
 Teams **2.** 46, 62; **4.** 44; **15.** 22, 25
Child Health Services (*see also* School Health Service) **2.** 62; **10.** 101; **15.** 3, 5, 10–12
Child Minders **5.** 69; **15.** 41
Children Acts (1948, 1963, 1975) **15.** 37

Planning of programmes within the **7.** 15, 27–8, 52; **8.** 11–12; **11.** *passim;* **14.** 9
Teacher training and the **12.** 8, 47, 51, 52; **13.** 9

Day Centres
Arrangements in **10.** 51–3; **11.** 59; **15.** 47; **19.** 23
Staff in **10.** 54; **12.** 74; **15.** 40, 47

Day Nurseries
Arrangements in **5.** 39, 43, 68–70; **9.** 24; **19.** 19, 22
Assessment in **4.** 42; **5.** 23–4
Staff in (*see also* Nursery Nurses) **4.** 2, 17; **5.** 71; **13.** 26; **14.** 30–1; **15.** 40–1; **16.** 25

Day Release **10.** 29, 34, 46, 90

Deaf Children (*see also* Hearing Disabilities/Impaired Hearing, Children with)
Category of deaf pupils **2.** 37, 45; **3.** 23; App. 2
Education for **2.** 1, 4, 7, 10–15, 25, 32, 34, 38, 46, 47, 50, 75; **5.** 64; **7.** 12(i), 51, 53; **8.** 13, 22, 56; **11.** 31–3
Research into needs of **18.** 2
Teachers of **2.** 7, 13, 35, 75, 76; **7.** 12(i); **11.** 37; **12.** 17–18, 22, 24, 28, 33, 41–5, 53
Training for other workers with **14.** 36; **15.** 48
Young people **10.** 47, 49

Deaf-Blind Children **2.** 83; **12.** 53

Delicate Children
Category of delicate pupils **2.** 45; **3.** 29; App. 2
Education for **2.** 12, 38, 46, 53

Denmark Intro. 7; **7.** 31, 37; **10.** 112, 114

Dental Services **2.** 71; **15.** 27

Department of Education and Science (*see also* Board of Education; Ministry of Education) **2.** 71; **3.** 29; **4.** 75; **8.** 30, 59, 61; **10.** 48, 113; **12.** 13, 32, 49, 50, 77–8; **14.** 35; **16.** 42, 44; **18.** 11, 12–13, 20; **19.** 20, 24
Circulars etc,

Circular 10/65 **2.** 82
Circular 15/70 **2.** 68
Circular 4/73 **7.** 23; **8.** 41, 71; **14.** 32, 35
Circular 3/74 **2.** 62; **8.** 73
Circular 5/74 **8.** 82
Circular 2/75 **2.** 73; **4.** 25, 27, 55, 58; **11.** 19; **14.** 6; **15.** 13
Circular 10/77 **10.** 33
Circular 11/77 **12.** 68n
Circular 14/77 **4.** 18; **10.** 13
Circular 15/77 **9.** 12
Circular Letter Schools Branch II (SE) 1/73 **8.** 72
Circular Letter Ref No S21/47/05 (1976) **5.** 59; **16.** 34
Circular Letter Ref No S47/24/013 (1978) **5.** 60; **16.** 34; **19.** 22
Further Education Circular Letter FECL 5/76 **15.** 21
List 42 **6.** 14

Surveys carried out by **4.** 58; **7.** 22, 41; **8.** 45; **11.** 48; **13.** 2; **15.** 31; **19.** 4

Department of Employment **10.** 94; **16.** 32, 36, 44

Department of the Environment **10.** 113

Employers **10.** 23, 29, 60, 61, 62, 76–83, 120; **11.** 9; **16.** 14, 32, 40

Employment of Young People with Special Needs (*see also* Work Preparation) **10.** 2, 8, 12, 17, 56–8, 76–90, 96; **17.** 21

Employment Medical Advisory Service **10.** 10, 102; **15.** 20; App. 4

Employment Rehabilitation Centres **10.** 22, 73, 75

Employment Service Agency **10.** 22, 59, 75, 78, 79, 80, 82, 120; **16.** 36

Epilepsy, Children with
    Category of epileptic pupils **2.** 37, 45; App. 2
    Education for **2.** 19–24, 25, 26, 42, 46, 51; **8.** 14, 27; **11.** 43–5

Equipment, Special (*see also* Aids, Special) **3.** 19, 40; **5.** 52; **6.** 4, 9; **7.** 12(i), (ii), 15, 32, 37, 48, 51; **8.** 13; **10.** 37, 41, 113, 115–20; **11.** 34; **13.** 14; **15.** 43; **19.** 25

Ethnic Minorities **4.** 51; **5.** 12, 16, 30; **9.** 5

Family Fund **17.** 24

Family Practitioner Committees **15.** 21; App. 4

Finchale Training College, Durham **10.** 63

Foster Homes/Parents **3.** 33n; **8.** 20; **15.** 44, 45

Further Education
    Preparation for **7.** 41; **10.** 7, 11, 19–20, 78; **11.** 4, 18, 19, 42; **13.** 23
    Provision of **10.** 25–9, 33–46, 74; **11.** 20, 30, 36, 42, 55; **12.** 84; **14.** 9; **17.** 13; **19.** 9, 11, 23–5

Further Education, Establishments of
    Health Services for **15.** 21
    Special units in **10.** 40; **11.** 36; **12.** 70; **19.** 23, 29
    Specialist **10.** 44; **11.** 20, 30; **17.** 13
    Staff in **10.** 37, 40, 41, 42, 54, 55; **12.** 66–74; **19.** 28

Further Education Review and Curriculum Development Unit **11.** 20

Further Education Staff College **18.** 19

Gaelic **4.** 50; **11.** 69

Garnet College, London **12.** 66

General Practitioners **4.** 2, 5, 8, 14, 34, 61; **5.** 5, 18, 23; **9.** 10; **10.** 99, 102; **15.** 5, 8, 9, 25

General Teaching Council (Scotland) **12.** 78, 80

Gifted Children **1.** 2; **12.** 5

Glasgow University **2.** 36; **8.** 54

"Good Neighbour Scheme" **17.** 27

Grant-Aided Residential Special Schools (Scotland) (*see also* Special Schools) **8.** 7, 21–3

Guidance Teachers **9.** 22; **14.** 1, 16, 22, 23

Handicap (*see also* Categorisation of Handicapped Pupils and handicapping conditions listed individually)
    Concept of **3.** 2–6

Handicapped Pupils and School Health Service Regulations 1945 **2.** 45

Handicapped Pupils and Special Schools Regulations 1959 **8.** 7, 21; **12.** 24; App. 2

402

Haringey, London Borough of **7.** 12(i)

Headteachers
    As Named Person and available to parents **4.** 61; **9.** 20, 27–8, 31, 32; **13.** 23
    Courses for **12.** 54
    In discovery and assessment **4.** 18, 36–9, 42, 53, 56, 59, 60–1, 66; **5.** 18; **10.** 10; **14.**7
    In organisation of school **4.** 23; **7.** 25, 28; **8.** 12; **11.** 14, 53

Health and Public Services Act 1968 **15.** 37

Health and Safety at Work Act 1974 **10.** 81

Health and Safety Executive App. 4

Health Boards (Scotland) **15.** 50; App. 4

Health Care Evaluation Research Team **5.** 34

Health Districts App. 4

Health Education **10.** 96; **15.** 7, 16, 29

Health Service (*see also* Child Health Services; Community Health Services; Primary
    Health Care; School Health Service)
    Organisation of **15.** *passim*; App. 4

Health Surveillance **4.** 6; **11.** 28; **15.** 9, 10, 15, 17

Health Visiting and Social Work (Training) Act 1962 **2.** 61

Health Visitors
    As Named Person **4.** 5, 61; **5.** 7, 13–18; **9.** 26; **15.** 15, 28
    Communication of information to **4.** 16
    In discovery and assessment **4.** 2, 8–11, 32, 42, 64; **5.** 5, 23; **15.** 9
    Other functions of **5.** 46; **10.** 95, 99; **13.** 33; **15.** 8, 33; **19.** 22
    Supply and training of **2.** 61; **4.** 9–10; **15.** 28, 34; **16.** 22

Health Visitors' Association **16.** 5

Hearing Disabilities/Impaired Hearing, Children with (*see also* Deaf Children; Partially
    Hearing Children)
    Education for **3.** 20; **5.** 35, 37; **6.** 5; **7.** 49, 53; **8.** 14; **11.** 13, 31–6
    Educational implications of hearing disability **3.** 4; **11.** 35
    Teachers of **11.** 54; **12.** 42–5
    Young people **10.** 9, 27

Her Majesty's Inspectorate **8.** 24–5, 59, 61, 65; **12.** 13, 23; **13.** 35; **18.** 12
    Survey of child care staff by **14.** 34
    Survey of handicapped students in further education by **11.** 20

Hereward College, Coventry **10.** 44

Hester Adrian Research Centre **5.** 44; **11.** 57

Higher Education
    Advice on opportunities in **7.** 41; **10.** 11, 17, 78; **11.** 4, 19
    Provision of **10.** 47–50; **11.** 36, 42

Higher Education, Establishments of (*see also* Colleges and Departments of Education;
    Polytechnics; Universities)
    Appointments in special education in **12.** 59, 83; **18.** 3–6, 22
    Health services for **15.** 21
    Provision for students with disabilities in **10.** 47–50
    Research in special education in **12.** 55, 59; **14.** 11; **18.** 5–6; **19.** 14

Highlands and Islands of Scotland **4.** 47; **10.** 46

Holidays
    Family **5.** 20; **9.** 35; **17.** 15
    School **8.** 18, 20, 37, 47–8, 85; **9.** 20, 29, 38

Holland Intro. 7; **12.** 57

Local Education Authorities *Cont.*

Planning of future arrangements for special educational provision **3.** 17; **7.** 43, 48, 59–60; **8.** 30–1, 32; **19.** 16, 25

Powers and responsibilities of (*present and proposed*), in relation to children with special educational needs **2.** 45, 67, 69, 83, 84; **3.** 22, 30–2, 42–4; **4.** 24, 25–6, 28, 40, 67, 69–74; **5.** 2, 27; **7.** 44–5; **8.** 60, 66; **10.** 28, 53, 55, 82, 103–8; **11.** 59; **15.** 47; **18.** 17

Support for training of teachers by **12.** 31, 38, 56, 64

Use of non-maintained special schools and independent schools by **8.** 24–7, 58, 60–5; **17.** 11

Variations in rate of ascertainment between **3.** 7

Local Government Training Board **14.** 19, 20, 28

Lunacy (Scotland) Act 1862 **2.** 6

McCann Committee, Report of (*The Secondary Education of Physically Handicapped Children in Scotland*) **2.** 83; **11.** 42

McNair Committee, Report of (*Teachers and Youth Leaders*) **2.** 76

Maddison, Mrs P M Intro. 5; **5.** 1n

Maladjusted Children (*see also* Behavioural Disorders, Children with; Emotional Disorders, Children with)

Category of **2.** 38, 45; **3.** 23; App. 2

Discovery and assessment of **2.** 74; **3.** 5, 7; **4.** 17; **11.** 60

Provision for **2.** 36, 46, 49, 55, 57, 65; **7.** 53, 59; **8.** 22, 56, 58; **11.** 13, 61–3; **15.** 25; **18.** 15

Teachers of **8.** 12; **12.** 30

Use of the term **3.** 27

Young people **10.** 90

Manchester University **12.** 17, 18, 22

Manpower Services Commission **10.** 59, 63, 67, 71–3, 75, 82

Medical Research Council **5.** 34; **18.** 10

Melville Committee, Report of (*The Training of Staff for Centres for the Mentally Handicapped*) **2.** 69; **10.** 52, 89; **14.** 38; **15.** 47

Mental Deficiency Act 1913 **2.** 27, 42

Mental Deficiency (Scotland) Act 1913 **2.** 28

Mental Handicap Hospitals **2.** 55; **8.** 79, 83, 86; **15.** 30

Mentally Handicapped Children (*see also* Educationally Sub-Normal Children; Learning Difficulties, Children with)

Category of mentally handicapped pupils (Scotland) **3.** 26; App. 2

Organisations for **17.** 7, 13, 14

Provision for **2.** 6, 9, 16–21, 24, 25, 27–31, 37, 38, 66–9, 74; **8.** 78, 79, 82; **11.** 57–9; **14.** 6, 12; **15.** 22, 26, 32, 33

Teachers of **2.** 68; **12.** 16, 18, 25

Young people **10.** 68, 76, 99, 109, 111, 114

Mental Health Act 1959 **2.** 66–7

Ministry of Education **2.** 46, 65, 71

Circular 324 **2.** 76

Circular 347 **2.** 60

Circular 348 **2.** 61

Circular 4/61 **2.** 65; **8.** 60

406

Scottish Education Department *Cont.*
    Circular 948 (1976) **10.** 20
    Circular 956 (1976) **10.** 22
    Circular 996 (1977) **10.** 33
    Consultative Document on the future of List D schools **8.** 77
    List G **6.** 14; **8.** 65
    Memorandum, Revision of Schools (Scotland) Code 1956 (1973) **7.** 23; **8.** 41, 71;
      14. 32, 35
Scottish Health Services Planning Council **10.** 117
Scottish Home and Health Department **10.** 116; **18.** 11
Scottish Information Service for the Disabled **10.** 115
Scottish Society for the Mentally Handicapped **10.** 111
Scottish Trades Union Congress **10.** 29
Scottish TUC/CBI joint committee on the employment of disabled people **10.** 79
SE Forms **2.** 73; **4.** 39, 57–68, 77; **5.** 26; **9.** 31; **13.** 10; **16.** 12
Seebohm Report (on Local Authority and Allied Personal Social Services) **2.** 64;
    14. 23; **15.** 37
Sheldon Working Party, Report of (on Hospital Facilities for Children) **15.** 13
Slow Learners (*see* Learning Difficulties, Children with)
Snowdon Working Party, Report of (*Integrating the Disabled*) **7.** 1
Social Science Research Council **18.** 10
Social Services Departments (Social Work Departments in Scotland)
    And communication of information **4.** 16, 66
    And co-ordinating machinery **8.** 30; **15.** 49; **16.** 32–3, 34–5, 36, 40
    Establishment of **2.** 63; **15.** 37; **17.** 6
    In discovery and assessment **4.** 46, 61, 63, 65; **5.** 23; **15.** 41–2, 44
    Responsibilities of/services provided by **2.** 70; **5.** 10, 68; **8.** 19, 20, 66; **9.** 24, 36;
      10. 37, 43, 51–3, 70, 90, 111, 113, 118; **11.** 38; **14.** 23; **15.** 37–40, 43, 45–8
    Social Services Committees **15.** 49; **16.** 33, 34
Social Work (Scotland) Act 1968 **2.** 63, 70; **14.** 12; **15.** 37
Social Workers
    As Named Person **5.** 15; **14.** 24; **15.** 41
    In discovery and assessment **4.** 2, 27, 32, 34, 42, 63, 65; **5.** 7; **13.** 22; **15.** 42–3
    School-based **9.** 22, 27; **14.** 22–3; **15.** 38
    Support provided by **5.** 46; **8.** 45; **10.** 94, 95, 114; **13.** 33; **14.** 8, 22–3, 27; **15.** 8,
      25, 38–43, 46
    Training of **2.** 61; **15.** 48; **16.** 20, 22, 25
Society of Friends **10.** 111
Southampton University **5.** 34
Spastic Children **8.** 57
Spastics Society **10.** 90; **17.** 5
Special Classes/Units (*see also* Teachers)
    Curriculum in **11.** 11, 15, 22
    Designated by LEA **7.** 2, 25, 34–9, 59; **11.** 31, 34, 53, 57
    Established on initiative of individual school **3.** 8; **7.** 12(ii), 30, 33
    Integration with rest of school **6.** 9, 11, 12; **7.** 7–8, 12(ii), (iii) and (iv), 21, 29;
      11. 23
    Links with parents **7.** 18
    Nursery **5.** 55–7
    Staffing of **7.** 21–4, 36; **14.** 32
    Support services for **7.** 41–3

413

Statistics
    Collection of   3. 29; 4. 75–8; App. 3
Summerfield Report (*Psychologists in Education Services*)   2. 61; 14. 4, 6
Supplementary Benefits Commission   10. 103, 109
Sussex University   10. 47, 49; 18. 7
Sweden Intro. 7;   7. 7

Tapton Mount School, Sheffield   7. 12(i)
Taylor Committee, Report of (*A New Partnership for our Schools*) 8. 49–51, 53; 9. 20
Teacher Training (*see also* Induction into teaching; Inter-Professional Training; Peri-
    patetic Teachers; Teachers)
    Admission of students with disabilities to   12. 75–80
    Initial   12. 4–23, 61–2; 19. 27
    In-service   8. 13, 72; 11. 37, 46, 48; 12. 2, 4, 31, 35–63; 13. 9, 12; 14. 11, 29;
        18. 16; 19. 27–32
    Training for further education teaching   10. 41; 12. 66–74
Teacher-Counsellors   9. 22; 14. 22, 23
Teachers (*see also* Advisory Teachers; Careers Teachers; Guidance Teachers; Home-
    School Liaison Teachers; Peripatetic Teachers; Teacher Training; Teacher-
    Counsellors)
    And communication of information   4. 21–2; 7. 16; 11. 43; 16. 5
    Associations   4. 3; 8. 70, 72; 9. 38; 16. 5
    Career structure for   12. 82–4
    Curriculum development and planning by   11. 2, 15, 65, 67, 68
    Discovery and assessment by   4. 2, 18, 24, 27, 30, 34, 36–9, 42, 46, 53, 63; 11. 60;
        14. 7; 15. 16
    In nursery schools and classes   5. 52–4, 56, 57
    In ordinary schools   3. 17; 4. 18; 7. 12, 13, 21–4, 30–3, 40, 48, 54; 11. 35, 39;
        12. *passim;* 13. 8–9, 21
    In special classes and units   7. 21, 34, 36, 41; 11. 11, 34; 12. 24, 29, 30, 33, 34
    In special schools   7. 41; 8. 10–13, 34, 41–4, 45, 47, 79, 85–7; 12. *passim;* 13. 4,
        11–12, 36; 14. 34; 15. 25; 19. 21
    Links between teachers in ordinary and special schools   8. 11, 12, 13, 87
    Research and   8. 13; 12. 59; 14. 11; 18. 7–9
    Special qualifications in special education for   2. 75–8; 5. 56; 7. 30, 54; 12. 24–34,
        37–50, 70; 13. 28; 19. 27–9, 31
    Views on aspects of special educational provision   7. 22, 41; 8. 45; 13. 2; 15. 31;
        App. 8
Teachers' Centres   11. 65, 66; 12. 56; 18. 17
Teachers (Education, Training and Registration) (Scotland) Regulations 1967   12. 79
Teachers' Workshops   11. 65; 13. 9; 18. 9, 17
Toy Libraries   5. 39, 43; 9. 10
Trades Union Congress   10. 29, 79, 82
    Trade union organisations   16. 32
Training for young people   10. 4, 29, 44, 52, 59–70, 80, 88–9; 11. 42, 59; 16. 35; 17. 13
Training Allowances   10. 72, 107
Training Council for Teachers of the Mentally Handicapped   2. 68; 12. 18
Training Opportunities Scheme   10. 62–3
Training Services Agency   10. 59, 62–9, 73; 16. 36

414

Produced in England for Her Majesty's Stationery Office by Commercial Colour Press, London E.7.
Dd.594499 C30 11/82

Corrections

Errors appear in the first impression (May 1978) of this Command paper and the following corrections have been incorporated into this reprint.

Page 72, paragraph 4.78, line 9: "simp ified" should read "simplified"
line 10: "assesseld" should read "assessed"

Page 151, paragraph 9.5, line 8: "servicss" should read "services"

Page 316, paragraph 17.25, line 7: "case" should read "care"

Page 319, paragraph 18.6, line 2: "sevrice" should read "service".

Page 321, paragraph 18.13, line 7: "Group" should read "group".

Page 321, paragraph 18.14, line 1: "group" should read "Group".

Page 347, 3rd line from the top: "pargaraph" should read "paragraph".

Page 361, paragraph 10, line 1: "playground" should read "playgroups".

Page 18, paragraph 2.39, line 2: *"Education"* should read *"Educational"*.

Page 18, footnote should read "[5] *Educational Reconstruction.* Cmnd 6458 (HMSO, 1943)".

Page 153, footnote should read "[1] DES Circular 15/77, Welsh Office Circular 201/77, Information for Parents (25 November 1977)".

Page 415, 4 lines from the bottom, "Circular 15/77" should read "Circular 201/77".